Transmedia Geographies

Transmedia Geographies

Decoloniality, Democratization, Cultural Citizenship, and Media Convergence

KEVIN GLYNN AND JULIE CUPPLES

Rutgers University Press
New Brunswick, Camden, and Newark, New Jersey
London and Oxford

Rutgers University Press is a department of Rutgers, The State University of New Jersey, one of the leading public research universities in the nation. By publishing worldwide, it furthers the University's mission of dedication to excellence in teaching, scholarship, research, and clinical care.

978-1-9788-3007-3 (cloth)
978-1-9788-3006-6 (paper)
978-1-9788-3009-7 (epub)

Cataloging-in-publication data is available from the Library of Congress.

LCCN 2024015341

A British Cataloging-in-Publication record for this book is available from the British Library.

Copyright © 2025 by Kevin Glynn and Julie Cupples

All rights reserved

No part of this book may be reproduced or utilized in any form or by any means, electronic or mechanical, or by any information storage and retrieval system, without written permission from the publisher. Please contact Rutgers University Press, 106 Somerset Street, New Brunswick, NJ 08901. The only exception to this prohibition is "fair use" as defined by U.S. copyright law.

References to internet websites (URLs) were accurate at the time of writing. Neither the author nor Rutgers University Press is responsible for URLs that may have expired or changed since the manuscript was prepared.

∞ The paper used in this publication meets the requirements of the American National Standard for Information Sciences—Permanence of Paper for Printed Library Materials, ANSI Z39.48-1992.

rutgersuniversitypress.org

For Tamara Dávila, Irving Larios, and all of the 222

Contents

Preface and Acknowledgments		ix
Introduction: Cultural Politics and the New Media Environment		1

Part I Popular Geopolitics and Cultural Citizenship in the Contemporary Media Environment

1	Transmediation, 9/11, and Popular Counterknowledges	13
2	The Gendered Geopolitics of Post-9/11 TV Drama	33

Part II Disaster Events, Participatory Media, and the Geographies of Waiting

3	Decoloniality, Disaster, and the New Media Environment	61
4	The Transmediation of Disaster Down Under	83

Part III Māori Media: Criminalization, "Terrorism," and the Celebrification of Indigenous Activists

5	Coloniality, Criminalization, and the New Media Environment	107
6	Indigeneity and Celebrity	132

Part IV Mediated Struggles for Democratization, Decolonization, and Cultural Citizenship in Central America

7	Authoritarianism and Participatory Cultures	155
8	Transmediation and New Central American Digital Activisms	178

Conclusion: Struggles over Modernity and the New
Media Environment   209

Notes   221
References   233
Index   265

Preface and Acknowledgments

This book has been more than a decade in the making. The authors, who both had academic training in cultural studies and met as members of the Board of Cultural Studies at the University of Canterbury in Aotearoa New Zealand, began collaborating in the early 2000s—Julie from the Department of Geography and Kevin from the Department of American Studies. The discipline of geography had undergone an intense cultural turn in the late 1980s and 1990s, borrowing heavily from cultural studies and trends in poststructuralism, while other disciplines in the humanities and social sciences were undergoing a kind of spatial turn, excited by the theoretical insights afforded by geography's close attention to space, place, and scale, and to the specific geographies in play that facilitate or hinder cultural and political change. It was also a time when the media environment was rapidly changing. We were moving into a post–network television era, new and more niche forms of media were emerging and converging with established forms, different forms of grassroots media were becoming affordable and accessible, and more and more people around the world were able to access the internet.

In 2007, collaboration between the authors took a decisive turn. After working for many years on U.S. popular media and cultural politics and theory, Kevin had started doing research on Māori media in Aotearoa New Zealand, while Julie continued to work in Nicaragua, her long-term field site, on questions of gender, revolution and counterrevolution, neoliberalism, municipal governance, disasters, and energy politics. In 2007, a visit to Nicaragua's Caribbean coast in the immediate aftermath of Hurricane Felix revealed the existence of a newly created intercultural television channel that was seeking to center Black and Indigenous perspectives, and a few months later we traveled there together to begin what would eventually be a long-term research project with Black and Indigenous mediamakers in the region, along with an intensification of our research with Māori mediamakers, especially Whakaata Māori (Māori Television). In the meantime, we were also combining our fandom and shared intellectual interest in TV drama, realizing that new and original insights could be developed when we brought concerns from geography on questions of development and postdevelopment into dialogue with the emphasis on entertainment television from media and cultural studies, or when we read contemporary drama on the post-9/11 world through the lens of popular geopolitics. All of this work was seeking to get to grips with the dynamics and cultural politics of the new forms of engagement, participation, interactivity, and technological development and deployment that were bringing the new media environment into being. Amid this ferment, the voices of ordinary people and of marginalized and subordinated populations were finding new ways of making themselves heard more widely and of engaging in various conjunctural, ideological, and discursive struggles. Our collaborative partnership became the basis for a successful grant from the Marsden Fund of the Royal Society of New Zealand entitled Geographies of Media Convergence (2013–2017), which aimed in part to advance incipient dialogues between human geography and media/cultural studies by asking to what extent and how practices within popular cultures of media convergence can contribute to the construction or renovation of cultural, even democratic, citizenship. Our aim too was to extend scholarship on media convergence in U.S. and European contexts by also exploring some of the key mediated cultural and political struggles unfolding in Central America and Aotearoa New Zealand, whose mediascapes were undergoing rapid transformation thanks in part to the rise of Indigenous broadcasting.

We would like to thank the Marsden Fund of the Royal Society of New Zealand for the initial generous funding for this project (grant number MAU1108) and for helping us to move the project to Massey University when post-disaster turmoil and particularly harsh forms of disaster capitalism made it impossible for us to carry out the proposed research at the University of Canterbury. Special thanks in this regard to Janet Sorensen and Ben Jeffares. We would also like to thank the School of English and Media Studies at Massey University and the School of English, Film, Theatre, Media and Communication, and Art History at Victoria University of Wellington, which provided the authors with a productive and stimulating intellectual home to carry out much of the research that appears in this book.

We would like to thank academic friends and collaborators who have worked with us on previous publications or fieldwork, read drafts of our work, discussed ideas with us, invited us to speak on their campuses, or provided emotional support as we navigate the pain that accompanies working in the contemporary university. Special thanks go to Paul Adams, Maria Borovnik, Joost de Bruin, Charlotte Gleghorn, Ian Goodwin, Jonathan Gray, André Jansson, Lynda Johnston, Simon Kelly, Simon Lambert, Eric Laurier, Howard McNaughton, Shaun

Moores, Marcela Palomino-Schalsha, Lisa Parks, Eric Pawson, Jan Penrose, Annie Potts, Mark Rahui, Raquel Ribeiro, Dennis Rodgers, Carlos Sandoval García, James Sidaway, Tom Slater, Simon Springer, Geoff Stahl, Mark Stewart, and Amanda Thomas.

In Aotearoa New Zealand, we would like to thank all the staff at Whakaata Māori, especially Mahuta Amoamo, Mihingarangi Forbes, Tepara Koti, Annabelle Lee-Mather, Jim Mather, Paora Maxwell, Piripi Menary, Coral Palmer, Haunui Royal, Erina Tamepo, and Julian Wilcox, as well as the Māori broadcasters working in independent production who spent time with us, especially Julian Arahanga, Armand Crown, Philip Crown, Kay Ellmers, Nicole Horan, Nix Jaques, Tearepa Kahi, Philly de Lacey, Hinewehi Mohi, and Jane Reeves, and also those working to fund Māori media, namely Larry Parr and Jane Wrightson. In the Tūhoe Nation, we would especially like to thank Mihihea Davies, Hemi Hireme, Tame Iti, Tracy Johnson, and Maria Steens. Thanks too to Janette Dalley of the *New Zealand Herald* for permission given for our cover image.

In Central America, we are indebted to Irving Larios and Dixie Lee in Nicaragua and Kendall Cayasso Dixon in Costa Rica, and their respective organizations, INGES, URACCAN, and Townbook Limón, whose incredible support made our research in this part of the world possible. In addition, we would also like to thank María Luisa Acosta, Margarita Antonio, Juana Bilbano, Michael Brittan, Deborah Bush, Shaun Bush, Rina Cáceres, Osorno Coleman, Avelino Cox, Lottie Cunningham, Raúl Davies, Tamara Dávila, Neyda Dixon, Aracely Reina Duarte, Ángel Gahona, Juan Herbacio, Juan Lorenzo Holmann, Alta Hooker, Leidy Jackson, Mike Joseph, Danilo León, Kenny Lisby, Guillermo Incer Medina, Dolene Miller, Sofía Montenegro, Nora Newball, Laura Wilson, Nayiba Witinia, and Yuri Zapata. Thanks too to Nicole Solano at Rutgers University Press and John Donohue at Westchester Publishing Services for their awesome support and hard work.

Finally, a note on authorship. This book is a collaborative and coauthored piece of work that we have created together in interaction with many research participants, media organizations, media texts, and academic publications. We have both done the fieldwork, the analysis, the reading, and the writing, and created a text that neither of us could have done alone. We have reversed our author names rather than present them alphabetically as is the norm in our field (and as we have usually done in the past) in response to our often difficult and unfortunate institutional location as cultural studies scholars in STEM-dominated departments, where first authorship tends to mean research leadership. There are no leaders here, or if there are, they are the Black and Indigenous broadcasters, activists, and civil society leaders with whom we have worked in Central America and Aotearoa New Zealand, and to whom we are forever indebted.

Some material in part I was previously published in an earlier form in Glynn, K. (2015), "Visibility, media events and convergence culture: Struggles for the meaning of 9/11," in S. Mains, J. Cupples, and C. Lukinbeal (Eds.), *Mediated Geographies and Geographies of Media* (pp. 293–311) (Dordrecht, Netherlands: Springer, reproduced with permission from Springer Nature); Glynn, K., and Cupples, J. (2015), "Negotiating and queering US hegemony in TV drama: Popular geopolitics and cultural studies," *Gender, Place and Culture: A Journal of Feminist Geography* 22(2): 271–287 (reprinted by permission of Informa UK Limited, trading as Taylor & Francis Group, www.tandfonline.com); and Cupples, J., and Glynn, K. (2020), "Drone queen of the homeland: The gendered geopolitics of TV drama in the age of media convergence," in A. Datta, P. Hopkins, L. Johnston, E. Olsen, and J. M. Silva (Eds.), *The Routledge Handbook of Gender and Feminist Geographies* (pp. 476–489) (London: Routledge, reproduced by permission of Taylor & Francis Group). Some material in part II was previously published in an earlier form in Cupples, J., and Glynn, K. (2014), "The mediation and remediation of disaster: Hurricanes Katrina and Felix in/and the new media environment," *Antipode: A Radical Journal of Geography* 46(2): 359–381. Some material in part III was previously published in an earlier form in Cupples, J., and Glynn, K. (2016), "Postcolonial spaces of discursive struggle in the convergent media environment," in P. Adams, J. Cupples, K. Glynn, A. Jansson, and S. Moores, *Communications/Media/Geographies* (pp. 52–94) (New York: Routledge, reproduced by permission of Taylor & Francis Group); and Cupples, J., and Glynn, K. (2019), "The celebritization of Indigenous activism: Tame Iti as media figure," *International Journal of Cultural Studies* 22(6): 770–787. Some material in part IV was previously published in an earlier form in Cupples, J., and Glynn, K. (2018), *Shifting Nicaraguan Mediascapes: Authoritarianism and the Struggle for Social Justice* (chap. 4) (Cham, Switzerland: Springer).

Transmedia Geographies

Introduction

Cultural Politics and the New Media Environment

This book is about the emergence of new transmedia geographies amid the "rise of a convergent media landscape" (Freeman 2017: 104) in the current century. It examines how the terrain of cultural politics has been deeply reworked and profoundly reconstituted in the new media environment. This environment is characterized by extensive digitalization and networking; enhanced technological mobilities and media ubiquity; expanded interactivity and participatory cultures; intensified citizen, consumer and audience/user tracking, monitoring, and surveillance; and rampant technological convergence, transmediation, and post-broadcast narrative forms. In the contemporary moment, stories, discourses, and discursive and narrative fragments spill readily across media platforms and geographical borders, are reworked and recirculated, and constitute continually emerging and mutating media events and transmediated moments.

We explore the cultural politics that have arisen and developed within this new media environment by moving across the mediated landscapes of the first, third, and fourth worlds, which are deeply intertwined and interconnected under contemporary conditions of neoliberal globalization and emergent regimes of authoritarian post-democracy.[1] We emphasize in particular the contexts upon which our research (both individually and collaboratively) has focused for decades: the United States, Aotearoa New Zealand, and Central America.[2] The spaces and terrains of the new media environment are deeply and intensely contested—they are indeed the products of ongoing struggles both *for* authoritarianism *and* for democratization; both *for* racialized modes of surveillant control *and* for decoloniality (which, in struggles for democracy and against coloniality, often involve forms of bottom-up or grassroots transmediation: media interventions and activism that are driven from below). Throughout this book, we attend both to the platforms and digital networks of the new media environment and to the cultural forms and practices that have constituted television as the dominant medium of communication throughout the second half of the twentieth century (as it still is in many parts of the world), for the latter have laid the foundations for the multitiered public spheres (Dayan 2009) and contested online sites of the former (see, e.g., Bolter and Grusin 1999). As John T. Caldwell (2003: 132) notes, "viewing new media through the lens of old media (and television in particular) can provide a range of insights into the increasingly complex strategies used in the deployment of digital media forms." In the new media environment, television "must be understood as a non-site-specific, hybrid cultural and technological form that spreads across multiple platforms" (Bennett 2011: 2). In the ever-expanding geographies of interaction between pre-digital and digital media systems that have taken shape in recent decades, transmediation works to promote the "expanded production of meaning" (Clarke 2013: 20) on behalf not only of those corporate megaconglomerates that have become all too familiar to media consumers around the world, but also by and for many communities and interests that have previously been fairly well excluded from access to the means of electronic textual production and circulation (cf. Martín-Barbero 2011). For the latter, grassroots transmediation has become an important technique for the production of cultural citizenship. For example, "in the new media landscape, historically marginalized voices rely on difference, that is, the Othered body and voice, along with discourses of the 'self', to present themselves to mass audiences on networked television" (Christian 2016: 96). Moreover, contemporary practices of cultural citizenship are often undertaken "at the intersection of television and new media," where "popular media and new information and communication technologies converge and contribute to ordinary citizens' political communication" (Wu 2012: 402–403).

Consider the rise of Donald Trump, who is a phenomenon of media convergence and was a transmedia president. After assuming a prominent place in tabloid media throughout the 1980s and 1990s (see Glynn 2000), Trump became the host of the successful reality TV show, *The Apprentice*, from 2004 to 2015. Just as Ronald Reagan produced himself through the roles he played in classical Hollywood Cold War movies at a time when U.S. politics was imagining itself and its strategies of "countersubversion" more than ever through cinematic screens (see Rogin 1987), reality TV made Donald Trump an authoritarian ("You're Fired!") megacelebrity. Trump thus ran a reality TV campaign and administration (which had a staff turnover rate worthy of *The Apprentice*), boasted incessantly that his rallies (which continued throughout his one-term [at the time of writing] presidency) are the "most entertaining," and tirelessly sent one outrageous tweet after another into the convergent mediasphere to "dominate the news cycle on the ever-proliferating mainstream media and social networking sites" (Kellner 2016: 5–6).[3]

As cultural studies has emphasized since its decisive turn to Gramsci in the 1970s, "domination," when theorized as hegemony, is never fixed or final, and is very rarely even particularly stable.[4] Thus, for cultural studies, hegemony requires constant and ongoing struggle not just to gain ground but even to defend that which dominant alliances have managed to hold for at least a time (see Fiske 1992: 219). Hence, while the new administration sought control over both the movement of people across national borders *and* narratives of race, gender, and religion, among others, multitudes within and beyond the United States who were concerned, disturbed, or terrified about what a Trump presidency would bring both turned to digital media and took to the streets to protest, express their anger, and satirize. Within hours of Trump's inauguration as president of the United States in January 2017, people around the world were using social media to point out that all references to civil rights, LGTBQ+ rights, and climate change, along with all Spanish language content, had already been deleted from the White House's web pages (see also Schilling 2017; Couzens 2017). On 21 January, the day after Trump's inauguration, an estimated five million or so digitally connected people in at least eighty-five countries marched to express their support for LGTBQ+ rights, immigrants' rights, reproductive rights, anti-racist initiatives, gender equality, the Affordable Care Act, and effective environmental protections in the face of expanding disasterscapes.

The idea for these marches began to circulate with a single Facebook post by a grandmother in Hawai'i on the day after the U.S. presidential election in November 2020; that post itself eventually garnered around half a million responses (Rafferty, n.d.; Hartocollis and Alcindor 2021). The marchers' banners and slogans protested, mocked, ridiculed, and parodied the new president, and many of them spread rapidly through the channels, pages, and networks of the print and digital press, broadcast, and social media. They were written in English, Spanish, French, Catalan, Serbo-Croat, Arabic, Māori, and many other languages, and they circulated easily throughout the convergent mediasphere and across all platforms, genres, and other (such as national) borders. A photo taken by a protestor in Wellington, New Zealand (where we marched that day), and uploaded to Twitter, wound up in the *New York Times* and was shared by other news agencies, websites, and dissident citizens via their own social media accounts. Hashtags such as #whyImarch, #alternativefacts, and #presidentfart began trending. If the White House deletions of Spanish- language pages and of references to progressive movements from its web pages were indicative of attempts to remove these things from the nation's political spaces and agendas, the social and other media engagements of millions of ordinary citizens kept them firmly there.

Accounts of the Women's Marches and the widespread use of the internet to protest Trump's first acts as president were accompanied by both political outrage and extraordinary levels of satire and parody, which took shape across global mediascapes, including in internationally circulated television, online magazines, and social media.[5] Even the Mexican Corona beer company piled on when it enacted a decolonial moment by reclaiming the concept of America/América from Trump's colonizing clutches, adopted the slogan *desfronterízate* (deborder yourself), and announced: "Basta de usar nuestro nombre para generar divisiones" ("Enough of using our name to create divisions"). Thus did Corona create a participatory online space for hundreds of Latin Americans to declare their status as "*Americans.*"[6] As one response to the Corona ad put it, "Long live America! We are more than a country, we are a continent and not a country that believes it owns the world and can separate us. It is not the country itself, it is the politicians who divide us and their ideologies of superiority. We are all equal and we can all help each other. Those who can destroy us can also save us and pride, arrogance and despotism will have a long and just decline. America for the Americans and not only for the US Americans. Long live America!"[7] An earlier border-interrogating video released by Mexican airline Aeroméxico in May 2016 also began to recirculate heavily after Trump took office, as did the multilingual and multicultural Coca-Cola "It's beautiful" ad, which was first released in August 2016 and also aired at the 2017 Superbowl.[8] Such practices of (counter)discursive hypercirculation around the dark forces that Trump (and Putin's Kremlin hackers) unleashed within and beyond the United States help to reveal the extent to which global cultures have entered a state of "maximum visibility," "maximum turbulence" (Fiske 2016a: 7), and intensely hypermediated contestation and struggle.

We begin this book with an extended investigation and analysis of arguably the defining transmedia event of the current century so far: the attacks of September 11, 2001, on the World Trade Center in New York and the Pentagon in Washington D.C. These attacks came at a key time for the emergence of new digital media networks (near the beginning of "TVIII" and on the eve of "Web 2.0's" emergence; cf. Pearson 2011; Creeber and Martin 2009) and at a time of geopolitical crisis for U.S. global hegemony (which these attacks deepened profoundly). On 11 September 2001, Wikipedia was a small, ten-month-old experiment in the crowdsourcing of knowledge; it subsequently exploded as a key element in the discourses of Web 2.0 and as a consequence, in no small part, of people's desire to use the site to cover breaking news and "to document the events, perpetrators, victims, and contexts, and the outpouring of collaborative effort in the aftermath" of the Twin Towers' collapse (Keegan 2020: 67).[9] Similarly, the 9/11 attacks and their impacts were major stimuli to the production of geopolitically oriented transmedia narratives and practices, and helped to bring the new media environment into being in terms of the transformation of television's narrative and ideological forms in what media analysts have called the "post-network age" (Lotz 2014: 9). TV storytelling "in the post-9/11 era experienced a profound shift in what was possible with regards to the narrative arc," as more "demanding storylines, diverse and complex characters, . . . geopolitical themes" and heightened ideological complexities began to emerge (Saunders 2019: 695). Moreover, the new media environment's popular geopolitical fallout from 9/11 included the world's "first Internet blockbuster" film (Dean 2009: 156), *Loose Change*, which appeared during the year when both YouTube and Google Video were introduced. At the same time, the imperatives toward securitization that lie at the heart of post-9/11 geopolitics have been key drivers of the massive technological expansion of a vast array of digital surveillance, data collection and storage projects, practices, and technologies, as states and corporations seek to subject activists, consumers and others to the powers of predictive analytics and algorithmic control. We chart a path through these developments in the opening years of the century by situating television and new media forms within the wider conjuncture and the emergence of new modes of popular geopolitics and cultural citizenship.

The attacks of 9/11 and the uncertainties and anxieties around global U.S. hegemony that they intensified and to which they gave expression were ultimately products of a 500-year history of coloniality that has culminated in our current, crisis-ridden era of neoliberal globalization, and we aim to show how the new media environment facilitates and accommodates forms of engagement, negotiation, and contestation over and around these developments. Widespread depictions of the 9/11 catastrophe in terms of its spectacular singularity enabled the event to interrupt "historical linearity" and so inaugurate an "exceptional political, economic, social, religious and cultural state, attenuated by the adoption of exceptional measures": a "state of exception" marked by intense contestation (Gonçalves 2012: 214), but from which we have yet to emerge. So, five years after the 9/11 attacks and three-and-a-half years into the long Iraq War, when Hurricane Katrina struck (see chapter 3), 63,000 National Guard troops were deployed across New Orleans, which was treated as a "war zone" whose residents were "regarded not as disaster victims or survivors but as 'urban insurgents'" (Holm 2012: 18). A survey of the "cultural history of catastrophes" reveals that "9/11 represented an exemplary catastrophe that marked the beginning of a series of crises" and "triggered new ways of thinking" about disasters and "new ways of documenting and ... representing" them; moreover, it "generated new insights into the possibility and role of media, aesthetic form and collective memory with respect to coming to terms with a tragedy as politically, socially and philosophically complex as 9/11" (Meiner and Veel 2012: 6–7).

We understand the 9/11 attacks and their geopolitical, security and military implications around the world as *the century's first globally mediated megadisaster*. In part II, then, we turn to broader questions and geographies of disaster, which is another byproduct of the social relations to which both coloniality and the globalization of neoliberalism (each of which we regard as entangled political projects of domination) have given rise.[10] We reject the notion of neatly and temporally contained disaster events that consist only of narrowly circumscribed and clearly defined periods of intense seismicity, storms that lead to flooding, or raging wildfires whose extermination marks the terminus of each event. Instead, we use the concept of *disaster* in definitionally, spatially, and temporally more expansive terms, and regard substantial disasters as long-term events with deep historical, social, and political roots and trajectories.[11] We therefore regard the disaster of 9/11, for example, as one that began long before the current century and continues to unfold today, and we apply similar analytical strategies to bear upon weather-related, climate-related, and seismic disasters, and upon their contested mediations and countermediations, in the Americas and in Aotearoa New Zealand. The ongoing and unfolding climate catastrophe, whose geographies cannot be disentangled from either neoliberalism or coloniality (and the variety of forms of persistent racism upon which both are built and to which both have given rise), has spawned a seemingly ever-intensifying and expanding planetary disasterscape within which the new media environment has facilitated forms of connectivity, contestation, and transmedia narrativity.[12] The new media environment has also, of course, *contributed* to the production of disasterscapes via its material imbrications within the geographies of neoliberalism and coloniality (on the environmental dimensions of this, see, e.g., Taffel 2019; Maxwell and Miller 2012). After the brutal Hamas massacre of Israeli citizens on 7 October 2023, for instance, the radical right-wing settler-colonial government of Israel declared that this was "Israel's 9/11" and began its disastrous, months-long, and indiscriminately genocidal onslaught against Palestinians in Gaza (and also, on a smaller scale, in the occupied West Bank), which mobilized new digital media technologies that deploy automated target generation by AI software capable of launching hundreds of "around the clock" bombings by airstrike each day (Davies, McKernan, and Sabbagh 2023).[13] We explore the mediation of and struggle over specific disasters in the United States, Nicaragua, and Aotearoa New Zealand, and show how the new media environment has changed the cultural politics of disasters by multiplying and transforming their representations and forms of narrativization, along with our modes of engagement and political contestation within and around them. As with other terrains, dimensions, and geographies of contemporary everyday life, the mobile and participatory realms of transmediation have facilitated the entry of previously excluded or marginalized voices and stories into the new media environment and its landscapes of disaster, including in the "quality" dramas of post-network TV and through the multiplatform mediascapes of Facebook fracases, YouTube mash-ups and muckraking, and social media-connected current affairs coverage, as we demonstrate in chapters 3 and 4.

In part III we show how the globally mediated catastrophe of 9/11 has been mobilized to extend coloniality in Aotearoa New Zealand by demonizing Indigenous people as "terrorists" and terrorizing their communities in the name of the securitization of settler-colonial nation-states (as has also happened in Latin America with regard to both Indigenous and Afrodescendant people, which we discuss in part IV). We also show how Indigenous media activists and broadcasters rearticulate and contest such terrorizing practices of coloniality in Aotearoa New Zealand, whose mediascapes have been profoundly transformed by the establishment and expansion over the past two decades of Whakaata Māori (which was previously known first as the Māori Television Service, and then as simply Māori Television; see, e.g., Smith 2016; Hokowhitu and Devadas 2013a). Indigenous people's access to the means of producing and circulating electronic media, including via television, has been extended partly as a consequence of digitalization and transmediality, which have expanded the range of things that "television" can mean and be, and have given rise to a variety of new tools and transmission channels, including social media and internet streaming platforms. Digitization has also radically extended television's multichannel technological environment in part by enabling new levels of signal compression and therefore the multiplexing of high-quality transmissions (see Hilmes 2009: 47–48). Matthew Freeman and William Proctor (2018: 1) note that "in the contemporary era of media convergence where the sharing of media across multiple platforms is increasingly accessible, transmediality has emerged as a global strategy for targeting fragmentary audiences and spreading content across a spectrum of media channels. But while scholarship continues to dwell on the commercial industry contexts of transmediality, smaller national communities and often far less commercial cultures around the world are now beginning to make very different and altogether nationally specific uses of transmediality."

One of the most characteristic and distinctive features of the new media environment is the global explosion of reality TV in the post-network age. Reality TV has "remained on the cusp of developments in media convergence, interactivity, user-generated content, and greater viewer involvement in television," and has served as "the principal testing ground for emerging convergence strategies such as podcasting, user-generated content, webisodes, and interactive computer games" (Ouellette and Murray 2009: 2).[14] Reality TV has, moreover, contributed to the emergence of new narrative forms across the landscapes of post-network television. Whakaata Māori has made innovative interventions into this cultural form by inflecting reality TV (including some of its most familiar international formats) with Indigenous accents and perspectives (see, e.g., Smith and de Bruin 2012). We examine an example of Māori reality TV, *Songs from the Inside*, which engages issues around racialized criminalization and incarceration. Racialized laws, policing, and penal systems have deep roots in coloniality and are tied to problems that confront many communities of color around the world, as the aftermath of the murder of George Floyd revealed in 2020. In our treatment of *Songs from the Inside*, we suggest ways in which the show reveals some of the promise, but also the limits, of transmediated decolonial struggle in a context where Indigenous broadcasters must rely to some extent on the support of the postcolonial state, as well as that of advertisers and mainstream audiences (cf., Abel 2011, 2013; Smith and Abel 2015). We also show how the forms of racialized monitoring, surveillance, policing, incarceration, and representation that are deeply rooted in the histories of coloniality have been extended to the designation of Indigenous dissidents as "terrorists" in the wake of 9/11, and explore the mediation and celebrification in mainstream, Māori, and digital platforms of one of Aotearoa New Zealand's most prominent decolonial activists, Tame Iti.

We then return to political struggles over coloniality and resurgent authoritarianism in the new Central American media environment in part IV. Here, as in our engagements with the new media environments of the Antipodean fourth world, we are in part continuing to respond to calls from scholars concerned about the heavy emphasis on the Global North and first world in the great bulk of scholarship on digital cultures and transmediality. Scholars have noted, for example, "a growing reaction against the self-absorption and parochialism of much Western media theory" developed "on the basis of evidence derived from a tiny handful of countries" (Curran and Park 2000: 1), and have called for a more "internationalized" approach to contemporary media research that "take[s] on board non-European trajectories" (Thussu 2009b: 23) and emergent "transnational networks" (Thussu 2009a: 2). Others have similarly called for more research that is sensitive to the "geographical variations" that differentiate many aspects and dimensions of the politics of the "newly structured communications environment" of global, digital, and convergent mediascapes (Couldry 2011: 498). "To look at media 'from' the South," writes one, "is today a necessary move to interpret the way media production and dissemination are transforming worldwide" (Jedlowski 2016: 178). In the Global South, the increasingly "re-invented media" environment unfolds within a variety of different "national projects of modernization" (Turner 2016: 59) and amid deep contestation over the very "notion of modernity," which "has been inescapably tainted by its historical and ideological association" with the Global North (71) and coloniality. Latin America is "an area in which a recognition of the mutual permeability of media must be enacted and addressed," for throughout the region, "the contemporary mediascape is a complex mix of traditional media and increasingly more visible processes of convergence, transmediality, and intermediality" (López 2014: 140). Others argue that in its necessary encounters with "questions of transmediality, intermediality, and media convergence" (Arellano 2016: 281), existing comparative media studies scholarship "has not sufficiently engaged with what we may identify as the *coloniality* of media change" (284). In this vein, Jenkins (2016: 14), whose work is central to debates on media convergence, but is overwhelmingly U.S.-focused, writes that he is "eager to see other scholars explore what it means to do participatory politics in other cultural, political, and economic contexts" outside the United States. We seek to address this insufficient engagement with the transmedial production of new media environments and intermedial struggles over coloniality in our examination of convergent Nicaraguan and Costa Rican mediascapes in particular. We begin with an analysis of conjunctural conditions and histories of the present in Central America, and with regard, in particular, to decolonial struggles for cultural citizenship undertaken by Afrodescendant and Indigenous peoples of the region. These struggles entered a new phase of resurgence in the wake of 9/11, which widely signified a failure of the project of modernity across Latin America, and which also therefore spurred a deepening of the critical interrogation of neoliberalism throughout the region that would become manifest in the wave of left-wing "pink tide" governments that subsequently came to power there (see Beverley 2011).

Meanwhile, new participatory media cultures were emerging and developing on foundations established through historical geographies of active radio use for purposes of cultural citizenship building and for lobbying authorities and officials who neglected the needs of local communities, as we explain in chapter 7. These participatory media foundations provided essential support and competencies necessary for the development of Indigenous and Afrodescendant community television operations, as we further elucidate, and later facilitated the emergence and formation of active movements mobilizing social media toward decolonial, democratizing, and anti-authoritarian ends. We therefore conclude the book by examining the growing importance in recent years of social media mobilization and transmediality for the defense of threatened Indigenous and Afrodescendant territories on the Caribbean Coast of Central America, and for anti-authoritarian mobilization, awareness raising, and solidarity building. These developments are tied to the "transmedia textures" of the contemporary media environment, whereby "virtual and corporeal mobilities are combined in increasingly diversified and open-ended ways as media users may access any virtual space (including 'news spaces') from any geographical location through their miniaturized transmedia technologies" (Jansson and Lindell 2015: 80). We further examine and analyze the uses of social media and strategies of digital activism during the Nicaraguan uprisings of 2018, as well as the transmedia expansion of this activism into the spaces of U.S. teen TV drama. We also explore the resurgence within the new media environment of an important Afrodescendant musical tradition that emerged among enslaved Trinidadians and spread more widely throughout the Central American Afrodescendant diaspora. Its earliest practitioners in the nineteenth century used calypso as a means of communicating in ways that could not be readily deciphered or decoded by their white "masters" and as a space for criticizing and satirizing these "masters," and so this cultural form became a key source of social and political commentary, a key node for the formation of grassroots information networks, and a central resource in the production and circulation of defiant pleasures and identities. Today, a new generation of contemporary Central American calypsonians are drawing upon both this important tradition and the affordances of the new media environment to revive and reforge participatory cultures for the production and assertion of new Black identities and communal bonds. The Global

South "is a place where alternative modernities are being fashioned and new humanity and thinking created" (Moyo 2020: 74), and the technological developments and mobilizations that continue to define and redefine the new media environment are "part of the problem that calls for" a "critical analysis and solution" that derives from, engages with, and draws upon the cultural practices of the Global South (58).

Part I
Popular Geopolitics and Cultural Citizenship in the Contemporary Media Environment

1
Transmediation, 9/11, and Popular Counterknowledges

> The number of contradictions in the official version of... 9/11 is so overwhelming that... it simply cannot be believed. Yet... the official version cannot be abandoned because the implication of rejecting it is far too disturbing: that we are subject to a government conspiracy of *X-Files* proportions and insidiousness.
> —Letter to the *Los Angeles Times* (quoted in Barrett 2005)

9/11 and the Popular Geopolitics of the New Media Environment

On 4 March 2001, Fox TV broadcast the first-ever episode of *The Lone Gunmen*, a spinoff from its iconic, conspiratorial 1990s global hit show *The X-Files*. *The Lone Gunmen* featured three countercultural computer and conspiracy geeks trying to salvage, as one of them puts it, "an American dream" of "a government as good as its people" from the corporations and corrupt leaders in control of the country. Viewers who tuned in for this first episode were treated to a fictional narrative preview of the revelations regarding the wholesale, covert, and illegal collection and storage of digital data by the U.S. government that Edward Snowden would disclose to the world some twelve years later (Greenwald 2013). This "premediation" (Grusin 2010) of illegal U.S. digital surveillance operations on an unimaginable scale was interspersed with the episode's main storyline about a U.S. govenment employee (who is the father of one of the show's main characters) who uncovers a plan by "a small faction" within the government to seize control of a commercial flight and crash the plane into the World Trade Center in New York. This plan was concocted and developed under the guise of a counterterrorism war game/simulation. The faction's calculation is that any one of "a dozen tin-pot dictators all over the world" will be "clamoring to take responsibility" for the terror attack after it's over. Once they do, it will present an astonishing windfall and bonanza for the U.S. government, the various branches of the U.S. military, and the arms industry, whose economic growth has been sliding dangerously toward stagnation in a post–Cold War world with no universally recognizable enemies against which a demagogue might rally the U.S. people. The faction's plot is averted only in its final seconds, as the commercial flight is narrowly diverted from its crash course and manages to take out just a single large antenna mounted on the roof of the World Trade Center. Six months later, on 11 September 2001, when fighter planes from the U.S. Eastern Seaboard were flown early in the morning to Canada and Alaska for a large-scale series of scheduled war games involving simulated terrorist hijackings of commercial flights, at least one of which is deliberately crashed into a building by the fictitious hijackers, nationwide audiences watching live breakfast TV just after 9:00 A.M. Eastern Time would see the second commercial airliner of the day crash into one of the World Trade Center's iconic "twin towers." It was eventually revealed that the absence of a preemptive military response during the morning of 11 September may owe at least in part to a widespread reign of confusion that prevailed among officers, technicians, and air traffic controllers throughout their operations at the Northeast Air Defense Sector that day due to their advance knowledge of the multiple war games and simulated hijackings that were already well underway by the time the "real" hijackings and attacks began (see, e.g., Bronner 2006).

The new media environment and the post-9/11 geopolitical world have developed alongside and mutually constituted one another. The emergent age of ubiquitous media was a core component of the conditions of possibility for the constitution of the 9/11 attacks as arguably the paradigmatic and defining geopolitical event of the new millennium. It was these ubiquitous media that enabled the 9/11 attacks, notwithstanding their fictional premediation on Fox, to constitute something like a two billion-gigawatt jolt to the expanding global image circulatory system at the dawn of the new century. In fact, this aspiration was a key design feature of the attacks, which were produced by techniques of visualization as much as by ones of terrorist violence, and which thus generated an image-event characterized by a strategy of visual terror, or of terrorizing visuality. At the World Trade Center, the timing and sequencing of the attacks were in themselves enough to ensure their spectacular instantaneous global visibility. The impact of American Airlines Flight 11 with the Center's North Tower, more than fifteen minutes prior to United Airlines Flight 175's collision with the South Tower, created an absolute guarantee that live video cameras would be in place, in abundance, and trained precisely on the second target in advance of its strike, and that the event would therefore be instantaneously visible—live and in real-time—from any position on the planet capable of electronic image reception.

In the new media environment, transmedia events such as the 9/11 attacks have become important sites of political activity, affective engagement, and cultural struggle. They involve (often spectacular) visibility, the articulation and circulation of meaning, and the formation of powerful discourses and counterdiscourses. The imaging technologies at the heart of transmedia events shape our encounters with place and our popular geopolitical imaginaries. This chapter thus begins our examination of the popular geopolitics of the new media environment by exploring the realm of visual media events through the lens of the attacks of 9/11. These attacks were profoundly mediated, and they generated complex reactions and ongoing political contestation across a diverse array of media realms. We therefore use this event to demonstrate the complicated and contingent politics of visual media at a time when media apparatuses have multiplied and saturated the world as never before. In the age of global visual cultures and media convergence, images and discourses spill interactively across digitalized, networked platforms and a multitude of screens, including televisions, computers, tablets, and smartphones. The new media geographies to which they give shape become invested with affects and meanings, as different groups and agents struggle to promote particular modes of sensemaking and political interests. These geographies define a terrain upon which dominant forces and interests work to establish and stabilize discursive control, but encounter image insurgencies and alternative knowledges that disrupt and contest such control through the disarticulation and rearticulation of its visual and narrative elements.[1]

In the next section of this chapter, we sketch the broad historical context of contemporary media events through a brief consideration of the centrality of vision and visuality within modernity and postmodernity, which has often been characterized as a state of image saturation and visual overload. We then briefly consider the affective intensity and complexity of the 9/11 iconography, which mirrored familiar patterns from extant Hollywood templates, and note its relationship to the emergence of an increasingly convergent mediasphere marked by new technological mobilities and interactivities. After that, we turn to John Fiske's (2016a) account of "democratic totalitarianism" and theory of media events as sites of discursive contestation between forces of domination and countervailing, democratizing energies. In the case of the 9/11 attacks, one of the most interesting formations of alternative discursivity and popular skepticism toward officialdom is that of the so-called 9/11 Truth movement, which alleges some degree of U.S. government complicity with or involvement in the attacks. The 9/11 Truth movement has found resonance with some of the most historically marginalized elements of U.S. society (African Americans, for example), and raises interesting questions about the production and circulation of alternative discursive and knowledge formations on the terrain of media convergence. We conclude by offering some remarks about the emergent geographies and topographies of the convergent mediasphere.

(Post)modernity and Visuality

The modern age gives a special place to visuality, human vision, and the process of visualizing, and this characteristic of modernity has played a prominent role in shaping the contemporary world as we experience it. Hence, the defining philosophical movement of early modernity was significantly called the Enlightenment, a designation that highlights the importance of vision and visuality as central metaphors within the modern epistemologies of the West, for which the "mind's eye" becomes a central figure. Early modern philosophers such as Descartes and Locke placed visuality at the apex of our senses, where it stood as a badge of rationalism and clarity of thought (see Jay 1993: 85). Hence, we refer to important thinkers as "visionaries" or "luminaries," we describe ways of understanding as "worldviews," and we talk about the importance of "keeping things in perspective," of not "losing sight" of our objectives and priorities. When we are looking for solutions, the first thing we do is try to "shed some light on the problem." When we achieve mutual understanding with another, we often proclaim "ah yes, I see," or "I get the picture." The predilection for the visual, which Jay (1993) and others call modernity's "ocularcentrism," impelled Martin Heidegger (1977: 115–154) to characterize the modern epoch as "The Age of the World Picture." In contrast, medieval thinkers such as Thomas Aquinas maintained a hermeneutic of suspicion in relation to the visual (Mirzoeff 1999: 5). Heidegger (1977) writes that "a world picture ... does not mean a picture of the world but the world conceived and grasped as a picture. ... The world picture does not change from an earlier medieval one into a modern one, but rather the fact that the world becomes picture at all is what distinguishes the essence of the modern age" (129–130, quoted in Mirzoeff 1999: 5). Calling our attention to the distinctive modern nexus of visuality and subjecthood, Heidegger (131) observed that the ancient Greeks characteristically understood "man" as "the one who is looked upon by that which is" (though he went on to note that Plato's allegory of the cave foreshadowed the modern thinking that would not become dominant until more than a thousand years later).

Michel de Certeau (1984: 187) states that while premodern cultures required of their members a belief in what cannot be seen, contemporary ones insist upon accession to all that can. Nicholas Mirzoeff (1999: 6) notes that the tendency to visualize the world and to conceptualize human understanding in terms of vision has in contemporary times become something of a compulsion. "Human experience is now more visual and visualized than ever before," he writes, so that "seeing is much more than believing. It is not just a part of everyday life, it *is* everyday life" (Mirzoeff 1999: 1, emphasis added). Consequently, contemporary societies invest astonishing levels of energy and resources into making things visible that otherwise wouldn't be. Such investments both symptomatize and intensify ocularcentrism, as an evermore dizzying array of new media technologies work overtime to deliver images of the insides of bodies, the furthest reaches of the galaxy, and the diverse spaces and surfaces of our planet, which are continually scanned, monitored, and subjected to the power of vision by increasingly sophisticated surveillance and remote sensing technologies, whether for purposes of investigation, examination, security-enhancement, reconnaissance, or entertainment. In the process, the development of such image-generating apparatuses and practices reveals that the drive to extend our "world picture" knows few boundaries; this drive is transforming our existing media environments in fundamental ways as it swamps distinctions such as public/private, interior/exterior, and surface/depth in "rituals of transparency" (Baudrillard 1988), a "fascination and ecstasy" of visibility, and an "obscene delirium of communication" (Baudrillard 1983: 132).[2]

For example, various governments have for decades attempted to develop surveillance technologies capable of identifying individuals across very great distances on the basis of "3-D body tracking" and "gait recognition analysis." As a 2003 U.S. congressional report put it, gait recognition surveillance aims to "identify humans as unique individuals ... at a distance, at any time of the day or night, during all weather conditions, with noncooperative subjects, possibly disguised" (Dowd 2003). In short, gait recognition technologies dream of making individual identity visible, even at a significant distance and under low-visibility conditions, and thus illustrate the use of visualization as a technique of security. While on one level such imagistic expansion of our contemporary "world picture" constitutes the development of new ways to exert and consolidate social control by intensifying the mechanisms of surveillance and reifying the identities it thereby establishes and catalogs (see, e.g., Andrejevic 2007), on another level the dialectics of this expansion lend to it a self-destabilizing dimension. As Mirzoeff (1999: 8) notes, contemporary levels of image saturation, overload, and hypervisuality, in a world where pictures are increasingly made to circulate everywhere instantaneously, mean that we have surpassed the concept of the "world picture" in our development of a constantly swirling global image flow. We have thus entered "an era in which visual images and the visualizing of things that are not necessarily visual has accelerated so dramatically that the global circulation of images has become an end in itself, taking place at high speed across the Internet." In order to stand out amid such seemingly self-justifying and self-perpetuating image flows (Mirzoeff 1999), any particular picture or set of pictures must work extremely hard to capture people's overloaded attentions. The 9/11 attacks were, as noted, engineered for maximum visual impact and thus supremely effective in this regard.[3]

The terrorizing visuality of the 9/11 attacks calls to mind Jean François Lyotard's (1984) "postmodern sublime" and Frederic Jameson's (1992) "technological sublime," which deploy excess, alterity, and allegory to "represent the unrepresentable" and thus to express the awesome "complexity and horrors" of an age characterized by blurred categories and multiple boundary implosions (Kellner 2003: 141). The postmodern and the technological sublime build upon traditional Kantian notions of a "strong and equivocal" aesthetic through which, paradoxically, "pleasure derives from pain" (Lyotard 1984: 77) and powerful dread combines with longing in its exploitation of the "sensual immediacy" of the visual (Mirzoeff 1999: 15–16; Freedberg, 1991). As Lisa Parks (2005: 176) writes, images of the attacks enlisted "the multiple discursive modalities of the televisual . . . in full force," as "commercial entertainment, public education, scientific observation, and military monitoring collided in . . . coverage that lasted not just for days but months," notably disrupting various familiar networks, circuitries, and rhythms of everyday life.

If the sublime technological power conveyed through the live, instantaneous, and global dispersion of images of the attacks combined pleasure with horror for some of their audiences, that pleasure led ultimately, and perhaps by way of the death drive and whatever requisite detours involving the serpentine and circuitous pathways of displacement and repression, to "the aesthetics of destruction" associated with visions of "wreaking havoc, making a mess" (Sontag 2004 [1965]: 102). Susan Sontag notes that certain science fiction films and thrillers provide a kind of "sensuous elaboration" that is unavailable in written texts, whereby "one can participate in the fantasy of living, through one's own death and more, the death of cities, the destruction of humanity itself" (101). According to Sontag, the spectacular and increasing "visual credibility" of contemporary films indexes the extent to which "modern historical reality has greatly enlarged the imagination of disaster, and the protagonists—perhaps by the very nature of what is visited upon them—no longer seem wholly innocent" (103). Such dynamics of the destructive image complicate and potentially intensify the critical charge associated with events such as the hypervisual 9/11 strikes against central icons of U.S. imperialism and global finance.

As Slavoj Žižek would write in a short piece that circulated widely through cyberspace in the days immediately following 9/11, to us, corrupted by Hollywood, the landscape and the shots we saw of the collapsing towers could not but be reminiscent of the most breathtaking scenes in big catastrophe productions. "Not only were the media bombarding us all the time with talk about the terrorist threat; this threat was also obviously libidinally invested—just remember the series of movies from *Escape from New York* to *Independence Day*. That is the rationale of the often-mentioned association of the attacks with the Hollywood disaster movies: the unthinkable which happened was the object of fantasy, so that, in a way, America got what it fantasized about, and that was the biggest surprise" (Žižek 2002b: 15–16). Or, as Jean Baudrillard similarly put it,

> the fact that we have dreamt of this event, that everyone without exception has dreamt of it—because no one can avoid dreaming of the destruction of any power that has become hegemonic to this degree—is unacceptable to the Western moral conscience. Yet it is a fact, and one which can indeed be measured by the emotive violence of all that has been said and written in the effort to dispel it.
> At a pinch, we can say that they did it, but we wished for it.... Without this deep-seated complicity, the event would not have had the resonance it has, and in their symbolic strategy the terrorists doubtless know that they can count on this unavowable complicity. (Baudrillard 2003: 5–6)

Notably, for Baudrillard, the universality of complicit desire for this "'mother' of all events" (2003: 4) does not require us to posit a death drive at its base; he instead asserts that the "countless disaster movies [that] bear witness to this fantasy" register instead an all-inclusive urge "to reject any system ... as it approaches perfection or omnipotence," a universal "allergy to any definitive order" or power (6–7). This of course is not to negate the difference between the experience of such images in fiction/fantasy and that of their "real" counterparts generated by the 9/11 attacks, nor to deny the incredibly shocking and disturbing force of the latter. Geoff King (2005) argues that as the 9/11 images were repeatedly re-edited and replayed in the days following the attacks, they were increasingly transmitted through familiar codes associated with Hollywood continuity editing and thus rendered less disturbing and perhaps even reassuring by their subjection to processes of ordering and control. In this way, television's treatment of the 9/11 images both provoked and assuaged intense shock and disruption (King 2005).

The San Francisco authorial collective that calls itself Retort (Boal et al. 2005: 26) suggested that the long-term geopolitical consequences of the worldwide circulation of images of a global superpower "afflicted" as on 9/11 are ultimately unpredictable. The animation of alternative possible eventualities depends in part upon the contingencies whereby such images are laden with meaning through their various subsequent discursive activations or, in other terms, subjected to the practices of semiotic struggle; this is why Žižek (2002a) exhorted us "precisely now, when we are dealing with the raw Real of a catastrophe," to "bear in mind the ideological and fantasmatic coordinates which determine its perception." But whatever narrative grooves may have been historically prepared in advance of the arrival of the attacks have also, through historical processes, been constituted in diverse and contested ways. For Žižek's "ideological and fantasmatic coordinates" are, as Boal et al. (2005: 26) put it, "bound up, in the longer term, with circuits of sociability—patterns of belief and desire, levels of confidence, degrees of identification with the good life of the commodity" and so forth, which are in their turn "aspects of the social imaginary still (always, interminably) being put together." That is to say, they are always in process, subject to the conflicts and struggles of sociality, and thereby constituted in heterogeneous and contingent forms.

A key consequence of these struggles, heterogeneities, and contingencies is that images of the attacks on the Twin Towers are widely available for a range of alternative discursive practices and enactments. For example, consider the famous "Satan in the smoke" (Phillips 2011) images that circulated widely on TV, in newspapers, and through the internet, such as figure 1.1, which was taken from CNN's live coverage of the attacks.[4]

This "face of Satan" image is fundamentally ambivalent with regard to its capacity for insertion into alternative and competing discursive structures. Its sensual immediacy and richly polysemic potential to convey powerfully condensed meanings and ideologies is thus available for semiotic and affective mobilization by different social formations and struggles. On the one hand, for instance, this picture of the doomed World Trade Center can be readily articulated to well-established Orientalist discourses that construct a racialized opposition between the wondrous achievements of Western civilization and the wicked barbarity of a demonic Other bent on bringing about its demise, all of which is registered in this and similar images of a spectacular yet ultimately fragile architectural grandeur under assault from the embodiment of absolute evil. Mark Phillips reports that he received more than 30,000 mostly emotionally laden messages after the widespread publication of his "Satan in the smoke" photograph. Some told Phillips that he "had been put on the earth to take this photo and that the photo showed who was really behind the attack" (Phillips 2011: location 191). One wrote, for instance, that

> If I were you, I would feel privileged (unfortunately) that the Lord used you to shed "the light on" darkness.... He used your picture to stir up a lot of Americans, Christian and non-Christian, as to who was really behind this whole traumatic event.... We have become so complacent to the fact that there really is a devil loose on this earth and you better believe he was behind this whole thing! The faith of Islam is rebellion towards God that goes way back and what better way to divide people on this earth than to use "religion." (Quoted in Phillips 2011: location 286)

On the other hand, figure 1.1 and similar images can likewise be mobilized within a very different set of discursive practices that associate the World Trade Center with global financial hegemony, whose true face is brought to the fore

Transmediation, 9/11, and Popular Counterknowledges • 21

FIGURE 1.1 The Devil in the Towers. (Source: CNN broadcast. Retrieved from http://www.youtube.com/watch?v=k3nLbc_8wfM.)

only upon the breach of its superficial facades. Thus, the Catholic website Guardian Angel asks,

> don't these photos of Satan at the World Trade Center catastrophe tell us that the current seat of Satan's power is the World Trade Center? Don't these photos depict Satan being awakened from his hiding place in the World Trade Center? For it is the international bankers who operate from Fed, the CFR

[Code of Federal Regulations] and the World Trade Center who create first, second and third world debt. Usury according to the Bible is Satan's method for enslaving the world under his priesthood, the accountants and bankers of the world (IMF, World Bank Group, WTO).[5]

Hence, the visuality that is central to modernity is a site of contestation between groups engaged in discursive practices that promote competing understandings of the world, and thus advance different social and political interests. This constitutes a (geo)politics of representation that comprises an important part of the terrain on which the meanings of place and control over space are struggled for. Therefore, the struggle to articulate images to one set of discursive practices or another is an extremely important one within the broader politics of a hypervisual and convergent global media culture (which constitutes, moreover, an increasingly contingent and open-ended cultural-political terrain).

Convergence Culture: Media Events, Democratic Totalitarianism, and Image Insurgency

Our use here of the concept of convergence is intended to include the various levels of expanding interconnective practices that have become associated with the term in media studies (see especially Jenkins 2008; see also, e.g., Kackman et al. 2011a; Meikle and Young 2012; Pearson and Smith 2015). Hence, convergence entails geographical, technological, social, and political dimensions, as consolidating systems of top-down control intersect with the increasingly interconnected yet multivalent and participatory practices and emergent mobilities of grassroots media users, giving rise to new forms, levels, and degrees of transmediation. Convergence also entails then the strange complicities and intersections noted above between, for example, Hollywood cinema audiences and Islamic fundamentalists (just as it entails the circumstance whereby in some cases these two identities are in fact the same convergent one). As Jenkins (2008: 3) notes, "convergence represents a cultural shift as consumers are encouraged to seek out new information and make connections among dispersed media content" and across different media platforms. Convergence brings cultural consumption and production together in ways that mobilize synergistic new regimes of "collective intelligence," which operate on the principle that, although no individual can possess complete knowledge, all have access to some; therefore, resource-pooling and task distribution across a broad base of people with unique and distinctive skills can generate alternative sources of media power (4). In an environment of intensifying media-cultural convergence, the field of potential discursive articulations into which images enter is a markedly expansive one. Thus, in relation to 9/11, as we will see, new knowledge formations have exploited the affordances associated with media convergence to generate and share forms of collective (counter)intelligence concerning the nature and perpetrators of the attacks.

Jenkins (2008: 1–2) cites the case of Dino Ignacio, a U.S. high school student who playfully created a photomontage that depicted Bert from *Sesame Street* cavorting with Osama bin Laden for his "Bert is Evil" website. As a consequence, an anti-American activist in Bangladesh wound up plastering images of Bert (and bin Laden) on placards and T-shirts that were distributed for use by marching protestors in numerous Middle Eastern countries. When global cable news networks transmitted the images of Bert and the protesters, *Sesame Street*'s producers were outraged at the apparent tastelessness of this intellectual property infringement, which in turn led tech-savvy observers to create new websites associating more *Sesame Street* characters with Al-Qaeda. Thus, "from his bedroom, Ignacio sparked an international controversy. His images crisscrossed the world, sometimes on the backs of commercial media, sometimes via grassroots media. And, in the end, he inspired his own cult following" (2). Here, media mobilities, images, discourses, platforms, connectivities, far-flung social collectivities, political constituencies, articulations, and complicities combine and combust in ways that are anything but predictable and that challenge traditional ways of understanding power, control, and meaning production in media culture.

Fiske (1998) noted an expanding regime of "democratic totalitarianism" in the United States that operates most intensively around racial difference, and whose core attributes include rampant technologized surveillance, escalated policing, and expanding "appeals to moral totalism." Under such conditions, visuality's power-bearing dimensions are exerted asymmetrically across racially differentiated populations. Fiske (1998: 69) characterized this social environment as "democratic totalitarianism" because its capacity to exert control depends upon the extent to which its key techniques of power can be operationalized "underneath the structures of democracy." For example, in November 2000, less than a year before the 9/11 attacks, the new millennium threw up one of its first major media megaspectacles: the intensively racialized Florida election debacle that swept Bush and Cheney into the White House by 537 votes, standing on the necks of tens of thousands of eligible African American would-be voters who were purged from the state's digital electoral rolls when a private computer firm hired by Jeb Bush falsely designated them to be convicted felons (Palast 2006: 240–246). Moreover, on election day, there were reports of the intimidating use of police roadblocks near polling places in Black neighborhoods of Miami, and seven whistle-blowers from the GOP-connected Sequoia Voting Systems would reveal in 2007 that defective ballots designed to produce "hanging chads" were deliberately manufactured and shipped only to Palm Beach County, a large, heavily Democratic district with a significant nonwhite population (Glynn 2009a: 229, 232). Thus would commence a decade that was soon to yield an even more disruptive media mega-event that would provide the basis and justification for manifold enunciations of moral totalism and media spectacle, and myriad extensions of imperializing surveillant, policing, and war-making powers that reached across geographical space and multiple axes of social difference, while extending the gulf between the haves and have-nots to levels unseen in the United States since the Great Depression, and perhaps since the Gilded Age of the late nineteenth-century robber barons.

In *Media Matters*, Fiske (2016a) explores the characteristics of media events and their relationships to the complex currents of meaning that comprise contemporary media cultures. Updating Raymond Williams (1997), Fiske argues that a media culture can be likened to a river of discourses that includes dominant, residual, and emergent streams that jostle, contest, and unsettle one another. A calm surface may at times mask and belie the churning forces and complexities below, though unexpected turbulence may suddenly bring to the surface deep, powerful, and well-established currents that had previously been all but invisible. Spectacular media events become focal sites of discursive and affective activity, maximal turbulence, and competing bids and counterbids for meaning and knowledge as they resonate powerfully with a culture's deepest fears, desires, and anxieties; the most powerful media events may therefore lead to significant shifts in a culture's overall structure of feeling. And yet to do so, they must break through a surface that is more image-saturated than at any time in human history. The new media environment is one of "affective 'surfeit'" (Andrejevic 2011: 610) and a "symphony of intensities" (616), where TV strives to "capture attention and modulate affect" via logics of "over- and under-exposure" that attach images and screens to bodies (Clough 2000: 99).[6]

The culture of the contemporary United States is one of "extreme multiplicity... of images, of knowledges, and of information technologies" (Fiske 2016a: 239). Contemporary strategies for its hegemonization must therefore seek to exert control over technology, visibility, knowledge, and information, and yet the multiculturalism implied by multiplicity means that such control can only ever be achieved in precarious, unstable, and contested forms. In such an environment, countersurveillance might contest and disrupt the imperializing management of visibility, and counterknowledges might be assembled through the technologically mediated disarticulation and rearticulation of fragments of information or repressed facts, perspectives and images (191–192). Practices of countersurveillance and the production of counterknowledge can become valuable weapons of the socially weak and of emergent social formations in the creation, expansion, and defense of localized and increasingly networked social spaces against incursion by colonizing and controlling forces.

Media and cultural theorists have noted the decline of what Daniel Dayan (2009) has called "central TV" as a source of hegemonic consensus, widely shared spaces of discursivity, and a sense of coherent national cultural vision. In the shift from central television to post-broadcasting, post-national, and convergent, networked digital media environments, multiplicity, contestation, and discursive collage have expanded possibilities for the rearticulation of information and images into contestatory counterknowledges and alternative countersurveillant practices of monstration and remonstration (Dayan 2009). Spectacularly disruptive media mega-events, such as the 2000 presidential election and the 9/11 attacks, may paradoxically recenter national attention for a time and, as Lynn Spigel (2004: 260) has observed, create opportunities for the mediated performance of "myths of reunification and nationalism," but they also inevitably provoke counternarratives and establish new terrains of political contestation, negotiation, and dialogue, particularly in the context of the "multitiered public sphere" (Dayan 2009: 20) of the contemporary media environment of convergence, digitalization, and post-broadcasting. While this dynamic necessarily gives rise to a degree of fragmentation often discussed in terms of media tribalism (Dean 2009) or referred to as "communities of dissensus" (Birchall 2006: 79), the contemporary media environment also creates new pathways for the assemblage of collective counterintelligence, new articulatory possibilities for alliance formation, and new techniques of countervisualization. The contemporary mediascape of "technostruggles" thus remains a politically vibrant terrain of contestation, where the motivation to participate in the formation and circulation of counterknowledges, alternative visibilities, and articulatory alliances is driven by and through the social relations and positions occupied by those engaged in these practices (Fiske 2016a). The means and ways of engaging in such technostruggles have expanded rapidly in the current century.

If Al-Qaeda drew upon and rearticulated a deeply familiar repertoire of Hollywood narratives and images to orchestrate a hypervisible spectacle of vulnerability that lay at the very core of the world's most powerful empire—an empire advanced by image-power as well as by economic and military might—then this might be understood as a kind of *image-insurgency*. As Marc Redfield (2009: 3) writes, the "space inhabited by the World Trade Center was (and is) so heavily mediatized, so utterly penetrated by representational technologies of global reach, and so symbolically at the heart of the world's various political, financial, and semiotic webs of power that the destruction of the towers could not help being at once the ultimate media event and (therefore) a haunting image of the deracinating force of communicational technology at work." The Bush/Cheney regime's response to the World Trade Center's collapse relied in turn upon the rearticulation of equally familiar and phantasmatic media images to imperializing discourses and narrative grooves capable of countering the event's disruptive force by reasserting Orientalist sensemaking categories organized around moralistic binaries such as "civilization versus barbarism" and "good versus evil." The cultural work of this moral totalism was to at once performatively constitute, underwrite, and justify the extension of new powers and expanded geopolitical practices of global and domestic policing and surveillance, and thus to initiate new modes of power-bearing visuality and control. The benefits and impacts of these measures were distributed in a wildly asymmetrical and disproportional manner across the social differences that regulate access to alliances that establish the corporate power bloc whose relations and interests were most active at the center of the Bush/Cheney regime.

Popular Counterknowledge: 9/11 Truth and the Geographies of the New Media Environment

In the face of this imperializing hegemonization of the 9/11 media event, another alternative image insurgency has formed that also appeals to a certain familiar media phantasmagoria and to an established counter-reading of U.S. history. The 9/11 Truth movement (see Bratich 2008) is a diverse global collection of people and organizations that reject the official accounts of the 9/11 attacks. Most adherents allege complicity of one sort or another in the planning and/or execution of the attacks by elements within the Bush administration motivated primarily by the potential to reap a variety of political, economic, and military opportunities and advantages in their wake.[7] Some within the 9/11 Truth movement articulate the spectacle of the collapsing towers to the counterhistories that have been generated in response to unresolved questions and suspicious circumstances around the assassinations of Presidents Lincoln and Kennedy, and of Robert F. Kennedy and Rev. Martin Luther King Jr., to evidence of the provocation of a Japanese attack on Pearl Harbor by the Roosevelt administration, and to suspected or actually documented "false flag" operations such as the attacks on the USS *Maine* and the *Lusitania*, the Gulf of Tonkin incident, and Operation Northwoods.[8] The 9/11 Truth movement thus draws upon, appeals to, and expands an established stock of popular skepticism around the secretive machinations and treachery of the powerful. It does this by articulating well-established histories of power bloc misdeeds and corruption, and of the exploitation and endangerment of the socially subordinated by the dominant, working through the established institutions and agencies of its domination, to the serious questions raised by willful gaps, shortcomings, and deep flaws in the official investigation of 9/11. These shortcomings, gaps, and flaws are in turn challenged by a substantial body of evidence, much though by no means all of it circumstantial, that has been amassed by a loosely affiliated group of 9/11 Truth movement researchers that includes both lay *and* well-credentialed, expert investigators, a significant number of whom are university professors working within and beyond the United States.[9]

The sprawling and expanding body of counterdiscourses and counterknowledges that are generated and circulated through the 9/11 Truth movement's articulatory practices and processes can be understood as both offensive and defensive weapons of sorts. They are weapons to use against the imperializing reach of hegemonic power. They are weapons of countersurveillance and countervisualization; weapons and tools for the expression of democratic impulses, desires, anxieties, and refusals; weapons and tools for the assertion of claims on behalf of particular normative visions of the world; and weapons and tools for the production of communal spaces, identities, affective energies, solidarities, and transformative popular imaginaries.

In this regard, the 9/11 Truth movement has interesting affinities and points of overlap and intersection with the ambitions, networked informational flows, and operational modalities of the multitude that articulated itself around and emerged expressively in the form of the Obama movement in 2008. As W.J.T. Mitchell (2009: 126) notes, Obama attained the presidency "on the crest of a wave of popular feeling that he helped to create, but that largely pre-dated his candidacy"—the "aura of a social movement being born" that surrounded the spectacular rise of the Obama movement was grounded in a deeply rooted and broad-based sense of popular longing for political transformation and for the rejection and expulsion of Bush-Cheney-ism. The Obama presidency was a product first and foremost of grassroots activism (Bobo 2009). During the campaign for his first presidential term, Obama achieved deep resonance with many who felt alienated by the political system and cynical about the depths to which it and U.S. society descended under the calamitously transformative Bush regime, which "in every conceivable way set the conditions for Obama's emergence" (Mitchell 2009: 128). Like the 9/11 Truth movement, the Obama movement constituted itself partly through mobilization of the affordances of convergent media (see, e.g., Everett 2009; Castells 2009; Cogburn and Espinoza-Vasquez 2011; Harris, Moffitt, and Squires 2010). Moreover, like widespread reactions to the 9/11 Truth movement (see Bratich 2008), conservative responses to the social movement that emerged around candidate Obama figured the phenomenon as a collective failure of political rationality that threatens the body politic (Spicer 2010). By the same token, the gun-toting, right-wing so-called Tea Party movement that, during the early days of the Obama administration, helped to launch a wider white supremacist backlash against the nation's first Black president would subsequently morph into the extremist, crypto-fascist authoritarian formation that eventually took over one of the two major parties in the United States under the guise of MAGA-ism.

The production and circulation of popular counterdiscourses and counterknowledges around 9/11 stepped up considerably after 2005, the year of the release of both the song "Bin Laden" by Mos Def, Immortal Technique, and Eminem, and the first of four versions of the feature-length film *Loose Change*, a kind of grassroots *Fahrenheit 9/11* for the convergence culture generation that was created on a laptop computer by twenty-one-year-old Dylan Avery with a total budget of about $2,000.[10] The viral YouTube vid "Bin Laden" features deep bass beats and a rapid-fire assemblage of miscellaneous images including heavy doses of TV journalists and Fox News commentators, Bush administration politicians, the World Trade Center attacks, corporate logos, third world military interventions, and death squad victims, all set to fiercely sardonic lyrics about "fake Christians" and "fake politicians . . . in mansions," the ongoing fight for survival in the ghetto, U.S. war mongering and covert paramilitary actions, and the recurring lines "Bin Laden didn't blow up the projects . . . Bush knocked down the towers." The feature-length *Loose Change* has circulated globally on the internet, where it has, as Avery told *ABC News Nightline* in 2010, "gone viral and back." It is, in the words of *Vanity Fair,* "the first Internet blockbuster" (quoted in Dean 2009: 156). The film has been translated into at least twenty-six languages, sold more than a million DVDs, and aired on TV in the United States, Portugal, Belgium, Ireland, the Netherlands, and elsewhere, and it has purportedly been watched more than 155 million times.[11] It is a central node in what Jack Bratich (2008: 135) calls the "conspiratology archipelago" that constitutes the discursive spatiality of the 9/11 Truth movement, which has emerged as a rhizomatic set of sites, researchers, knowledges, and practices linked through decentralized media distribution. Mark Fenster (2008: 278) suggests that among the core messages of the film "is that we are all Dylan Avery now—a laptop battalion prepared to go into battle, armed with information, insight, and an interpretive method that *Loose Change* has provided." By 2006, the virality of the 9/11 Truth movement had made multiple incursions into media outlets such as CNN, HBO, Comedy Central, and ESPN, as the movement's celebrity spokespeople (including Ed Asner, Rosie O'Donnell, Ed Begley Jr., and Martin Sheen) and nationwide commercials imparted to it a different form and level of visibility (see Bratich 2008: 132–133). That same year, on the fifth anniversary of the collapse of three World Trade Center towers, thousands marched on New York City from around the world wearing the movement's trademark black T-shirts emblazoned with the words "Investigate 9/11."

In November 2007, the third version of the film, entitled *Loose Change, Final Cut,* was released with an eye toward the 2008 U.S. campaign season. In this third version, several speculative assertions about the 9/11 attacks from the film's first two editions were dropped and the film's arguments were honed in response to criticisms from within and beyond the 9/11 Truth movement. The element of political critique directed against the Bush administration was sharpened as well. *Final Cut*'s closing lines of narration state that "the government designed by the people, for the people, has turned its back on us. Or have we turned our backs on it? They spy on us. They torture and imprison innocent civilians. Ask yourself: what's happening? Where are we headed? And would we be here today without 9/11?" The *Loose Change* films incorporate images from Google Earth and NASA satellites to enact a kind of countersurveillance that questions the *official* conspiracy theory of 9/11—the one about a conspiracy among nineteen Islamic terrorists armed only with box cutters who successfully demolished three World Trade Center towers and a sizeable chunk of the Pentagon before any effort at a U.S. military intervention could be mustered. *Loose Change: Final Cut* also samples and mashes up clips to illustrate the inadequacies of mainstream media coverage of the attacks and their aftermath, thus performing a kind of media criticism that might also be read as countersurveillance. The soundtrack over the final credits consists of a hip-hop theme song whose chorus announces, "We say no more! We're gonna fight back! We want the truth out, we want our rights back! . . . Change is loose don't stop it now!"

Like the YouTube vid by Mos Def, Immortal Technique, and Eminem, the *Loose Change* series draws on a remix aesthetic with a very long history that passes through the Caribbean, and includes the creation of Haitian vodou from a hybrid assemblage of West African, Indigenous Hispaniolan, and Northern as well as Southern European Christian religions, and to which some scholars attribute the social solidarities, communities, and identities necessary for the eventual emergence and success of the Haitian Revolution, which gave the world its first Black people's republic in 1804. This long history of remix culture also passes through Jamaica and New York in the birth of hip-hop, through the culture of vidders,[12] through that key site of Bush era social commentary, political critique, and satire, the *Daily Show*, and through the internet branches of the Obama movement throughout 2008. The multifarious instantiations of this variable remix culture must be understood as being rooted in the specific social relations of particular historical and geographical conjunctures and material conditions of existence. In their 2007 appearance on *Real Time with Bill Maher*, Mos Def and Cornel West provide a glimpse into the articulation of material conditions of existence to the forms of 9/11-oriented popular skepticism that are expressed through remix practices in the "Bin Laden" vid:

MAHER You have to admit that there are people who do want to kill Americans.
MOS DEF Yeah, some of them are called the police.
MAHER But that's apples and oranges.
MOS DEF Uhhh, uhhh, you know, coercion apparatus: one is endorsed by the state and the other is not. You know, when the Revolutionary War was going on, George Washington and all them dudes was terrorists, as far as the queen was concerned. . . .
MAHER But you don't want to get blown up by a bomb.
MOS DEF . . . Listen, I'm Black in America. I live under *constant pressure*. I don't believe in that bogeyman shit. . . . I don't believe that was bin Laden [in a videotaped message] today. I don't believe it was ever him. . . . I'm from the projects—I *know* danger. . . .
MAHER You don't think bin Laden knocked down the World Trade Center?
MOS DEF Absolutely not! . . . Go to any barber shop. I am *so* not alone! . . . Highly educated people in all areas of science have spoken on the fishiness around the whole 9/11 theory. It's like the "magic bullet" and all that shit! . . .
CORNEL WEST I think that bin Laden . . . had *something* to do with the buildings, 'cause he said so, and I believe it. But the thing is that if at the same time, you have multiple sources of force, coercion and terror coming at you, which many Black Americans do—prison-industrial complex, racial criminal justice system, . . . disgraceful school systems—to what degree do you begin

to think: my paranoia is actually justified, because if *they* can sustain this level of psychic and physical terror against *me*, and *they're* obsessed with the terror that's against *them*, then maybe they might not be believable and credible.

Mos Def's invocation of the founders of the republic of the United States is interesting in relation to widespread dismissals of the 9/11 Truth movement as an unfounded "conspiracy theory," a phrase that, at this point in history, seems capable by its mere invocation of rendering dissident perspectives and counterknowledges illegitimate a priori. As Bratich (2008) has shown, this denunciatory discourse of "conspiracy theory" is part of a larger discursive apparatus that works to keep U.S. politics "within reason" and thus to exert control and discipline over dangerous forms of thinking. This power-bearing "reasonability" expresses of course not a universal position but rather an historically specific (and contested) formation of reason. While the Enlightenment was surely indispensable for the American Revolution, so too was the highly active conspiracy-mindedness of leading colonists bent on discerning obscure patterns of orchestrated deceit, manipulation, and treachery in the machinations of key British parliamentarians of the day (see Dean 2002: 54–57). If the American Revolution was a product of both Enlightenment rationalism and colonial conspiracy theorization, today it is the shadow cast by a particular historical formation of "reasonability" that makes it difficult for mainstream U.S. media outlets to contemplate either the possibility or the evidence of something deeply rotten at the core of the nation's democracy. Indeed, responses to the 9/11 attacks across, broadly, the white and middle-class United States are particularly revealing in this regard. Unlike other events that have been the objects of high-profile conspiracy theories, such as the assassination of JFK or the HIV pandemic, the 9/11 attacks seems to be unique in the sense that there has never been *any non-conspiratorial* official explanation of them against which we might set the popular "conspiracy theories."[13] Even the official explanation of the 9/11 attacks is a conspiracy theory, which raises the following question: In the face of what Bratich (2008) calls "conspiracy panics" that render virtually all "conspiracy theories" beyond belief in "respectable circles," what explains the almost immediate and all-but-unquestioning acceptance, in such circles, of one conspiracy theory and the equally immediate and steadfast refusal to even contemplate or consider alternative conspiratorial explanations of the same events purportedly explained by the official conspiracy theory? And what role do the racial identities of the principal actors play in producing this differential fate of two competing conspiracy theories?

The World Trade Center attacks and the 9/11 Truth movement also enable us to make some observations on the relationships between the different elements of the contemporary media environment—that is, of Dayan's (2009: 20) "multitiered public sphere," with its remnants of "central TV" in the major networks, and its exuberantly expanding rhizomatic margins which, through their constant fragmentation and dispersal of attention, increasingly threaten to swamp the center out of existence. One key feature of this environment is the role of spectacular media events as rejuvenators of attention centers, where centralized dominant forces concentrate their efforts to re-stabilize hegemonic regimes of power, social formations, and discourses, and to repress or vanquish marginal ones. The relatively socially weak forces and voices, in turn, radiate outwards toward the networked margins, which provide a kind of safe harbor of enclaves and opportunities for growth and development through processes associated with convergence culture (Jenkins 2008), such as collective intelligence and creative remix, which are increasingly important for the production of counterdiscourses and counterknowledges, for the practices of rearticulation and resignification, and for the generation of oppositional identities and the maintenance or protection of endangered solidarities.

The new media environment has seen the rise of traffic between the rhizomatic, deterritorialized, and networked margins consisting of podcasts, blogs, vid sites, and social networks, on the one hand, and the mid-sized juncture points that provide what we would like to call (with pun intended) *medium visibility*, on the other. The latter might include, for instance, cable TV outlets such as HBO, Comedy Central, MSNBC, and Fox News (the last of which is an important mediating and somewhat moderating node of the most radically extreme right-wing, white supremacist fringe movements in the United States, including the conspiratorially-minded proponents both of the "great replacement theory" and of that 4Chan-driven movement known first as "Pizzagate" and later as QAnon),[14] as well as non-prime-time programming such as *Nightline* and *The View*. Though such sites of medium visibility may be consumed "tribally" by relatively homogenous niche audiences, they nevertheless expand visibility in relation to the smaller clusters on the deterritorialized capillary margins, and so provide opportunities for the formation of new alliances across social difference, and perhaps for eventual break-through emergence within the attention centers associated with "central TV." The appearance of professional physicists, architects, and engineers in media such as CNN and national network breakfast TV to discuss the publication in 2009 in a peer-reviewed scientific journal of an article offering strong evidence of the use of super- or nano-thermite, a high-tech explosive produced by only a handful of military contractors such as Livermore Labs, in the destruction of the three World Trade Center towers represents one such moment of *medium visibility* capable of generating new articulations and political alliances across social differences.[15] Another such moment occurred on 13 November 2010, when the father of a man killed in the 9/11 attacks and a mechanical engineer appeared together on the Fox News show *Geraldo at Large* to discuss their criticisms of the official story of the attacks and their ongoing efforts to bring about a new investigation into the strange collapse of World Trade Center Building 7, late in the afternoon of 11 September 2001.[16] By the same token, Fox News has been operating as a site of *medium visibility* for Donald Trump's increasingly extreme and openly fascistic pronouncements in 2023 and January 2024 (at the time of this writing), when the former president and would-be dictator told the network's "town hall" audience, for example, that "Democrats are 'killing babies after birth'" (see Hall 2024; Media Matters Staff 2024), a claim that has circulated on the fringes and margins of the internet for years, according to the fact-checking website Snopes (see LaCapria 2015, 2016).

The first decade of the new millennium in U.S. political culture was in many ways bookended and defined by two key, counterposed spectacular media events. First, the collapse of the World Trade Center in 2001. And second, the twin moments of high spectacle associated with the hopeful transformation of the dark nightmares of the Bush/Cheney regime into the age of Obama: Obama's speech accepting his party's nomination for the presidency at Denver's Mile High Stadium during the 2008 Democratic National Convention, and his electoral victory speech in Chicago's Grant Park just over two months later.[17] The attacks of 9/11 constituted a geopolitical transmedia megaspectacle that generated struggles to put its images into discourse in a manner capable of shifting the U.S. culture's central structure of feeling—whether this is understood to entail an effort by Al-Qaeda to shift it away from an interventionist, Orientalist, and American exceptionalist swagger toward a newfound sense of vulnerability and humility in the face of an angry world and God, or alternatively, to entail the Bush/Cheney regime's efforts to shift this structure of feeling through shock and awe toward a sense of deep and widespread fear in the service of democratic totalitarianism and war without end. By contrast, the remix-driven counter-mobilizations of this media event by the 9/11 Truth movement and the mashups and counterspectacles that constituted the high moment of the Obama movement (which re-formed subsequently in the Occupy movements) must be read as major popular efforts to reclaim and redirect the structure of feeling, and to reconstitute the political conditions of possibility within and beyond the United States for the new millennium.

2
The Gendered Geopolitics of Post-9/11 TV Drama

While television may be losing its centrality within the contemporary media environment, it nevertheless remains an important site of popular geopolitical engagement. In an influential paper published more than four decades ago, Horace Newcomb and Paul Hirsch (1983) argued that television should be understood as an important cultural forum because it tends to raise questions rather than answer them, and opens spaces where thought, imagination, and the deconstruction of "common sense" can take place. For Stacy Takacs, whose work has dealt in depth with geopolitically inflected entertainment television (see especially Takacs 2012), TV drama has "functioned admirably as a 'cultural forum' for the ethical contemplation of dilemmas raised by the Bush Doctrine," especially given the amount of material we were not allowed to see in news and current affairs media after 9/11 (Takacs 2010: 154). The Iraq War, for instance, was characterized by extreme attempts at "perception management" (Mirzoeff 2005) and a tightly prescribed set of "protocols for looking" (Macdonald, Hughes, and Dodds 2010: 8–9), including the use of embedded journalists, the staged destruction of the statue of Saddam Hussein, the faked rescue of Jessica Lynch and the coverups, violations of protocol and suspicious circumstances surrounding the killing of Pat Tillman by so-called friendly fire (see Glynn 2009a), Bush's "Mission Accomplished" spectacle, and the ban on news media covering funerals or displaying the coffins of U.S. soldiers killed in combat (see also Butler 2010). Especially under such conditions of U.S. government obstructionism, orchestrated trickery, and enhanced control, entertainment media became an important site where the public could "see" and "watch" outside of such protocols and constraints, such that "its role in framing and re-framing 9/11 and its aftermath is of vital concern" (Takacs 2010: 154). Therefore, in this chapter, we examine of the role of entertainment television and its associated sites of online engagement in the formation of landscapes of popular geopolitics within the new media environment.

Popular Geopolitics, Gender, and Post-9/11 TV Drama

Post-9/11 interactions between TV drama and geopolitics have occurred in parallel with, and are facilitated by, a range of contemporary transformations within the practices of television production, distribution, and reception. Dramatic changes in the contemporary television and wider media environment are closely associated with, but not reducible to, technological innovations and processes of media convergence. Hence, there has been an expansion of various forms of user-driven interactivity and transmedia practices, facilitated in part by social media and the spread of devices such as tablets and smartphones. New modes of media consumption, modification, and recirculation have enabled audiences to appropriate and rework content produced by media companies and to "speak back" to these massive global megaconglomerates. In television's network and "multi-channel transition" eras, spanning from roughly the 1950s to the start of the new millennium (Lotz 2007: 8), many viewers watched TV shows at the time of broadcast and discussed them in person with family, friends, and colleagues. These audience reception practices are still widespread but are now increasingly unmoored from broadcasting schedules and are accompanied, or even replaced, by online conversations. The "channel surfing" of television's early age of abundance has given way to the binge-watching associated with DVD box sets, smart TVs, and digital streaming, for instance. Today, many viewers are likely to have watched a show that their family, friends, and colleagues have not (yet) seen but are able to listen to podcasts about it and engage in discussions about it with distant friends and family members, or with people they have never met on Facebook, Twitter, Tumblr, show-related wikis, internet forums, digital newspaper comment sections, and online dedicated fan forums such as Digital Spy, TV Time, Overclockers, and the once-brilliant but now defunct Television without Pity.

Furthermore, the mass audience of the old media environment has given way to a post-Fordist logic of extreme fragmentation of audiences and revenue streams, which has in turn led to an expansion of nichification, cultification, and greater openness toward experimentation within the TV industries (see, e.g., Reeves, Rodgers, and Epstein 1996; Gwenllian-Jones and Pearson 2004; Mittell 2006). While audiences for commercially successful shows are now much smaller than they once were, they are also likely to be more loyal, to stick with their shows over multiple seasons, and to engage with programming across multiple media platforms. To promote audience loyalty and even cultish devotion, producers have intensified the complexity of narrative forms and serialization practices (see, e.g., Mittell 2015a; Dunleavy 2018; Clarke 2013). This has led to the emergence of new modes of ideological complexity and innovation, and new ways of exploring serious social and political issues (see, e.g., Creeber 2004; Mittell 2006; Cupples and Glynn 2013), such that the new media environment has arguably enhanced the importance of television for geopolitical analysis and critique. New modes of complexity in fictional television seriously challenge the Habermasian separation between factual and entertainment media that has allowed political economists and elite commentators to construe the former as making important contributions to a rational public sphere, while dismissing the latter as a mindless distraction incapable of promoting the formation of responsible and well-informed citizens (Gray 2006). Gray offers a nuanced account of *24*, whose contradictions enable him to grasp the show's role in the complex constitution of cultural citizenship via its production of "dialogic spaces" and "cultural forums" wherein the resolution of persistent ambiguities is consistently refused, and audiences are thus invited to imaginatively explore a range of political identifications and outcomes:

> The show is rife with conservative sentiment on racial profiling and on torture, and with racial fearmongering. The 2006 and 2007 seasons also told the story of an incompetent president led by a secret organization that is complicit with numerous terrorist activities, and in 2007 the vice president was painted as a dark and sinister figure pulling many of the strings behind this network. And while Arab Americans are being rounded up, the president as moral authority voices his displeasure, as do other likeable characters. . . . *24* refuses to resolve these varying strands, instead keeping to an ambiguous line whereby neither conservative nor liberal viewers could in good faith and full knowledge allege clear "bias." (Gray 2008: 140)

By placing competing political voices and perspectives in conflict and dialogue with one another, *24* offers not so much "proclamations" as "*resources* for arriving at our own answers, and *testing grounds* in which we can see various answers interplay" (Gray 2008: 141, emphasis in original). In this way, television provides audiences with a space for "working through" (Ellis 1999) complex issues.

In the multiplatform television era, then, narrative forms and reception practices that scholars have long associated with cult TV and media fandom have expanded and become increasingly mainstream. While television has long trafficked in hybrid narratives that combine and experiment with various forms and permutations of serialization, it has in the age of media convergence departed farther than ever before from both linearity and the episodic structures that once defined its most recognizable conventions. Like the cult TV that forms one node in the prehistory of TV's new modes of complex seriality, the latter often prominently foreground moral ambiguity, transgression, supernaturalism, characters who defy normalization, and multiple, simultaneously unfolding narrative arcs the stretch over numerous episodes and entire seasons (Dunleavy 2018). This complex seriality also often plays with alternative epistemologies that constitute the otherworldly televisual equivalent of magic realism that Glynn (2003) has characterized as "popular subjunctivity." Television's complex seriality has developed alongside new practices of "forensic fandom" whereby "dedicated fans embrace" narrative complexities "and seek to decode a program's mysteries, analyze its story arc and make predictions" (Mittell 2015b). The show *Lost* (2004–2010), for instance, which attracted a large multinational audience that stretched across many parts of the world, is often held to exemplify the complex seriality of the new multimedia environment. *Lost* engaged amply, albeit often in displaced and allegorical ways, with myriad aspects of post-9/11 geopolitics, and gave rise to a sprawling online repository of diegetic knowledge and fan speculation known as Lostpedia. In the words of one blogging devotee, Lostpedia "became an incredible resource for fans to keep track of all the twists and storylines within the show as they obsessively documented everything from the number of crash survivors still on the island, to more bizarre stuff like how many times a season [fan favorite character] Hurley said 'dude'" (Baker1000 2015). Through their narrative and fan engagement practices, *Lost*, its paratexts (see Gray 2010), and its viewers, who vigorously and extensively discussed all aspects of the program online, participated in constituting and reshaping the discursive and imaginary terrains of post-9/11 geopolitics, as when, for example, they conjectured and debated over the nature and significance of links between the crash of Oceanic Airlines Flight 815, the objectives of the mysterious DHARMA Initiative, and the involvement of its funders, the secretive Hanso Foundation.

One important feminist critique of the discourses and practices associated with the age of media convergence concerns gendered distinctions that have formed around what has often been called television's "third golden age" of the past twenty or so years. During this period, the cutting-edge technologies and narrative forms associated with digitalization and media convergence have been frequently touted as "cinematic." Cinema has long been regarded as a more "legitimate" (and "masculine") "art form" than television; "cinematic" has thus become a key adjective in the contemporary discourses that reproduce cultural hierarchies, and therefore inequalities, by differentiating between television's texts and audiences that are more worthy and those who are less so (Newman and Levine 2011). As Michael Newman and Elana Levine (2011: 10) write, "that television has been classified as feminine, and therefore as a less worthy, significant, and serious medium, has been a fact of its history." TV has, perhaps more than any other medium, been consistently identified with cultural decline, "massness," and feminization. Prominent discourses of television's "third golden age" thus reinscribe gendered distinctions and hierarchies within domestic spaces of media consumption by mobilizing the emergence of new televisual technologies and narrative forms that ostensibly transcend (mere) television-ness to achieve cinematic heights and dimensions. Newman and Levine's analysis of convergence-era TV thus demonstrates how it has been positioned as new and improved television in relation to earlier and more feminized forms of TV such as soap opera.

There are parallel hierarchizing discourses that differentiate the "serious" and worthy from the insignificant and trivial in the realm of geopolitical analysis. Traditional geopolitics has historically emphasized statecraft, the realm of the traditional public sphere and policymaking, and the terrains of war and conflict—in short, the core concerns of "statesmanship" and of the "hard news," in tellingly masculinist journalistic parlance. As regards televisual taste and "quality programming," the often derisively used terms "soap opera" and melodrama neatly capture the confluence of feminization and trivialization widely invoked to derogate programming that falls outside the category of "serious" (masculine-oriented) fare of one sort or another. In this way, *gender* and *genre* form intertwined and co-constitutive systems of categorization and distinction in relation to television production, circulation, and consumption.[1] Programs like *Homeland* and *Commander in Chief* are of interest in part for their deconstruction of such categories and distinctions. As Diane Negra and Jorie Lagerway (2015: 131) argue, *Homeland* is "a consummate example of melodramatic political discourse ... that does not seek to and never can quell the anxieties of the present moment with which it so forcefully engages." Similarly, *Commander in Chief* is a popular text that is rife with contradictions and complexities that animate a range of potential subject positions that are offered for audiences to take up as points of identification and conjecture.

Our view is that the social struggle for resources, including semiotic ones (in other words, *meanings*), is so thoroughgoing and socially pervasive that even individual texts and subjectivities are necessarily riven by competing and contradictory elements, the division and the clamor between which cannot fully be domesticated, even via the processes of cultural commodification—at least, not if the "culture industries" hope to attract popular audiences to their products. For those products must contain at least the faint traces of popular perspectives and ways of knowing, and such traces provide points of purchase for diverse audiences in the contestation for competing modes of sensemaking. Media industries have found that providing audiences with space for semiotic maneuvering is one way to engage them effectively. Consequently, it is vital that we develop complex accounts of cultural citizenship, negotiation, and articulation that will enable us to examine the ways in which texts of popular culture stage conflict between competing political discourses and perspectives, and thus facilitate audiences' engagements with different ideological orientations.

Since the 9/11 attacks, television has engaged amply with the gendered consequences of the so-called war on terror. Fictional television's activities in these regards have been particularly important in light of the "absence, erasure and invisibility" (Stubblefield 2014: 4) that was characteristic of the approach of conventional news and current affairs programming in the face of the Bush administration's massive information and image management efforts (Mirzoeff 2005; Glynn 2009a; Takacs 2010). During the Bush years, for instance, journalists were, as noted previously, banned from accessing, photographing, or filming the arrival of coffins of fallen soldiers at all U.S. military bases (Vann 2003). Paradoxically, Thomas Stubblefield (2014: 4) argues, this invisibility, erasure, and absence were products of the logic of spectacularization that engulfed the 9/11 event itself and engulfed, by implication, many events that followed in its wake, including the spectacle of the Iraq War: Following the logic of implosion rather than explosion, the World Trade Center withheld its contents from view as it fell; its stories "pancaked" on top of one another rather than turning themselves inside out. With the vast majority of the dead dying behind the curtain wall of the towers' facades, "the most photographed disaster in history" failed to yield a single noteworthy image of carnage.

Nevertheless, while sometimes succumbing to it, television drama also found ways to circumvent spectacularization and invisibility, and to interrogate dominant post-9/11 geopolitical logics and images. It often did this by exploring how geopolitical dynamics reshape intimate relationships and position women, men, girls, boys, sisters, and brothers differently in relation to significant events. A 2006 episode of long-running hospital drama *ER*, for example, plumbs the emotional depths surrounding the loss of a major character, Dr. Michael Gallant, when a roadside bomb explodes near his position while he is offering medical assistance in the war zone near Mosul (season 12, episode 22, "The Gallant Hero and the Tragic Victor"). Gallant's young widow, Dr. Neela Rasgotra, then finds herself in the same place as many other post-9/11 U.S. military families who are left emptily to mourn fallen loved ones with only funereal military spectacle offered to them in lieu of adequate explanation, compensation, justification, or political accountability (season 12, episode 23, "Twenty-One Guns"). Consequently, Neela joins the anti-war movement (season 13, episode 23, "The Honeymoon Is Over"). Similarly, *Six Feet Under*, a show about a family-run funeral parlor in Los Angeles and that is in many respects taboo-breaking (see Akass and McCabe 2005), also began to connect with gendered dynamics of the war on terror. In a 2005 episode (season 5, episode 11, "Static"), the daughter/younger sister of the family, Claire Fisher, who is high on drugs at the time, yells at the grieving sister of a deceased soldier who was euthanized in the hospital after losing all of his limbs in Iraq. The soldier's sister is driving an SUV sporting a "Support Our Troops" bumper sticker, which provokes Claire into an enraged tirade that covers a range of political angles on the war in Iraq: "Why don't you try driving something that doesn't consume quite so much gas for starters, if you're so fucking concerned?" "Dozens of fucking Iraqis are dying every day. The whole world hates us for going in there in the first place!" "They bring the wounded soldiers back at night, so the press can't even film it and nobody sees!" Viewer commentary in response to a clip of this scene recirculated on YouTube reveals the modes of civic engagement with the geopolitical that Claire's impassioned speech provoked:[2]

> Let's be honest, she made a good point. The Iraqi War was nothing but a bunch of bullshit, causing mass suffering and great hostility among the young generation of adults who have no way of stopping it. What have we done in Iraq besides given the middle east more motivation to oppose us? Oh and spending $3 trillion of tax.
> This episode affected me deeply at the time as a cousin of mine was serving in Iraq, and the fact that I was pissed about Bush being re-elected the year before.

The following comment, which was posted on the Internet Movie Database (IMDb) in response to the series finale, captures the show's resonance with the gendered and familial realities of the Iraq War, including for those serving in Iraq:

> I've watched plenty of show finales in my lifetime. Many had great endings and some had decent ones. I recently finished watching every episode of all 5 seasons of this amazing show while deployed in Iraq. From start to finish, I was completely captivated by the characters as they went about their every day lives. After the credits commenced to roll in Season 5's Series Finale "Everyone's Waiting." I just sat there in my chair completely flabbergasted at "Alan Ball's" incredible and yet honest ending. Of course, that is after I wiped the tears from my eyes and took an enormously deep and saddened "SIGH." I replayed that ending over five other times and still felt the same chills as though it was the first time. The Series finale has inspired me to regain my artistic composure, which I had temporarily lost for the last year and a half. It motivated me to call my wife and kids every day to tell them I missed and loved them so much. It very well has changed the way I look at life itself. I know it sounds kinda weird but it did. "Everyone's waiting" is the best ending I've ever seen in any medium of entertainment.[3]

While *Six Feet Under* and *ER* were shows that predated 9/11 yet began to engage with its politics, others such as *Friday Night Lights*, *Battlestar Galactica*, *Brothers and Sisters*, and *Boston Legal* all launched in the aftermath of the war on terror and were built to one degree or another upon premises that centered around it. *Friday Night Lights*, for instance, featured the ongoing difficulties between a high school quarterback and his father, who was caught in an interminable series of tours of duty in Iraq. When his father's face is blown off by an improvised explosive device (IED), the beleaguered son is confronted by a profiteering funeral director hawking an "American Hero Memorial Package" on the exaggerated premise that the Department of Veterans Affairs will pick up most of the tab. *Battlestar Galactica* deeply explored many issues that were central to the Bush/Cheney terror war, including an astonishing story arc that involved a society of fervently Christian androids who occupy and struggle to convert a group of polytheistic humans to monotheism. When the humans, with whom we are generally invited to identify, undertake an insurgency in the face of the ongoing occupation, as was occurring in Iraq at the time, and resort even to suicide bombing, audiences are confronted with "an extended opportunity to consider what they might do under similar conditions," and an invitation to empathize with and contemplate the perspectives of "the Iraqi peoples subject to U.S. military authority" in the post-9/11 world (Takacs 2012: 198; also see Potter and Marshall 2008).

Brothers and Sisters explored the lives of the large and affluent Walker family of Pasadena, California, and emphasized that while post-9/11 military interventions may well be happening "over there," the impacts of the war on terror nevertheless permeate family life at home in the United States. In the Walker family, everyday dramas and arguments over such things as business and professional life, marital affairs, and terminal illness are shot through with and shaped by the legacies and impacts of the war on terror. These include son Justin Walker's deployment to Iraq and subsequent battle with PTSD, high-flying daughter Kitty Walker's professional and political entanglements with and passionate support for the Republican Party, and matriarch Nora Walker's staunch opposition to conservative politics in general and the Bush/Cheney administration in particular.

Boston Legal also returned repeatedly to the geopolitics of the post-9/11 era. As a legal drama, the show's generic conventions suited it well for the detailed exploration of competing positions and perspectives on a wide variety of topical issues. For instance, in one episode from the first of *Boston Legal*'s five seasons, a corporate CEO who was born in Sudan but raised in the United States from the age of five entreats his lawyers to bring a suit on his behalf against the U.S. government for its failure to intervene in the genocide that is taking place in the country of his birth. Viewers hear a harrowing account given by the CEO of his recent visit to family members in Sudan, of whom he has lost eleven to the genocide thus far. The man explains that, while he was with his family, the Sudanese army arrived to tell them all that they are unwelcome slaves who are occupying cattle-grazing lands. When the man's uncle objected, he was taken behind a barn and burned alive while the family was forced to endure his screams. The man's cousin was then raped.

His lawyers develop a novel legal theory based in tort law to establish the man's standing to sue the U.S. government. This theory turns upon the U.S. government's constant trumpeting of its "war on terrorism" and promise to intervene whenever and wherever terrorization occurs, and particularly on the premise that this constant trumpeting leads other nations to expect action from the U.S. and therefore decline themselves to intervene in humanitarian crises. In short, then, the lawyers seek to turn the power of this discourse of the war on terror against the U.S. government's refusal to intervene in oil-free lands on behalf of African populations undergoing "ethnic cleansing." While this episode reproduces discourses of American exceptionalism, it uses these discourses to shame the U.S. government (and public) for not caring enough about or tending to the injustices taking place in Sudan. As the judge in the case states when she surprisingly rules in favor of the man's standing to sue the U.S. government:

> Why does every crisis automatically fall to the United States to solve? We've got Iraq, Iran, North Korea—and *these* are people who might murder *us*. We're supposed to tend to a bunch of Africans killing each other? Why? Because we're Americans? The answer is: yes, because we're Americans. Because we're a nation—perhaps *the* nation—that's supposed to give a damn. What's going on is an organized extermination of an entire race of people. We're the country that is supposed to give a damn.... Maybe the American people don't care about what's happening over there, but for today, here, now, at least one federal court judge does. [The U.S. government's] motion to dismiss: denied.

This speech reveals something of the complexity of *Boston Legal*'s navigation of these geopolitical waters. While, as noted, the show affirms American exceptionalism, it turns the power of the discourses of American exceptionalism against those in the Bush/Cheney regime, which typically mobilized this power only to reap vast geopolitical advantages and financial gains.

Another *Boston Legal* episode explored the use of false promises and manipulative recruiting techniques by military personnel to sustain a war without requiring broad sacrifices (or even engagement and understanding) by the wider public (such as a draft would entail), which would risk provoking widespread opposition to the war (as during the war in Vietnam). Here, the lawyers represent a woman suing the U.S. military over her brother's death in Iraq, after he was sold an enlistment contract called "Try One," which allows recruits to leave the service after a year if they are not happy. In the case at hand, though, when the brother wished to leave at the end of his year, the military unilaterally extended his commitment by an additional *26 years* under its Stop-Loss program (which was in fact invoked very liberally throughout the Iraq War), and the man was subsequently killed while attempting to disarm an IED, a task for which he had never been trained. Other episodes raised and examined issues such as widespread backlash against criticism of the Iraq War and of the Bush regime in general (a major issue during the Bush years and a constant theme in *Boston Legal*), the infringement of U.S. citizens' rights via securitization measures in the post-9/11 world, and massive Iraq War profiteering by Dick Cheney's former oil services company, Halliburton.

These are a handful of the numerous post-9/11 TV dramas that have delved serially and melodramatically into the complex modes of geopolitical, familial, and gendered sense-making that have circulated around issues such as sacrifice, security, nationhood, and terrorist threats in the contemporary world. These shows have strong female protagonists, deal with some of the war on terror's impacts on both family and professional lives, and have invited substantial online (and presumably offline) audience engagement. We now turn to a closer examination of two more such shows: *Commander in Chief*, which revolves around a matriarch who is also president of the United States, and *Homeland*, which features a female CIA agent whose work involves putting the war on terror into practice.

Semiotic Maneuvering and Unstable Hegemonies: *Commander in Chief*

Commander in Chief is an ABC drama first broadcast in 2005, in which Geena Davis plays Mackenzie "Mac" Allen, the first female president of the United States. Set in the post-9/11 world, Mac, a political independent and vice president serving under Republican Teddy Bridges, becomes president when Bridges dies in office. The series charts the challenges Mac faces after she moves into the White House with her husband and former chief of staff, Rod Calloway, and their three children, Horace, Rebecca, and Amy. The drama of the show emerges from an ongoing series of domestic and foreign geopolitical conflicts to which Mac must respond. We also see her attempting to manage her family life, in particular dealing with her emasculated husband, who is struggling with his new position as the first "First Gentleman," and her three children, who are endeavoring to adapt to the difficulties that come with being the president's son and daughters. There are also ongoing conflicts between Mac and her arch-nemesis, House Speaker Nathan Templeton (played by Donald Sutherland), who embodies a very different political style. While Mac is principled, moderately progressive, suspicious of partisanship, and committed to human rights, equality, and the advancement of women, Templeton is a conservative, hardened, and sexist politician who thrives on backroom deals and underhanded methods in his drive to discredit and derail Mac by whatever means are available. In its eighteen episodes (despite solid ratings and reviews and the 2006 People's Choice Award for "Favorite New Television Drama," the show was cancelled after only one season), *Commander in Chief* deals with a number of contemporary political issues, including relations between the United States and North Korea, China, and Latin America; homegrown and Al-Qaeda style terrorism; the Israeli-Palestinian conflict; the Kurdish separatist movement; the politics of oil; homeland security and U.S. military activity; the war on drugs; disaster management and environmental catastrophe; the politics of race, gender, and sexuality; homelessness; incarceration; healthcare and education; and constitutional law. In many ways, *Commander in Chief* follows in the generic footsteps of *The West Wing*, but much of the work it does around issues of cultural citizenship involves the exploration of what it might be like for the United States to have a female president, while providing a broader commentary on the politics of gender, race, and sexuality in the contemporary United States.

Commander in Chief appeared at a time when the United States' place in the world and position as a superpower had become increasingly uncertain. As such, it evinces interesting textual negotiations over the implications and consequences of the ongoing emergence of a more volatile and multipolar geopolitical environment. Sharp (2000b: xix) has shown how the dominant anti-communist discourses of the Cold War had a containing effect on U.S. national identity and thus helped to construct the nation as a "coherent moral agent—with a clear sense of mission and inevitable destiny." In the post–Cold War period, this position of moral authority and leadership began to unravel as international respect for the United States declined and global contestation of its hegemonic position increased (Sharp 2000b). Attempts to re-secure a hegemonic U.S. national identity under the Bush administration brought renewed political struggles over gender and sexuality that were transcoded into the realm of geopolitics. Nicholas Mirzoeff (2006: 36) has described the Bush regime as one of imperial masculinity characterized by military aggression abroad and the reassertion of heteronormativity at home; "sustaining America's place as the leading nation within empire depends on the doubled performance of feminized consumers and masculine soldiers of all genders. All those who refuse this performance, whether domestic queers or overseas insurgents, must be denied if the self-sustaining image of empire as equivalent to the United States is to continue."

Commander in Chief also appeared just before both Hillary Clinton and Sarah Palin made serious bids for presidential and vice-presidential office. While polls conducted after 9/11 showed that many U.S. voters had no reservations about electing a female president, some citizens stated that the United States was "not ready" for a woman president and that men were better able to handle issues relating to terrorism and national security (Han 2007: 5; Heldman 2007: 19). Caroline Heldman (2007) documented the continued persistence in U.S. society of substantial structural and attitudinal barriers to a female presidency, among which are the close relationship between militaries and masculinity, and the fact that the president of the United States occupies the position of commander in chief, the highest military rank. Hence, forms of entertainment television that envision and work through the prospects of a moderate female president of the United States hold some promise for the renegotiation and reworking of gendered geopolitical imaginaries.

It is thus within a context of renewed masculinism and militarism that *Commander in Chief* tackles (without ever resolving) some of the cultural and political implications of the declining hegemony of the United States, as well as some of the consequences of economic and political transformations underway in China, Latin America, and the Middle East. The show engages with and at times appears to reinforce aspects of American exceptionalism, while inviting viewers to imagine the United States in an era of geopolitical crisis under the leadership of a competent and confident woman rather than George W. Bush. Mac's archrival Templeton, by contrast, routinely puts forward more conservative, aggressive, and Bush/Cheney-like responses to situations. The show frequently stages confrontations between competing perspectives, discourses, and ideologies, at times leaving viewers to ponder and debate the merits of alternative positions.

An interesting feature of the negotiatory work that *Commander in Chief* textually enacts involves its intertwining of parallel familial and geopolitical narratives. Much of the action takes place in the White House, which functions as a central locus of both national geopolitical dramas and the quotidian, domestic tribulations of Mac's family. Consequently, major foreign and domestic policy decisions are made alongside everyday domesticities and family struggles. As a female president with an emasculated husband and sometimes unruly, sometimes anxious children, Mac cannot neatly separate geopolitical matters from the travails of everyday life. Indeed, these areas of her life are so thoroughly entangled that they shape and influence one another in a variety of ways. As Mac moves between the Oval Office and her children's bedrooms, *Commander in Chief* explores and negotiates some of the ways in which the spheres of family life and formal politics spill over into and mutually constitute and implicate one another.

Some episodes deal with U.S. military activities abroad. In "First Strike," Mac and Templeton clash over the issue of how the United States should respond to the murder of three DEA agents attempting to shut down a drug cartel in San Pasquale, a fictitious, composite Latin American country whose democratically elected president has been deposed in a military coup. While this episode draws on well-established tropes of Latin America as drug-ridden and politically unstable, it also amply calls our attention to some of the complexities associated with DEA activities in the region and invites viewers to ask whether the U.S. war on drugs might do more harm than good there. Over the course of the episode, Mac must weigh up the demands of San Pasquale's people for the restoration of democracy, their resentment of a U.S. DEA presence there (voiced in particular by the deposed president, who is now living in Georgetown), the devastating impacts of U.S.-led coca eradication schemes on the livelihoods of small-scale coca farmers whose use of their crops is legitimate, and a felt need to respond to an egregious act of violence against U.S. citizens serving their country abroad.

In "Sub Enchanted Evening" and "No Nukes is Good Nukes," a U.S. spy submarine carrying nuclear weapons is sent into North Korean waters by male military commanders who have neither sought Mac's approval nor even informed her of the mission. When the sub becomes critically damaged, Mac must devise a plan to rescue the troops on board without revealing their violation of North Korean maritime limits and thus potentially provoking a nuclear confrontation. Mac negotiates a deal that involves important concessions to China, who would like the United States to allow them to sell arms to Myanmar and Algeria in exchange for assistance with a covert rescue operation. While the Chinese are thus represented in what might be read as an Orientalist vein via their calculatingly ruthless willingness to put more weapons into the third world, this episode also draws attention to equally unethical behavior by the United States, which is in turn shown to be linked to the sexism of military leaders who go behind the back of their commander in chief out of disrespect for her capacity for command. The situation escalates when Chinese leaks alert the North Korean government to the violation of their waters. While Templeton and U.S. military leaders respond with excitement over the prospect of a "winnable" (if nuclear) war, the president adopts a less masculinist and more cautious, flexible approach; indeed, she even offers a public apology to the North Korean people (in stark and direct contrast to Bush's intransigence and monolithic, confrontational approach to this third member of his "axis of evil"). In the midst of the crisis, Mac goes to say goodnight to her children, who are anxious about the situation. She tries to reassure her youngest daughter, Amy, that the trouble is brewing far away in Asia and would not affect the United States; Amy's reply suggests that we should worry as much about people in Asia as we do about Americans.

Other episodes negotiate issues such as the value of torture as a means of responding to terrorism, the *legitimacy* of grievances that may motivate both international and homegrown "terrorists," the decline of the United States' capacity for moral leadership in the world at large, the country's inadequate healthcare system, and the poor treatment of military veterans and their families by the U.S. government. Mac's combination of traditionally "masculine" and "feminine" attributes in handling such situations often shows how a less intransigent style of leadership could potentially serve the United States very well, while her status as a political independent is often used to illustrate the obstructions to good governance that stem from the corrupting influence of big money, special interests, slick professional handlers, and excessive partisanship. There are typically a range of possible ways in which audiences might position themselves in relation to the program's storylines, and key issues are often raised without being fully resolved. When Mac and her attorney general disagree over the use of torture to gain information about a suspected impending terrorist attack on a U.S. elementary school, the latter asks why a detainee would "talk when he's being wined and dined by the anti-torture statutes?" Mac is left to assert that "other nations follow us. If we torture, there's nothing to prevent other nations torturing our citizens." As Gray (2008: 141) notes in a different context, "prominent voices may well be lacking from this dialogue, so we must avoid characterizing the cultural forum [to which it contributes] as complete or wholly open, but it nevertheless can often offer a space for the (limited) rehearsal, vigorous testing, and development of political beliefs."

Commander in Chief thus embeds narratives linked to "homeland security" in the performative, gendered, and racialized politics of Washington, DC and the White House. In this way it concretely embodies, grounds, and materializes what is often understood as the abstract work of government. On one level, the show appears to promote an identifiable feminist subtext. It displays a woman confidently, competently, and decisively executing the role of commander in chief, depicts the kinds of everyday overt and covert, recoded sexism that women who work in Washington, DC (and beyond) have to deal with routinely, and suggests that the heterosexual economy within which women perform roles as wives and mothers can be drawn upon as a strategic resource.

Commander in Chief also calls into question the idea that the politics of gender are only an issue for women, particularly through its treatment of Mac's husband, Rod Calloway, the nation's first "First Gentleman." The First Gentleman becomes an object of late-night television comedy and high school ridicule, to which Horace and Rebecca are exposed. For instance, Horace gets into a fight at school over this issue and tells his father that the latter has become a national joke and is partly to blame since, as a "wuss of a husband," he is a "pretty easy target." So while the show stages commentary on the attitudinal and structural barriers facing women presidential candidates and professional women more generally, it also shows the president's husband being forced to negotiate gender too, possibly suggesting that the United States is even less ready for a First Gentleman than it is for a female president. When Rod is offered a much more "manly" position as Commissioner of Baseball, he is forced to decline because of his responsibilities in the White House. Rod's emasculation is a challenge for Mac, who attempts to bolster his wounded masculinity by giving him an official position in the administration in charge of strategic planning—which ends up being a mistake both personally and professionally.

In the small body of scholarship that exists on *Commander in Chief*, some have criticized the show for sometimes appearing to promote an anti-feminist message. In her discussion of the program's familial narrative, Michelle Adams (2011) objects to the way in which it depicts Mac as a competent political leader, but as a failing and guilt-ridden wife and mother whose three children are suffering because of her job as president. Horace gets into fights and cheats on his essays at school, Rebecca objects to how the Secret Service's security detail imposes tight restrictions on her social life, and Amy always seems to be having nightmares. Judith Walzer (2009: 104) is concerned that such "proof of maternal neglect" suggests that it would be too difficult for a woman with children to be president. But without these troubling representations, some audiences might not connect with the text and thus be denied an opportunity to reflect on and negotiate important gendered experiences because juggling home and work, trying to appease sexist husbands, and feeling guilty will be familiar to many female viewers. The show thus works to invite critical reflection on such familiar gendered experiences.

Commander in Chief's gendered and racialized narratives also encourage viewers to negotiate the show's geopolitical dimensions. One storyline deals with a Nigerian woman who has been condemned to death under Sharia law for adultery. The U.S. response to this state of affairs is presented as politically complex. On the one hand, Mac asserts in a principled fashion that she will not see a woman put to death for having sex, and sends in the Marines, who successfully rescue the prisoner from what appears to be a brutally inhumane Lagos jail. Clearly, one possible reading is that of the United States as triumphant and morally superior to Nigeria, which is depicted as underdeveloped and backward with respect to the rights of women. Such meanings, however, are complicated and open to negotiation, particularly in light of the way the episode has amply exposed entrenched sexism and racism at work in Washington, DC, the capital of what many consider to be the most politically advanced and democratic nation in the world. This episode also asks viewers to consider whether and in what circumstances military intervention in other sovereign nations is justified. Mac's speech after the rescue is peppered with such gems of American exceptionalism as "freedom is our gift to the world," but the episode's primary narrative strongly and ironically suggests that U.S. political culture is still not advanced enough to treat women and African Americans as equals. For instance, Nathan Templeton states his aversion to wasting U.S. resources on a Nigerian "lady who couldn't keep her legs together," thus demonstrating how sexist discourses frequently inform and shape foreign policy responses.

Queering Popular Geopolitics

It's worth reflecting on geopolitically inflected TV drama's potential for queering U.S. foreign policy and hegemony, which we take up as a further strategy for advancing the critique of masculinist geopolitics initiated by feminist scholars some time ago (see, e.g., Sharp 2000a). We draw in particular on the work of Cynthia Weber. Weber shows how queer practices disrupt the conventional codings of international relations (IR) identified by feminist IR scholars. Moreover, Weber understands queerness broadly; while maintaining a focus on sexuality, she sees queerness "as something that doesn't fit and therefore confuses and confounds the norm and normativity" (Jauhola and Pedersen 2010: 5). It is this broad conception of queerness that is useful for extending our analysis of the popular geopolitics of TV drama in the contemporary media environment as we seek to identify the queering of U.S. hegemony in a show such as *Commander in Chief*. In *Faking It: U.S. Hegemony in a "Post-Phallic" Era*, Weber (1999) analyzes U.S. invasions and interventions in the Caribbean between 1959 and 1994 to show how attempts by the United States to recover a lost phallic power and affect a straight masculine hegemonic identity have paradoxically entailed the adoption of a set of queer compensatory practices. These practices are products of the doubts the United States has about its place in the world. Although *Faking It* was written before 9/11, it is not hard to see how the Bush administration's response to the World Trade Center attacks performed what Weber characterizes as simulated modes of hypermasculinity, particularly through its interventions in Iraq, Afghanistan, and at home. These interventions intensified questions about the role of the United States in the world, thus creating the context of uncertainty within which *Commander in Chief* takes place.

A number of feminist scholars have made the point that the forces of homophobia, sexism, and racism are not external, but rather integral to the workings of foreign policy. What is interesting about *Commander in Chief* is how it exposes these forces at work within the geopolitical realm (and as Weber argues, the power of the phallus is deflated through exposure). In *Commander in Chief*, we see Washington struggle as much with its internal others (feminist resistance in the White House, and differently embodied people) as with its external ones (Muslim fundamentalist terrorists, a rising China, North Korea, Latin American coca farmers). The show thus reveals the relationship between the U.S. government's anxious interactions with the wider world and its inability to extend full inclusion to differently gendered/embodied U.S. citizens. In this way, *Commander in Chief* suggests that U.S. geopolitical anxiety contributes to the reproduction of differential citizenships with respect to race, gender, and sexuality. So, for example, Mac's arch-nemesis Templeton concocts a plan to damage the president when he learns of the HIV status of White House staffer Vince Taylor, who failed to disclose that he is gay and HIV-positive on his national security application. These events generate discussions about political ethics, security, disclosure, and privacy rights, and ultimately lead Mac to the defense of her aide.

Weber (1999) shows that a sovereign nation-state is usually coded in two opposing ways: as internally female/feminine and externally male/masculine. Hence the feminine/domestic space is the site from which a nation-state projects itself into the masculine/international arena. In practice, however, the domestic and the foreign, the public and the private, are constantly combined, deconstructed, and therefore queered. *Commander in Chief* is full of such queerings, not only because the boundaries between domesticity and politics are blurred to an exceptional degree, but also because Mac (and other characters in the show) deploy both masculine and feminine attributes in dealing with geopolitical threats from overseas others, as well as the turbulence of family life. In this regard, the show, and the figure of Mac in particular, persistently foregrounds the incredibility of binarized genders. In *Commander in Chief*, the "domestic" constantly intervenes in and disrupts the phantasmagoria of the United States as a morally superior global hegemon. Mac contributes to this disruption *and* draws on discourses of American exceptionalism in order to project herself in a masculine manner to the world just as previous male presidents have done. In the process, issues and sites are engendered and queered in unpredictable ways. Mac can be masculine in her removal of her husband from a position in the White House and maternal and feminine in her dealings with a would-be terrorist. Similarly, in his efforts to achieve his political ambitions, the hypermasculine and sexist Templeton must express feminized concern toward Colombian subsistence farmers whose livelihoods are destroyed by the U.S. war on drugs, calling into question a masculinist foreign policy objective.

Weber's (1999) broad understanding of queering, noted earlier, means that U.S. hegemony can be queered by anybody who disrupts the white masculine script that underpins foreign policy actions. Thus, it includes Muslim Americans as well as gay ones, along with undocumented migrants and disabled or mentally ill war veterans. And U.S. hegemony is also queered by the way in which dominant political actors paradoxically adopt queer subjectivities in their attempts to restore lost or endangered phallic powers. In "Sub Enchanted Evening," for example, the U.S. government must appease the Chinese in order to keep its botched reassertion of phallic military power in the waters off North Korea under wraps. For Weber (1999), a loss of phallic power means that the United States is unable to have the last word in contemporary geopolitical affairs, and indeed it is from this loss and inability that some of the semiotic fluidity in *Commander in Chief* flows. Because nobody in the U.S. administration is able to have the last word on any geopolitical matter, anxieties about the United States are only ever *temporarily* suspended. We wonder if the repeated queerings in *Commander in Chief*, which draw attention to the uncertainty of the United States' place in the world, contributed to its falling ratings. Did the show make some viewers feel uncomfortable? Could it be that U.S. TV audiences might be ready for a female president, but are not yet ready for a lack of national phallic power to be so exposed?

It is our view that a renewed focus on the negotiatory complexities of television texts can make substantial contributions to future intellectual developments in the arena of scholarship on popular geopolitics and bring the latter into closer dialogue with media and cultural studies. Television's texts facilitate negotiated responses, along with (counter)hegemonic and queer readings, which are often the very stuff of citizen engagement. While our focus here is on TV drama, and we believe substantial further work could be done on the large corpus of post-9/11 TV drama that is now available, we also believe scholars interested in popular geopolitics should also pay greater attention to other kinds of entertainment television, including soap operas, sitcoms, and reality TV shows, all of which are often marked as "feminine," as we have noted above. If we ignore such "delegitimated" albeit popular genres, there is a risk of residual masculinisms being sedimented in other ways. Characters in soap operas also get killed or injured in roadside bombs while fighting in Afghanistan (such as *Coronation Street*'s Luke Quinn and Gary Windass), so it is incumbent to focus on the geopolitical textualities at work in ordinary/feminized entertainment television. It is in part through them that the geopolitical permeates everyday life in real and televisual families and communities.

Drone Queen of the Homeland

Homeland (Showtime, 2011–2020) is focused on U.S. counterterrorism strategy in the aftermath of 9/11 and in particular on the work of the CIA. Its protagonist, Carrie Mathison, begins the series as a CIA agent who struggles, unbeknownst to the agency, with bipolar disorder. Seasons 1–3 are focused on her complicated entanglements with a former U.S. marine turned Al-Qaeda sympathizer, Sergeant Nicholas Brody. Prior to his rescue and return to the United States in 2011, Brody had been held hostage by Al-Qaeda for eight years, during which time he converted to Islam. He also lived for a time with Al-Qaeda commander Abu Nazir and taught English to Nazir's son, Issa, who was later killed by a U.S. drone strike, an event that impacted Brody profoundly. Carrie correctly suspects that Brody has turned against the United States and is planning a terrorist attack; she subsequently manages to recruit him to work for the CIA. Brody and Carrie then embark on a sexual relationship, as a consequence of which Carrie becomes pregnant and gives birth to Brody's child, Frannie, shortly after he is publicly executed in Iran for treason at the end of season 3.

As Trisha Dunleavy (2018) notes, contemporary TV narratives often feature morally complex and transgressive figures who invite awkward and uncomfortable forms of identification. Carrie does her best intelligence work when she is "off her meds," at which times she experiences heightened states of both mental acuity and instability and is capable of making brilliant insights into cases that her colleagues and superiors have misunderstood, and of breaking open difficult and extraordinarily complex investigations. She is often sexually manipulative and sometimes sleeps with CIA assets and informants. She drinks a fair amount (we often see her pouring herself a very large glass of white wine to wash down her medication), and she routinely defies normative notions of "good mothering" by, for instance, repeatedly abandoning her daughter Frannie to the care of Maggie, Carrie's sister. Indeed, in season 4, Carrie takes a seductively challenging and dangerous CIA station chief posting in Afghanistan that precludes Frannie from joining her, even though she could have chosen a safer (but duller) chiefship in Istanbul that would have allowed the two to live together. There is a chilling scene in season 4 when Carrie almost drowns Frannie in the bath. At other times, Carrie's intelligence work actively puts Frannie in serious danger. In season 6 (episode 5, "Casus Belli"), for example, Frannie is effectively taken hostage in her own home, which is surrounded by police snipers, after Carrie leaves her in the care of former CIA colleague and PTSD sufferer Quinn, in an incident the *Baltimore Sun* characterized as asking "the unhinged professional assassin guy [to] watch your child" (Renner 2017). Robyn Longhurst

(2008: 117–129) argues that discourses of "bad mothering" generate moral panics that target those seen to be "lacking" in relation to norms of femininity and familiality. Carrie lacks a husband, lacks neurotypicality, and lacks a normative "maternal instinct" capable of regulating her threateningly excessive professional devotion and aspirations. The simultaneous absence and excess of maternal normativity poses a threat to the stable familial order that often stands metonymically for the nation in popular geopolitical narratives and representations.

Homeland's representational politics are highly complex, though many viewers object to its depictions of gender, race, and religion, and some have carefully detailed factual and geographical errors they have identified in the show.[4] Carrie is a professional woman who works in the aggressive, dangerous, and male-dominated world of anti-terrorism and national security. The fate of the nation, and indeed even of Western democracy, often hang on her ability to perform beyond competently. She sometimes, as noted, puts her work ahead of her relationship with her child, and some suggest that *Homeland*'s depiction of Carrie's "hysterical" mental instabilities dovetail too neatly with patriarchal discourses of women's madness (see, for example, Strauss 2014, who nevertheless recognizes, as we argue below, that such a reading is not easily sustained). Kathleen McInnis (2012), who has worked in national security, believes that what she views as Carrie's blatant lack of professionalism ("making passes at the boss" and "taking classified materials home and displaying them on" her wall) does a disservice to women who work in this field. While Carrie resists domestication, she does so in the name of a racist and imperialist war. Thus, Carrie is an unstable figure who challenges both overtly feminist and anti-feminist readings; that she makes available a range of contradictory potential meanings is symptomatic of ongoing gender trouble that has been active for decades, but roiled in particular ways in the post-9/11 geopolitical climate. As Gargi Bhattacharyya (2014: 378) argues, *Homeland*'s narrative suggests that "femininity and feminism—both female bodies and a discourse of women's rights—can become central elements of the project of securitization. What appears to be a development is the use of familiar tropes of women's unreason to serve as an alternative justification of irrational actions by the state. The femininity that serves the security state here is the unruly femininity of the hysteric."

As regards representations of race and the war on terror, criticism of *Homeland* is widespread. The *Washington Post* claimed that *Homeland* was "the most bigoted show on television," and accused the show of churning out "Islamophobic stereotypes as if its writers were getting paid by the cliché" (Durkay 2014). The *Guardian* has asserted that *Homeland* offers nuance, as in its depiction of how Brody was "turned" in part because of the murder of an innocent child by a U.S. drone, but also espouses "a dangerous set of lies about terrorism, American omnipotence and the very nature of international politics" (Cohen 2013). Pakistani officials objected loudly to *Homeland*'s depiction of a devastating U.S. drone attack on a wedding in Pakistan in an episode from season 4 that we discuss below. One diplomat complained to the *New York Post* that "Islamabad is a quiet, picturesque city with beautiful mountains and lush greenery.... In *Homeland*, it's portrayed as a grimy hellhole and war zone where shootouts and bombs go off with dead bodies scattered around. Nothing is further from the truth" (Schram 2014). Such criticisms have been echoed in some of the academic media studies literature. James Castonguay (2015: 139), for example, writes that *Homeland* "successfully exploits post-9/11 insecurities, psychological trauma, and narrative complexity to produce "quality" television propaganda for the Obama administration's "overseas contingency operations" and its unprecedented domestic surveillance on the home front under the umbrella of an $80 billion US security state."

In season 5, *Homeland*'s producers hired several street artists to embellish a Syrian refugee camp set with Arabic graffiti. Unbeknownst to the producers, the graffiti artists inscribed, "Homeland is racist" and other comments critical of the show on the walls of their set. After the scenes set in the camp aired, one of the artists, Heba Amin, stated, "We think the show perpetuates dangerous stereotypes by diminishing an entire region into a farce through the gross misrepresentations that feed into a narrative of political propaganda. It is clear they don't know the region they are attempting to represent. And yet, we suffer the consequences of such shallow and misguided representation" (Quoted in Phipps 2015). This act of creative subversion highlights that the modes of sense-making associated with popular geopolitical texts are both dispersed across and contested at a variety of different sites and levels, including those of production and the industry, of the text and its multiple and often contradictory discourses, and of audiences and their multifarious reception practices (see, e.g., Fiske 2011; Gledhill 1988). Indeed, commercially successful TV dramas of the media convergence era tend to promote controversy and the formation of coalition audiences by staging confrontations between competing perspectives, discourses, and ideologies, and to eschew binary frameworks of understanding. While it is thus possible to argue that *Homeland*'s storylines circulate and reinforce discourses that proclaim "the need for increased homeland security and the use of force in counterterrorism operations," and open up alternative possibilities only to then shut them down (Castonguay 2015: 141), we are suspicious of forms of textual determinism that seek to read audiences' meaning-making practices off media texts themselves. Indeed, one study of *Homeland* audiences' reception practices found that fans frequently read the text against the grain and produced a range of oppositional positions regarding CIA operations (Pears 2016).

In our view, *Homeland* continually evades black and white political binarisms. As Richard McHugh (2016: 163) writes, the story arc that deals with Brody's radicalization at the hands of Al-Qaeda reveals that Brody "was already radicalized as a US marine through the same government system that radicalizes the CIA agents as patriots." The show makes clear that this patriotism involves the murder of innocent children with drones, which constitutes an "act of violence that pushed Brody further into his alternate-radical self" (164). In addition to its highly critical treatments of U.S. drone warfare in Pakistan, *Homeland* also engages critically with Zionist attitudes toward Israel's West Bank occupation. It is difficult to argue that *Homeland* valorizes the CIA, whose agents the show routinely depicts as flawed, corrupt, duplicitous, predatory, racist, and villainous.

The entanglement of and interplay between motherhood, mental health, and counterterrorism function as key narrative drivers in *Homeland*. Some of the existing feminist literature on *Homeland* captures these textual complexities and underscores why the gendered dynamics of this show are of theoretical importance. Alex Bevan's (2015) discussion of *Homeland* emphasizes how gendered embodiment functions "as a nexus point for geopolitical discourses" (151), as the pathological, "reproductive and sexual currencies of Carrie's body are burdened" with the symbolic task of territorializing and representing the "elusive terms of twenty-first-century warfare and geopolitical power" (148). The management of Carrie's bipolar disorder, for instance, volatilizes the distinction between being surveilled and doing surveilling in ways that raise but do not settle questions about the degree of surveillance needed in the post-9/11 world and the consequences of its intensification. *Homeland* reveals not only how women's bodies are central rather than incidental to the project of securitization (for example, they are sometimes invoked as figures of fragility that stand metonymically for the vulnerability of the nation, and thus in support of calls for a general restoration of traditional masculinities), but also how the "unruly hysteric is an unexpected complement to the securitized state" (Bhattacharyya 2014: 378). Indeed, audiences might come "to inhabit the logic of securitization" (382) through identification with Carrie but are just as likely to accept the text's implicit invitation to reflect critically on the security state and its gendered logics in ways that leave them more unsettled with regard to U.S. foreign policy directions and actions. The text of *Homeland* permits a range of political positions with respect to both women's rights and the war on terror, and so remains polysemous and multidiscursive in its constant engagements with the multifaceted relationships between gender and geopolitics. We now turn to a discussion of one highly gendered geopolitical instrument, the drone, in order to develop an analysis of its treatment in the show.

Unmanned aerial vehicles (UAVs), also known as drones, first entered the war on terror as a consequence of two U.S. government surveillance and assassination programs launched in 2002 to target Al-Qaeda sympathizers in Pakistan and Yemen—two countries *not* at war with the United States. The use of drone attacks as an instrument of U.S. foreign policy was escalated dramatically during the Obama presidency and was mostly shrouded in secrecy until 2012, when the U.S. government admitted the existence of the program, but refused to say how many terrorists and civilians were killed by UAV strikes, a choice the government defended by invoking Orientalist, masculinist, and medicalized discourses. Obama propounded the view that Pakistan's Federally Administered Tribal Areas, near the border with Afghanistan, constituted the world's most threatening and dangerous locale and must be brought to order; he thus established a space of exception amenable to missile penetration from above (Gregory 2017: 31), through the mobilization of "new visibilities" that "produce a special kind of intimacy that consistently privileges the view of the hunter-killer" (Gregory 2011: 193). As one drone operator put it, "sometimes I feel like a God hurling thunderbolts from afar" (192). U.S. officials have also commended drones for the "surgical precision" that enables them "to eliminate the cancerous tumor called an al-Qaida terrorist while limiting damage to the tissue around it" (John Brennan, Obama's counterterrorism advisor, quoted in Crawford 2012). Nevertheless, U.S. drone strikes have, of course, killed hundreds of civilians, including hundreds of children (Gregory 2017: 29), and provoked substantial protests and political opposition in areas subject to attack.

The CIA's use of drones for both surveillance and targeted killing has been a recurring feature of *Homeland*'s narratives. The first episode of season 4 ("The Drone Queen") deals with faulty intel that leads Carrie to order a late-night missile strike on a farmhouse in Pakistan, thus killing forty innocent civilians attending a wedding there. Just before she turns in for the night, Carrie's colleagues surprise her with a birthday cake decorated with the moniker, "The Drone Queen." The scene of Carrie getting into bed for a restful night's sleep cuts to images of community members frantically searching through piles of rubble for the bodies of the dead and injured at what is left of the farmhouse. The next day, Carrie scrutinizes the live video feed that is relayed by drones trawling the scene of the previous night's strike and is clearly able to see row upon row of corpses, along with a young medical student, Aayan Ibrahim, who is looking through the bodies for his mother and sister, both of whom were killed in the attack. In a chilling moment that literalizes the reversal of surveillance practices that occurs when the watched becomes watcher, Aayan stares bitterly up at the encircling drone and into its camera as if to lock eyes on Carrie and the entire U.S. military industrial apparatus with an accusatory look that clearly, momentarily unsettles Carrie (see figure 2.1). The previous night, Aayan was using his cellphone to film children dancing at the wedding party when the U.S. missiles struck. After Washington issues vehement denials of claims that their missiles hit a wedding party and anti-drone protests ensue outside the U.S. embassy in Islamabad, Aayan's roommate uses a proxy server to upload Aayan's cellphone video of the attack on the celebrants to YouTube without Aayan's consent. The video quickly goes viral and generates a major political conflict for Carrie and the CIA. In the storylines that ensue, Carrie seduces and becomes sexually involved with Aayan in her efforts to use him to gain access to his uncle, the U.S.-trained terrorist, Haissam Haqqani, who had been the original target of the missile strike on the farmhouse, but who survived the attack. Her deception

FIGURE 2.1 Aayan returns Carrie's gaze via the drone's camera in *Homeland*.

and betrayal of Aayan leads ultimately to his murder at the hands of Haqqani, which takes place in full view of an overhead drone as a horrified Carrie and her colleagues look on.

Just as drones respatialize war, so does *Homeland* respatialize drones and the techniques and consequences of their use in the media. Drones destabilize the boundaries between battle zone and non–battle zone, and render ambiguous the difference between combatants and non-combatants. Furthermore, they participate in the manipulation of "the visibility and concealment of socially sanctioned forms of killing" (Asaro 2017: 286). Peter Asaro writes that "even while the work of drone operators has become increasingly important to the military, and to national and international politics, the actual work of drone operators has remained largely hidden from public view and increasingly protected from the prying eyes of journalists and social scientists. And even within the military, drone warriors are subject to powerful social pressures not to reveal or discuss their work or its psychological or emotional stresses" (286). Consequently, surveillance and killing by drones are rendered resistant to sustained public debate and made "difficult to perceive, bear witness to, or even conceive of" (Bevan 2015: 148). But while neither drones nor anti-drone protests in Pakistan have received much media coverage in the West (Parks 2017: 23), they have been subject to sustained fictional exploration in *Homeland*. In "Drone Queen," for example, Carrie is directly confronted and challenged by the distressed and irate U.S. soldier responsible for delivering the missile strikes on the wedding party and others, who tells Carrie he is "sick to the stomach" over these killings and calls those ordering the attacks "fucking monsters, all of you." The respatialization of drones in TV drama thus helps audiences "imagine and speculate about covert US drone attacks in Pakistan through multiple positions and modalities—the air or ground, perpetrator or victim . . . as part of the process of grappling with the killing of thousands of people, including civilians and children, that US officials have refused to account for" (Parks 2017: 23).

Lisa Parks (2017: 15–16) discusses what she calls "drone media," a category that includes grassroots and activist-made "photographs, video, maps, data visualizations, and infographics" that circulate on internet sites such as YouTube, "convey grounded dimensions of drone attacks," and "challenge the widely-held assumptions that US military drones enable a remote and precise form of warfare that minimizes casualties and collateral damage." Drone media participate in exposing "how deeply and profoundly this 'surgical' method of warfare has affected lifeworlds on the ground," and thereby "model the kinds of knowledge practices that are needed when democratic states fail." Drone media can thus be considered as a form of counter-media that generates an alternative scopic regime wherein the very apparatus of state-sanctioned visualization, surveillance, and killing becomes the object of a critical and interrogatory gaze. While Parks does not include TV drama in the category of drone media, our view is that shows such as *Homeland* participate in and extend a similar project of counter-visualization that constructs spaces amenable to a critical and interrogatory gaze, but also, through television's emergent narrative modalities, to forms of identification and affective engagement with remote sufferers and suffering. Lilie Chouliaraki (2013) argues for the importance of the "mundane acts of mediation" that, through everyday storytelling on TV and elsewhere, offer a kind of "moral education" in the form of "a series of subtle proposals of how we should feel and act towards distant suffering" (57). Such acts of mundane mediation are necessary, she argues, for the production of a "humanitarian imaginary" capable of stimulating forms of "sympathetic identification that may lead to action" (44). Such identifications and solidarities are routinely provoked through TV's new modes of narrative complexity and participatory reception practices.

As scholars have noted, television in the age of media convergence is marked by the development of new strategies of diegetic elaboration that facilitate intensified modes of audience engagement and the creation of "worlds that viewers gradually feel they inhabit along with the characters" (Sconce 2004: 95; Cupples and Glynn 2013). In the case of *Homeland*, we experience the devastation and suffering that missile strikes produce on the ground through the eyes and voices of characters we have gotten to know and maybe care about, such as Aayan Ibrahim or Abu Nazir and his young son, Issa. Moreover, as the camera's gaze shifts between the often abstract, top-down, surveillant perspective of the CIA command center and the quotidian routines and relationships of the people living within the drone's field of vision—whom viewers have come to know as parents, friends, sons, daughters, and lovers—we are invited to draw connections and bear witness to juxtapositions between the deterritorialized discourses of counterterrorism and the strategic exertion of control, on the one hand, and the grounded and embodied experiences of those unjustly targeted, on the other. We might read such interplays as the televisual and popular cultural equivalent of the sorts of connections and juxtapositions that have long been at the heart of good feminist geography and media scholarship. As regards ongoing U.S. military interventions in South and Central Asia, *Homeland* can thus be read as a kind of response, in its own way, to the fact that "the space in which these continuing operations have been brought into public view remains strikingly limited," and that "the space of the [drone] target has been radically underexposed" in Western media (Gregory 2011: 204).

Homeland and *Commander in Chief* help us to illustrate some of the ways in which popular culture in general and television in particular function as spaces of ideological mobilization, discursive struggle, and gendered geopolitical deliberation in the age of media convergence. While expert and specialist knowledges are mobilized in the construction of official policy documents and proceedings in ways that preclude widespread participation and minimize opportunities for the involvement of "ordinary people," popular culture circulates discourses of securitization and surveillance, war and conflict, gender and geopolitics, and race and religion in ways that invite popular affective engagement and contestation. Joke Hermes (2005: 3–4) uses the term "cultural citizenship" to explore the "democratic potential of popular culture" as a terrain where, "regardless of the commercial and governmental interests and investments that co-shape its forms and contents," space is nevertheless continually made for "implicit and explicit social criticism" from a variety of locations and perspectives. Hermes's reading of popular culture as a space of affective engagement, discursive contestation, and political negotiation follows a well-established scholarly tradition associated with cultural studies. Feminist cultural studies, like feminist geopolitics, has long sought to trace the complex and often contradictory connections between the micropolitics of everyday lives, struggles and pleasures, and the macropolitical realm where the structuring forces of political and economic institutions operate most powerfully and effectively. By problematizing the geopolitics of gender, surveillance, securitization, and remote-controlled, state-sanctioned killing, television in the post-9/11 age of media convergence constitutes a key site of both popular cultural citizenship and critical scholarly investigation and analysis.

Part II

Disaster Events, Participatory Media, and the Geographies of Waiting

3

Decoloniality, Disaster, and the New Media Environment

Disaster Events in the New Media Environment

Major disasters have long been heavily and often globally mediated events, and the new media environment is changing the way disasters are experienced, made sense of, and responded to. Marita Sturken (2007: 29) notes that even people in the vicinity of a disaster tend to watch it unfold on television, and increasingly they experience disaster events through streaming services and social media as well. Like other media events, disasters do not come pre-equipped with meanings; rather, they must be put into discourse in order to *mean* or to *make sense*, for "nondiscursive reality may never be accessible in its own terms and never has an essential identity of its own" (Fiske 2016a: 5). When a disaster strikes, its survivors, politicians, emergency managers, reporters, and others struggle to put its events into established frames of meaning and so make sense of their unfolding. Such sensemaking struggles turn disasters into sites of semiotic contestation as events are inserted into competing and often contradictory discursive frameworks. For as John Fiske (2016a: 4) observes, "we can know an event only by putting it into discourse, so an event is always continuous with its discursive construction, but it still always contains the potential to be differently constructed." Furthermore, disasters such as hurricanes and earthquakes are not only mediated but also mediating—they mediate relationships between states and their citizens, and in the process often produce new forms of political engagement and mobilization. Rebecca Solnit (2010: 163) writes that "disasters are ultimately enigmas: it is not the disaster but the struggle to give it meaning and to take the opportunity to redirect social meaning that matters, and these are always struggles with competing interests."

Hegemonic discourses and narratives that make sense of disasters as highly localized and sometimes "natural," inevitable, and one-off disruptions that are beyond human control generally circulate widely and predominate in mainstream media. Of course, disasters might alternatively be represented and narrated as phenomena that do not simply and suddenly happen, but rather unfold in historical time and across space as manifestations of established and ongoing forms of social and economic neglect, inequality, and marginalization; geopolitical dynamics, strategies, and machinations; racial and ethnic discrimination and domination; and the authorization of particular kinds of knowledges and ways of knowing, and the corresponding delegitimation of others (Oliver-Smith 1986). Mainstream media representations of disasters also often tend to exaggerate chaos, suffering, and social breakdown. For example, journalistic pieces-to-camera often take place in front of collapsed buildings or piles of rubble. Additionally, there is a tendency to fetishize individuating discourses of "resilience" and "heroism." Disaster events are often articulated with pervasive neoliberalizing and racializing discourses that assert some places and even people are not worth saving, or that individuals are to blame for their hardship as a result of a failure of self-responsibilization (see Elliot 2010). For example, during the 2020 COVID-19 pandemic, prominent conservatives in the United States and the United Kingdom asserted (and heavily funded think tanks, lobbyists, protest groups and movements, and media networks promoted the view) that older people would be best sacrificed for the good of the stock market or the economy, as it would be too financially costly to protect them (see, e.g., Levin 2020; Paton 2020; Bragman and Kotch 2021). Similarly, Diane Negra (2010: 16) notes that a set of deeply racialized neoliberal narrative figures and patterns differentiated coverage of the 9/11 disaster from Hurricane Katrina. Mainstream media stories about the 9/11 attacks tended to focus on "suburban breadwinners ... linked to the idealized daily rhythms of American capitalism and seats of financial and governmental power" who were simply going to or about their work when disaster struck, and on the heroism of "an intensely re-valorized class of white male firefighters and police officers" who responded to this disaster. By contrast, "Katrina victims were presented in compliance with a set of preexisting stereotypes about the idle urban poor in a city where 'black gangsterism' was understood to thrive." But in the contemporary media environment, alternative and popular discourses and knowledges concerning the long-term causes of devastation and vulnerability, and the (in)adequacy of emergency response, informed by lived experiences of specific material conditions of existence, also circulate, although they might be discredited by official discourses, knowledges, and authorities. The mediation of disasters necessarily unfolds within socially constituted power relations, but the discursive circulation of competing discourses means that the potential always exists for more inclusive, alternative, and democratizing perspectives and forces to gain traction.

The unfolding of a disaster event in the context of neoliberal capitalism produces important continuities and ruptures. We do not see neoliberalism as a monolith that takes the same form and has the same effects everywhere in the world. Rather, we see neoliberalism as "a complex assemblage of ideological commitments, discursive representations, and institutional practices, all propagated by highly complex class alliances and organized at multiple geographical scales" (McCarthy and Prudham 2004: 276). While neoliberalism has some core defining features, including the rigorous and persistent dismantling of the (welfare) state, privatization, deregulation, and trade liberalization (Hall 2011), individuals position themselves within and against neoliberal policies and practices in a range of compliant, resistant, and contradictory ways. Thus, contemporary neoliberalism has been stretched, for example, to accommodate a widespread expansion of deeply racist formations of authoritarian nationalism in many parts of the world, including the United States and the United Kingdom. Hence, neoliberalism has many varied contours, is never finished, and is highly contradictory and unpredictable in its outcomes and effects (Larner 2003; Hall 2011).

The social groups most excluded or harmed by neoliberal processes and initiatives are also often the worst affected by disasters, which frequently exacerbate existing inequalities and vulnerabilities. But ruptures to the social fabric associated with disasters sometimes enable survivors to find new sources of strength and solidarity, and to mobilize for political change. Significant disasters variously contributed to the toppling of the Somoza dictatorship in Nicaragua and of the Partido Revolucionario Institucional (PRI) in Mexico and constituted major turning points for the fortunes of the presidencies of George W. Bush (Solnit 2010) and Donald Trump in the United States. Disasters such as hurricanes rupture physical and material landscapes when they flood or wash away homes, other buildings, roads, and bridges. Ensuing crises are often seized opportunistically by governments, planners, and think-tanks to advance neoliberal agendas in ways that might have been politically impossible absent a crisis (Peck 2006; Klein 2007; Cupples 2012a; Johnston, Sears, and Wilcox 2012). Disasters do, however, also produce discursive ruptures, and therefore opportunities for the expanded circulation of residual popular or subaltern ways of knowing that may ordinarily remain latent under neoliberal or neocolonial conditions, and for emergent discourses that may be repressed or marginalized by official knowledges to find spaces of more open and sometimes effective articulation. At such moments, long-term deprivations and vulnerabilities that were invisible to some groups may become more visibly manifest and indeed may become sites of intense contestation. The media and mediation have a crucial role to play in the realization (or not) of such possibilities.

Hurricanes such as Katrina, which hit the Gulf Coast of the United States (and especially New Orleans) in 2005, and Felix, which hit the Caribbean Coast of Nicaragua and the port city of Bilwi (Puerto Cabezas) in 2007, took place in quite particular socioeconomic and epistemic conditions and amid a rapidly shifting and increasingly complex media environment. The hegemony of the extractive economy since the colonial era and of neoliberalism since the 1980s has condemned too many people to life below the poverty line or to extreme conditions of labor precarity. But contemporary socioeconomic exclusions are now being enacted in a moment of deep conjunctural and epistemological crisis, in which many things once confidently presumed have been put in question (Quijano 2007). On the one hand, the contemporary era is arguably one in which many states are becoming less responsive to the demands and needs of their citizens. At the same time, the hegemony of Eurocentric rationality and the "violent concentration of the world's resources under the control and for the benefit of a small European minority" (Quijano 2007: 168) are now more contested than ever. For Jesús Martín-Barbero (2011: 41), the innovative and inspirational forms of Indigenous, African American, and Afro-Latinx mobilization taking place in the Americas constitute the reappearance of a politics that "breathes fresh life into the atmosphere, expanding the horizons not only of action but of thought." For Aníbal Quiijano (2005: 55), the "discontented population . . . is starting to organize itself in new ways and to present demands which its oppressors clearly do not expect." However, while some countries are seriously engaging with redistributive policies, much of the Americas continues to be characterized by further concentrations of power and wealth, accompanied by the erosion of democratic processes in order to minimize popular opposition. As Stuart Hall (2011) remarked in an article that reflects on the situation in Britain after the debt-driven boom, the crisis of the banking sector, New Labour's defeat in 2010, and the 2011 U.K. "riots" (which we might alternatively term "uprisings"), the deep problems with neoliberalism have been more than amply revealed, but "so far it is a crisis which refuses to 'fuse'" (705). It is still unclear, based on available evidence, whether neoliberalism is unravelling or reconstituting itself in more dangerous and authoritarian ways (Peck 2012). In the contemporary Americas and beyond, there is abundant evidence in support of both possibilities, and it was in this conjuncture that Hurricanes Katrina and Felix made landfall. These hurricanes also occurred at a time, as noted in part 1, when centralized forms of media began to give way to an increasingly complex communication environment marked by the emergence of new connectivities and networked spaces. This chapter explores the potential for democratizing and decolonizing forces to gain steam in the context of a shift in how different groups use media to produce and circulate knowledges, construct and promote identities, engage as citizens within increasingly complex political cultures, and understand and confront disasters and crises. In what ways might the contemporary rapid circulation of responses to disasters across multiple media platforms—including YouTube, blogs, Indigenous community television, and mainstream TV news, current affairs and drama—facilitate the disruption and rearticulation of Eurocentric modes of understanding, and promote the spread of decolonizing and democratizing discourses and knowledges of disaster?

The contemporary, globalized media environment is undergoing rapid transformation under the pressure of continuing expansion, fragmentation, digitalization, and technological elaboration. Television has gone from "a network to a postnetwork institutional structure" and been transformed by "the appearance of digital and web-based delivery platforms" (Gray 2012). We are witnessing the growth, densification, and "complexification" of interactions between different media technologies, and the development of new media mobilities and user-driven processes. Under such conditions, the changing landscapes of the world's diverse and complexly mediatized societies are increasingly disrupting the credibility of various official narratives of (national) consensus. In the current environment, "old" media such as newspapers, radio, and television compete with "new," including blogs, podcasts, and a host of other so-called Web 2.0 applications, while all media are transnationalized and dispersed across proliferating channels and multiple niche audiences (Tay and Turner 2008). As we have argued in chapter 1, what Daniel Dayan (2009: 20) has called "central television," which helped to focus "collective attention," has given way to an expansion of "conflicting versions" of "the same situations" and a range of alternative media, so that "the activity of displaying has become a globally sensitive battlefield" to a greater degree than ever before. Amid this fragmentation and disruption of the relative stability associated with central television, media convergence is giving rise to new interconnections, divisions of labor, and mutually transformative interactions between different media; to new forms of networked social relations, nodes or points of media densification, and participatory agglomeration; and to new ways of generating and circulating knowledge (Bruns 2008; Burgess and Green 2009; Jenkins 2008).

In this context, the various economic, epistemological, and identity crises that have accompanied the neoliberalization and de-democratization of some spheres of everyday life in the past few decades, have also seen a rapid expansion and democratization of access to technological and media resources by some of the world's most marginalized populations. Colombian author Frances Njubi refers to this as "the counter-penetration of information technology by people of African descent" (quoted in Jordan 2004: 21), a process that facilitates forms of connection between people with a shared "racial" identity (Quijano 2005: 71), exemplified, for example, in the way that events in Ferguson and Gaza became articulated on platforms such as Twitter and resulted in the #Ferguson2Palestine solidarity movement.[1] While on the one hand, the contemporary media environment markedly extends the reach of surveillance and control networks into new corners and modalities of everyday life (see, e.g., Andrejevic 2007, 2013), at the same time, this mediasphere is providing ordinary people with new forms of voice, new technologies of countersurveillance, and new ways of making and interacting with content. Media forms such as blogs and YouTube create space for reactionary rants and the reproduction of dominant discourses, but also enable marginalized people to speak back to power. It is interesting to note that YouTube hit the mediasphere in the same year as Hurricane Katrina and provided a new way of responding to the disaster and to the inadequate emergency management efforts mounted in its wake. It is important, however, not to set up a binarism between so-called old and new media. As Bolter and Grusin (1999: 55) argue, "all mediation is remediation," and "at this extended historical moment, all current media function as remediators" of earlier media forms, just as "older media can also remediate newer ones." Similarly, it is important to recognize that alternative and subaltern perspectives have always circulated, to a degree, in media both "old" and corporate/mainstream. Furthermore, as Martín-Barbero (2004b: 312–313) argues, popular consumption, including that of media, cannot be adequately grasped as mere social reproduction or "the acceptance of the values of other classes"; rather, "it is a production of meanings and the site of a struggle" that "expresses just aspirations to a more human and respectful life."

Fiske's (2016a) work has explored the cultural and political struggles waged in and around the media by tracing the circulation of power through discourses and counterknowledges that readily cross the boundaries between different media forms, platforms, and genres. Thus, for example, he shows how cultural and political contestation around the meanings of race and gender was waged through such events as the Senate hearings on the appointment of Clarence Thomas to the U.S. Supreme Court and Anita Hill's accusations that he had sexually harassed her. The discourses, counterknowledges, and cultural struggles at work in this event spilled readily across a range of media forms, including the mainstream and alternative press, news and current affairs programs, sitcoms, documentaries, daytime talk shows, and even a prime-time cartoon. In a media-saturated world, media events, which erupt transmedially across such ostensibly distinct generic realms as news and drama programming, constitute key sites of cultural politics where society's deepest divisions, anxieties, and aspirations are expressed, debated, contested, and played out against each other. Adopting a poststructuralist epistemology and framework that combines core insights from Foucault and Gramsci, Fiske shows that media events are neither straightforward reflections of some underlying reality nor diversions from a more "authentic" or effective politics. Rather, the discourses, knowledges, and counterknowledges that circulate through and comprise transmedia events are agents and conduits for the exertion of power, control, and opposition. Discursive diffusion in the media (and therefore socially) is, for Fiske, an inherently political practice through which power-bearing discourses "work to repress, marginalize, and invalidate others; by which they struggle for audibility and for access to the technologies of social circulation; and by which they fight to promote and defend the interests of their respective social formations" (2016a: 4).

In the wake of disaster, survivors that have not lost access to their sources of media tend to become heavy users for multiple reasons that shift across the short, medium, and long terms. In the immediate aftermath of disaster events, those involved often use media to seek information they need to survive and recover, including announcements about where to find shelter, water, fuel, and other necessary supplies, and whether schools, universities, and roads will remain open or not. They listen to the radio or watch TV to learn about the scale of damage caused by a disaster, the implications for their lives and livelihoods, and the progress being made to restore order and daily routines. They use social media or local radio to search for missing family members or friends. Crowdsourced mapping technologies that involve Volunteered Geographic Information (VGI) such as Open Street Map or Ushahidi often become crucial to relief efforts. As Aswin Punathambekar (2017: 84, emphasis added) writes, after major flooding in Chennai, India in 2015, "a tech-savvy group of people mobilized" through the use of "Twitter, various messaging services, Facebook pages, Google Docs, and crowdsourced maps ... to produce *an infrastructure of care* that the government simply could not."

In the medium and long term, disaster survivors also use the media to speak back to power, and to lobby the authorities or insurance companies about addressing local needs. They rely on news and current affairs teams to call the government, insurers, and other entities to account in cases of incompetence, corruption, or failure to act. In the wake of disaster, people use the media in a variety of ways to advance their own or others' efforts to rebuild or raise funds, and to memorialize those who have died and places that no longer exist (see, e.g., Kirshenblatt-Gimblett 2003: 11, on the extraordinary popular exuberance that emerged all around Ground Zero and wider Lower Manhattan in the wake of the 9/11 catastrophe, where "grassroots responses to the trauma" were "spontaneous, improvised, and ubiquitous," and where "every surface of the city—sidewalks, lampposts, fences, telephone booths, barricades, garbage dumpsters, and walls—was blanketed with candles, flowers, flags, and missing persons' posters"). The extension of such practices into digital media spaces includes the production of YouTube videos and documentaries, the creation of memes and hashtags, and the recording of music that frames, reflects upon, and commemorates disasters. Some of these user-generated media texts are sad, serious, or sentimental, while others deploy humor and satire. Finally, people use media to participate in shared experiences with others, to find cultural and informational resources that explicate their ordeals, and to validate their reactions and efforts toward recovery. The ongoing construction and reconstruction of cultural citizenship are important to those recovering from disaster events, and the media are among the key sites where this recovery takes place. Indeed, a body of scholarship has emphasized how disastrous phenomena produce interesting forms of political mobilization as survivors struggle for resources and political redress, and in the process learn how to lobby authorities and insurance companies who are responsible for meeting key post-disaster needs, but have been negligent in their responsibilities (as in, "Brownie, you're doing a heck of a job!"; see Enarson and Morrow 1998; Poniatowska 1995; Solnit 2010). Disasters often reveal and exacerbate a wide array of social and cultural fault lines, and thus facilitate the exposure of deeply sedimented forms of exclusion or racism that had previously been less visible or even unknown to the more privileged sectors of the population.

The political terrain formed by media events and discourses has rapidly expanded in the new media environment. As Martín-Barbero (2011: 42) argues, the convergence of new media technologies and their appropriation by "groups from lowly sectors" is enabling counter-hegemonic activities across the globe. By tracing the recirculation and rearticulation of discourses and counterdiscourses across media platforms and generic forms, we can begin to grasp one aspect of the process whereby alternative, Indigenous, and popular ways of knowing that are closely tied to specific material conditions of deprivation, continue to survive and become socially and politically active despite their constant devaluation by dominant social groups. While the struggles over discourses and knowledges at the heart of disaster media events are not in themselves sufficient to constitute decolonization, they can nonetheless contribute decisively to the formation of new modes of common sense whose creation is a key prerequisite to the expansion of participatory democracy and the reformulation of economic and social policies and practices that racialize, harm, and exclude.

Disaster and Decolonization

In recent years, a set of interesting theoretical developments coming out of Latin American cultural studies have coalesced into what is referred to as the decolonial option, or the modernity/coloniality/decoloniality (MCD) research program. This body of literature, which has been advanced by scholars such as Walter Mignolo, Arturo Escobar, Aníbal Quijano, Catherine Walsh, and Nelson Maldonado-Torres, is particularly useful for thinking through the disarticulation and rearticulation of conventional disaster and crisis narratives in the Americas. While MCD scholars have some sympathy with theoretical developments in postcolonialism, they draw primarily on bodies of Latin American Indigenous, popular, and subaltern thought rooted in dependency theory, philosophy of liberation, and debates on Latin American modernity and postmodernity. Key influences on decolonial thought include Carlos Mariátegui, Enrique Dussel, Rodolfo Kusch, and Gloria Anzaldúa. MCD work is also inspired by what Escobar (2007: 184) refers to as "landmark experiences of decolonization," such as the 1780 Tupac Amaru rebellion in Peru and the 1790s Haitian slave rebellion, and by contemporary decolonial activities in Latin America, including the Zapatista insurgency in Chiapas, the presidency of Evo

Morales in Bolivia, and a variety of Indigenous, Afro-Latinx, and African American social movements. The decolonial option attempts to promote alternative forms of intellection, and encompasses a range of concepts including border thinking, an other thought (*pensamiento otro*), transmodernity, and interculturality (see Dussel 1995, 2002; Escobar 2007; Mignolo 2000, 2007; Quijano 2007; Walsh 2007). Indeed, the aim, according to these scholars and others associated with the project, is to promote non-linear, situated, and non-Eurocentric modes of thought, to enact a pluriversal social order, and to read modernity "from the perspective of the excluded other" (Escobar 2007: 10).[2]

A central tenet of decolonial theory is that modernity and coloniality are inextricably linked and mutually constituted, and that there is, therefore, "no modernity without coloniality" (Escobar 2007: 185). Indeed, from the perspective of MCD thought, modernity began not with the Enlightenment but with the conquest of America in the fifteenth century, and the failure to recognize coloniality as modernity's underside—that modernity meant colonizing and dominating others—inhibits our political and cultural analysis and imagination to such an extent that a new kind of thinking is required. For Maldonado-Torres (2007), modernity/coloniality produces "misanthropic skepticism" (the idea that the humanity of the colonized is constantly under question). Maldonado-Torres notes that the *ego conquiro* (certitude in one's status as conqueror, which obtains security for some at the expense of others) precedes the *ego cogito* and self-doubt put forward by Descartes. As Escobar (2007: 183) puts it, by "refracting modernity through the lens of coloniality," we might be able to access alternative ways of thinking.

Coloniality became entrenched in U.S. and Latin American societies because of the way in which elites of European descent embraced a Eurocentric modernity as the primary mode of nation-building, which at its core entailed marginalizing or erasing Indigenous and African populations. Just as Europe peripheralized the colonies, the white European populations in Latin America and the United States absorbed the logic of modernity, fulfilling their "dreams of becoming modern" by dominating Indigenous and Black populations (Mignolo 2005: 58). They became the internal colonizers, so both internal colonialism and race are central to the reinscription of colonial logics after independence and to nation-building throughout the Americas. As Mignolo (2005) emphasizes, the "Latin" in Latin America becomes a useful rhetorical device through which to erase the Indigenous and African population and elevate the European. A similar erasure and permanent subordination of Native American and African peoples, and a corresponding valorization of whiteness has been central to the production of North American modernity in the United States and Canada. It is within this context, which Derek Gregory (2004) calls the "colonial present," that disaster strikes in the Americas.

New Orleans, Bilwi, and the Black Atlantic

New Orleans on the Gulf Coast of the United States, and Bilwi on Nicaragua's Caribbean Coast (RACCN), are both part of what Paul Gilroy (1993) calls the Black Atlantic and what Rodolfo Kusch (2010) calls América.[3] Thus despite the many economic, political, and cultural differences between them, both places are part of the same matrix of domination, shaped by the same colonial history, and subject to the same imperializing logics underpinned by legacies of slavery and racism.[4] New Orleans became part of the United States as a direct result of the Haitian slave rebellion in the 1790s and the Louisiana Purchase of 1803. It was not until the mid-1800s that the notion of a singular "America" began giving way to the sense of a continental division based primarily upon colonial roots that established an Anglo-American North and a Latin American South (Mignolo 2005: 57). In the twentieth century, a consortium of New Orleans companies established highly profitable banana and lumber operations in and around Bilwi. They built port facilities and a railroad, and brought in many Black workers from the U.S. South and other parts of the Caribbean (Pineda 2006).

Given the significant yet underrecognized shared history of Bilwi and New Orleans, it is, we hope, something of a decolonizing move to bring these two sites together in this chapter. For as Mignolo (2005: x) notes, there is a need to rethink the American continent and put in question the "excess of confidence... regarding the ontology of continental divides," as we have noted in the introduction. There is also a need to "place Afro-Latinidades... in the context of the global African diaspora as a key geo-historical field within the modern/colonial capitalist world-system" (Lao-Montes 2007: 309). Both Louisiana and the RACCN share joint Indigenous and African American heritages based on intense cultural interactions and mixing between Blacks and Native Americans. Their local histories are *inter-related by imperial/colonial relations of power* through which their inhabitants have been subject to the same "civilizing mission... advanced by elite Americans of European descent" (Mignolo 2010: xliv, emphasis in original). But they are also related through shared forms of grassroots struggle, bottom-up agency, and collective cultural practices and creativities. The power blocs in each site have "depended on peripheral populations whose racialization facilitates their hyper-exploitation" and expendability (Saldaña-Portillo 2007: 504), particularly in the extractive economy around fishing (in both places), logging in Bilwi, and oil in New Orleans. As Mignolo (2005: 55) states, "the entire Atlantic economy, from the sixteenth century until the dawn of the twenty-first, was founded on the increasing devaluation of whatever did not sustain capital accumulation." The linkages between economic imperatives and cultural assumptions, and between capital accumulation and racist discrimination, create the situation often referred to as *internal colonialism*. The peoples of the Caribbean Coast of Nicaragua, also known collectively as Costeños, usually assert that they were never colonized by either Spain or

Britain, but since the region was annexed by Nicaragua in 1894, they have been subject to internal colonialism and racial discrimination by Spanish-speaking Pacific Nicaraguans. Black and Indigenous agency is threatening to the governments of both the United States and Nicaragua, so we find there ongoing attempts to contain and reorder the meanings of local cultural politics. Both Bilwi and New Orleans are places in which the inhabitants experience the persistent condition of living *entremundos*, or between worlds (Mignolo 2005), which produces the mode of subjectivity famously described by Du Bois (1903) as "double-consciousness."

There is an explosion of interculturality underway in the Americas. There is as well a growing convergence there between Black and Indigenous struggles that is reflected in recent scholarship (Anderson 2009; Escobar 2008). As Mark Anderson's (2009) work notes, groups such as the Garífuna in Central America, who identify and mobilize as both Black and Indigenous, disrupt the binary thinking that sees Indigenous peoples as embedded in place and having deep cultural roots, but views Black populations as diasporic, uprooted, and less place-connected. In both Bilwi and New Orleans, the population can be considered to be both Black and Indigenous, with a wide variety of shifting and fluid racial identifications at work. In recent decades, the demographic growth of both Indigenous and non-Indigenous Latin Americans in the contemporary United States means that after centuries of being pushed southwards by U.S. imperialism, there has been a renewed geographic displacement northward (though this has stalled in the past few years). In cultural terms at least, the United States is becoming a Latin American country, while the growing visibility of Indigenous and Afrodescendant populations in Central and South America is "making 'the idea of Latin America' obsolete" (Mignolo 2005: xv).

Both Bilwi and New Orleans are places frequently understood not to properly belong to the nation-states in which they are located. Julie Leyda (2012: 244) writes that New Orleans is often viewed as somehow separate from or outside the United States, and Jacob Leland (2009: 123) notes that both the U.S. government and the nation's popular cultures have since 1803 imagined the city as a "less developed, foreign territory at the boundary of the US proper." By the same token, Barón Pineda (2006: 3) states that the historical relationship between the Caribbean Coast of Nicaragua and the Anglophone world provokes suspicion among mestizo Nicaraguan elites and "serves to place Costeño society as a suspect internal other." Both cities are exoticized and othered as sites of sin and excess: hybridity, gambling, drinking, and carnivalesque exorbitance in the case of New Orleans; drug dealing, addiction, prostitution, and Anglophilia in the case of Bilwi. Both places are also widely seen by the mainstream as sites of bizarre, supernatural cultural and religious practices, including voodoo in New Orleans, and *sihkru tara* (a celebration involving communication with spirit ancestors) and *lasa* (supernatural protectors of the natural world) in Bilwi (see Dennis 2004; Fagoth, Gioanetto, and Silva 1998; Jamieson 2009; Cupples 2012b). Their respective national mainstream societies seem to view both cities as worthy of disdain but also pride, as they provide "exotic" ethnic color to the nation-state (see Negra 2010; Pineda 2006; Leyda 2012).

Ongoing coloniality in these two sites creates the conditions for border thinking. Both New Orleans and Bilwi reveal evidence of what George Lipsitz (1988: 101) calls "the emancipatory potential of grassroots cultural creation." Cultural practices such as New Orleans' Mardi Gras Indians and Bilwi's King Pulanka festival are celebrations of Black/Indigenous and subaltern cultural values that involve the subversion and hybridization of dominant iconographies and a blending of diverse cultural influences (Lipsitz 1988; Glynn and Cupples 2011). As Lipsitz (1988: 102) writes, the Mardi Gras Indians project a "cultural indeterminacy, picking and choosing from many traditions in order to fashion performances and narratives suitable for arbitrating an extraordinarily complex identity." The Black working classes involved in the celebration "collectively author an important narrative about their own past, present and future" (102). Similarly, the Costeños identify with and are known for their historical and cosmopolitan embrace of hybridities that can be seen in festivals such as King Pulanka and in the region's participatory media culture (see Glynn and Cupples 2011). The persistence of reciprocal economies based on collective and horizontal solidarities (such as the practice of *pana pana* [I help you, you help me] in the RACCN) provides clear evidence of how Indigenous and African "thoughts and ways of thinking survive with bodies" (Mignolo 2005: 9). What we have in both New Orleans and Bilwi—consequent to the combination of decades of disempowering neoliberalism, resilient cultural formations, and new communication networks—are societies that are "structurally broken" (Martín-Barbero 2011: 43), but politically and culturally vibrant.

Disaster Denaturalized: The Racialization of Neglect

For decades, disaster scholars in many fields have been attempting to take the *naturalness* out of disaster (see, inter alia, O'Keefe, Westgate, and Wisner 1976; Hewitt 1995; Hinchliffe 2004; N Smith 2006), because of the ways in which blaming nature tends to absolve human responsibility for disaster and obscure the political, social and economic conditions, practices and processes that turn "hazards" into "disasters." Despite the influence of this scholarship, the misnomer of "natural disasters" has survived, and it is common for media commentators and ordinary people still to talk in such terms, even though "nature," however one conceptualizes it (and it is at best a highly problematic and contested concept), might not even be the biggest contributing factor.[5] In other words, a large magnitude hurricane or earthquake is only part of the story, and loss of lives, homes, or livelihoods is a product as well of the long-term economic and social vulnerabilities and forms of political neglect that often pre-exist a disaster-event "itself" (and which might be better understood as parts of the disaster event).

Felix and Katrina were both large hurricanes that caused extensive damage and devastation. Katrina was a much bigger disaster than Felix in terms of loss of life, livelihoods, and ongoing impacts. Nevertheless, deaths and damage in Bilwi from Felix were also significant, and the death toll is intensely contested by locals who assert that many more people died than were accounted for in the official statistics. Both hurricanes revealed remarkably similar forms of racialization and racialized neglect. These include government failures to evacuate or rescue people known to be in harm's way, which exacerbated long-term forms of official negligence that had placed many residents in precarious positions to start with. The failure to rescue was compounded by characterizations of victims as blameworthy, irresponsible, and failed citizens who pathologically insisted on staying put despite public warnings to evacuate, and was further aggravated by an overall lack of government concern for the suffering and urgent material needs of these victims. While the inadequacy of the Bush administration's response to Katrina has been widely castigated, it is less well known that Nicaraguan president Daniel Ortega, in a speech to the United Nations just after Hurricane Felix, delivered an anti-imperialist diatribe against the United States and the European Union, but controversially neglected to mention the people of Nicaragua's Caribbean Coast who had recently been devastated by the storm there (Marenco 2007; Cupples 2012b).

"Katrina and its aftermath exhibited one of the most astonishing media spectacles in US history" (Kellner 2007: 223), revealing in the process both racism and the consequences of a lack of public investment (Dyson 2006). After Katrina struck, New Orleans bloggers quickly began to refer to its impacts not as phenomena of "nature" but rather as an "engineering disaster" and a "federal flood" (Brodine 2011: 90). It thus became quickly apparent that it was the breach of inadequately engineered levees, along with deep-rooted and multifaceted forms of racialized socioeconomic inequality, that turned the storm from a hazard into a disaster. On television, we saw widespread death, devastation, and an incompetent, uncaring government response. Although there was much media coverage characterized by racist understandings of the inhabitants of New Orleans (the Superdome, for example, was treated as a site of anarchy, civil unrest, and lawlessness), alternative perspectives underpinned by an awareness of race and class disadvantage began to break through. Reporters such as CNN's Anderson Cooper got visibly upset and outraged by the government nonresponse. Internet users noted that media coverage described Black people as "looting" and white people as "finding" or "carrying" food, while Kanye West famously went off script at a televised Katrina fundraiser and announced that "George Bush doesn't care about Black people" (see Dyson 2006).

The intense mediation and remediation of Katrina continued over the years that followed, particularly through both user-driven content on the internet and the dramatization of the hurricane on television. A YouTube search for "Hurricane Katrina" produces hundreds of thousands of videos. Many key

FIGURE 3.1 Photoshopping neglect: Poppy Bush and W haul in the big ones while New Orleans drowns. (Source: http://asay.blogspot.com/2005/09/picture-george-bush-fishingkatrina.html.)

moments, statements, and images have circulated repeatedly, including the Kanye West appearance noted above (which was watched by millions of viewers on YouTube); the infamous image of George Bush looking down on the devastation from a safe distance on Air Force One; a widely circulated, parodic, photoshopped image of Poppy Bush and W fishing in the streets of New Orleans while African Americans wade through waste deep flood waters in the background (see figure 3.1; Mikkelson 2005); Bush hugging Black people as a PR stunt; Bush's infamous and widely circulated, "Brownie, you're doing a heck of a job" commendation;[6] Barbara Bush's equally infamous statements about those who ended up on the floor of the Houston Astrodome;[7] and a widely recirculated interview with Katrina survivor Hardy Jackson, who became the subject of international news reports, about which we will say more below. In addition, there have been Katrina-themed episodes across a range of reality TV and drama shows, including *Extreme Makeover*, *America's Most Wanted*, *House*, *CSI*, *Law and Order: Special Victims Unit*, *Bones*, *Boston Legal*, *K-Ville*, and *Treme*. Unlike most of the other shows, which feature single episodes dealing with Katrina, *Treme* revolves entirely around events in post-Katrina New Orleans. Many of the characters in *Treme* are based on real people and some play themselves. There have also been a number of important documentaries about Katrina, including Spike Lee's *When the Levees Broke* (filmed immediately after the hurricane) and 2010's *If God Is Willing and Da Creek Don't Rise* (in which Lee revisits the survivors from the first film), as well as Harry Shearer's *The Big Uneasy*, which focuses on the engineering errors that turned a hazard into a major disaster. Harry Shearer and *Treme* star John Goodman are high-profile New Orleans residents and Katrina activists. Harry Shearer is also a New Orleans blogger who for many years has tweeted about post-Katrina New Orleans. Both Shearer and Goodman are well connected with web-based organizations such as levees.org, which has done substantial mobilization around the U.S. Army Corps of Engineers' mistakes and neglectfulness in particular and which has been "making sure New Orleans and America get the safe levees we deserve" since 2005. In the wake of Katrina's spectacular mediatization, most people stopped regarding it as a "natural" disaster and many began to refer to it as a "federal fuck-up" or something similar.

Spike Lee's documentaries make connections between Hurricane Katrina and the city's colonial history, as well as its links to other parts of the Atlantic Basin, including Haiti. Harry Shearer's film also makes these connections, and one participant compares Katrina's aftermath with the history of slavery: "We are on a plantation right now and I'm trying to run." Shearer's film also deals in-depth with questions of engineering, the levees, the faults in MR-GO,[8] and the way in which scientists who tried to report on scientific findings about the engineering failures and the hazardous elimination of wetlands were gagged, discredited, and even dismissed from their academic positions. In the first episode of *Treme* ("Do You Know What It Means?," first broadcast 11 April 2010), Tulane English professor Creighton Bernette (John Goodman) responds angrily as follows to a British journalist who characterizes Katrina as a "natural disaster": "The flooding of New Orleans was a man-made catastrophe of epic proportions and decades in the making. The levees were not blown, not in '65 and not three months ago. The flood protection system built by the Army Corps of Engineers, a.k.a. the federal government, failed and we've been saying for the last 40 years, since Betsy, that it was gonna fail again, unless something was done. And guess what? It was not." Hence, the coloniality of social relations in New Orleans is exposed by attention paid to the role of political and human neglect in the precipitation of disaster by the likes of such media figures as local bloggers, documentary filmmakers and their interviewees, and a fictional character (Creighton Bernette) in an HBO drama who is based on one of the original bloggers (about which we will say more below).

Unsurprisingly, Hurricane Felix did not produce anything like the same volume of coverage, but the region has a strong tradition of participatory media that was for a long time rooted in radio and has more recently expanded to include community and Indigenous television and online activity. After Felix, locals made use of the radio, internet, and YouTube in particular to speak back about the disaster and related issues, and to comment on coverage of the event (a YouTube search for "Hurricane Felix" produces 1,840 videos). As well, one of Bilwi's two Indigenous television channels, TV7, produced a short documentary called *La Vida Después Del Viento* (Life after the Wind), which focuses on the aftermath of the disaster rather than the event itself and juxtaposes ordinary people's testimony with expert opinion. Hence to different degrees, both Felix and Katrina have remained in the media in ways that have been atypical for disaster coverage in general.

We do not wish to exaggerate the value of contemporary television and participatory media in challenging coloniality and embedded forms of racism. As María Brodine (2011: 88) warns, we must not assume that blogs and other citizen media are intrinsically democratic. She also points out that there are digital divides at work, as blogging requires access to both technology and time (95). Nor should there be any doubt that many of the TV shows dealing with Katrina have facilitated quite ideologically conservative narratives and readings (Fuqua 2010). Lindsay Steenberg (2010), for example, points out how the crime dramas dealing with Katrina treat the storm as a forensic event that can be addressed through a series of neoliberal checks and balances, while Brenda Weber (2010: 176) asserts that Katrina makeover shows tend discursively to construct New Orleans "as a typically racialized body in need of a makeover," while simultaneously highlighting the value of privatization in sites where the state has absented itself. *Treme* is probably one of the most innovative Katrina-related dramas on television and has attracted substantial critical and scholarly attention, as well as local popular approval. But even though *Treme* might produce a counter-aesthetic of New Orleans, it is not entirely free of discourses that exert internal colonialism (see Schiwy 2003). Herman Gray (2012), for example, is concerned that *Treme*'s frequent focus on rebuilding, return, and individual enterprise, might undermine or displace the critical attention to power relations that the hurricane called forth. But Gray (2012: 273) also acknowledges that the show "helps viewers affectively connect to New Orleans." Residents of New Orleans have engaged heavily with the program; for example, important local opinions and audience observations on things such as timeline errors in the show were published in the *Times-Picayune* and elsewhere.

Similarly, Spike Lee's documentaries, which underscore the knowledges and agency of survivors (such as how people used all kinds of makeshift flotation devices in the absence of a state-led rescue), can also be seen as promoting a kind of neoliberal self-responsibilization (Elliot 2010). As Jane Elliot (2010: 96) reminds us, an emphasis on agency in the context of neoliberal crisis is highly problematic and will not necessarily lead to a "reprieve from the structures of domination." Nevertheless, the contemporary extension of disasters as transmedia events expands the terrain of discursive struggle and cultural contestation around matters such as racial and economic inequality and enables us to glimpse certain intriguing moments of decolonial strife. While we concur with Peck (2006) and Klein (2007) that Katrina was seized by right-wing developers and think tanks to further entrench and extend key neoliberal agendas, we also believe that in the context of the new media environment, the ongoing remediation of these disasters has facilitated the advancement of certain decolonial perspectives and interests that we will discuss in the remainder of this chapter.

The ongoing remediation of Katrina and Felix creates spaces of decoloniality as it draws attention to the racialization of neglect and underscores the open-ended character of disasters for those caught up in them. Most disaster events tend to disappear from most mainstream (including international) media within a matter of days, which creates conditions of possibility for many people outside disaster zones to imagine disaster events as singular, contained, and finite, and to imagine life as having "gone back to normal" upon the completion of disaster coverage. But Katrina and, to a lesser extent, Felix have retained an important media presence, both in grassroots media such as YouTube and in contemporary commercial TV programming. TV7s documentary *La Vida Después del Viento* deliberately begins with the aftermath of the disaster, rather than with the hurricane making landfall, thus demonstrating the point that for many people the real disaster is still to come, as biodiversity, harvests, and livelihoods are lost and aid disappears. *Treme* is particularly innovative in this respect, as the first episode of season 1 starts three months after the hurricane and deliberately avoids the event itself, focusing instead on the ongoing difficulties of return and recovery. Even a complex flashback sequence covering the hours leading up to the storm in the season 1 finale refuses to show the hurricane itself. As we noted in chapter 2, TV scholars have noted the development of new forms of narrative and ideological complexity in the era of abundant television and media convergence, including the expansion of storytelling strategies that complicate or refuse closure (e.g., Mittell 2006). The refusal of closure is particularly significant in the context of the official memorialization of Katrina. Lindsay Tuggle (2011) describes the Katrina memorial on the outskirts of New Orleans as a kind of "architectural whitewashing" (72) that demonstrates "a bizarre fixation with the event itself" (75) and a desperate search for closure. She sees this memorial as part of a number of state-led attempts to erase the memories of Katrina and its victims, even though the disaster is far from over for many New Orleanians (especially as it began long before Katrina made landfall). Yet, on YouTube and elsewhere on the internet, and in TV drama, we find an ongoing commemoration and mourning that is not eclipsed by the spectacle of the event itself. For example, Hardy Jackson, from Biloxi, Mississippi, who reduced a white reporter to tears when he was interviewed by her moments after losing his wife and his house, was present across a range of grassroots and mainstream media (see figure 3.2). Ordinary citizens set his story to music, and mainstream (including international) news covered his life after Katrina until his death in March 2013 (see Mayerle 2015).

Cultural Struggles for Alternative Modernities

In much of the media discussed thus far, we also observe the assertion of different ways of knowing and being, and the formulation of imaginaries that gesture toward alternative modernities. Alongside the pathologization of Katrina victims, we also see articulate survivors who have extremely valuable knowledges

FIGURE 3.2 Hardy Jackson is interviewed by TV news reporter Jennifer Mayerle in the wake of Katrina.

about disaster survival, who sometimes move from victimhood to agency and speak back to the racialized system that has subordinated them. In Bilwi, women have attracted media attention by contesting gendered and racialized efforts to stop them from returning to the work on which they depend in the Miskito Keys, which were heavily damaged by the hurricane.[9] Such protests have found their way onto YouTube as well as into the national press (see Cupples 2012b; López 2007). Consider, for example, a Miskito Felix survivor (see Cupples 2012b; López 2007) who moves from "disaster victim" to dissident agent status in the presence of the camera that enables her to speak back.[10] Such speaking back challenges a number of colonizing assumptions about the sites of these disasters and the people affected by them. One clear theme that emerges is the importance of a sense of place, and the insistence that the sites where people live and work are clearly worth saving and rebuilding. Discourses asserting that New Orleans should be moved further from the coast or that the destruction of the Miskito Keys was to be welcomed in light of the "sinful" activities (drug taking, prostitution) that take place there circulated in the aftermath of both hurricanes. In *Treme*, a group of local musicians led by Davis McAlary records a song that both criticizes Bush's non-response to the disaster ("shame, shame, shame on you now Dubya") and protests the fact that many New Orleans residents are unable to return home because of the destruction of the housing projects (season 1, episode 5, "Shame, Shame, Shame," first broadcast 9 May 2010).[11] This articulation of a deeply rooted

FIGURE 3.3 John Goodman as Creighton Bernette reaches out to the world through YouTube in *Treme*.

sense of place is an important challenge to the idea that it is somehow acceptable for African-descended peoples to be displaced because they are already diasporic. Such a view underpins Barbara Bush's unfortunate comments about people housed in the Astrodome (noted earlier). *The Big Uneasy* also shows that New Orleans cannot simply be moved, that it is not possible to pick up neighborhoods and put them elsewhere, and that the eradication of coastal wetlands has undermined the natural flood protection these wetlands historically afforded the city.

Dramas like *Treme* that emphasize the food and music cultures of New Orleans demonstrate that "culture" is not just a colorful backdrop to action, or something that exists to be consumed or exoticized by tourists, and that it is through culture that the city and its inhabitants come into being and sustain themselves. The cultural economy is central to the survival and recovery of New Orleans. Such an approach counters the criticism made of New Orleans for going ahead with Mardi Gras after the storm. The significance of carnival, culture, and a sense of place is articulated in *Treme*, for instance, by Creighton Bernette, who is modelled on real-life New Orleans blogger Ashley Morris (who died in 2008). In season 1, episode 4 ("At the Foot of Canal Street," first broadcast 2 May 2010), Bernette discovers YouTube on his daughter's computer and records his feelings (see figure 3.3). The following lines of dialogue from *Treme* are a transmediated adaptation of Morris's widely circulated FYYFF (Fuck you, you fucking fucks) blog.[12]

> Hello, YouTube. This is Creighton Bernette from New Orleans. Yeah, we're still here. I just want to say something to all you all trying to figure out what to do about our city. Blow me. You say, why rebuild it? I say, fuck you. You rebuilt

Chicago after the fire. You rebuilt San Francisco after the earthquake. Let me tell you something, anything that's any fucking good in Chicago came from someplace else, and San Francisco is an overpriced cesspool with hills. To Houston and Atlanta, may I say, lick my hairy balls. You took in thousands of our people, but guess what? You still suck. We got more culture in one neighborhood than you got in all your sorry-ass sprawling suburbs put together.
To New York, fuck you too. You get attacked by a few fundamentalist fucking assholes and the federal money comes raining down like rose petals. Our whole fucking coast was destroyed and we're still waiting for somebody to give a good goddamn. But you want to write off New Orleans, cancel carnival. Well let me tell you something. Tuesday February 28th, wherever the fuck you all are, will be just another gray, dreary, sorry-ass fucked up Tuesday. But down here, it'll be Mardi Gras. Fuck you, you fucking fucks.

Not only has *Treme*'s incorporation of Morris's original blog helped to ensure that it has been visited countless thousands of times, but so too has the YouTube clip from *Treme* of John Goodman as Creighton Bernette speaking on YouTube.

The significance of the cultural economy is also illustrated by late TV gourmand Anthony Bourdain's visit to New Orleans in his show *No Reservations* (first broadcast 4 February 2008), where it is emphasized that chefs and musicians are vital to both the national interest and disaster recovery. As well, there is a detailed storyline in *Treme* about a group of Mardi Gras Indians who attempt to go ahead with their annual celebration despite the everyday challenges they face. This celebration involves arduous and painstaking preparation and commitment. Neoliberal rationalities that concern what is conventionally understood to be "useful" or "productive," and which are often articulated in highly racialized ways, are intensely contested in this narrative and more reciprocal alternative economies that affirm and celebrate Black humanity are envisioned and commended.

In such media, we can observe what Rodolfo Kusch (1975) has termed "*la negación en el pensamiento popular*" (the negation in popular thinking), which for Mignolo (2010: xxx) is an epistemological position that both negates "imperial epistemic supremacy" and affirms "an-other way of thinking and of living." The defense of carnival, wetlands, and a right to place, asserts epistemic structures and entitlements that have been "violated by imperial epistemology" (Mignolo 2010: xxx). It is important to stress, however, that in the affirmation of other ways of living, the negation of coloniality and neoliberal rationalities, and the expression of identities that refuse to assimilate, we do not find a totalizing rejection of the "emancipatory potential of modern reason" (Escobar 2007: 184). For example, the response to disasters by survivors involves vocal calls for the non-racist application of modern engineering practices, and especially the construction of levees that do not fail. Indeed, in all the documentaries mentioned here, *When the Levees Broke, If God Is Willing and Da Creek*

Don't Rise, The Big Uneasy, and *La Vida Después del Viento,* we see the juxtaposition of expert and popular knowledges in ways that finally privilege neither over the other. New Orleans needs both Mardi Gras and adequately engineered levees. Bilwi needs its traditional medicine and supernatural creatures, as well as modern marine biology and forestry.

Katrina and Felix revealed the coloniality of being that is active in the idea that some Nicaraguan and U.S. citizens are more expendable than others. For Maldonado-Torres (2007: 247), coloniality can be grasped as "a radicalization and naturalization of the non-ethics of war. This non-ethics included the practices of eliminating and slaving certain subjects—e.g., Indigenous and Black—as part of the enterprise of colonization." Disasters such as Felix and Katrina can also be understood as consequences of a non-ethics. Maldonado-Torres (2007: 254) draws on Fanon's notion that the lives of colonized populations involve "a permanent struggle against an omnipresent death"; hence the importance of the cry (*el grito*) that calls "attention to one's own existence" (256). In a later paper, Maldonado-Torres (2008: 66–67, our translation) asserts that the "de-colonial attitude is born when the cry of fear in the face of the horror of coloniality is translated into a critical position in the face of the world of colonial death and into a search for the affirmation of the life of those most affected by such a world." Right from the time of the hurricanes up to the present day, Katrina and Felix victims and survivors have called attention to their existence by writing on rooftops, making graffiti, preserving search and rescue markings on homes and buildings, and speaking back through both mainstream and alternative media. In the process, the "ontological excess" (Maldonado-Torres 2003, quoted in Escobar 2007: 185) exposed through disaster has produced outrage, concern, tears, and indignation in reporters and ordinary people, as a means to restore ethics. As noted, Hardy Jackson's call of attention to his existence, moments after his wife and his home had been swept away in the flood, produced a dramatic affective response and has continued to do so via YouTube. Although he emerges first as a *damné* (wretched), his appearance and story immediately resonate affectively with Jennifer Mayerle, a white WKRG reporter.[13] She is visibly shocked and horrified by his experience, by what Maldonado-Torres (2007: 263) calls the "scandal of death." This footage has been remixed, recirculated, and watched thousands of times on YouTube, incorporating both mainstream news coverage and uploads by ordinary YouTube users. Footage of Hardy Jackson spills over from mainstream news reporting to YouTube and back. The reporters and those who have circulated Hardy Jackson on YouTube (often set to music) become part of "the search for love and human filiality" (see Maldonado-Torres 2007: 117).[14] Because dehumanization is central to the coloniality of being, the rehumanization of Hardy Jackson through mediated recirculation is significant. It demonstrates how media can be used to urge critical reflection and promote an ethic of solidarity in the face of the denial of humanity (see Maldonado-Torres 2007).

A similar piece pertaining to Hurricane Felix was posted to YouTube by U.S.-based Costeño Zabu6269. This video is set to local music and contains images of the devastation caused by the hurricane, but also emphasizes a culturally vibrant community that is deeply rooted in place and for whom everyday life continues.[15] So while the governmental non-responses to these disasters reproduced what Mignolo (2018: 370, emphasis in original) calls *"epistemic and ontological colonial differences,"* these remediations of disaster begin to do something quite different. Nigel Clark (2010) asserts that caring responsiveness to those devastated by periodic planetary destabilization is the source of a "will to justice" (72) and "an impetus for the emergence of communal being" (140). Outsiders have recirculated footage of Hardy Jackson because they are moved by his plight and believe that his suffering must be responded to. Such remediations can provide important correctives to official modes of sensemaking that emerge after disaster, and potentially allow new forms of understanding and engagement to emerge.

So far we have emphasized the politically productive convergence between Black and Indigenous struggles, particularly in terms of contesting disaster-driven displacement. The cultural struggles engaged through the ongoing remediation of these disasters have revealed how it is not only people who identify/are identified as Indigenous that are deeply rooted in and connected to place. Deeply felt connections to place are also powerfully mobilized by African American and Afro-Latinx inhabitants. While studies of globalization have emphasized the movement of human populations across a stable ground, it is equally important to analyze the political and ethical possibilities and liberation of meaning generated by those "trying to stay put" on an unstable ground or next to an unstable sea (Clark 2010: 198). We now shift our attention to the postcolonial South Pacific nation of Aotearoa New Zealand, where seismic instabilities generated a series of disasters through which we both lived, and which exposed deep social, cultural, and economic fault lines not unlike those dredged up in the wake of Felix and Katrina.

4

The Transmediation of Disaster Down Under

Decolonizing and Democratizing Disaster Down Under: The Christchurch Earthquakes (2010–2012)

Christchurch is a medium-sized city in the Canterbury region of the South Island of Aotearoa New Zealand. Like many other Christchurch residents, we experienced the trials involved in dealing with a substantially damaged home and interminable tribulations of struggling with the neoliberal "public/private partnership" formed by the New Zealand Earthquake Commission (EQC) and our under-reinsured insurance company.[1] As faculty members at the University of Canterbury, we were also confronted by the higher education variant of what Naomi Klein (2007) has called "disaster capitalism" (which also struck at Tulane and three other New Orleans universities in the wake of Hurricane Katrina, as has been widely discussed and documented, and which led to an American Association of University Professors censure that was in place for years against Tulane and the others; see Jaschik 2007). At our institution, the administration seized upon the opportunity space opened by disastrous events to enact otherwise politically unpalatable and deeply destructive forms of "restructuring" under the guise of purported financial exigencies and a drive to impose the conservative New Zealand government's ideological zeal for gutting ostensibly "useless" humanities and social sciences departments in favor of a so-called STEM (science, technology, engineering and math) agenda (see Cupples 2012a; Johnston, Sears, and Wilcox 2012; Matthews 2012; Dean 2015). These moves were exacerbated by the fact that in its deliriously wholehearted embrace of neoliberalism during the 1980s and beyond, the government of New Zealand Thatcherized its universities by following in the footsteps of the "Iron Lady's" complete abolition of formal legal academic tenure throughout the United Kingdom in 1989, thus producing a permanent professorial precariat that is, for the entirety of each and every academic career, vulnerable to the budget-slashing zeal associated with whatever intellectual and political prejudices or fads and fashions happen to tickle the fancy of this or that senior university administrator. These developments should serve as a cautionary tale to faculty members everywhere, and made it intolerable for us to continue our research collaboration where we were, so at the start of 2013 we fled (taking with us a major research grant we had just been awarded) for greener pastures (and new institutions). Nevertheless, like the disaster scholar and survivor Susana Hoffman (who lost her home and all her belongings in the 1991 Oakland firestorm), we endured life for two-plus years in a disaster zone composed of our broken city and its university's neoliberal administration, and thus bore "witness to the reformulation of a social," professional, "and cultural milieu" (Hoffman 1999: 174). Kevin Fisher (2015) notes the strong similarities (including the suspension of democratic rights and the privatization of public education) between the responses of the New Zealand government to the Christchurch earthquakes, those of the Bush administration in the wake of Katrina, and Naomi Klein's account of disaster capitalism on a wider geographical and historical scale: "In Canterbury, as in the other locations described by Klein, a state of precariousness becomes the 'new normal', as perpetual fear of aftershocks, job loses, demolitions, and social restructurings become intertwined" (167). For us, these experiences of neoliberal crisis exploitation, market engineering, and right-wing "creative destruction" were both emotionally troubling and intellectually fascinating.

Christchurch is built on at least two precarious foundations: one geomorphological, and the other cultural, historical, and colonial. The Canterbury plains that surround Christchurch are composed of postglacial alluvial sediment that renders the city prone to intense shaking and liquefaction when there are earthquakes (as there commonly are throughout New Zealand, since the country straddles the subduction zone between two tectonic plates). Christchurch is in fact a city that is both built on a swamp and swamped by its own colonial history. It has a long history of celebrating a particular mode of middle-class Englishness that is embedded in local, colonially imposed place names, Gothic architecture, and "exotic" plants and trees brought by settlers. Christchurch is known for its persistent enactments of nineteenth-century emblems of Britishness (such as "punting" on the River Avon), for an obsession with English-style schools and schooling, and for colonial fantasies of the "First Four Ships" of British settlers to land there, all of which have worked to marginalize and erase the area's Indigenous Māori histories and cultures. The city's British colonial history and façades of Englishness were, however, already contested and precarious before the quakes, in particular as a consequence of the presence of the Ngāi Tahu *iwi* (tribe), the region's native Māori inhabitants, whose tenure there long predates that of European settlers, as well by a range of urban subcultures, including those of immigrants, skinheads, graffiti artists, young skateboarders, and working class residents (see Cupples and Glynn 2009; Cupples 2009a; Ginn 2009; Glynn 2009b; Kobayashi 2009; McNaughton 2009; Pickles 2016). Christchurch's dominant place meanings have also frequently been put in question by disruptive media events that reveal the city's dark and troubled cultural currents and countercurrents. These include a grisly 1954 murder/matricide that captured international attention and inspired both a 1971 French film, *Mais ne nous délivrez pas du mal* (Don't deliver us from evil), and Peter Jackson's 1994 movie *Heavenly Creatures*; the notorious Sunnyside psychiatric hospital, which was captured in the autobiographical work of the internationally celebrated New Zealand author Janet Frame, and in the 1990 Jane Campion film, *An Angel at My Table*; and various high profile sex abuse cases, such as the 1999 Morgan Fahey affair (about which see Cupples and Harrison 2001; Cupples and Glynn 2009; Pickles 2016) and the Christchurch Civic Creche case of the early 1990s.

On 4 September 2010, a 7.1-magnitude earthquake shook buildings and buckled roads in Christchurch at 4:35 in the morning. The quake involved intense ground movement acceleration and thus caused strong and persistent shaking throughout the city. While a number of people were injured, the depth and distance of the epicenter from the city combined with the early morning hour of the strike to ensure that there were no fatalities. This initial shake was, however, followed not only by many thousands of smaller aftershocks, but also by another five major seismic events, the most significant and destructive of which was a 6.3-magnitude quake on 22 February 2011.[2] This intense quake occurred at lunchtime on a working day, and its epicenter was much shallower and closer to the heart of the city of Christchurch. It caused 185 fatalities, thousands of injuries, and the collapse of major multi-storey buildings in the city, including the Canterbury Television building, which housed a television station, an English-language school, and a medical clinic, and where 115 people died as a result of the building's deficient engineering design and faulty construction. The quake also damaged many other buildings beyond repair (including the iconic Anglican cathedral in the heart of the city center) and left the city's transportation, water, and sewage infrastructures in a state of near collapse.[3] The aftershock sequence lasted for years and produced more than 17,000 aftershocks that kept residents on high alert and contributed to widespread and persistently heightened levels of anxiety, depression, insomnia, and PTSD. More than a decade later, Christchurch is still in recovery.

Shortly after the earthquakes, the City Council produced a Christchurch City Plan based on extensive and widely embraced community consultation, but this participatory, bottom-up blueprint for regeneration was displaced by a top-down, national government-decreed agenda, the Christchurch Central Recovery Plan

(CCRP), which was imposed through special emergency legislation that overturned and suspended key democratic institutions and processes through its declaration of a state of exception (see Agamben 2005). This legislation ran roughshod over the people-centered approach adopted by the City Council, allowed for the forcible expropriation of landowners by the national government, and prioritized the interests of large investors over the needs of residents and small businesses. The CCRP has been described as a "colonial project" (Blundell 2014), as it views the city as a "blank canvas for new beginnings" (see Sutton 2014). Despite the rationalist, top-down approach imposed by the conservative government of New Zealand, the Christchurch central business district (CBD) has for years remained a scattered and messy assemblage of damaged and graffiti-covered buildings awaiting demolition (many of which are behind fences), buildings in the process of being demolished, shipping containers that are propping up dangerous buildings, and empty spaces where buildings once stood. In front of building sites, there are billboards with anticipatory glossy images of the city (supposedly) to come, and there are ample "for sale," "for lease," and "development opportunity" signs that underscore the reluctance of private sector investors. Weeds, grass, pools of stagnant water, and other "natural" elements have emerged through the damaged concrete and asphalt to produce a rather dark, post-apocalyptic, and cinematic feel in places. This landscape of destruction is interspersed amid the handful of buildings that survived the disaster, a number of shiny new buildings and businesses (including a small shopping mall built from recycled shipping containers), lots of murals and artwork on the sides of buildings (so many, in fact, that *Lonely Planet* designated Christchurch a "global street art capital"; see Gates 2017), and a number of temporary experimental participatory projects led by grassroots post-disaster organizations such as Gap Filler, Life in Vacant Spaces, and Greening the Rubble (which was renamed "the Green Lab" in 2019). These projects included initiatives such as the Pallet Pavilion, a live music venue made of building pallets; Dance-O-Mat, a large, outdoor coin-operated speaker system and dancefloor powered by a washing machine, into which participants plugged their own devices and danced; the Super Street Arcade, a large retro videogame screen with a massive joystick; and the outdoor Cycle-Powered Cinema, which both ran on electricity generated by and featured films about bicycling (see www.gapfiller.org.nz). As Cloke, Dickenson, and Tupper (2017: 10) note, these temporary and subversive Gap Filler projects "inevitably counterpose the lack of progress going on around them."

In the suburbs, the picture has been more mixed. The city's eastern suburbs endured more physical damage and liquefaction, and these impacts were exacerbated by the higher levels of preexisting racialized socioeconomic deprivation there. Consequently, houses in these neighborhoods have been left to rot, empty former businesses have been boarded up or covered in graffiti, and roads have remained in a calamitous state that may take decades to remediate (Hayward

2018). Some suburbs such as Addington have, however, become more economically and culturally vibrant, as some businesses displaced from the CBD have successfully relocated there. Like Managua, Nicaragua, whose urban center was destroyed in the massive earthquake that struck there in 1972, Christchurch has become a polycentric city with economic activity and entertainment dispersed across a number of suburbs; this phenomenon possibly contributed to the glacial pace of regeneration in the city's CBD.

These transformations reveal how disaster events tend suddenly and dramatically to rework geographies and cultures of everyday life. Rather than changing gradually as other cities do, Christchurch has been rapidly and profoundly transformed by the earthquakes and the processes of mediation and remediation that both coproduce and accompany them. The spaces and places that complexly constituted Christchurch, which we took for granted and on which we built not only our everyday experiences but also the narratives of our lives, were reworked, disarticulated, rearticulated, disfigured, and reconfigured. We permanently lost access to numerous places where we worked, shopped, ate, socialized, swam, watched films, and borrowed books. Indeed, much of what had been a vibrant central city was razed to the ground, so that many of our memoryscapes are no longer physically manifest apart from the variety of media forms they assume: videos, films, photos, recordings, digital platforms, and so forth. Although we have returned to visit the city on a number of occasions, we find it hard to do so because, in the face of the gaps and empty urban spaces that still define much of the CBD, any sense of nostalgia for things we used to do and places we used to go requires an unusually strong imaginative effort. Such experiences become central to post-disaster place-(re)making for many residents. They become part of struggles for new forms of sociality and belonging, and have produced a vast outpouring of media texts and artistic material artefacts that seek both to remember Christchurch as it was and to create ways of moving forward in place.

Our experiences of media began to shift significantly in the midst of the earthquakes. Like the city's authorities and risk experts, we were largely unprepared for the first major quake that woke us in dramatic fashion on 4 September 2010, despite having lived up until then with an awareness of the seismic activities throughout the country and even credible scientific forecasts that our region was statistically highly likely to experience "the big one" sometime before 2055. The September 2010 quake caused our electricity to fail and with it our television, radio, and broadband services. Our son did however have a 3G phone and began to read out the social media reactions from his friends, who were posting statuses that said things like "Fuck you, Mother Earth." We eventually used our landline to speak with family members in Wisconsin, who relayed to us that the damage was far more extensive than we were aware, as they had seen an outpouring of Christchurch cell phone videos that had been uploaded to YouTube and depicted such things as collapsed chimneys, crashing bookshelves, and surprisingly intense perturbations in swimming pool water. Once our power grid and broadband access were finally restored days later, we began to encounter increasingly dense layers of mediation through which our experiences of the disaster were constituted, reconstituted, and textured. Similar processes began again anew in the immediate aftermath of the much more devastating February 2011 quake event, when even the region's cell phone networks collapsed due to extreme levels of demand that overloaded the network. In the wake of this and the subsequent tens of thousands of seismic shakes and aftershocks, the Christchurch disaster has generated a diverse profusion of media (and mediating) materials.

When we returned to our quake-impaired home in February 2011 after a few nights in a local motel, we engaged in compulsive media consumption, as the badly damaged downtown area of the city was completely cordoned off. Thus, the ongoing flow of TV news reports (which was somewhat reminiscent of that which ensued in the wake of 9/11, as noted in chapter 1) provided our only visual access to what had become of it. The quakes made heavy Twitter users of some Christchurch residents, as the hashtag #eqnz became a key site of mediated intervention into the unfolding disaster taking place around us. News and current affairs shows offered sweeping coverage that returned repeatedly to the quakes, to ongoing recovery efforts, and to ordinary people's struggles with authorities. Additionally, Christchurch earthquake videos eventually numbering in the hundreds of thousands were uploaded to YouTube. They take many forms and engage many types of subject matter, but the majority fall into at least one of the following categories: (1) videos taken of the immediate aftermath and chaos; (2) CCTV and citizen footage of indoor and outdoor shaking; (3) mash-ups of Christchurch before and after the quakes; (4) clips and mash-ups of news footage that provide insight into the disasters or critical commentary on their coverage; (5) footage of residents offering reflections on their experiences and on what has become of the city; (6) videos that celebrate grassroots community projects undertaken by artists and activists; and (7) videos that commemorate those who died in the quakes. As well, many Christchurch people created or participated in Facebook pages dedicated to the February earthquake, some of which remain active today. The earthquakes also led to the production of a number of documentaries, including *When a City Falls* (2011), *Five Days in the Red Zone* (2011), *A Shocking Reminder* (2012), and *The Day That Changed My Life* (2015); a four-part TV drama miniseries, *Hope and Wire* (2014); a fictional feature film, *Sunday* (2014), which is set in Christchurch in February 2012, amid the destruction and ongoing recovery efforts in the city and which, according to its producers, received "the largest multiplatform release of a film ever";[4] and an ongoing web series known as *Christchurch Dilemmas* (2016–2017). All of these media texts and more have produced substantial engagement and have proven to be highly "spreadable." As Jenkins, Ford, and Green

(2013: 13) note with regard to "spreadability," which they take to be a key attribute of impactful media in our networked culture, there is no

> single cause for why people spread material. People make a series of socially embedded decisions when they choose to spread any media text: Is the content worth engaging with? Is it worth sharing with others? Might it be of interest to specific people? Does it communicate something about me or my relationship with those people? What is the best platform to spread it through? Should it be circulated with a particular message attached? Even if no additional commentary is appended, however, just receiving a story or video from someone else imbues a range of new potential meanings in a text.

In post-disaster Christchurch, spreadable media of many different sorts became vital tools in struggles to survive, recover, and thrive. These media enabled survivors to renew old, and generate new, post-disaster social relations with others; to provide mutual assistance and forge solidarities across social differences; to highlight the implications of coloniality for disastrous practices and events, and to promote forms of decoloniality in the spaces opened by disaster; to rethink taken-for-granted, commonsense aspects of social life in heavily commodified, postcolonial consumer societies; and to engage in struggles with corporations and political authorities over the inadequacies of their visions for contemporary social life and its renewal in the wake of profound disruption.

Some of the scholarship on the Christchurch earthquakes usefully approaches them as rupturing events whose consequences apply across a range of sites, scales, axes of social difference, and domains of experience. For instance, Terry Austrin and John Farnsworth (2012: 78) suggest that the earthquakes constituted and brought forth mash-ups across multiple dimensions, including the "geological, experiential, mediated and sociotechnical," which both generate and demand new forms of urban thought and analysis necessary to understand "the significance for urban life of such traumatic events." Some find that these rupturing events hold forth a potential to remake Christchurch in more inclusive, democratizing, and decolonizing ways, in spite of the all the trauma, sadness and difficulties the disasters have brought in their wake. Katie Pickles (2016: 18) argues that the earthquakes deeply undermined the colonial confidence on which Christchurch was founded, which entailed powerful commitments to a "belief that nature could be controlled and conquered" and that Indigenous culture could be ignored and destroyed. She suggests that the importance of this "postcolonial moment" was most aptly encapsulated in the way the quakes brought down the statues of male colonial administrators and explorers, including John Robert Godley, William Rolleston, and Robert Falcon Scott.[5] For all their monumentalization, the colonial settlers and their ancestors failed to come adequately to terms with their place in the world. For Pickles, the disruption brought by the quakes thus presents an opportunity to enact a different kind of future. Cloke, Dickenson, and Tupper (2017: 2) also see the disaster as an event that "announces itself by forming a clear disruption of the status quo." It is an event "that has ruptured the foundations, structures and assumed relations that previously made the world of Christchurch legible," and hence these ruptures hold "the potential to open up new beginnings and new imaginations" (2–3). Cloke, Dickenson, and Tupper do not suggest that pre-quake Christchurch was particularly stable and secure in its hegemonic coloniality, but that its instabilities and insecurities were fairly well obscured beneath the city's dominant, triumphalist colonial narratives. Among all of New Zealand's cities, Christchurch has long been noted as a particularly Anglophilic site and has often been described as "more English than England" (see Glynn 2009b; Cupples and Glynn 2009; Cupples and Harrison 2001), so the fallen statues built to commemorate colonial founding fathers were, unsurprisingly, ultimately restored to their positions of urban prominence—but not without the addition of new reminders in the built environment of the Indigenous inhabitants whose presence long predated that of the British colonists, thanks to the long-standing and ongoing efforts of many local Māori activists to bring more balance to the city's landscapes (see, e.g., RNZ 2020; Hunt 2021). As local Māori leader Karaitiana Tickell put it in 2020 during a nationwide debate over the retention of statues commemorating colonial founders amid raging international controversies over those celebrating slave traders, Confederate insurrectionists, and colonizers of Africa (see, e.g., Morris 2020; Grey 2020; Chaudhuri 2016), "the history of New Zealand as told in the popular story and as represented in those statues excludes an entire history pre-colonisation. It starts with their arrival . . . the four ships . . . and it trivialises anything that came before that" (Broughton 2020, ellipses in original).[6]

Melodramas of Postdisaster Waiting and the Participatory Cultures of Current Affairs TV

In the new media environment, discourses and ways of knowing multiply, spread promiscuously across a dizzying array of media and platforms, and are subject to a range of bottom-up, participatory practices that include sharing, commenting, reworking, resignifying, and rearticulating. These processes and practices allow for the reconfiguration of dominant discourses and narratives of disaster, and thus intervention into the power relations they enact and sustain. In Aotearoa New Zealand, one site of participatory media culture that created space around the Christchurch earthquakes for the assertion of alternative meanings, knowledges, and practices that the power bloc ordinarily works hard to marginalize and exclude was the nightly current affairs show *Campbell Live* (2005–2015), which featured an affable anchor with a nationwide household name (see figure 4.1). During its decade on air, *Campbell Live* dealt with important political issues, including government surveillance and spying, child

FIGURE 4.1 John Campbell on *Campbell Live*.

poverty, exploitive labor relations, and, in great depth and detail, the Christchurch earthquakes. John Campbell, the show's eponymous, muckraking host, rejected the discourses and pretenses of journalistic "objectivity" and embraced what he referred to as "advocacy journalism." As New Zealand journalist Jane Bowron (2013) wrote, "increasingly, *Campbell Live* has become a last-ditch appeal court serving as a platform for the poor, the desperate and the not listened to, where they can present their case through national television exposure." *Campbell Live* accordingly kept its focus on the Christchurch earthquakes for years, tenaciously scrutinized quake survivors' circumstances and living conditions, and worked tirelessly to hold key agents and officials involved in the reconstruction of the city to account. These agents and officials included Gerry Brownlee, a controversial right-wing politician who was appointed government minister for Canterbury Earthquake Recovery (a position that became widely and colloquially known as "Earthquake Czar"), EQC, Fletcher Building Limited, and the private insurance industry. EQC is a public entity whose main role "is to provide natural disaster [*sic*] insurance for residential property." In 1993, at the height of New Zealand's ongoing neoliberalization, EQC was legislatively restructured to tighten its links with private construction and insurance companies in order to limit risks to the public purse. It is funded by a levy that homeowners must pay through their private home insurance premiums; people without paid-up private home insurance receive no coverage from EQC. EQC insurance cover was capped at a maximum of NZ$100,000 per claim, beyond which any damage becomes the responsibility of the private insurer. Fletcher Building, a large corporation, was appointed by EQC as its agent to repair all homes whose damage fell entirely under the NZ$100,000 cap. Because of widespread questions about Fletcher's capacity and the quality of its work, the issue of whether a given homeowner's damage was over or under the cap became a subject of intense negotiation and struggle in the years after the most destructive quakes.

While the early *Campbell Live* episodes immediately following the quakes were very similar to other news coverage and thus generated conventional stories of loss, heroism, and community spirit filled with dramatic images of spectacularly damaged buildings, the show moved on to the production of different kinds of earthquake stories that were bottom-up, grassroots-driven, highly participatory, and affectively charged. In particular, the show began to provide a platform for disaster survivors to talk about their experiences not so much of the initial quake event itself, which had already received ample coverage across a range of mainstream media, but rather of the aftermath and ongoing failure of various authorities to respond promptly and adequately to the conditions in which they now found themselves living. *Campbell Live* mobilized, boosted, and amplified the affective energies generated by a participatory culture of local citizens that the government sought actively to dampen, control, and suppress. This participatory culture is theoretically and analytically important, not only because it both helps us to better understand the shifting relations of power within the new media environment and challenges the neoliberal discourses of "resilience" and preparedness that now dominate emergency management planning in New Zealand and elsewhere (see, e.g., Glynn and Cupples 2024), but also because it reveals the potential to extend the incipient scholarship on geographies and politics of waiting into the arena of media and disaster. Through *Campbell Live* and the grassroots convergent media activity surrounding it, not only were the voices of ordinary people given extended circulation, but a different set of disaster narratives and affects were asserted, particularly in relation to experiences of waiting. As John Campbell said on air at the start of the 13 June 2013 installment of the show, more than two-and-a-quarter years after the "big one,"

> tonight, *Campbell Live* presents some brilliant dark comedy from our friends in Christchurch. It's the waiting that's most likely to drive earthquake survivors mad. First, it was waiting for the shakes to stop. Then for zones to be decided. Then for EQC to visit, and insurers to visit, and EQC to visit again. And EQC to answer the phone. And find your file. And insurers to pay you out. And TC3 land [damaged by liquefaction] to be remediated. Or not. And then, when you want to start over somewhere, you have to wait for building consent, which is the council's department. And it's slow.

Understanding *waiting* is useful for thinking through postdisaster experiences and the dynamics of media convergence culture that have helped to facilitate the public articulation and rearticulation of the frustrations and power relations that official delays and inaction engender and enact. A long line of social and cultural theorists have placed waiting within the panoply of techniques of temporality and relations of power that define characteristic experiences of modernity. As Barry Schwartz (1974: 869, quoted in Auyero 2012: 34) wrote fifty years ago, "far from being a coincidental by product of power ... control of time comes into view as one of its essential properties." Javier Auyero (2012: 9) identifies "toxic waiting" (for state services) imposed upon the poor of Argentina as a strategy for the production of submissive "patients," whose patience works to incarnate a recognition and acceptance "of the established political order." Pierre Bourdieu (2000: 228) writes that waiting "implies submission" and is "one of the privileged ways of experiencing the effect of power." Bourdieu avers that imposed waiting "modifies the behaviour of the person who 'hangs,' as we say, on the awaited decision. It follows that the art of 'taking one's time,' of 'letting time take its time,' as Cervantes puts it, of making people wait, of delaying without destroying hope, of adjourning without totally disappointing, which would have the effect of killing the waiting itself, is an integral part of the exercise of power. . . . An art of 'turning down' without 'turning off,' of keeping people 'motivated' without driving them to despair" (228).

It is perhaps this link with motivation, however, that generates complications in and around the relationships between waiting and power. Like its affective twin *boredom*, in Walter Benjamin's account, waiting can stimulate *critical reflection* and subversive impulses. As Joe Moran (2003) notes, Benjamin "stresses that boredom can reveal the traces of a communal everyday life which ordinarily remains invisible" (174–175), is "a key to opening up neglected stories and memories" (176), and contains a "revolutionary promise" that stems from its "capacity to dispense with the often mistaken convictions and assumptions which give meaning to our lives, and to require us to face the fundamental question: how should we actually spend our time?" (179). Benjamin (1999: 105) writes that "we are bored when we don't know what we are waiting for. . . . Boredom is the threshold to great deeds. . . . Boredom is a warm gray fabric lined on the inside with the most lustrous and colorful of silks. In this fabric we wrap ourselves when we dream." Benjamin's account of boredom resonates with Catherine Brun's (2015) work on "protracted displacement." Brun (2015: 19) emphasizes the feeling of being stuck and of not being able to move forward, while "everyday time" nevertheless "continues to flow through routinized practices and survival strategies," so that the waiting experienced by displaced peoples often involves projecting and imagining alternative possible futures. Similarly, Alison Mountz's (2011) work explores the topographies and counter-topographies of power associated with migrant waiting, and shows how such waiting modifies time-space trajectories in significant ways; she discusses how migrants get trapped in different sites and between states as they encounter and negotiate power, including in the forms of physical and legal barriers to movement. Mountz finds that waiting is a far from passive practice for the migrants she studies, and notes the various kinds of activism and political participation they undertake while they wait. Jeff Scheible (2010: 207–208) recounts the performance of *Waiting for Godot in New Orleans* that Paul Chan staged "in front of a barren home in the devastated landscape" of the city's Lower Ninth Ward more than two years after Katrina struck. Like many of the scholars we have cited, Chan understood Katrina as an episode in a much longer narrative that had been unfolding for decades and chose Beckett's source text because he found an "uncanny" and "terrible symmetry between the reality of New Orleans post-Katrina and the essence of this play, which expresses in stark eloquence the cruel and funny things people do while they wait: for help, for food for hope."

Regarding the intersections of coloniality, disasters, and waiting, Yarimar Bonilla (2020: 2) has placed Puerto Rico, a vast chunk of whose infrastructure was destroyed when Hurricane Maria struck in 2017, within a racialized archipelago of disastrous U.S. neglect that also includes New Orleans after Katrina, and Flint, Michigan, whose water supply has been toxic ever since a 2014 Republican-led public utility privatization project left it unsafe for human consumption. Bonilla notes that in Puerto Rico, as in other parts of the "archipelago of racialized neglect" (4), urgency has been "met with a crushing wall of inaction," so that "the present did not expand in its eventfulness but in its persistence. Time passed, and nothing changed," which "created a frenzied state of repetition in which each day felt eerily like the last" (3). But there is, Bonilla asserts, a widespread hope among many Puerto Ricans that the current "period of extended waiting, this arrested postcolonial present, is actually a period of gestation" that just might transform this "stalled present" into "the dawn of a new political future" (10). As Bourdieu (2000: 209) argues, "relations to time such as waiting or impatience," which evince frustrated expectations, tend to generate states of "boredom or 'discontent'" that call forth "a dissatisfaction with the present that implies the negation of the present and the propensity to work towards its supersession."

Between September 2010 and May 2015, *Campbell Live* repeatedly covered the situation in Canterbury. This coverage captured the anger, frustration, and sadness associated with *waiting* for authorities such as EQC and insurance companies to respond. Indeed, *Campbell Live* patiently documented, often in melodramatic style, how myriad institutional failures plunged individual homeowners into frustrating, soul-destroying, and emotionally exhausting spaces of bureaucratic incompetence, official indifference, and legal liminality or ambiguity. These people were forced to endure cold, damp, moldy, millipede- and slug-infested conditions in homes that had become uninhabitable and a city that had been damaged beyond recognition and lost hundreds of its citizens in the disaster. The disaster survivors had undergone substantial emotional loss and in many cases were displaced not from their nation-state but internally from their homes. Many indeed found themselves in the ambiguous and paradoxical state of being *displaced at home*: consigned to live without plumbing in camper trailers, garages, or tents, and unable to move forward in the face of commercial and institutional powers serving up a toxic mix of neglect, indifference, corruption, and incompetence. Hundreds of disaster survivors contacted *Campbell Live* by text, email, social media, and other means in order to tell their stories on national television. One *Campbell Live* innovation was the so-called Caravan of Complaint, a roving, camera-equipped vehicle where disaster survivors could come to provide accounts of their experiences given at their own pace and in their own words. A characteristic example of the work of the Caravan of Complaint comes from a May 2013 episode, which opens with a shot of John Campbell standing in front of a hastily erected, makeshift plywood wall and announcing, "our program is about people living with this kind of thing [gestures toward the plywood wall]: half-done repairs. Or not even something this good: uncertainty. Waiting, waiting, waiting. Remember: the first earthquake, September 2010. The second major earthquake: February 2011. It is now *thirty-two months* since that first, big shake. We begin tonight with stories of people waiting for EQC to act and reaching the end of their tether." The image track then cuts to the inside of a vehicle, and we see and hear from a parade of survivors in various states of emotional distress relating their experiences of desperation and interminable waiting to the camera. Some are wiping tears from their eyes, others are holding small children, still others wear expressions of disbelief, frustration, exasperation, weariness, and anger. Many explain that they have been trying for more than two-and-a-half years to get an adequate response from EQC and its agents. They variously proclaim that they feel "stuck," are a family "still living in our garage," "are no further forward" than they were more than two years earlier, that they "haven't seen a cent" yet to help with their recovery from disaster, and that they have "rung up every day" without satisfaction, trying just to get their roof repaired. They explain that "after two-and-a-half years, still not knowing" is unbearable, that they cannot even get an answer about whether they are "under cap" or "over cap," and that the government has "just been using stalling tactics." They exclaim that they feel like they have "got nowhere to go" because the government and EQC "have all the power," and wonder "how urgent is 'urgent'" after they have been told that they have been on a list for "urgent" action that has still not arrived after years of waiting.

Another *Campbell Live* story from May 2013 chronicled the experiences of Sasha and Steve Bell, two Christchurch "quake refugees" who had been displaced at home and whose lives were profoundly disrupted as a result of EQC failure and so who were now waiting interminably for reparative action. In November 2011, EQC sent a team of builders to repair the earthquake damage to the Bells' home. For three days, the interior of this home, which had been earthquake-damaged but was otherwise habitable, was dismantled by the repair crew, who then abruptly announced that they could proceed no further and departed. Eighteen months later, at the time of the 2013 story, the repair crew had still not yet returned; however, their work on the building had transformed it from a livable (albeit quake damaged) home to an uninhabitable shell, which forced the Bells to move into their detached garage. Now, on the cusp of their second bitterly cold Southern Hemisphere winter spent living in a garage with no insulation and only a tin door between themselves and the world beyond, the Bells have found themselves stuck in a "bad dream ... they can't wake from," characterized by "achingly slow progress" toward a restoration of their lives. Steve says that "home is where the heart is," but EQC "ripped it out" and now "we just want our lives back."

While Sasha and Steve have not been rendered stateless nor caught between jurisdictions like other refugees, they have been caught between alternative everyday geographies, between public and private insurance, and between competing expert opinions, and have thus been effectively stripped of core markers of citizenship and belonging such as access to a warm and habitable home. While they wait, we see Sasha and Steve living in their garage, but working to replicate key routines of everyday life, such as making coffee, getting ready for work by putting on makeup, and making the bed (see figure 4.2). Such quotidian routines are in this story spatially and temporally rearticulated to signify the inadequacies of bureaucratic indifference, official neglect, and post-quake *displacement at home*. Near the end of the story, Sasha becomes very emotional and reveals how her orientation toward the future has been thoroughly disrupted by EQC's failures. But she also asserts her intention to fight back. Despite the new vulnerabilities that have been inflicted upon her, Sasha imagines and articulates a future in which she and others who have been displaced at home will triumph over the indifference of the neoliberal officialdom and the profiteering insurance industry: "You can't even think too far ahead, that's the thing. It's like you just go day to day. I can't think beyond probably the end of the week really. . . . I'm not gonna

FIGURE 4.2 Post-quake everyday life as seen on *Campbell Live*: Sasha prepares in the garage to go to work.

let these people win. They're not go to beat me. They've made our situation bad enough and it's just—you know, I'm gonna fight through everything. It's just not right, you can't do this to people."

As *Campbell Live* was broadcast live on national television, and the show generated an avid following of social media users around it, there was an outpouring of instantaneous Twitter responses to the situations of Christchurch quake refugees from audience members across the country. Some of these responses were selected for inclusion in the broadcast by *Campbell Live* staff, such as "in other countries there would be rioting in the streets . . . we should all be standing up and fighting," and "someone needs to . . . kick arse down there and clear out all the petty bureaucrats who have been sitting on their hands letting people suffer for years." Consequently, EQC was forced to shift rapidly into damage control mode and issue a similarly prompt (and highly uncharacteristic) response via *Campbell Live*: "EQC apologises unreservedly for the way the Bell's [sic] claim has been dealt with. There were significant technical issues and differing expert opinions but, at the end of the day, it was completely unreasonable to leave the Bells in a position of prolonged uncertainty after the repair was discontinued. EQC acknowledges and accepts that this has caused unnecessary stress and hardship for the Bells. We will be contacting the Bells immediately and working with them to resolve their claim as quickly as possible." *Campbell Live* and its audience were thus able to collectively call EQC to account in a way that the Bells alone could not. Some of the vast amounts of online engagement with the show's quake coverage took place on the official *Campbell Live* Facebook page. Facebook discussions and comments about the show's stories are key sites of participatory and affective investment that both enliven and augment the more measured on-air coverage. These responses angrily indict bureaucratic incompetence, neoliberal politicians, disaster capitalism, and misplaced priorities that put profits before people:

> Just watched Campbell Live and the EQC CEO, what a load of bureaucratic bullshit he spouted, couldn't answer a question with a straight answer . . . EQC get your bureaucratic finger out of your arse and pay up so people can get on and recover [Respondent #1]

> JUST on CAMPBELL LIVE. Yes EQC, get your bloody act together, there's alot of people still hurting! [Respondent #2]

> Watching Campbell live regarding chch earthquake, EQC sort your shit out and do your f. . . . . . job [Respondent #3]

> Caught a bit of Campbell Live tonight re Christchurch! Our wonderous government, [Prime Minister] John Key and the EQC! What the fuck is wrong with you? Where is all the money we donated to get these people in

homes? Sitting somewhere getting you interest? This is a supposedly western country, what the fuck is taking so long? Why are our fellow New Zealander's suffering? NO excuse will do JK, no excuse, not good enough.... I bet you have running water and a proper loo for xmas... dam I forgot, its more important to demolish the CBD! [Respondent #4]

Did you see those poor people on Campbell Live tonight. EQC needs a real kick up the a—and some body should really take charge. We don't live in a 3rd world country, but after looking at tonights programme I think we do, what's wrong with you people. Please get your heads out of the clouds and help these people and the many others that you have put to one side. We are becoming a sick nation and it's not funny anymore [Respondent #5]

It seems like you need to appear on Campbell Live before EQC will acknowledge you exist! [Respondent #6]

It seems wrong that to get anything done by EQC you need to be highlighted by Campbell Live. [Respondent #7]

Ppl of Chch, trouble getting yr EQC or insurance claim sorted? You know what to do, form an orderly queue to go on Campbell live. [Respondent #8]

Campbell Live's disaster mediation reveals that being made to wait constitutes a power-bearing technique of temporality that brings its own sort of disastrous violence. In the Caravan of Complaint footage and in Sasha and Steve's story, we encounter not only a "resilient" Canterbury population, but also people who have been made vulnerable, devalued, mistreated, and even brutalized—not so much by the quakes themselves as by the power bloc's responses to disaster, which we might characterize as a strategy to advance disaster capitalism and agendas of privatization, to suppress critical publicity and erode remaining remnants of a public sphere, and to limit or neutralize the quakes' potential to provoke mobilization and to catalyze movements for democratization and decolonization. *Campbell Live* opened a media space for the voices of the vulnerable and clearly took the side of ordinary people, who resisted what they were expected to endure. When Campbell himself was criticized by the *New Zealand Herald* for abandoning journalistic "objectivity" and siding "with people against power," he responded by asking rhetorically, "Am I not meant to give a shit?" (quoted in Wichtel 2012). As a result, the *Campbell Live* team, the ordinary people featured on the show, and other digitally active and engaged viewers began to reimagine and enact a collective form of disaster experience, including that of waiting, and thus began to shift the discursive terrain and to displace neoliberal discourses of resilience and "the new normal."

Campbell Live's post-quake coverage leaves at least three important legacies. First, it has rearticulated the spatialities and temporalities of the experience of being "in limbo" or "waiting" in terms of the inadequacies of neoliberal disaster response. Second, in the context of media convergence culture, which has dramatically transformed the nature of post-quake recovery, lobbying, and activism, *Campbell Live* has participated in and strengthened existing connectivities and engendered new ones. The mediated interactions between bottom-up and top-down discourses have, we believe, been disruptive to ongoing projects of de-democratization and the coloniality of power. Finally, *Campbell Live* reveals what can be achieved when flawed notions of journalistic objectivity are abandoned and TV shows take it upon themselves to speak back to power. As many people of Canterbury recognized, if you wanted to shake things up and force the authorities to do their jobs in the wake of the quakes, you needed to get on *Campbell Live*.

Despite or, as in the views of many, *because of* its muckraking success, *Campbell Live* was axed in 2015. Its cancellation provoked substantial opposition and protest as Kiwis across the country signed petitions calling for the show to be kept on air. Many New Zealanders are convinced that the cancellation was politically motivated. It was widely rumored that *Campbell Live* was detested by many conservative business and political leaders such as Earthquake Czar Gerry Brownlee, who had already in 2012 stated publicly that he was "sick and tired" of the "carping and moaning" of Christchurch residents whose homes had suffered liquefaction damage, who were critical of the government's authoritarian responses, and who had too much time to "buggerise on Facebook all day" (quoted in Dally 2012). But while the *Campbell Live* website has now been removed and there is no easy way for ordinary people to gain access to previously broadcast material, the complete erasure of such content is difficult if not impossible in the contemporary media environment. As the remnants left on YouTube and elsewhere demonstrate, cancellation does not eradicate all digital traces of *Campbell Live*, nor prevent the continuation of the conversations it helped to stimulate and for which it created spaces. After the cancellation of *Campbell Live*, John Campbell became the host of *Checkpoint*, a new multiplatform show simulcast on radio and in online live-streaming video format, and continued to pursue the many active issues plaguing the people and disaster recovery of Christchurch. As viewer "Lew" tweeted of the show in March 2018, "another day, another monster instalment in the all-encompassing clusterfuck that is the EQC from John Campbell and the Checkpoint team, who Gerry Brownlee won't talk to for some reason." A group of Christchurch citizens, including Sasha and Steve Bell, went on to sue EQC and Fletcher Building for breaches against their human rights. And the New Zealand Labour government that was elected in 2017 established an independent enquiry into EQC, which found that the organization "was poorly prepared for the Canterbury earthquakes and has left people with a 'deep mistrust of government' that will take years to overcome" (Todd 2020). The transmediated activist muckraking practiced through and around *Campbell Live* (and *Checkpoint*) by journalists and audiences formed a complex assemblage marked by expanded engagements with the conjunctural crisis around EQC's failures and, more broadly, ongoing efforts to enact, advance and contest everyday forms of coloniality, neoliberalism, and de-democratization in twenty-first-century Aotearoa.

Disasters, Decoloniality, and Popular Media Culture

In this and the preceding chapter, we have attempted to identify the decolonizing and democratizing potentials associated with forms of cultural struggle visible in the mediation and remediation of disaster. By considering sites with broadly similar and interconnected colonial and neoliberal histories that are geographically dispersed across the first, third, and fourth worlds, we have drawn attention to shared struggles to dismantle ongoing modes of domination and control. Tragedy in the so-called third and fourth worlds is often viewed as more acceptable by many people in the (self-designated) first. But Katrina posited the convergence of New Orleans (and other cities affected by the hurricane such as Biloxi, Mississippi) as a city located at once in the United States and the third world. As Richard Rodríguez (quoted in Saldaña-Portillo 2007: 504, emphasis in original) noted: "It is insufficient to say that the first world population got out of town and left New Orleans to become a third world capital, flooded and stinking and dangerous. It is truer to say that we discovered that New Orleans, *like any other city*, had been in the third world all along. These faces of terror and want and despair and menace and stoicism are faces from the third world. They are American faces." The idea that any U.S. city belongs as well to the third world undermines common sense binaries and American exceptionalism, thus reinscribing the nation within "a continental history of labor flows" (Saldaña-Portillo 2007: 504). Similarly, the protracted displacement and waiting endured by citizens of Christchurch in the wake of the earthquakes—and particularly endured in the racialized Eastern suburbs of the city—accompanied the physical destruction of long-standing colonial landscapes in the South Pacific and spurred many Kiwis both within and beyond Christchurch to question and ponder whether Aotearoa New Zealand is a first, third, or fourth world nation. We might say that these disasters amply revealed the extent to which it is all three.

Hurricanes Katrina and Felix and the Christchurch earthquakes all occurred under conditions created by not only coloniality but also ascendant (albeit contested and perhaps unravelling) neoliberalism. Indeed, the 2020 COVID-19 disaster has inspired many to consider whether the neoliberal conjuncture may well be on the verge of giving way to something else, such as a resurgent global socialism (as more cities, regions, and countries think seriously about enacting universal basic income programs), pluriversality, or, alternatively, something more along the lines of democratic totalitarianism (as we suggested in chapter 1), authoritarian capitalism, or neofeudalism. But just as neoliberalism and coloniality modify spaces and subjectivities, so too do spaces and subjectivities modify neoliberalism and coloniality, and produce ways of understanding and ways of being that are not always straightforwardly negative or oppressive. Disasters and crises provide ample opportunities for neoliberal revanchism and the reproduction of racist pathologization, and we must, as Jamie Peck (2006) has urged, remain vigilant and bring analytical capacities to bear on how such processes are made politically and culturally possible. At the same time, crises and disasters also create openings and spaces for decolonial projects, which depend in part on both histories of anti-colonial struggle and, increasingly, the dynamics and affordances of the new media environment. This is exemplified not only by the ways in which the mediation of Katrina, Felix, and the Christchurch quakes (as well as the COVID-19 pandemic) revealed long histories of neglect and racial exploitation, although this dimension is significant, but also by how the infrastructures of convergent media and contemporary modes of electronic engagement have redistributed representational agency in such disasters in highly complex ways. For example, groups such as Gap Filler and levees.org make full and effective use of Facebook, Twitter, and other social media to inform and mobilize, while bloggers, vloggers, and YouTubers produce content that crosses media platforms and genres into TV dramas dealing with disaster, which in turn spawn online debates and new affective engagements among audiences. We saw in chapter 3 how Ashley Morris, a real-life blogger with a highly influential internet presence, inspired a fictional character on *Treme*, played by an actor (John Goodman) who is also a Katrina activist. Like the footage of Hardy Jackson, a YouTube clip from *Treme* that is based on Morris' blog gets thousands and thousands of views and comments and is repeatedly reblogged and reposted. The persistent remediation of Katrina, Felix, and the Christchurch quakes put these disasters and their consequences back into public and popular circulation for renewed struggle and ongoing reworking and engagement, thereby generating cultural resources for survival and resistance. Disaster victims' and survivors' struggles for dignity and justice thus challenge and disrupt spatiotemporal and discursive containment.

The remediation of disasters is contributing to the ongoing erosion of boundaries between "old" and "new" media, between "factual" and entertainment genres, and between expert and popular or Indigenous knowledges. In 2016, Māori Television (which is now called Whakaata Māori and which we will discuss at greater length in the next chapter) told the story of how traditional Indigenous knowledges of the land, including accounts of Rūaumoko, the *atua* (supernatural being or god) of earthquakes and volcanoes (stories of whom circulated amply in the wake of the Christchurch quakes), were helping Māori children in Christchurch cope with and heal from post-quake PTSD (see

Timutimu 2016, which includes video of the Māori Television story).[7] Indeed, in the wake of both the Christchurch earthquakes and the COVID-19 pandemic, Whakaata Māori gave notable emphasis to perspectives and approaches to Indigenous *aroha* (love) and caring practices, and social media were mobilized similarly by many Māori people (see, e.g., Cram 2021). Twinkl, an international online distributor of educational content founded in 2010, the year the first of the major earthquakes hit Christchurch, now distributes a PowerPoint slide show designed to teach children about Rūaumoko.[8] A bilingual and bicultural interactive book *Te Hīkoi a Rūaumoko/Rūaumoko's Walk* was later produced by the Hawkes Bay Emergency Management Group (Andrews and Graham 2014), and Rūaumoko features in the interactive museum Quake City in central Christchurch (which is dedicated to remembering the earthquakes), indicating the incipient Indigenization of a highly Eurocentric field (see figures 4.3 and 4.4). The decolonizing potential of cultural struggles engaged through practices of recirculation and remediation can be seen in the way decolonial discourses, narratives, bodies, and voices spread across media platforms, entering mainstream news and current affairs, "quality" HBO and other TV dramas, documentaries and feature films, Indigenous and community television, blogs, and social media sites such as YouTube. This transmedia deluge argues that emergency management and disaster relief and recovery must be informed by popular and Indigenous as well as expert knowledges in ways that avoid privileging one over the other *a priori*.

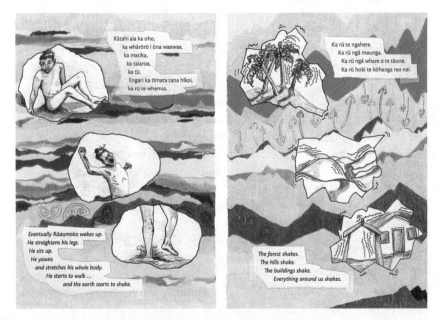

FIGURE 4.3 Rūaumoko wakens. (Source: Andrews and Graham 2014.)

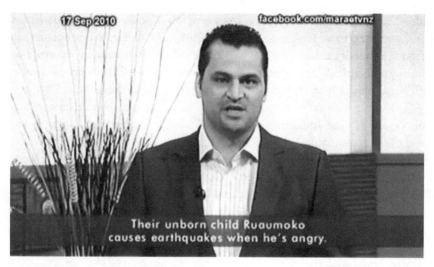

FIGURE 4.4 Covering the story of Rūaumoko with Marae TV.

Scholars working in and with decolonial and other critical approaches must take popular media culture seriously. Commercial and social media cultures can indeed be as important as community, grassroots, and Indigenous media, and the blurring between these realms increasingly thwarts their categorical delimitation. As Lipsitz (1988: 100) wrote many years ago,

> Storytelling persists, even inside the apparatuses of commercial mass culture. Indeed, commercial culture expressly depends upon the residues of local popular narratives for its determinate forms and themes.... But the pervasiveness of popular narrative forms and themes is not just a matter of the sedimented residue of historical communities and cultures. Mass society and commercial culture provoke a new popular narrative response, one that draws upon both old and new forms of cultural creation. By circulating the stories of particular communities and cultures to a mass audience, the culture industry invites comparison, interpretation and elaboration.

In the new media environment, people's capacities to engage in such practices of interpretation, comparison, and elaboration are substantially expanded, and the possibility of determining categorically just where a popular culture that is genuinely "of the people" ends and commercial culture begins is correspondingly diminished. This is not merely an historical observation, but also a theoretical one, for the binarism of "ersatz commercial" versus "authentically popular" culture has always been incorrectly conceived. As Stuart Hall (2019: 354) writes, "If the forms of provided commercial popular culture are not purely manipulative, then it is because, alongside the false appeals, the foreshortenings, the trivialization and short-circuits, there are also elements of recognition and identification, something approaching a recreation of recognizable experiences and attitudes, to which people are responding. The danger arises because we tend to think of cultural forms as whole and coherent: either wholly corrupt or wholly authentic. Whereas, they are deeply contradictory; they play on contradictions, especially when they function in the domain of the 'popular.'"

The alternative rationalities and ontologies expressed in the celebrations of the Mardi Gras Indians, the King Pulanka festival, stories of Rūaumoko, and the community projects of the Gap Filler and Greening the Rubble/Green Lab collectives (like all popular cultural texts, according to Jameson 1979) "contain a radical utopian kernel that contrasts the indignities of the present social order with the possibilities for happiness conjured up by collective and individual imagination" (Lipsitz 1988: 101, summarizing Jameson 1979). The recirculation and rearticulation of such celebrations and undertakings in diverse media spaces expands their reach as cultural resources that can be put in the service of decolonial and democratizing projects. As Stuart Hall (2019: 360–361) observes, popular culture matters deeply because it is a site where struggles "for and against a culture of the powerful is engaged," and is "one of the places where socialism might be constituted." In the contemporary media environment, where images and narratives can be reposted, remixed and reblogged, where struggles across geographical space can be more easily connected and brought into dialogue with each other, and where it is easier for some ordinary people to self-publish and interact in other ways, the potential to redirect the meanings of disaster is enhanced. In this context, "common sense" forms of racialization and economic exploitation that enable disaster to unfold and devastate can be contested in new and powerful ways.

Part III
Māori Media

Criminalization, "Terrorism," and the Celebrification of Indigenous Activists

5
Coloniality, Criminalization, and the New Media Environment

The Coloniality of the New Zealand Mediascape

As we have argued, the contemporary media environment is changing in ways that create new forms of and possibilities for practices of cultural citizenship. One dimension of these changes, as we have noted in relation to disaster events, involves the ways in which new media resources are increasingly harnessed by Indigenous and Afrodescendant populations in pursuit of decolonization at a time when Eurocentric thought and practices are increasingly subject to challenge in many parts of the world (see Quijano 2007; Martín-Barbero 2011). In recent years, to note another kind of example, the democratization of access to media by racially subordinated populations has facilitated the expansion of grassroots countersurveillance of police forces, whose most famous precursor, perhaps, is the home video of the beating of Rodney King (see Fiske 2016a, 2016b; Thompson 2005; Goldsmith 2010).[1] Ordinary citizens are thus filming police violence with their cell phones and distributing these images widely, where they can be shared, commented on, and amplified through mainstream media in ways that reshape our understandings of public space, authority, and racialized policing, and that often demand some form of political response. Widespread protests engulfed the United States in 2020 after ordinary citizens filmed the murder of African American George Floyd by a white police officer in Minnesota. In this chapter, we explore the racial politics of the changing media environment within the wider neoliberal and postcolonial conjuncture of Aotearoa New Zealand, and with particular emphasis on the struggle for and interventions of and around Whakaata Māori (Māori Television), which has been broadcasting now for two decades.

The postcolonial settler state in New Zealand emerged from violent, state-sponsored racism carried out by European (Pākehā) settlers against Māori populations in the island territory the latter called Aotearoa, from the colonizing endeavor to replace Indigenous forms of governance with European ones, to Indigenous struggles in the face of this violence to retain the land rights and sovereignty they had enjoyed prior to colonization, and through (often awkward) political, cultural, and legislative accommodations with Indigenous ways of knowing and being by Pākehā colonizers and their descendants. New Zealand's founding document, the Treaty of Waitangi, which was signed in 1840 between the British Crown and some 500 Māori chiefs, was supposed to provide Māori with ongoing control of their land and other *taonga* (treasures). In the ensuing decades, however, Māori treaty rights were repeatedly breached and, despite intense and frequently armed resistance by Māori to colonial rule, large tracts of Māori land were confiscated and Māori populations were decimated. Colonial governments passed laws such as the 1870 Native Schools Code, which mandated that all instruction be conducted in English, and the 1907 Tohunga Suppression Act, which was designed to undermine Māori epistemologies and cultural practices.[2]

Colonial violence sent Māori society into decline. While Māori continued to resist racism, hostility, and colonization throughout the nineteenth century, it was not until the second half of the twentieth century that Māori protest gained powerful traction and Māori began successfully demanding recognition of and redress for some of the land and treaty rights that had previously been violated by the colonizers. They achieved a series of political gains, including the creation of the Waitangi Tribunal in 1975 to address treaty violations, and the more overt and violent forms of racism that had characterized earlier historical periods gave way to "biculturalism," which became a key emergent discourse and official policy. These shifts facilitated some reparations for historical grievances gained through the work of the Waitangi Tribunal, helped to generate legislation and state funding to protect the Māori language (*te reo*), and resulted in a growing presence and acceptance of *tikanga* Māori (correct Māori procedure) such as *pōwhiri* (welcoming ceremonies) in many cultural, political, and educational spaces. While serious forms of discrimination persisted, Māori began to experience a cultural, political, and economic renaissance (Poata-Smith 1996). The growing political visibility and representation of Māori and other Indigenous groups around the world has gained strong impetus from both national and international struggles. International and multilateral initiatives to end discrimination against Indigenous peoples, such as International Labour Organization Convention 169 on Indigenous peoples' rights, the UN

Permanent Forum on Indigenous Issues, and the UN Declaration on the Rights of Indigenous Peoples, have helped to consolidate and legitimize the recognition of past injustices gained by Māori at the national level.[3]

It ultimately became apparent that the European settlers' claims on sovereignty and subordination of Māori populations were never fully realized, and that many Māori had neither assimilated nor accepted coloniality as many of the colonizers had imagined. Māori epistemologies continued to be articulated in ways that challenged Pākehā hegemony, and Māori modes of governance were still practiced in many places. While widespread recognition of the collective and still palpable pain inflicted by colonialism on Māori is not yet fully apparent across mainstream New Zealand society and many Pākehā remain ignorant of their obligations under the Treaty of Waitangi,[4] there is a growing awareness and acceptance among some sectors of New Zealand society that many Māori grievances are legitimate. This emergent recognition of the validity of treaty grievances does to some degree put the very legitimacy of the settler state into question, which of course produces anxieties among many Pākehā New Zealanders. Such anxieties are often expressed through institutional and everyday forms of racism. So although the idea that Māori have rights which must be protected is now fairly uncontroversial, loud right-wing voices railing against "special privileges," the "treaty grievance industry," and "racial separatism" are still frequently heard (Walker 2002).

Since the dawn of the colonial era, Eurocentric and Pākehā-dominated media have played a central role in "securing ... settler domination over the landscape" (Hokowhitu and Devadas 2013b: xxxi). A significant body of literature has emphasized how mainstream New Zealand media have collaborated in epistemic and other forms of colonial violence enacted by the postcolonial settler state and have constructed demonizing representations of Māori characterized by an excessive emphasis on family dysfunction, domestic abuse, and general criminality (Abel 2008; Walker 2002; J Smith 2006; Nairn et al. 2012; Hokowhitu and Devadas 2013a). Linda Tuhiwai Smith (2012) draws attention to colonial culture's pervasive *problematization* of Indigenous peoples. Smith outlines the imperializing work performed by discourses of "the Indigenous problem" and notes the role of the media in extending the reach of these discourses: "Concern about 'the Indigenous problem' began as an explicitly militaristic or policing concern. The problem was articulated in terms of 'putting down rebellions' or getting rid of recalcitrant rebels. Individual chiefs or leaders who resisted various attempts to control them were labeled as rebels and the 'real problems' and the media accounts helped whip up a frenzied hatred of these individuals by white settlers" (Smith 2012: 94).

Suzanne Duncan (2013: 93) expresses concern about the excessive targeting of Māori in public health and social marketing media campaigns aimed at encouraging productivity or reducing smoking, drinking, and domestic violence, as such campaigns depend on a dominant construction of Māori as "undesirable, impoverished, uneducated and socially deficient" citizens and consumers. This is a good example of the "inferential racism" Stuart Hall (1981: 37, emphasis in original) identifies in "social problem" shows on TV whose "every word and image... are impregnated with unconscious racism because they are all predicated on the unstated and unrecognized assumption" that non-whites "are the *source of the problem.*"

Ranginui Walker (2002: 217–218) writes that an ethnocentric and monocultural press has played a key role in "supporting the hierarchy of Pākehā domination and Māori subordination." Walker discusses how the colonial press represented leading Māori activists, such as Te Whiti of Taranaki in the 1880s or the prophet Rua Kenana of Mangapohatu during World War I, as extreme and fanatical threats to European social order. Walker believes that such representations helped facilitate repressive police invasions at Parihaka in 1881 and Rua Kenana's commune in 1916. More recent forms of Māori activism, such as the Ngā Tamatoa protests on Waitangi Day, have been depicted in similar ways that mobilize "public opinion against Māori self-determination" (Meek 2013: 26).

In addition, there has been Pākehā resistance to Māori-language media. In the 1980s, when TVNZ (Television New Zealand) began to broadcast programs such as *Te Karere* in *te reo*, they received complaints from Pākehā audiences (Lysaght, 2010). Māori have struggled for recognition of broadcasting rights under the Treaty of Waitangi, in order to control their own representation in contemporary media; interject Māori language, discourses, identities, and perspectives into national and international spaces; promote redress for historical injustices; and achieve other favorable social, cultural, political, and economic outcomes for Māori. After overcoming substantial political obstacles (see Walker 2004 for an overview and discussion of these obstacles), Māori Television began broadcasting in 2004. In the words of Jo Smith (2006: 27), Māori Television "can be seen as a strategy of decolonisation that must, by necessity, inhabit the very thing it might seek to critique or interrupt." Despite a difficult start, Māori Television has over the past two decades established itself as a credible and innovative public broadcaster that has put important issues on the political agenda, covered stories ignored by mainstream media, and inflected national news with Indigenous accents and perspectives. Māori Television has underscored both Māori success and Pākehā state failure. In addition, the channel has delivered a range of entertainment programs that foreground Indigenous epistemologies and aesthetics. It has surprised many observers by drawing substantial Pākehā as well as Māori audiences.[5] By the early 2010s, Māori Television had developed around itself an active participatory culture of digitally engaged audiences making avid use of Twitter, Facebook, and YouTube to comment on shows, trade perspectives, share experiences, and suggest stories and programming ideas to the network.

Throughout the entire existence of the channel, the contemporary global media environment, including the medium and institutions of television, has been undergoing rapid and profound transformation under the pressure of continuing expansion, fragmentation, digitalization, and technological elaboration. As we have argued in previous chapters, "media convergence" has emerged amid these changes as a central concept for grappling with a range of shifts in how we use media to produce and circulate knowledges and identities, engage as citizens within increasingly complex political cultures, and understand and confront crises. The concept of media convergence has acquired several different meanings and frames of reference that include the development of new media mobilities and the expansion of new forms of participation and interactivity. Media convergence entails modes of hybridization between "old" and "new" media, between different media genres, and between media producers and media consumers/users. As we have suggested in previous chapters, the forms of centralized television that once arguably served to generate (at least the semblance of) a national consensus has fragmented, as expanded multichannel environments, niche programming and TV in social media and other online spaces enable a range of participatory activities by viewers and allow a wider array of voices to circulate and sometimes contribute to the emergence of "collective intelligence" (see Lévy 1997; Jenkins 2008). Kackman et al. (2011b: 11) ask, "if broadcast television had cohered a national community around a simultaneous engagement with shared texts, then what kind of communities form in response to the multiple screens, interfaces, and media platforms of our contemporary mediascape(s)?" One answer, judging from the Aotearoa New Zealand media environment, is that cultural communities that have resisted assimilation into dominant national narratives and identities, and have developed new spaces and practices for the ongoing production and circulation of alternative ones.

Key features of the twenty-first-century media environment include the digital proliferation of distribution channels associated with post-broadcast media forms, intensified geographical connectedness, and expanded possibilities for transcultural dialogue as images and discourses spill interactively across a multiplicity of networked screens and platforms. One important dimension of the new media environment has therefore been the extension of Indigenous media in different parts of the world. Indigenous TV channels such as Whakaata Māori have deployed emergent technological affordances to forge new ways of maintaining, asserting, and reconfiguring traditional knowledges, languages, and identities. Whakaata Māori often leverages the growing digital competencies of Indigenous viewers and their willingness to participate in online spaces to contest Eurocentric figurings of Indigeneity, and to reveal how the imposition of coloniality continues to subordinate Indigenous peoples and deprive them of cultural (and other dimensions of) citizenship. Indigenous mediamakers and viewers deploy media within contexts of epistemic crisis characteristic of postcolonial settler states constituted through violence and dispossession, where discursive and institutional spaces for the articulation of Indigenous rights have been forced open in recent decades. While Indigenous cultures continue to be marginalized by resilient colonial worldviews, the ongoing production and circulation of alternative discourses creates new opportunities for the rearticulation of hegemonic forms of common sense. How, we ask, has the existence of Māori Television in the wider convergent media environment disrupted some of the ways Indigenous peoples are inserted into media discourse? Two sites of intervention into dominant discursive practices we explore in this chapter involve historically entrenched modes of representing Māori criminality, and the conventional, post-9/11 recoding of Indigenous activism as "terrorism." Our aim here is to use the lens of media convergence to explore how Whakaata Māori is contributing to the reconfiguration and reassemblage of dominant media geographies.

Māori Television, Crime, and Policing

Whakaata Māori has engaged actively in the negotiation and rearticulation of Māori criminality in ways that raise questions about the complex relationships between Indigenous people, colonial criminal justice systems, and the media. Their practices invite consideration of how prevalent racist associations between Indigeneity and criminality might be disrupted. Both the media (as noted) and the criminal justice system in Aotearoa New Zealand have functioned as instruments of coloniality and continue to do so, but they are also subject to persistent decolonizing challenges and pressures. It is well documented that the European colonization of what is now referred to as New Zealand involved the systematic and violent erasure of Indigenous modes of governance along with their systems of justice and reconciliation, which were replaced with imported European ones. Howard McNaughton (2009: 51) notes, for instance, that "traditional modes of punishment among Māori—and many other colonized peoples—find no place for incarceration," and John Pratt (1992: 45) observes that during the early decades of the colonial period, jailing was seen as a "culturally unacceptable sanction" by Māori, who expressed a "deep-rooted antagonism to the idea of prison." The criminalization of struggles for Māori sovereignty, in particular, was and is a key colonial strategy. Contemporary crime statistics, which must of course be approached with extreme caution (see Jackson 1988), show that Māori constitute 15 percent of the total population, but that half of all men and more than 60 percent of women in prison are Māori. This statistic bears grim witness to the ways in which coloniality continues to produce persistent social disadvantage, stigmatization, and often the criminalization of practices for the defense of Indigenous rights.

The starkly disproportionate incarceration of Indigenous and Aboriginal populations is also a key feature of other postcolonial settler societies such as Canada and Australia, while elsewhere, most notably in the United States, Brazil, and South Africa, it is people of African descent who are disproportionately imprisoned. Incarceration is of course accompanied and abetted by state-sponsored racial profiling and surveillance, targeted stop and search actions, and other forms of police harassment, which create a situation in which Black and Indigenous populations develop a generalized fear and distrust of police and criminal justice systems (Hall et al., 2013). Furthermore, incarceration statistics are in many countries, including New Zealand, becoming more, rather than less, racially asymmetrical. As Ruth Wilson Gilmore (2007) argues with respect to the mass incarceration of African Americans in California, the imperatives of predatory neoliberalism, which include the withdrawal of state social safety nets, have turned prisons into holding sites for "surplus" populations unable to access the fruits of capitalist (over)development.[6] Moreover, the privatization and outsourcing of incarceration and securitization services to companies associated with the prison industrial complex of contemporary authoritarian formations of neoliberal racial capitalism (see Robinson 1983), such as the GEO Group (formerly Wackenhut) in the United States, Australia, and South Africa, and Serco in the United Kingdom and New Zealand, generates impressive profits and return rates for the investor class.

As struggles for political redress by Indigenous populations have gained momentum in many countries, we have witnessed a concomitant increase in the criminalization of Indigenous activists. Racialized incarceration intensifies the social fragmentation of Māori communities that are already severely fragmented by myriad mechanisms of coloniality, and thus serves the useful purpose, for the Pākehā power bloc, of sustaining coloniality and weakening the threat that Māori activism poses to systems of white privilege. Dominant Pākehā discourses of Māori crime, which assert that Māori are more prone to criminality, serve to obscure or invisibilize violence enacted by the state against Indigenous communities, leave many Māori families in a state of economic and cultural deprivation, and help maintain Pākehā imaginaries that locate coloniality in a distant past that has long since been eclipsed. They also evade the question of the legitimacy of colonial and Eurocentric justice, particularly when it is exerted over Māori communities that never signed the Treaty of Waitangi, as it was in the Tūhoe Nation in 2007 to devastating effect (as we discuss further on).[7] Indeed, the incarceration of Māori by a European-imposed justice system enacts, in the words of late Māori legal scholar Moana Jackson (1998: 71), "the assumption by the colonising states that they have a right to dispossess us."

This state of affairs is however increasingly precarious, thanks largely to the efforts of Māori leaders, activists, intellectuals, lawyers, and mediamakers who have drawn attention to the colonial and imperializing powers whereby large numbers of Māori are imprisoned and crime statistics are produced and circulated. In their efforts to highlight and disrupt problematic associations drawn between Indigeneity and criminality, they have identified racisms embedded in asymmetrical policing and sentencing practices. For example, Moana Jackson's (1987, 1988) seminal work in the late 1980s, which gathered Māori experiences of and perspectives on the criminal justice system through a series of *hui* (gatherings or meetings), demonstrates how the social and cultural construction of crime and the application of "justice" in New Zealand overwhelmingly benefits Pākehā populations and disadvantages Māori. For Jackson, institutionalized racism is central to Māori experiences of the criminal justice system, Indigenous crime rates reflect Pākehā priorities as much as they do Māori offending, and much research that seeks to explain Indigenous criminality is founded in sociocultural biases. Jackson argues against what he calls the "offender-based methodology," which detaches criminalized individuals from broader social and cultural forces and structures, overlooks how cultural difference and socioeconomic deprivation are entangled, and understands Māori criminality as the product of a stubborn inability to assimilate or adapt to social and economic change. Furthermore, mainstream media representations have been key agents in the production and maintenance of Eurocentric commonsense associations between Indigeneity and criminality. Jackson observes that the mediated spectacularization of violent Māori crimes such as child abuse, for instance, means that Māori child abusers become household names while Pākehā child abusers do not (see New Zealand Drug Foundation 2009). Analysts such as Chris Cunneen (2013: 396) argue that since colonization entailed the racist "imposition of an alien justice system," it is imperative that researchers focus not on Indigenous crime, but on the complex interactions "between colonial processes, Indigenous people and criminal justice systems." The rise of Māori media is driven in part by a desire to engage issues around Māori and the criminal justice system through alternative cultural discourses and representations, and it is not difficult to identify key differences between, for example, crime reporting on Whakaata Māori and that found on New Zealand's mainstream TV channels.

As a result of ongoing cultural and political struggles and interventions by Māori activists, mediamakers and others, there is now greater awareness, among at least some sectors, of the need for structural reform. For example, the Just Speak network, which is based in New Zealand's capital city of Wellington, seeks to rethink questions of criminal justice and reformulate policy. Just Speak (2012) lauded important initiatives such as the introduction of tribal *rangatahi* (youth) courts, family conferences, and Māori-focused corrections units, but also noted persistent failures to adopt many of the proposals that have been put forward for decades by Māori legal experts such as Moana Jackson. Just Speak (2012) has made specific calls for both the government and the media to promote, for instance, the creation of spaces in which Māori offenders can speak about their experiences. Following Nick Couldry's (2010: 7) analysis in *Why Voice Matters*, both neoliberal and colonial rationalities undermine *voice*, which Couldry understands at its core as "people's practice of giving an account, implicitly or explicitly, of the world within which they act" in ways that can in turn be understood and acted upon by others. Like Couldry, Just Speak favors both broader structural reforms *and* more localized, scaled-down initiatives, particularly as New

Zealand's size lends itself to "small-scale activism and discussion" (39). For Couldry, *voice* as *process* and *value* can form the basis for the production of counter-rationalities that challenge neoliberal (and, we would add, colonial) modes of spatial organization, which generally work to exclude some groups' and individuals' voices from effective participation. Couldry (2, emphasis in original) posits *voice* as a "*connecting* term" that "challenges neoliberalism's claim that its view of politics as market functioning trumps all others, enables us to build an alternative view of politics that is at least partly oriented to valuing processes of voice, and includes within that view of politics a recognition of people's capacities for social cooperation based on voice."

While there's ample evidence that New Zealand television has functioned as an agent of coloniality through its general marginalization or outright exclusion of Māori voices and perspectives, and through its representations of "Māori criminality," it is also clear that television can serve decolonizing aims, particularly in the contemporary media environment, which facilitates the transmediated circulation of texts and discourses across an expanded array of genres, platforms, and technologies. It is important not to overstate the capacity of media to bring about political transformation—though media, including television, can contribute to or hinder such efforts. As John Fiske (2011: 45) writes, "the arguments that television is always an agent of the status quo are convincing, but not totally so. Social change does occur, ideological values do shift, and television is part of this movement. It is wrong to see it as an originator of social change, or even to claim that it ought to be so, for social change must have its roots in material social existence; but television can be, must be, part of that change, and its effectivity will either hasten or delay it." Similarly, Lynn Spigel (2015: 50) suggests that while television cannot by itself produce social or political transformation, it nevertheless exerts transformative pressures that lie in its capacity to intervene in the circulation of discourses and the representation of social relations, and in its power to encourage people to question and sometimes reformulate their views and understandings of things.

Our view is that television and other media are made and consumed within a complex, multidiscursive terrain comprised of a range of political and cultural resources that can be put to diverse uses. Television is a site for the circulation of multiple and often contradictory and competing discourses. It is a site of cultural contestation and for the negotiation of, and struggle over, meanings, including the meanings of Indigeneity, criminality, and imprisonment. We are particularly interested in the practices of articulation, disarticulation, and rearticulation that comprise the terrain of cultural struggle in the contemporary, convergent media environment. Some of the media we examine in this chapter invite engagement in ways that disrupt imperializing and colonial narratives of criminal justice in general and Māori offending in particular. We thus explore here (and in the next chapter) the extent to which decolonial interventions into the criminal justice system are abetted by the practices being mobilized by Māori filmmakers, broadcasters, and activists working within a rapidly changing and convergent media environment to produce alternative visions of policing, criminal justice, and prisons. In the next section, we focus in particular on a prison-based reality TV series broadcast on Whakaata Māori entitled *Songs from the Inside*.

Songs from the Inside and the Reconfiguration of Indigenous Criminality

Since its inception in 2004, Whakaata Māori has attempted to reconfigure the ways in which stories about policing, criminal justice, and prisons are framed and told. For example, the network has run two reality TV series that seek to rearticulate the confrontational relationship between Māori and police forces, and to encourage the recruitment of Māori officers in order to increase the organizational diversity and what Ruth Frankenberg (1993: 15) calls the "race cognizance" of the police and so promote the improvement of law enforcement practices. Both shows end with onscreen information on how to go about joining the police force. The first of these policing shows, *Kaitiaki o te Maungarongo* (Guardians of the peace), which was made by Maui Productions and broadcast in 2006 and 2007, followed a number of Māori police officers going about their work and revealing, for example, that the small town of Taneatua in the heart of the Tūhoe Nation is not the crime-ridden place that many Pākehā imagine it to be, and exploring how Pākehā drivers put others' lives at risk every day through excessive speed or alcohol consumption. In 2011, Māori Television screened the second of these policing shows, *Ngā Pirihimana Hou* (The new police), which follows Māori police recruits through their nineteen-week training course.

More innovatively, some Māori mediamakers have taken their cameras inside prison walls to focus on Māori who have been incarcerated. In 2008, Māori filmmaker Tearepa Kahi made a documentary entitled *First Time in Prison* for TV3. For eleven months, Kahi followed an eighteen-year-old Māori inmate in Mt. Eden Prison, capturing his experience from sentencing to release, a program that sought to disrupt the way that incarceration of Māori was usually represented. As he explained to us:

> My approach was about intimacy as opposed to seeing what's sensational. I just wanted to sit in there with him and my directing approach was to get rid of the camera crew, it was just me and a tiny little handheld camera and we just sat like that. We had a big couple of *whānau hui* [family meetings] at the start, telling him what was going to happen. Meet with the parents, meet with his *whānau* [family] and explain that we weren't trying to sell anything you know. This is me, this is you so there were *mihi* [introductions] and exchanges, but I think there was an in-depth ... or, well, I tried to be a lot more sincere. I don't mean it was more sincere than Pākehā [programs], but tried to be sincere through the filming of the program. There were things that I could have been

interested in, like the sexual practices of prisoners on the inside, but I wasn't, because I was more interested in this young guy, his girlfriend on the outside, making it through the day, and how it was for his father (interview with authors, 2010).

From 2012 to 2015, Māori Television screened three seasons of *Songs from the Inside*, produced by Julian Arahanga and Maramena Roderick of Wellington-based production company Awa Films. *Songs* takes a group of well-known Kiwi musicians into both men's and women's prisons in Wellington, Auckland, and Christchurch (see figure 5.1). These artists help the inmates to write and perform their own songs and more broadly to tell their stories. We believe that *Songs* conveys a powerful but limited decolonial ethos. While it obviously cannot restore Māori communities' management of their own legal and penal practices, processes, and affairs, it nevertheless promotes smaller-scale changes and opens spaces for discussions of the sort that Moana Jackson, Just Speak, and other activists have called for.

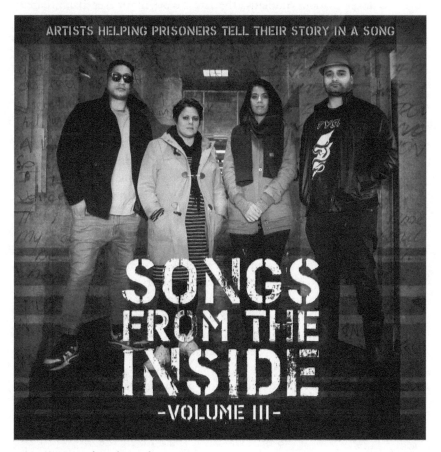

FIGURE 5.1 *Songs from the Inside.*

Sending television crews into prisons is, of course, not a new innovation. The lives of inmates have featured variously in a range of TV genres, from documentaries and reality TV shows to comedies and dramas. Examples include documentaries such as *Inside Death Row* and *Women behind Bars*, hosted by veteran British newsreader Trevor McDonald, and the *Lockup* franchise that airs on MSNBC. These shows, like many others of their genre, seek to reveal everyday life behind bars, as well as the motivations and circumstances that led to serious crimes. TV prison dramas have a long history, but the Netflix hit *Orange Is the New Black* was particularly innovative in drawing attention to the social contexts, especially those shaped by gender, race, and sexuality, which result in and impact upon incarceration.

It is interesting to consider what happens to the prison genre when cameras are put into the hands of Indigenous mediamakers who belong to a disproportionately incarcerated group. As Faye Ginsburg (2002: 50) writes, media produced by Indigenous people can "reverse and resignify the history of colonial looking relations," and put alternative knowledges and discourses into media, and therefore social, circulation. Similarly, the late Māori filmmaker Barry Barclay (2003) noted that white and masculinist imperial-looking relations are unsettled when the filming is done by "the natives." Since its inception, Whakaata Māori has become particularly adept at taking globally familiar generic media templates and inflecting them with Indigenous accents, interests, imaginaries, and desires (Glynn and Tyson 2007; Smith and de Bruin 2012). Examples include the karaoke talent show *Homai Te Pakipaki*, cooking shows such as *Marae Kai Masters* and *Cam's Kai*, and the makeover show *Marae DIY*. The packaging of Indigenous content within the trappings of familiar global genres has proven capable of increasing the appeal of such programming among both Māori and Pākehā audiences, as well as articulating and rearticulating both the generic frameworks and Māori cultural meanings, practices, and identities in ways that value and endorse the latter, rather than denigrate or sideline them. For instance, *Marae DIY* involves the collective restoration of both Māori meeting houses and their communities, and thus substitutes extended families and shared community spaces for the single, nuclear family houses of Western home makeover shows. Through interviews with *kuia* and *kaumātua* (elders), the show incorporates Indigenous reflections on the historical changes and challenges affecting Māori communities, and often brings younger members of the *iwi*, who are now living and working in urban centers, back home, for a time at least, to their traditional tribal lands and into renewed contact with their tribal spaces, stories, histories, affiliations, and identities. When Indigenous knowledges are foregrounded within entertainment television, possibilities and spaces are opened for the disarticulation and interrogation of racist and colonial discourses and attitudes. The convergent media environment, and social media in particular, give us some insight into the engagements with such programming that are enacted by audiences and community members.

While in our view *Songs from the Inside* constitutes a decolonial reimagining of key aspects of the Pākehā criminal justice system, director Julian Arahanga insisted in an interview with us that he had not set out to "shift any perceptions": "I don't have an agenda really. We're just doing what we're doing and we're focused on what we're doing. If that does build into some sense of a community and national or international changing of perceptions then, you know, that's a bonus, but I'm definitely not looking that big." Nevertheless, he noted later in the interview that "when we went into *Songs from the Inside* I was thinking, the very first one, my thing was, if we change *one* life then that would be enough, you know. I was like if we just, if one of these people gets it and then like stays out of prison and that, then that will be the reward. Currently *no one* after two seasons has gone back to prison."

While Whakaata Māori has a non-commercial mandate and is therefore not primarily ratings-driven, it does of course seek, not least for political reasons, to attract large audiences, as well as to make money, and *Songs from the Inside* has been one of the channel's highest-rating programs. It was named "Best Reality Series" at the 2017 NZTV Awards (Koti 2017). Its success lies in a number of factors, significant among which is, we believe, its decolonial ethos. The show is emotionally powerful and underpinned by a strong and overt *kaupapa* Māori (Māori methodology or way of doing things) approach. The show gives equal attention to both male and female inmates, who establish reciprocal and non-hierarchical working relationships with *Songs'* featured musical artists. The groups of prisoners and artists operate as a *whānau*, use *te reo* (Māori language) frequently, and create a space for the inmates to relate their often-harrowing personal histories and to articulate their hopes for the future. The gradual unfolding of inmates' back stories, as in *Orange Is the New Black*, is intensely humanizing by dint of the multidimensionality and emotional complexity it brings to their depiction. These stories thus challenge the collective pathologization of Māori offenders, which is common in mainstream New Zealand media and other institutional discourses, and give Pākehā viewers a chance to get to know the criminalized and imprisoned as people with complicated, unique, and socially situated biographies. The songs crafted by the inmates over the course of each season are rooted in expressive storytelling practices, personal experiences, and a struggle to forge an effective musical voice. These endeavors can be understood productively in relation to the claim made by one of Jackson's (1988: 157) *hui* participants that, in dealing with "Māori crime," it is crucial to find ways for people to "retain *mana*" (authority, status) and to gain "insight regarding... [their] own *mauri*, ... [their] own particular life force ... [and] self-esteem." The use of speech and song to articulate the social and cultural contexts and life histories that led to incarceration and the concomitant pain endured, potentially constitutes a step toward the restoration of *mana*, partially or temporarily at least. The inmates often describe this process as an invaluable opportunity or a "last chance" in ways that provide a revealing glimpse into the more ordinary conditions and consequences of life and imprisonment as a Māori in Aotearoa.

A central component of Indigenous media is, as Barry Barclay (2003) made clear, that Indigenous people are able to speak for themselves and articulate their perspectives in their own words. In *Songs from the Inside*, the participants are able to speak (and sing) for themselves, and to give expression to their own pain, instead of being pathologized as individuated case studies of (post)colonial maladjustment, or aggregated into problematic crime statistics, as is often the case in many Eurocentric, journalistic, and academic modalities for the discursive production of criminality. Through both interviews and song, inmates who are more typically consigned to voicelessness are here given a space for the emergence of voice. As Jackson (1987: 12) writes, a "recognition of the pain caused by this experience" of incarceration is central to the Indigenous reformulation of the justice system. The forms of self-narration available in *Songs* often challenge the rationalities of Eurocentric legal discourse in much the same way that "voice," as *process* and as *value*, in Couldry's (2010: 12–13) account, challenges neoliberalism: "Valuing voice means valuing something that neoliberal rationality fails to count; it can therefore contribute to a counter-rationality against neoliberalism.... Articulating voice—as an inescapable aspect of human experience—challenges the neoliberal logic that runs together economic, social, political and cultural domains, and describes them exclusively as manifestations of market processes." In particular, the relationships of mutual reciprocity and reciprocal exchange formed between students and artists on *Songs* can be understood to constitute a kaupapa Māori alternative to Eurocentric, disciplinary, and normalizing discourses of "rehabilitation." A central theme of the show is that the professional artists are transformed through their shared experiences with the prisoners in the same degree as are the latter. This approach is then quite different from that of a social worker, therapist, or "corrections officer," for instance, who oversees processes of "rehabilitation" that are designed to change the behaviors and subjectivities of inmates without problematizing those of the professionals. Nevertheless, *Songs* does not articulate a radical structural critique of the prison system or of its role in the reproduction of coloniality, which would perhaps be too much to expect from a production that depends upon the cooperation of the New Zealand Corrections Department, and from a broadcaster whose very existence, like that of public service media organizations in other countries, has often been threatened by neoliberal and right-wing politicians. *Songs* works not by radical critique, but rather through forms of ideological negotiation and progressivism to facilitate the creation of spaces of expressivity and voice for small groups of prisoners, and potentially for the rearticulation of commonsense understandings of Indigeneity and criminality among wider viewing audiences.

The progressivism of *Songs from the Inside* lies partly in its refusal to dwell fetishistically on the spectacularization of crime and criminality. Indeed, the crimes that have been committed are often not mentioned at all or are revealed only after we have gotten to know an inmate well. By contrast, the sensationalization of Māori crime has become an all too familiar feature of the wider New

Zealand mediascape, where journalistic reporting, for instance, has conventionally served to "remind Māori people of their 'shortcomings' and 'weaknesses'" (Jackson 1987: 17). *Songs* defies such conventions by reminding audiences of Māori talents, cultural resilience, and strengths. Additionally, *Songs* reveals a set of hidden spatialities that have the potential to remake the prison in Pākehā imaginaries. In contemporary New Zealand, Māori are heavily surveilled, policed, and targeted by welfare regimes, the criminal justice system, and the media. Since 1995, when television cameras entered New Zealand courtrooms, audiences have become well accustomed to seeing Māori defendants in the docks. But once incarcerated, they are rendered invisible and inaudible. The intense stress and suffering that imprisonment imposes on offenders and their *whānau* are easily ignored, but just as important, their voices are substantially silenced.

When the artists are welcomed by the inmates onto the prison grounds, an inhospitable site of punishment is transformed temporarily into a space of *manaakitanga* (hospitality). *Songs* reminds us that the criminal justice system is not a monolith but a complex assemblage, which suggests that it might be possible to disarticulate, rearticulate, and thus transform some of its dimensions and components in at least partially decolonizing ways. Arahanga observes that through the production of *Songs*, the show's producers developed a positive working relationship with the Department of Corrections, who are, as he notes, positioned in the political environment quite differently from the police and courts: "Our relationship with the Corrections Department has strengthened. They see us as quite a good ally to have. They don't have many allies out there, Corrections, you know. The Police and stuff, *they* have allies, but the Corrections Department don't, and the Corrections Department's job is to just *house* these people and try and keep them safe and the community safe. But they didn't actually put them there. So through, you know, continual dialogue with them and building relations, we were able to push the boundaries a little bit further."

As Jackson (1987, 1988) made clear, Māori forms of justice and reconciliation differ substantially from European ones, and have been largely, but not comprehensively or irrevocably, destroyed by colonialism (see also New Zealand Māori Council and Hall 1999). While European law is based on individual rights and offending, Māori law is based on collective rights and decision-making, and justice is served through interactions between the families of the offender and the victim in ways that ensure the integrity of the social fabric and restore the *mana* of each *whānau* involved. New Zealand Māori Council and Hall (1999: 27) describe criminal justice in the precolonial era as follows:

> Essentially the system was akin to what is now referred to as restorative justice. There were a number of important elements in this. When there was a breach, community process enabled a consideration of the interests of the social group (whanaungatanga) [kinship] and ensured the integrity of the social fabric. Through whanau or hapu [clan] meetings, and on occasion iwi meetings, the

voices of all parties could be heard and decisions arrived at by consensus (kotahitanga). The aim was to restore the mana of the victim, the victim's family and the family of the offender, and to ensure that measures were taken to restore the future social order for the wider community. Because these concepts were given meaning in the context of the group, retribution against an individual offender was not seen as the primary mechanism for achieving justice. Rather, the group was accountable for the actions of the individual (manaakitanga) and that exacted compensation on behalf of the aggrieved.

Reconciliation and social restoration thus lie at the heart of traditional Māori justice and are mobilized for the collective good. Eurocentric incarceration practices work against such reciprocities and physically sever inmates from their *whānau* and communities, which might otherwise contribute to the restoration of mana, help avert reoffending, and restore the sociality of the wider collective. Through its use of social media, *Songs from the Inside* promotes the reestablishment of disrupted networks of social and spatial connection, and opens spaces for the acknowledgement of pain, the celebration of inmates' achievements, and the contestation of state-sponsored racism. These subsidiary convergent media thus contribute to the show's partial reversal of the forms of social invisibilization and silencing that incarceration enforces. There is a tangible spirit of *whanaungatanga* on the *Songs* Facebook page that is evident in the many likes and messages of love and support sent by the inmates' friends, family members, and others, who also actively share and thus recirculate the contents of these pages:

Loving this show . . . in a way we all can relate to their stories and its just awseome to be able to use their story into music . . Mean x

what a privilege it is to see these two groups of survivors start to get back their mana and dignity. what grace and integrity. thank you so much for making the world a better place, song by song.

i forgot the name of a song mayb from the first album. . . . but it goes wake up mums on te corner of the begging please stop hurting me. . . . who sings this song and wats the name please her song helped my sister thru a very ruff time . . .

Big love's to Odean, I love you and am praying for you my girl. Xox

My Blutiful Lil Sis Abi x

Love u my sista.xx

> About a month ago i was wondering where + what ya were doing with ya life Trecita, tried to find ya on fbk lol.—Then a week or 2 ago i seen this program .. & you .. loved ya 30min challenge rap! will continue to watch the series x

> Naaaw ... miss my girls handwriting ... love u cita

Julian Arahanga says of the Facebook page:

> Yeah, we have a Facebook page, and it's a small audience, but it's very loyal. I think a lot of them are family and friends or people of the mind that, you know, our judicial system and the corrections system, you know, needs reform, and needs to find ways to better do its job. But yeah, there are a range of comments and commentary, you know, right from how people are inspired to go and write their own songs through to people loving seeing the journey of the students, and the change over the course of two or three months and how those kind of things are good to see.

In their call for the establishment of a Māori-centered system of restorative justice, New Zealand Māori Council and Hall (1999: 29) emphasize some of the elements that we can glimpse in *Songs from the Inside*. These include the shift from "cognition or 'head-thinking' to affect or 'heart-feeling,'" the emphasis on healing through collective and bottom-up processes, a respect for the cultural and community context in which offending has occurred, and the ability to speak freely, each of which is in some ways and to one degree or another denied by the official court and parole systems. In these ways, *Songs* provides a counterpoint to the dominant biopolitical modes of framing offenders in both research and policy. It offers a set of affective geographies and sense-making practices rooted in mutual reciprocity and recognition, sharing and horizontal power relations, and efforts to restore the dignity and mana of the imprisoned. Moreover, *Songs* offers Pākehā viewers a glimpse of the fact that the application of "justice" is not culturally neutral, and that those criminalized by a colonial justice system are also confronting social deprivation exacerbated by racial inequality. While both prisons and much crime research seek to "depersonalize social control" (Robinson 2014: 184), *Songs* repersonalizes and rehumanizes, giving inmates and viewers a space in which to imagine a life beyond and after prison.

Indigenous Struggle as "Terrorism"

Indigenous struggles for sovereignty are frequently understood by settler populations as threats to the Eurocentric nation-state. As Jackson (2008: 2) puts it, Indigenous peoples have always been "defined as a threat whenever they have questioned their dispossession or whenever the colonisers wanted to keep them in a position of political powerlessness and economic inequality." Since 9/11, there has been a growing tendency to insert Indigenous activism into discourses of "terrorism."[8] This practice can be readily understood as exemplary of the *recoding of racism* (Fiske 2016a), which exerts racial power through discourses that are not explicitly about race, and therefore masks that racial power is at work at all. In Latin America, Indigenous groups "demanding not just 'rights' but a reinvention of the state along deeply democratic lines" are increasingly labeled as terrorists by governments (Klein 2005). Indigenous peoples in Colombia, Chile, and Ecuador have been subject to surveillance, securitization, and criminalization under anti-terror legislation, and a number of U.S. and Latin American government, intelligence, and military agencies have classified the activism of Indigenous peoples as a threat to national and global security alongside al Qaeda–style terrorism (González 2005; Radcliffe 2007; Zibechi 2011; Wadi 2011). The use of 9/11 and the war on terror to perpetuate what Derek Gregory (2004) calls "the colonial present" extends far beyond Iraq, Afghanistan, and Palestine. It has facilitated the criminalization of Indigenous peoples in countries such as New Zealand. Although the latter did not support the U.S. invasions of Iraq and Afghanistan, the New Zealand government nevertheless passed legislation known as the Terrorism Suppression Act (TSA) in 2002. This law bore many similarities to New Zealand's 1863 Suppression of Rebellion Act, and many prominent Māori lawyers, including Annette Sykes and Moana Jackson, correctly predicted that it would be used against their people.

That the recoding of Indigenous activism as "terrorism" has occurred in conjunction with growing formal national and international recognition of the rights of Indigenous peoples suggests that new modes of political recognition enjoyed by Māori and other Indigenous groups have their limitations, and that alternative forms of racial power and control have emerged to perpetuate entrenched inequalities. The recoding of racism enables dominant racial groups to discursively mobilize covert forms of racism that support their racialized dominance, while simultaneously proclaiming that the end of racism has been achieved. By the same token, expanding racialized economic inequalities function covertly to sustain racial hierarchies in otherwise officially "race-neutral," "colorblind," and "post-racial" societies whose laws and formal political apparatus may even be overtly anti-racist in important ways (see Fiske 2016a). Frankenberg (1993: 14–15) discusses the dominant discourses and sensibilities around race and ethnicity in contemporary Western societies in terms of "color evasiveness" and "power evasiveness." By this she means that whites must actively "repress," "avoid," "conceal" (1993: 33), and thus *evade* recognition of the structural racial privileges accorded to whiteness on an ongoing and everyday basis, for non-whites do not have the luxury of the "color-blindness" that is proclaimed by many whites in post-civil rights societies. The recoding of racism through discourses of "terror" also instantiates, operationalizes, and extends white people's fear of people of color, which is, as Frankenberg (1993: 54) notes, both central to the maintenance of racial hierarchy in contemporary societies and constitutive of a form of imaginary social inversion, since historical analysis shows that people of color have had far more to fear from white populations than the latter have had to fear from the former. Moreover, fear/terror resonates with racialized discourses of "savagery" and performs discursive "animalization" (Fiske 2016a), which sustains racial hierarchies by connecting white, racialized meanings and intense affects with an imagined "Other." As Frankenberg (1993: 54) writes, "white people's fear of people of color is an inversion ... linked to essentialist racism, or the idea that people of color are fundamentally Other than white people: different, inferior, less civilized, less human, more animal than whites." Thus, "history is marked by many moments when the power of racist imagery constructing men of color as violent, dangerous, or sexually threatening has been renewed, as rationale or pretext for white hostility, in the context of political and economic conflicts between particular communities of color and white" populations (1993: 60–61). As we saw earlier in this chapter, and in the 2020 global eruption of Black Lives Matter protests, the renewal of such racist imagery is often closely linked to practices and representations of policing, and to the commemorative representation of colonial histories involving projects of enslavement and of the "civilization" of various peoples of color.

There is evidence that state-endorsed bi- or multiculturalism can be used to promote a domesticated conception of Indigenous identity that operates in conjunction with the marginalization and stigmatization of more threatening Indigenous identities. Charles Hale (2004, 2005, 2006) shows how neoliberal multiculturalism makes room for a politics of cultural recognition for Indigenous populations, while simultaneously limiting the field of what is politically imaginable and achievable, thus, in Jack Bratich's (2008) apt formulation, keeping political discourse "within [Eurocentric] reason." Hale argues that while Indigenous subjects may no longer face demands for cultural assimilation, they are nevertheless pressured to adopt the nonthreatening identity of the *indio permitido* (authorized Indian), who is allowed to enjoy certain rights and a degree of respect from settler populations, as long as they question neither neoliberal economic models nor the territorial integrity of the colonial nation-state. Thus, state support for Indigenous rights "comes with an equally weighty investment in the boundary that separates permissible from proscribed rights" and "acceptably moderate from radically threatening social transformation" (Hale and Millamán 2006: 301). The obverse of the figure of the *indio permitido* in the white imagination is the radical, unruly, or insurrectionary Indian: the *indio insurrecto*, who must be kept under strict regimes of surveillance and control. Indigenous peoples who too forcefully articulate political demands or otherwise threaten white imaginaries with the specter of a loss of Eurocentric order and control thus become subject to potential stigmatization, repression, and criminalization. The figure of the disruptive Indigene appears most frequently in mainstream New Zealand media in the guise of the (presumably violent, *moko*-bearing [traditionally tattooed]) Māori gang member or the *moko*-bearing, politically engaged activist who uses forms of direct action or struggle for Māori rights outside of sanctioned political means, and often draws on historical and tribal meanings, knowledges, and identities of which most Pākehā are ignorant.

On 15 October 2007, heavily armed police using warrants obtained under the TSA entered the town of Ruatoki in the land of the Tūhoe people and proceeded to lock it down. The raids were the culmination of a year-long covert surveillance program called Operation 8. During the raids, doors and windows were broken, homes were ransacked, all vehicles entering and leaving town were stopped, and drivers were photographed. Townspeople, including children, were held at gunpoint, searched, and questioned. Some families were forced to endure hours without food or water. In their first press conference following the raids, the police claimed that Tūhoe were operating guerrilla training camps in the Urewera bush and that members of the tribe were being taught to use firearms, Molotov cocktails, and napalm there. Simultaneous raids and arrests took place elsewhere in New Zealand that day, but it was only the people of Ruatoki who awoke to roadblocks and riot police (Jackson 2008). A total of seventeen activists, twelve of whom were Māori, were arrested. One of the arrestees was the well-known Māori activist, Tame Iti. In the wake of the raids, Howard Broad, commissioner of the New Zealand Police, described Tūhoe behavior on Tūhoe land as "unacceptable" and insisted that the terror-raiders were acting "in the public interest." Prime Minister Helen Clark stated that "paramilitary training in the Ureweras by disaffected people of many ethnicities is distressing and abhorrent to our people" (*October 15: After the Raids* 2010).

For many Tūhoe, the raids constituted a clear case of history repeating itself. Tūhoe did not sign the Treaty of Waitangi and have repeatedly resisted colonial incursions into their lands, which can be understood in Valerie Kuletz's (1998) terms as a "sacrifice zone," a site where colonized peoples and places are subjected to exploitation and control in the name of a "national interest." Over many, many years, Tūhoe have faced police repression, land confiscation, and scorched earth strategies. The Ruatoki valley is divided by a "confiscation line" created by the Crown's brutal 1866 seizure of roughly 7 percent of Tūhoe nation lands. The lands taken consisted of the tribe's flattest and most fertile agricultural territories, as well as its only access to the coast and therefore seafood. This confiscation thus contributed to the impoverishment of generations of Tūhoe people and precipitated subsequent periods of starvation. Historian Judith Binney (2010: 288–289) notes that to this day, the confiscation line remains visually "very similar to the US-Mexico border, for those who have seen how the land changes at that point: visible farming wealth on one side, relative poverty on the other." Many Tūhoe have been killed in conflicts with colonial forces (Hill 2008; Keenan 2008; Devadas 2013). It was in Te Urewera where Tūhoe prophet and land rights activist Rua Kenana set up a peaceful commune in opposition to

World War I. The movement he launched was brutally suppressed by armed police in a military-style invasion in 1916. Kenana was imprisoned and two Tūhoe, including his son, were killed (see Hill 2008). Kenana was not officially pardoned until 2019.

In the days, months, and years that followed the terror raids of 15 October 2007, the occurrences of that day and the criminal charges pursued against those taken into custody became important events that were narrativized and examined across the New Zealand broadcast, online, and print mediascapes. As a number of scholars have indicated, the mainstream media coverage of the raids and their aftermath largely reproduced conventional, power-bearing, and sensationally racialized depictions of Māori as criminals and dangerous extremists (see Abel 2008, 2016; Jackson 2008; Morse 2008; 2010; Devadas 2013). In particular, Tame Iti was framed as the insurrectionary Indian who must be domesticated or "tamed" (Fiske 2016a: 87) through arrest and imprisonment. Vijay Devadas (2013: 4) writes that "the media reportage of the event on that day connected and amplified a moral panic of 'terror' around the figure of Iti." In 2005, Iti had shot at a New Zealand flag during a visit to Ruatoki by members of the Waitangi Tribunal (about which we will say more below). Footage of this incident was shown repeatedly without explanation of its context or relevance by both TV1 and TV3 in October 2007. This flag-shooting incident became a widely reproduced signifier of and metonym for "extreme Māori radicalism" (Abel 2008: 120–121). While the majority of New Zealand Members of Parliament (MPs) interviewed by the media after the raids endorsed the police action, some prominent MPs (including those from the Māori and Green Parties, and the Labour Minister of Māori Affairs, Parekura Horomia) criticized the suggestion that Tame Iti was a terrorist. The story of the raids was also picked up by international news media. NZTV1 reporter Francesca Mould clearly endorsed a "war on terror" mode of geopolitical rationality when she said that "a key point of interest" made by international commentators is that the country's geographical isolation has led New Zealanders to believe they are "immune to terrorism. But uncovering of this plot shows we clearly aren't" (*ONE News at 6 P.M.*, 16 October 2007). For Valerie Morse (2010: 15), who was arrested and imprisoned during the raids, "the trial-by-media had the desired effect: it vindicated the police and condemned the arrestees." In contrast, Sue Abel (2008: 116) observes that Māori-produced news shows' coverage of the raids provided "completely different" maps of meaning and sense-making codes "and a very different explanatory context."

Hence while mainstream media generally played to white fear in its discursive encoding of the terror raids, Māori Television was struggling with the challenge of narrating events that to many Māori seemed so ludicrous as to be laughable, were it not for the brutal treatment inflicted on the people of Ruatoki through the paramilitary tactics of the police raiders. When a Māori Television reporter phoned the TV network from Ruatoki to report that Tame Iti was under arrest, the Manager of News and Current Affairs put the reporter on loudspeaker in the newsroom so everybody could hear her. According to the manager, upon hearing that "they've got Tame" and are "accusing him of running terrorist camps in the Urewera," the entire newsroom "cracked up laughing. And we thought it was ridiculous, it was really stupid" (interview with authors, June 2013). Laughter may be one way of powerfully subverting the affective energies associated with white fear of the Other. As Allon White (1983: 9) writes, "seriousness always has more to do with power than with content. The authority to designate what is to be taken seriously (and the authority to enforce reverential solemnity in certain contexts) is a way of creating and maintaining power." Laughter, by contrast, is a "vital source of social renewal" that "restores the community to itself in physical convulsions which revive our untheorised sense of solidarity in embodiment," so that we "may have to learn to laugh our way around whatever sense of dread and crisis may afflict us" (Hebdige 1988: 243). Nevertheless, the Māori Television staff immediately grasped the potential danger to Māori posed by wall-to-wall mainstream media reports of "Terrorism in Tūhoe Country," and set out to preemptively counter the imperializing narrative their history had taught them to anticipate. As the News and Current Affairs Manager explained to us, "(a) knowing Tame, (b) knowing the community and (c) knowing how the community was reacting to the way the cops had been in, and (d) the whole kind of lining up of the confiscation line and knowing the history of all that, we had a whole bunch of other stories that we had to tell. Rather than "this is a terrorist plot," which is what I think everyone else focused on, we had to focus on the history of the Tūhoe/Crown relationship, and we did that" (Interview with authors, June 2013).

It thus became incumbent upon Māori Television to counter the racialized narratives and discourses circulating through mainstream New Zealand media coverage of the terror raids. So, for instance, footage of pots and pans from the "training camp" that was shown repeatedly in a TV3 newscast as though it offered potential material documentation of "terrorist" activities (*3 News at 6 p.m.*, 16 October 2007) was made an object of Indigenous laughter in a Māori Television piece the following week. In this piece, reporter Semiramis Holland accompanied Tūhoe hunter Te Rangi Kepa to the spot of the alleged "military-style camp," near which 3 News reporter Amanda Gillies had recently done a piece-to-camera (Māori Television 2007). There, Kepa told Holland that when he saw the TV3 story, he experienced a "mean shock" and said to himself "that's my pots; what are they doing there?" Kepa stated that the site was "our little retreat, not a terrorist camp," and said, "all these pots . . . these are ours. This is our smoko billy [container for boiling water to make tea during a smoking break]. These are always here for when we stop for a cup of tea." More broadly, *Native Affairs'* "Guerrillas in the Mist" (Māori Television 2007) coverage makes a profound intervention into the media activity surrounding the Urewera raids, and into the terrain of discourses circulating publicly around Indigeneity and coloniality in the New Zealand mediascape. *Native Affairs'* coverage includes commentary by

Indigenous leaders from different parts of the world about the treatment they routinely undergo at the hands of postcolonial nation states. For example, Kevin Barlow, a Mi'kmaq man from Canada, asserts that "the state seems to misinterpret how Indigenous people choose to defend themselves and treat their homeland with the same security needs as the government does. And somehow when we do it, we're called 'terrorists.'" Tūhoe spokesperson Tamati Kruger notes that, for 150 years, Māori have repeatedly been confronted by the same issues raised by the raids, and that in the case of Tūhoe, these issues stem from ignorance on the part of the Crown: "Tūhoe knows all about the Crown. But the Crown knows nothing about Tūhoe." When asked by reporter Mere McLean about the existence of the alleged training camps, Kruger first notes that there are no such camps in Te Urewera, then states that

> the question shouldn't be about where these camps may be, but what has led to their presence? If people are learning how to kill or become terrorists, why do such sites exist? There's no point in trying to find where these camps may be. What should be explored is why these sites would even be conceived. Then there is the reason for police claims that terrorist training camps have been set up. I say that it surrounds the Māori promotion of Tūhoe independence and sovereignty, and their fear of that. That's what the real issue is. They fear the strength and principle of Tūhoe independence and sovereignty. What they don't understand is that we know our people. And we also know that you can't extinguish our beliefs. There will always be someone to hold onto that belief. If you get rid of one who holds the position, then another will cement that position in their place. Hence the utterance of our ancestors: "When one fern frond withers, another fern frond grows." So those who think that taking Tame Iti and others away will destroy our confidence in sovereignty and independence are misguided. (Māori Television 2007, translation from *te reo* by Māori Television)

Foucault's (1978, 1979) work shows that power is exerted through discourse. The circulation of discourse and counterdiscourse is thus an important dimension of both cultural struggles and conjunctural analysis. The different cultural, institutional, and economic positioning of mainstream commercial media in relation to Whakaata Māori led each to adopt different discursive, narrative, tonal, and representational approaches to their coverage of the terror raids. One Māori journalist explained to us that most mainstream media reporters have lives that are so far removed from those of the people of Ruatoki and speak little or no Māori, so that when the raids unfolded, they "just tell the story that they are capable of telling that day, which is there are terrorists in here, they are looking for guns and Molotov cocktails, and they wouldn't know what happened to any of the people" whose homes were raided (interview with authors, June 2013). By contrast, many Whakaata Māori personnel have close connections to rural Māori communities like Ruatoki and therefore gathered lots of on-the-ground stories told in the Māori language about the violence of the raiders and the traumatization of children and other villagers. Māori Television also later aired two documentaries, *October 15: After the Raids* (2010) and *Operation 8* (2011), which demonstrated the suffering and trauma to which the people of Ruatoki had been subjected, and revealed how the "training camps" were being used to teach bushcraft skills to Tūhoe youth in order to keep them connected to their *iwi* and their culture.[9] These documentaries discussed the loss of *mana* felt by those who were "dragged handcuffed from their homes" in front of their children.[10] Moko Hillman, whose children were locked in a shed by police for seven hours during the raids, asked why they had to smash down doors and windows and "tip *kai* [food] all over the place" rather than simply knocking on the door and taking him in for questioning (*Operation 8* 2011). Both documentaries raise the question of Tūhoe sovereignty over their lands and note that weapons have been used by *iwi* members for hunting and defense against colonial aggression for more than a century. The parallels and similarities between the 2007 raids and the 1916 police invasion of Tūhoe territory are drawn out to undermine the imperializing force of racializing discourses of "Indigenous violence" and of settler affectivities associated with white fears of people of color. These documentaries suggest that Tūhoe need weapons not because Tūhoe are violent, but rather because coloniality is.[11]

We broadly agree that mainstream coverage of the terror raids represented events in racially problematic ways, and that Māori Television's coverage circulated a different set of meanings and discourses, but we also think that mainstream coverage was more complex and conflicted than some have suggested. Both Abel (2008) and Devadas (2013) recognize that mainstream New Zealand media have become less monocultural and more "balanced" in recent years, and Devadas (2013: 19) has identified the circulation of alternative meanings and narratives of Tame Iti in some mainstream media. In the days after the raids, mainstream media reproduced imperializing images and discourses of Māori extremism and dysfunction, but there is also evidence of what we will describe as an epistemological crisis afflicting the postcolonial settler state that is increasingly played out in a range of cultural and institutional spaces, including media. Thus the imperializing narratives of "terror" that circulated widely after the Urewera raids did not go uncontested, as a range of alternative voices and discourses made their way into both mainstream and Māori media.

For instance, mainstream news and current affairs programming on both TV1 and TV3 raised concerns about children who were traumatized by the raids, covered protests against the police actions and expressions of support for those arrested, and included the voices of Ruatoki citizens, including Tame Iti's partner Maria Steens, who spoke about the heavy-handedness of the paramilitary approach to law enforcement exercised that day. Reporter Francesca Mould's uncritical mobilization of a geopolitical discourse of "war on terror" as a means to make sense of the raids, noted above, followed the observation by Māori MP Tariana Turia that Māori have been labeled as "terrorists" before, and that such labeling has never been substantiated.[12] Just four days after the raids on Ruatoki, a report on TV2's satirical *Eating Media Lunch* interjected a note of playful skepticism when it explicitly posited equivalences between Iti and Bin Laden, Tūhoe and Al-Qaeda, and New Zealand police commissioner Howard Broad and Donald Rumsfeld. Skeptical laughter and satirization were also mobilized in other mainstream media treatments of the raids. For example, Labour MP and Minister of Māori Affairs, Parekura Horomia's comparison of Tame Iti to an "aging rocker" (*ONE News at 6 P.M.*, 16 October 2007) amusingly invokes media celebrity (about which more follows below) to undermine the characterization of Iti as a "terrorist." Similarly, when asked about the possibility of Tūhoe terrorism, Ruatoki resident Te Kanapa Tamaki laughingly conjectured that the entire "guerrilla training camp" alleged by the police may have been nothing more than an anxious fantasy conjured up by the sight of a "*hāngī* [traditional Māori earth oven] blowing up too hot" (*ONE News at 6 P.M.*, 17 October 2007). Alternative discourses on the "terror raids" were then present in mainstream media and constituted significant spaces of contestation and discursive rearticulation even in the immediate aftermath of the 2007 events.

Conjunctural analysis presumes that there is no "unified and racist 'ruling class' conception of the world" that can underpin and guarantee our anti-racist analyses of the media (Hall 1981: 35). As Stuart Hall, one of the key advocates and developers of a neo-Gramscian conjunctural analysis for cultural studies argues, the purpose of critical theory must therefore be "to produce as accurate a knowledge of complex social processes as the complexity of their functioning requires," because "differences and complexities have real *effects*, which ought to enter into any serious political calculation about how" the tendencies at work in a hegemonic social formation or conjuncture "might be resisted or turned" (Hall, 1981: 35–36, emphasis in original). Since October 2007, Māori Television has worked actively to rearticulate and resignify the terror raids in the media. Throughout this period, counterdiscursive constructions of the raids persistently multiplied and circulated widely throughout the country to such an extent that a significant shift in the discursive terrain became palpable. Tame Iti, indeed, emerged increasingly as the celebrity face of Māori resistance reimagined.

6
Indigeneity and Celebrity

Celebritizing Indigenous Activism

According to Graham Turner (2016), the expansion of celebrity culture is a central characteristic of the "re-invented" mediascape of the digital, post-broadcast era. Both within and beyond Aotearoa New Zealand, we have in recent years witnessed what we might refer to as the celebritization of Indigenous activism. Tame Iti is thus one of a number of Indigenous activists around the world who have become household names both nationally and globally. Others are Kayapo chief Raoni Metuktire from the Brazilian Amazon, Ecuadorian Kichwa activist Marlon Santí, Maya Guatemalan Rigoberta Menchú, Mirrar Australian Aboriginal anti-mining activist Yvonne Margarula, Honduran Lenca activist Berta Cáceres, and Subcomandante Marcos of the Zapatistas from Chiapas in southern Mexico.[1] The ways in which these celebrity-activists challenge(d) the capitalist and colonial status quo generate extensive solidarity and media attention, especially in alternative and social media spaces, as well as in mainstream media. Turner (2004: 8, 13) writes that "modern celebrity is ... a product of media representation," and "those who have been subject to the representational regime of celebrity are reprocessed and reinvented by it. To be folded into this representational regime ... changes how you are consumed and what you can mean." At the same time, the new media environment creates unprecedented opportunities for celebrities to intervene in and redirect the discursive and representational forces generated through celebritization. Some of the Indigenous celebrity-activists noted above are mediamakers in their own right and make extensive use of both "old" media, such as radio and television, and social media such as Twitter, YouTube, and Facebook to intervene in terrains of cultural and political struggle.

As we have suggested, struggling in defense of Indigenous people's rights to full cultural citizenship is a risky undertaking in many parts of the world. Many Indigenous activists are subject to state-sanctioned racism, criminalization, and incarceration as a consequence of their opposition to destructive neoliberal forms of development that threaten Indigenous lands and lives (OHCHR 2018). In the worst cases, such as that of Berta Cáceres, they are brutally murdered (see Cultural Survival 2012; Lakhani 2020). State-led or -endorsed violence often increases global solidarity and further builds the profiles of Indigenous activists and their causes. Consequently, it can in part constitute or accelerate processes of Indigenous celebritization. That the politics of celebrity culture can be multifaceted and contradictory has been recognized by scholars such as Turner (2004) and Chris Rojek (2001). In spite of the work it does on behalf of global media conglomerates, celebrity culture also often functions as a site in which meanings of affluence, visibility, accountability, value, talent, and inequality are contested and struggled over (see, e.g., Glynn 2008). In this chapter, we adopt Olivier Driessens's (2012) distinction between the processes of "celebrification" whereby particular individuals achieve fame or notoriety, and the "meta-process" of "celebritization," which entails "societal and cultural changes" (643) associated with the expansion and "embedding" of celebrity, including the "diversification" that ensues as celebrity penetrates "social fields" that have traditionally been "less permeated by celebrity status" (645). We nominate the ongoing emergence of Indigenous activism as a terrain for the production and consumption of celebrity as one such site of contemporary diversification in Driessens's sense.

McCurdy (2013) distinguishes between two different forms of celebrity activism: that associated with celebrities who harness their fame to promote political causes (which he calls CA1), and that associated with those who achieve prominence or notoriety as a consequence of their political activism (which he labels CA2). There is a significant body of literature on celebrities who embrace and publicly promote humanitarian and political causes (see, e.g., Brockington 2009, 2014; Brockington and Hensor 2015; Chouliaraki 2013; Cooper 2007; Hasian 2016; Kapoor 2013; Markham 2015; Richey and Ponte 2008; Tsaliki, Frangonikolopoulos, and Huliaras 2011), but there has been much less scholarship on CA2 or on Indigenous celebrities (see McKee 1999; King 2009; York 2016), and even less work that focuses specifically on the celebritization of Indigenous activism (but see di Piramo 2010; Krøvel 2011). This absence is surprising in light of widespread criticism of the strong colonial, "white saviour," and neoliberal implications of much CA1 activism (see, e.g., Kapoor 2013). These critics have emphasized how CA1 activism often eclipses or marginalizes local and Indigenous struggles for development or justice (Hasian 2016). What work has been done on Indigenous celebrity, nevertheless, does help us to understand its differences from other forms of celebrity and is suggestive of ways in which Indigenous celebrity can be constituted and mobilized in counterhegemonic ways.

Like mainstream celebrities, Indigenous activists become the focus of public attention, appear across the convergent mediascape, and become implicated in the sense-making practices of media audiences and commentators, state actors, and political activists. But because Indigenous activism generally entails resistance to both colonialism and neoliberalism, its celebritization is potentially productive of a quite different cultural politics than that typically enacted around celebrities who become known for their music, movies, or sporting talent (or who become "well-known for their well-knownness," in Daniel Boorstin's famous phrase [quoted in Turner 2004: 5]), and who then publicly embrace an activist cause. Celebrified Indigenous activists have the potential to draw attention to anti-capitalist and anti-colonial struggles without being seen as engaged in problematic and hypocritical modes of brand-building. As Jane Stadler (2009: 323) writes, prominent Indigenous activists' "ability to embody ideas and identities from the periphery, to revalue cultural difference and enable recognition of the rights of the disadvantaged, and to inspire social change is perhaps the ultimate potential of the postcolonial celebrity." Nevertheless, Indigenous activism is not immune to commodification, nor to the complex interplay of both top-down and bottom-up forces that drives all celebrity culture (see Couldry and Markham 2007). While the celebrity status of Indigenous activists is not industry-driven in quite the same way as that of mainstream celebrities, celebritization enables activist performances to provide good material for ratings-driven television that can complicate the grassroots underpinnings of this activism. While not all Indigenous media forms should be understood as reactions to non-Indigenous media and society (York 2016), the celebritization of Indigenous activism cannot always be separated easily from other forms of celebrity activism that may be more complicit with the forces of commercialization and neoliberalism (see Krøvel 2011). For instance, Sting's support for the Kayapo cause brought about the celebrification of Chief Raoni, though the latter then became a compelling media figure capable of attracting global attention without the presence of the former.

A major problem for CA2 activists of all sorts concerns the forces of individualization that are central to celebrity culture (McCurdy 2013; di Piramo 2010; Stadler 2009). Because the Zapatista struggle, for instance, strives for both collectivism and leaderlessness, and rejects capitalism's "hyper-individualism" (McCurdy 2013: 322), Subcomandante Marcos sought to avoid celebrification and presented himself simply as a spokesperson (albeit a highly articulate and media-savvy one) for the movement. But the cult of personality that surrounded Marcos dominated the Zapatista rebellion in problematic and often distracting ways (di Piramo 2010; Hesketh and Morton 2014). In May 2014 he therefore terminally interrupted his own celebrification by announcing that "Marcos" was no more and would be replaced by Subcomandante Insurgente Moisés (see Desinformémonos 2014).

We explore here the figuration and celebrification of Tame Iti in a rapidly changing media environment and political context, in order to understand how his activism and criminalization both shape and are shaped by the celebritizing and neoliberal conjuncture within which they are constituted. This approach enables us to see how the mediation of Māori struggles can exploit opportunities to unsettle persistent colonial confidence. We therefore draw upon a large number of media texts featuring Tame Iti, as well as the discursive activity conducted around these texts in the convergent mediasphere. Additionally, we have spent time talking with Tame about his activism and its mediation and remediation, which take place within a complex conjuncture marked by the fluid and contradictory dynamics of media convergence and the generation of new spaces of material and discursive struggle, whereby neoliberal capitalism and coloniality are both intensively contested *and* reasserted.[2]

In our discussion of celebritization/celebrification, we draw on the concept of the *media figure* to explore how larger historical forces and social dynamics come to be embodied in and represented through particular individuals. "Figure" is both a noun and a verb, and media figures always operate as both objects and agents of struggle who at once intervene in and shape, while also being shaped by, key terrains of contemporary discursive and cultural politics. As Fiske (2016a: 69) writes, media figures are products of our hypermediated age, and a figure is thus "a hyperreal person whose reality includes both a body . . . composed of flesh, bone, and blood and a body of infinitely reproducible signifiers or electronic dots on a . . . screen." Although the body of an individual who becomes a media figure may be "comparatively powerless in determining the way he or she is to be figured, it is extremely powerful in giving the histories" and social alliances with which it is associated "a material presence, in making them live, in making them visible and audible, and in making them matter in, and become the matter of, everyday life" (70–71). Media figures become terrains of struggle, as well as points of articulation through which social interests and alliances speak and can be heard. It is the physical and electronic embodiment of social and historical interests in media figures that makes them popular sites of engagement, for in "an age of electronic figures and of hypervisibility, embodied histories and politics are the ones that matter . . . because alliances, for or against, are more easily formed with a figure" than with an abstract political position (76). Media figures resonate with viewers, audiences, and citizens because they tap into a society's deepest fault lines, axes of division, and reservoirs of affective and discursive energy.

Writing in the context of neoliberalism in the United Kingdom, Imogen Tyler (2013: 10) develops what she calls a "figurative method" that traces the "fabrication and repetition of abject figures across" multiple sites such as the popular media, government policy formulations, and the discourses of academic experts. These abject figures, including immigrants and welfare recipients, function as "ideological conductors" that are "mobilized to do the dirty work of" neoliberalism, by serving to justify punitive economic, social, and political measures (9). In our case, the figure of Tame Iti is mobilized as an ideological and discursive conductor of both colonial and decolonial forces and meanings. Tame Iti is a flesh and blood person (in Māori, a *tangata*), but he is also a mediated assemblage composed of "all available public texts" about him, and is therefore subject to diverse modes of political and discursive activation and rearticulation (see Molina-Guzmán 2010: 51–52). The concept of the media figure is theoretically useful for engaging with the celebritization of Indigenous activism because it helps to account for the impossibility of finally and definitively distinguishing between the reality of the individual and the discursive mediation of the figure, as well as helping to understand the ongoing capacity of the figure to serve as a terrain of struggle across a variety of sites and issues.

Figuring Tame Iti

Iti has been fighting for Māori sovereignty for more than four decades. He is also an accomplished artist, a radio broadcaster, and a social worker. Our reason for focusing on "Tame Iti" as a media figure, far from wishing to individualize the generations-long collective struggle for Māori sovereignty, is aimed precisely at the demonstration of how social and historical forces come to be condensed and embodied within particular sets of texts and images that thereby themselves constitute terrains of contestation where political victories and losses accrue and contribute to the production, reproduction, or destabilization of this or that conjunctural assemblage. Iti is of course not the only famous Māori activist, although he certainly is one of the most recognizable of the current generation, and is sometimes described in the media as *the* face of Māori activism. He is well known for his disruptive, hyperperformative, theatrical, and media-savvy style of protestation. His full facial *moko* makes him easily recognizable and, in the eyes of many Pākehā, dangerously radical (see cover image). His methods have frequently unsettled many New Zealanders, including some Māori, and have often attracted condemnation from conservative sectors of the political and media establishments.

Tame Iti was born in Rotorua in 1952 and raised in the Tūhoe nation, which covers the Bay of Plenty and Ureweras on the East Coast of the North Island of Aotearoa New Zealand. He was politicized at an early age, when his *whāngai* (adoptive) father drew his attention to the colonial violence and land dispossession their *iwi* had endured, and from his experience of attending school in the small Tūhoe town of Ruatoki—"the school that colonized Tūhoe" (TVNZ 2010)—where Māori children were punished if they spoke Māori on school grounds. Tame has also lent his support to a number of radical and anticapitalist actors and movements around the world, including the Black Panthers, the Zapatistas, the Cuban Revolution, and the fight against apartheid in South

Africa, and has travelled to China, Nepal, Fiji, Tahiti, and the United States in support of Indigenous and revolutionary causes.

Iti became visible in the media in the 1970s through his membership of Ngā Tamatoa (the Warriors), a group of young activists who fought for Māori land and language rights. Tame was inspired by Aboriginal activism in Australia and tired of being treated, as he put it, "like foreigners in our own land" (*Ngā Tamatoa: 40 Years On* 2012), so in 1975 he established a "tent embassy" outside New Zealand's parliament building in Wellington. The embassy consisted of a banner affirming "Māori control of Māori things," flying over a borrowed tent where Iti introduced himself to visitors as the Māori ambassador. Years later, Iti recalls that "most Pākehā were quite shocked by that," as Māori "were meant to be very obedient" (*Ngā Tamatoa: 40 Years On* 2012).

In 1981, Iti was on the front lines of the nationwide anti-apartheid protests against the visiting South African Springboks rugby team, which drew global media attention to Aotearoa New Zealand. These protests against apartheid are widely understood to have sparked a modern Māori cultural and political renaissance. They were crucial to the creation of the conditions of possibility for sharpened discussion and debate among New Zealanders about forms of pervasive but mostly unacknowledged (in mainstream discourse) racism. At the time, the predominant mythologies of the Pākehā majority cast New Zealand race relations in Panglossian terms. The nationwide protests against the South African rugby tour, captured in Merata Mera's film *Patu!* ruptured these racial mythologies in ways that would facilitate important advances in Māori struggles for cultural citizenship rights and the redress of historical grievances concerning land and resource privation stretching back nearly a century and a half. Moreover, the intensification of transnational affective alliances between Māori and Black South Africans contributed to a growing Māori political will and sense of righteous indignation, while Pākehā protestors' concerns for the plight of racially subordinated peoples half a world away lent enhanced moral leverage to Māori demands for racial justice closer to home.

Over the course of the 1980s, Iti continued to engage in public activism and decolonial struggles. For instance, he protested against the establishment of commercial pine tree stands on a sacred Tūhoe mountain (1985), established a roadblock in the small town of Tāneatua on Waitangi Day to raise awareness of the many historical violations of Māori treaty rights by the Crown (1988),[3] and stood in the Whakatane River to protest against the pollution of waterways by commercially operated jetboats (1989). In the decades since, Iti has developed a shrewd sense of theatricality and of what we would like to call media tricksterism, through which he has intervened within the realms of politics and media in ways that have been challenging and that have both drawn upon and contributed to wider social transformations within Aotearoa New Zealand. As William J. Hynes writes, the trickster is a "border breaker" (1993a: 33), "transforming bricoleur" (1993a: 43), "situation-invertor" (1993a: 37), "metaplayer," "revealer" (1993b: 202), and agent *"of creativity who transcend[s] the constrictions of monoculturality"* (1993b: 212, emphasis in original). Through his media presence, tricksterism, and sense of theatricality, Iti has come to figure and personify a century and a half of colonial violence, dispossession, and struggle for wider contemporary New Zealand publics, including even a Pākehā "antifandom" for whom his modes of performativity serve as unwelcome reminders of historical and persistent inequities and injustices.

In a TEDx talk, Iti (2015) recounts one of his interventions vis-à-vis attempts by a conservative New Zealand government to put a premature end to Māori claims for compensation in relation to a century and a half of treaty violations by the Crown. In 1994, the conservative National Party government sought to establish a permanent, absolute total budget cap on any and all future claims before the Waitangi Tribunal. All future payments in compensation for past land thefts and other treaty violations against Māori by the Crown would therefore be abruptly and permanently terminated as soon as the amount of money allocated arbitrarily in 1994 was entirely spent. During a *hui* (assembly) held in the town of Ōpōtiki to discuss this so-called fiscal envelope proposal, Iti performed a characteristic form of political theatrics. While a group of tribal elders were discussing stolen Tūhoe lands with government officials on the stage of the assembly hall, Iti was gradually moving from the back of the audience in the hall toward the stage with a stepladder. The audience became increasingly distracted from the official proceedings by Iti's deliberate and incremental advancement with the ladder toward the stage. When Tūhoe leaders finished their formal presentation to the government and the crowd stood in support, Iti mounted his ladder in the front of the hall and made clear that he had no intention of looking up toward the Crown officials, but instead "wanted to look down on" them as he intoned, "Ko ahau te rangatira i tenei wa. Naku te korero. I am the chief now. It is my turn to speak" (Gardiner 1996: 86–87). Iti then went on to present the government minister in charge of Treaty of Waitangi negotiations with a horse blanket inscribed with a list of Tūhoe grievances, including a reminder that more than 50,000 acres of prime agricultural and coastal lands had been stolen from them by the Crown. Inverting the colonial custom of purporting to offset the colonizers' thefts and atrocities with gifts of blankets, Iti was now offering the Crown "a blanket for my land back" (see Emmerson 2011). The Crown kept the gift and even hung it on the wall at the Office of Treaty Settlements, but failed to return the stolen lands, so in 1998, Tame sent the government an invoice for NZ$11,250 (Iti 2015).

Such activist theatricality and tricksterism have garnered media attention throughout Iti's career and have helped him to amplify and more widely circulate Māori perspectives on coloniality as violence and injustice. In 1999, for instance, in order to raise awareness of the history of colonialism in the Tūhoe nation, Iti issued eviction notices to Pākehā farmers living on land confiscated from Tūhoe in violation of the Treaty of Waitangi, and announced that those living on these stolen lands had twelve months to vacate them. He then waited for a call from the media, which came early the next morning from Radio Pacific. When he was asked on air why he had issued these eviction notices, Iti replied, "Well, let me tell you this story. In 1860 we too were also issued an eviction notice. We were only given three months to vacate the place. And so they came through and those who refused to move after three months, not only were they shot on the spot, but their homes were burned to the ground. And their gardens were burned to the ground." As Tame said to us of this event, suddenly "you've got 35,000 people [listening to the radio] who had never heard that story before. So, you capture your audience" (interview with authors, July 2015).

In 2004, Iti held an art exhibition in Auckland that he called "Meet the Prick" (see Peters 2004). He invited the conservative National Party spokesperson for Māori affairs, Gerry Brownlee, to open the show. Brownlee is one of the politicians who frequently expressed vociferous opposition to the creation of Māori Television (see also chapter 4 on Brownlee's controversial service as the Christchurch "Earthquake Czar"). In a documentary bearing the same title as the exhibition, Iti emphasizes how the use of the word "prick" (along with the ambiguity over *which* of the two men *is* "*the* prick") is a tactic of "manipulation" that attracted substantial mainstream media attention to both his exhibition and his activism (*Meet the Prick* 2005).

In 2005, members of the Waitangi Tribunal travelled to Ruatoki to meet with Tūhoe, and Iti was in charge of organizing the welcome party. He decided to create on the confiscation line a theatrical enactment of the 1860s scorched earth policy. The Crown representatives arrived to shouting, burning cars, and Tūhoe on horseback. They witnessed Iti performing a *whakapohane* (bearing of the buttocks), which is, according to Māori scholar Pat Hohepa, "the ultimate culturally sanctioned Māori way of displaying opprobrium" (Mihaka and Prince 1984: 15), and brandishing a shotgun, which he used to fire at a New Zealand flag that was lying on the ground. For Iti, these displays were necessary to remind the Crown of its history of atrocities against Tūhoe: "A hundred years ago they burned this place down. So, the Crown is coming here to hear your story. So, we need to create tension, firearms, guns, because that all happened in 1860. Fire, smoke, yelling, screaming, all of that" (interview with authors, July 2015). After filmmaker Robert Pouwhare's footage of the reenactment was shared with mainstream media, the images of Iti shooting the New Zealand flag were, as noted earlier, shown over and over again on national television where they provoked Pākehā rage. Nevertheless, Iti's reenactments also exposed the violence and brutality of New Zealand's colonial histories and "opened the space of the political to create a new reading of the past" (Edmonds 2015: 189). This new reading would become increasingly significant as Tūhoe moved closer to settling its differences with the Crown through the Waitangi Tribunal.

Actions like flag shooting, calling someone a prick, and performing a *whakapohane*, which may be deemed outrageous or "vulgar" by Pākehā, thus give targeted offence that necessarily unsettles the dominant Pākehā discourse of New Zealand as a harmonious bicultural nation. Amber A'Lee Frost (2016) has emphasized the importance of vulgarity as a political weapon that helped to dismantle royal privilege during the French Revolution. Iti's "vulgarity" is counterposed to the colonial façade of civility and politeness that masks violence, socioeconomic exclusion, and other atrocities. It might indeed be read as a counter-discourse through which the disproportionate incarceration, unemployment, poor health outcomes, and social marginalization of Māori are resignified as unacceptable and intolerable colonial vulgarities. Nevertheless, while Tame had already been established as a figure of Māori radicalism in the media by 2005, this figuration was reconfigured, intensified, and contested in the wake of the 2007 Urewera terror raids, after which the footage of his previous flag shooting was enlisted in the ongoing production of Iti as a figure of terrorism (cf., Devadas 2013: 9). This footage was replayed endlessly on mainstream national TV in ways that refigured its meanings through its recontextualization within post-9/11 discourses of a "war on terror." However, Māori Television, which was well-established by 2007, worked hard, as we noted in chapter 5, to disarticulate Iti in particular and Tūhoe in general from discourses of terrorism, and to rearticulate the meanings of the raids themselves by linking them to the nation's long histories of colonial violence. Moreover, the raids drew damning criticism from many Māori leaders, whose voices circulated through both Indigenous and mainstream media. For Jackson (2008: 2), for example, they constituted "a terrible cost to have imposed upon such people for aims that are unclear and operational decisions which were unwise, unacceptably belligerent, and ultimately racist." Increasingly, as a consequence of such discursive contestation, the police actions began to appear excessive, unjustified, and terroristic in their own right, and all charges of terrorism against Iti and the others were ultimately dropped.

Despite the collapse of the terror case, Iti was tried and jailed in 2012 on firearms charges arising from the raids. The trial and its coverage provided media with a new opportunity to figure Iti as a violent extremist, but also to interrogate coloniality and police brutality, and to explore Tūhoe history and cultural practices. This came about partly as a consequence of contestation over the application of discourses of terrorism to Tūhoe, but also partly as a consequence of negotiations between the *iwi* and the Waitangi Tribunal, so that the 2007 terror raids and the much longer history of colonial terrorization of Tūhoe by the Crown became increasingly intertwined constituents of a common discursive terrain. While the negotiations were an attempt to settle grave historical injustices, the 2007 terror raids, which were undertaken on unceded Tūhoe land, became increasingly available for media figuration as an instance of a long colonial history being rerun in full color. The verdict and sentencing in the firearms trial were of interest to all New Zealand media, so Tame took advantage of the television cameras both inside and outside the courtroom to display his lack of deference to the colonial legal system, to emphasize that the application of justice is not culturally neutral, and to draw attention to the fact that the New Zealand justice system was imported from Britain and should not be applied to Indigenous peoples. When he left the courtroom after the verdict in March 2012, he spoke only in Māori to the large phalanx of assembled media, which was heavily armed with cameras and recorders (see this book's cover image). After thanking all the Māori around the country that had supported him, he recited: "Hei tira tira, te poti me te whira, te kau hūpeke te maramu...." This is the Māori translation of the English nursery rhyme, "Hey Diddle Diddle," which he was taught in English at the primary school where students were forbidden from speaking Māori. Tame later explained to us that he understood the use of such nursery rhymes to be part of a larger colonial strategy that attempts first to disorganize or "scramble" the minds of colonized peoples ("hey, diddle, diddle, the cat and the fiddle, the cow jumped over the moon...") so they could then be put together differently (personal communication, July 2015). At the moment of his sentencing in May 2012, Tame performed a loud *haka* (Māori war dance) that disrupted the constructed and enforced solemnity of the courtroom.

In 2022, Tame reprised his role as a Pākehā-media figure of post-9/11 "Māori terrorism" for the remarkable Aotearoa New Zealand film *Muru* (2022), directed by Tearepa Kahi. *Muru*, which was filmed on location at the site of the 2007 terror raids, presents a strikingly dark figuration of twenty-first-century coloniality in Aotearoa New Zealand that, therefore, further disarticulates Iti's figuration as a "terrorist" from its 2007 official framing and repositions it within a framework of deeply corrupt state-led violence against a generally peaceful Tūhoe community whose members draw routinely upon their memories of past atrocities as they continue to struggle against a long history of colonial appropriations and impositions exerted through racist regimes of media representation and discursive circulation, sophisticated technologies of digital surveillance, long-standing historical treatment by the colonial state of Tūhoe "like dogs" (a motif that recurs throughout the film), and the formation of alliances between white leaders and a small number of key Māori collaborators who have been carefully placed in positions of military and policing authority by the colonial state (which is embodied here in the form of a shadowy political figure who pulls strings from his office rooted deep in that archetypal metonym of colonial power, the New Zealand House of Parliament). New Zealand's Parliament building, which is nicknamed "the Beehive" for its characteristic shape, is in *Muru* figured as a site of toxic and corrupt coloniality. This colonial Beehive is contrasted against the film's figuration of Tame as a beekeeper who produces his own mānuka honey, which is widely associated with healthfulness and healing in Aotearoa New Zealand and is used by Tame to help heal his sick friend and old comrade from Ngā Tamatoa (an organization we have noted earlier in this chapter) who is suffering from kidney failure. The film repeatedly exposes the continual use of Tame's 2005 protest action by mainstream media to figure him as a "terrorist," and also engages

FIGURE 6.1 Tūhoe, led by Tame Iti playing himself, rise up against injustice in *Muru* (dir. Tearepa Kahi, 2022).

with the April 2000 police killing by a Māori officer of a young Māori man armed with only a golf club who had gone on a window breaking spree in the small New Zealand town of Waitara (see Braddock 2003). In this way, *Muru* (which is the Māori word for a traditional form of restorative justice whereby a transgression is redressed by "returning the affected party back to their original position in society")[4] powerfully articulates twenty-first-century New Zealand coloniality and state-led violence not only to the production and digital surveillance of Indigenous "terrorism" in the post-9/11 world, but also to the scourge of police killings of people (and especially young men) of color in the age of Black Lives Matter. *Muru*'s images of Tame in a beekeeper's suit as he tends to his hives lends him a sheen of quotidian caretaking benignity and ordinariness that contrasts sharply with both the recurrent and spectacular media images of his purportedly "terroristic" 2005 assault on the New Zealand flag, and with the forces of corruption and destruction that the film depicts as emanating from the colonial Beehive. Tame Iti's appearance *as himself* in *Muru* (see figure 6.1) also speaks to his celebrification in the new media environment, just as Taffy's (played by Māori Hollywood star Cliff Curtis) outburst of laughter when elite Special Tactics officers tell him they suspect Iti of "terrorism" reflects both the laughter of the Māori Television news staff when confronted with the same accusation (as we noted in chapter 5) and of wider Māoridom in general.

Conjunctural Struggles, Colonial Ambivalence, and the Politics of Estrangement

The same structural forces that marginalize some groups in society, politics, and the economy also work through the media; hence, mainstream TV typically pushes the voices and perspectives of the relatively socially weak to the margins of both the mainstream media text and the overall broadcasting schedule. When it does appear on mainstream commercial TV in New Zealand, programming that foregrounds Māori voices, language, and perspectives has generally been relegated to non-primetime "ghetto" slots on weekend mornings, weekday afternoons, or late at night (Fox 1993: 135). This pattern has been replicated in mainstream New Zealand media's treatment of Tame Iti, as is illustrated by the fate of *Tame Iti: The Man behind the Moko*, a 2005 TV2 documentary program that depicts Iti sympathetically and centrally features his own account of his life and of Tūhoe history, as told in his own voice, which aired on a Wednesday night at 11:30 P.M. Similarly, in 2010, the long-running TV1 news and current affairs show *Waka Huia* dedicated one of its installments to Iti's life and struggles for Māori cultural rights (TVNZ 2010). However, like other Māori-oriented shows that air on mainstream New Zealand TV, such as *Marae* and *Te Karere*, *Waka Huia* was consigned to a non-prime-time (Sunday morning) slot.

Tame Iti states that the mainstream media "use what they've captured to belittle us" (TVNZ 2010) and notes that "the majority of the people in this country, particularly Pākehā and Māori too, well they view me from split second images, six o'clock news TV1, TV3, it's all crap. They got it wrong, I'm a nice guy, yeah true, I'm a pussycat" (*Tame Iti: The Man behind the Moko* 2005). As Rojek (2001) writes, "celebrity status always implies a split between a private self and a public self" (11), such that people who are celebrified "surrender a portion of the veridical self, and leave the world of anonymity and privacy behind" (20). Iti has developed strategies for the reclamation and rearticulation of his figuration—and that of Māori more broadly—in much mainstream media. Moreover, there is some evidence that the growing visibility of Whakaata Māori within New Zealand's contemporary convergent media environment, and the consequent expansion of dialogical relations between Māori and mainstream media, have begun to shift the wider discursive spatialities of the nation's media landscapes. These shifts have entailed the movement of some Māori voices and perspectives from the margins toward the center of the New Zealand mediascape in ways that bear some similarity to the topographies of the new media environment that we discussed in chapter 1.

Consider, for example, the primetime coverage given to the story of Tame Iti by NZ TV3's news and current affairs show *3rd Degree*, which sent journalist Michael Morrah into the Ureweras for an extended interview with Iti in August 2013. Morrah's exploration of much of the ground that had been broken by Māori Television expanded discursive space for the presentation of a Tūhoe perspective in response to the historically decontextualized coverage of the terror raids carried out by commercial media outlets in 2007. Iti and his partner Maria Steens welcomed Morrah with warm Tūhoe hospitality, and Morrah recounted how "Iti's now famous execution of a flag," during a visit by members of the Waitangi Tribunal to Ruatoki in 2005, "seared an image into the New Zealand consciousness and made Iti the face of Tūhoe protest." Iti then carefully situated the flag shooting within the context of Tūhoe's painful colonial history, as he explained to Morrah that the incident was a theatrical "recreation of the scorched-earth policy. The burning of the cars was the burning of our gardens, the burning of our nation. So we as artists had to create the space so that you can feel it." The oft replayed footage of Iti's demonstrative protest was thus torn from its anchorage in discourses of Indigenous "terrorism," and resignified through its insertion into a narrative of colonial violence inflicted on Tūhoe by European settlers and a discourse of artistic and performative activism. This disarticulation and rearticulation of the discursive locus of terror continued when Morrah asked Iti whether he is a threat to New Zealand and Iti replied, "no, I'm not. I have not stolen any Pākehā lands. I have not killed any Pākehā. I have not punched any Pākehā." Iti thus raised the question of who has been terrorizing whom and challenged mainstream New Zealanders' refusals to acknowledge the colonial violence that has accompanied their presence in New Zealand. As Iti tells Rawiri Patene in *Ngā Tamatoa: Forty Years On* (2012), "Tūhoe has been terrorized, the whole country has been terrorized." These interventions, moreover, highlight the imperializing force of mainstream modes of media representation and celebritization.

As a great deal of cultural studies work demonstrates, discourse is always both a sensemaking practice and an agent of power that exerts control on behalf of one set of social interests or another. Since multicultural societies are necessarily multidiscursive, it is crucial for both a geographically sensitive media studies and a geography that engages with the spaces and places of media, to understand the media conjuncturally as sites of discursive contestation, for the politics of meaning that motivate discursive contestation are central to the establishment and disruption of predominant forms of common sense, and thus of political relations and the boundaries of the thinkable more broadly. If nations are imagined communities, narrative and discursive contestation are core to the practices of imagination that enable a sense of the national to emerge and to be challenged and reformulated (see, e.g., Anderson 2006; Hartley 2004). Thus on the one hand, suspicious colonial imaginaries of Indigenous "terrorism" are discursively invoked in *3rd Degree*'s story on Iti, as the show's in-studio host raises questions such as, "who is Tame Iti? Personal trainer or paramilitary trainer?" and "what was he doing running around in the bush with guns and Molotov cocktails?" On the other hand, *3rd Degree* performs the important function of spatially and temporally extending Māori discourses into the terrain of mainstream and primetime television as it explores issues that had previously been examined in Whakaata Māori documentaries such as *Operation 8* (2011) and *October 15: After the Raids* (2010), and in Whakaata Māori programs such as *Te Kāea* and *Native Affairs*, including the subjection of Tūhoe children to inhumane treatment during the raids, the role of Iti's "training camps" in the development of bushcraft and self-reliance skills among Tūhoe youth, and the question of why concerned police seeking answers did not simply knock on Tūhoe doors rather than kicking them down.

In its visualization of the Urewera landscape, *3rd Degree* depicts this locale as a site of Tūhoe hospitality, painful colonial histories, and anti-colonial resistance, thus disrupting dominant Pākehā place-imaginaries that figure the site as a space of recreation and relaxation or, since 2007, of terrorist activity.[5] We argue that the conditions of possibility for the resignification and reconfiguration of spatial imaginaries in mainstream commercial media, and for the practices of discursive disarticulation and rearticulation described above, are partly themselves a product of Whakaata Māori's interventions into this field of representational politics, which have altered the cultural terrain upon which all New Zealand media operate. As Vijay Devadas (2013: 9) notes, Tame Iti was resignified by mainstream media in 2007 "from campaigner for Indigenous rights and sovereignty into the figure of the terrorist." By contrast, we might say that *3rd Degree*'s 2013 interview participates in moments that deconstruct the resonant figure of the white imagination—Iti as "terrorist"—into a set of multiplicities and plural identities: Iti as artist, social worker, diabetes sufferer, loving partner, stepfather, hunter, activist, and defender of his *iwi* and *hapu* (subtribe).

The interplay and struggle between imperializing discourses of Indigenous problematization and Māori discourses of decolonization and sovereignty are extended into the convergent mediasphere in spaces such as *3rd Degree*'s website and Facebook page. Thus, for example, one Tame Iti anti-fan posted the following comments, which received two "likes": "he might be getting fit, but he is still a thug and always will be. you can dress him up as much as you like but he is and always will be a disrespectful, arrogant man who has no respect for anyone, he lives in the past and its [*sic*] about time he got over the colonisation of NZ. But I bet you he is more than happy to monetary accept handouts for the very governments he despises. I dont [*sic*] know why you even wasted air time on him."

Such comments are symptomatic of Pākehā anxiety regarding Māori struggles for sovereignty and redress of historical wrongs, which involve the engagement of, among other things, questions of stolen land and of the historical foundations for the asymmetrical accumulation and distribution of wealth. Nevertheless, *3rd Degree*'s Facebook page attracted a very diverse set of comments, and there is evidence there of viewer interactions involving challenges to neocolonial or racist discourses, and of attempts to address the consequences of Pākehā ignorance:

Poster #1: Boycotted your programme tonight TV3, you want to glorify a person who intentionally wishes to dishonour the flag of my country and then takes a handout from the government even though his tribe weren't at the Treaty signing. Disgraceful!!!

Poster #2: I didnt think the programme glorified Tame Iti . . . it simply gave him an opportunity to give his side of the story . . . and it is his country too, and hes not the only person having to take a "handout". . . .

Poster #3: Yes Tuhoe never signed the treaty and yet we are still made to live by what it stands for!

Poster #4: Some people are so uneducated they can't even understand what is under their noses—go figure! SNOBS is what they call them—hahaha!

Poster #5: Wow he shot a flag big deal. And don't the point of the Tūhoe settlement, they don't sign the Treaty yet govt still confiscated their land. Bigots is what they call them, don't want to understand like [Poster #1], ignore! (From *3rd Degree*'s Facebook page, 7–8 August 2013)

Senior Māori mediamakers express support for the attempts made by mainstream media to deal more adequately with Māori stories. As one Māori Television journalist said to us while the *3rd Degree* report was in preparation:

I know that there's a [mainstream] current affairs show at the moment that's working with Tame Iti, and gone back up there to ask what—the only question left unanswered is—what the hell was going on up there? Which is a fair enough question, and I'm hoping that he's answered it so people can get a sense of how ridiculous or scary it was. So I think that this is how many years later and we're just starting to ask these questions, five years later. . . . So it's good that these kind of things are happening and I think in mainstream if they can tell these stories that's brilliant.

Similarly, a Whakaata Māori manager believes that there has been a recognizable and favorable shift in both the level and the nature of Māori visibility in mainstream New Zealand media, and that the existence of the network has played a role in provoking and contributing to this shift. He suggests that mainstream commercial broadcasters in New Zealand have begun to find new ways of telling stories that often involve more detailed research into both Māori perspectives and historical contexts:

I think if you take news as it was before Māori TV started . . . most of the stories were negative Māori stories, but there has been I think an impact from Māori Television—well, from the establishment of Māori Television in news anyway, because you've got people who will actively now try and beat us on Māori stories. And the competition wasn't there before. And so because there wasn't any competition a lot of people would just not do them. And now we've seen a lot of stories. And a lot of it is to do with I think a wider kind of change and shift in the public perception of things Māori generally speaking in New Zealand. And so maybe just good timing is another issue about it. . . . So there's a change there, but also I think there's been a bit more competition in terms of getting Māori stories now which simply wasn't there before. And I think in spite of the fact that there are reports that say that the stories are still negative, I think you find a lot, TVNZ, TV3 they do a lot more research on their stories now on Māori issues than they did before, so if you had a look at the Tūhoe claim, I mean you had TVNZ actually and TV3 who both had guys talking about what happened to Tūhoe in the 1800s, and the history being told really well. I mean their stories were great on the Tūhoe claim when it got signed off and how it went. And I don't think that would have happened before. Personally, I think you wouldn't have had the time investment done before. And whether or not that's a direct influence of Māori Television or not I'm not too sure, but it's coincidental that I think you've seen a change in the way Māori stories are told on mainstream for the time that Māori television has been here to before that.

It is worth noting that conjunctural analysis avoids conventional logics of "cause" and "effect" in its approach to the relational links between events and opts instead for an alternative understanding, whereby conjuncturally related events are grasped as mutually determinative via their colocation within a particular historical conjuncture (see Hall 1996). Another Whakaata Māori manager thinks that the channel's success at attracting Pākehā audiences has encouraged mainstream TV to "'brown up' their own thing. Using Māori words that they would never have done before, and that's part of the effect. The effect is not immediate or large, but what it is, is very subtle. But you start seeing it. You know, I've seen programs where they would never have done that before on TVNZ, before we arrived. And suddenly they've got a brown face doing a thing instead of a Pākehā guy doing it. So just little things you notice that are influences on other broadcasters."

The year 2015 saw the release of a new documentary, *The Price of Peace*, which explored Tame Iti, the Tūhoe communities that were turned upside down by the terror raids, and the work done by police to repair the damage they had inflicted upon these communities. The film's director, Kim Webby (2015), sought to counter dominant mainstream media depictions of Iti by revealing a "softer man" who wears "many hats" and is "a father, grandfather, artist, health worker, radio announcer, community leader and, these days, a *kaumātua*" (elder). The film's premiere in Tāneatua (which we were fortunate to attend) was a deeply moving event for Tūhoe. This film then screened in cinemas across the country and was broadcast on Whakaata Māori. Social and other media activity around *The Price of Peace* suggests an expansion of Iti's celebrification, a growing appreciation for his activism, and a widening recognition that colonial violence continues in New Zealand. *The Wairarapa Times-Age* reported that a Masterton cinema "ignited a social media frenzy after posting to Facebook a trailer of festival film *Price of Peace* that drew more than 100,000 views" (Norman 2015). The Facebook post also sparked a lengthy conversation thread that captured the positive energy, excitement, and interest surrounding the film. The cinema's social media manager said they had "not had a reaction like this to a movie before," and that *The Price of Peace* attracted more engagement than a typical Hollywood blockbuster. This kind of convergent media activity reveals that Tame Iti as celebrity activist media figure is beginning to occupy a different location within both the New Zealand mediascape and society more broadly. In recent years, Tame has been invited to do longer interviews on radio and television and to give prestigious public lectures. Iti's 2022 art exhibition drew attention to the status of *te reo* (the Māori language) in New Zealand society and involved the creation of a screen print stating "I Will Not Speak Māori," the line that Tame was forced to write on the school blackboard hundreds of times as punishment for speaking his own language at school;[6] this intervention was picked up across the mainstream mediascape in print, radio, and television (see, e.g., Brebner 2022; RNZ 2022; TVNZ 2022). A version of the exhibition was also displayed on the Wellington waterfront with the support of Wellington City Council as part of its Māori Language Week activities (see Wellington City Council 2022). Tame was named a New Zealand Arts Foundation Laureate in September 2022 (Irwin 2022). In 2023, after declining invitations to appear on other reality TV shows such as *Dancing with the Stars*, Iti accepted the challenge of becoming a contestant on *Celebrity Treasure Island* in the hope of winning NZ$100,000 for the I Am Hope mental health charity founded by fellow Māori media personality and comedian, Mike King (Jack 2023). While it is now hard to believe that Tame was incarcerated by the New Zealand state as recently as 2012, competing figurations of Iti—as troublemaker or extremist, for example—do nevertheless continue to resurface. That is to say, he continues to be a socially resonant and contested figure.

Like other celebrity activists, Iti must negotiate the tension between his firm commitment to collective struggle and celebritization's drive to produce a "spectacle of individuals" capable of reproducing "the code of hyper-individualization pushed by consumer culture" (McCurdy 2013: 322). He is acutely aware of the ways in which his activism has been repeatedly refigured and disfigured in order to sell newspapers and TV advertising, and emphasizes to us that he is "passionately committed to the liberation of the Tūhoe nation" and that he is just "another little dot of the story" (interview with authors, July 2015). It is striking that his paintings seem often to depict large crowds filled with multitudes collectively peopling the landscape, and he stresses that decisions about the future of Tūhoe are being taken by the *rangatahi* (younger people), with *kaumātua* like him helping with "fine-tuning" (personal communication, May 2016).

The figuration of Iti as dangerous radical, extremist, or terrorist facilitates the erasure of the violence of colonialism. This figuration enabled and legitimized the terror raids and Iti's incarceration. But media figures can only function as ideological conductors for dominating powers for as long as conjunctural conditions allow it. Conjunctural shifts have facilitated new figurations and called forth new strategies. Lilie Chouliaraki (2013), while highly critical of the past and present forms of solidarity that develop around celebrity humanitarianism, and in particular the narcissistic cultural dispositions that they engender, ends her book *The Ironic Spectator* by suggesting that engagement around Indigenous activism might produce a progressive or even radical mode of estrangement. Such estrangement involves three elements: "exposure to otherness," "engagement with argument," and the "reversal of humanization" whereby sufferers who are different from an implicitly Western "us" are "endowed with a sense of... humanity" through depictions of their asymmetrical power relation with a dominating figure who is "like 'us'" (Chouliaraki 2013: 199–200), as in some of the media coverage of the terrorizing aspects of police raids on ordinary Māori members of the community of Ruatoki. While Chouliaraki is focused on *distant* suffering, there is some evidence that gaining familiarity with Iti's activism and engaging with arguments around sovereignty, racism, and coloniality are producing a progressive kind of estrangement among at least some New Zealanders.

The figure of Tame Iti thus forms part of a "symbolic battleground" (see Beltrán 2002: 89) upon which New Zealand's colonial past and colonial/postcolonial present are continually negotiated and renegotiated. Iti struggles upon this battleground and is constituted by it. He is figured and constrained by colonizing discourses and practices, but also subjects them to interrogation and destabilization, and takes advantage of the convergent media environment to engage in practices of articulation, disarticulation, and re(con)figuration. One study of Iti's tweets from prison, for example, shows how his social media strategies "dismantle[d] the communication barriers of spatial confinement and... counter[ed] dominant narratives" (Elers and Elers 2018: 81) by offering audiences insights into the solidarities and communities formed inside the prison, by working to maintain key Māori cultural practices, and by providing alternative commentaries on wider New Zealand social issues. Hence, while much of the media activity around Iti enacts the resilience of coloniality in New Zealand, the figuration of Iti as radical extremist or terrorist has been impossible to sustain as the conjuncture has shifted, in part as a consequence of Tame's modes of celebrity activism. As the Tūhoe chief negotiator Tamati Kruger noted during the Urewera trial, the current generation of New Zealanders is "more open and comfortable about dialogue and debate around Treaty issues" (Thorby 2012). These changes influence how people engage with and understand Iti's activism, and require mainstream media to shift, too, or risk losing both viewers and influence. The stigmatization of Iti that worked in one conjunctural moment begins to lose its discursive force in another, somewhat reconfigured and shifting one.

By the same token, the intense criticism of the New Zealand terror raids by Māori leaders was eventually (partially) endorsed by New Zealand's Independent Police Conduct Authority (IPCA) after their enquiry into Operation 8. The report they released in 2013 established that the roadblocks and personal searches conducted by police were "unlawful, unjustified and unreasonable" (IPCA 2013). Police commissioner Peter Marshall was forced to apologize publicly for officers' failures to uphold appropriate professional standards while establishing roadblocks and conducting searches of private property (Quilliam 2013). Despite this finding, nobody within the police or government has been held accountable for these unlawful actions.[7] However, the New Zealand Police and Tūhoe were able to agree on a settlement regarding the damage inflicted by Operation 8, and in 2014, police commissioner Mike Bush personally apologized to the Tūhoe communities and families impacted by the raids (Ihaka 2014). New Zealand police even organized a trip to the national capital, Wellington, for the Tūhoe children affected by Operation 8.

The shifting conjunctural assemblage noted above is also revealed clearly in the official apology to Tūhoe made in 2014 by the Crown representative, Treaty of Waitangi Negotiations Minister Chris Finlayson, at the time of their settlement concerning the long history of Treaty violations against the *iwi*. This apology, which was all but unimaginable in 2007 when the police conducted their terror raids, included admissions of responsibility for the unjust seizure and sale of the tribe's best lands, and for the Crown's long and "brutal military campaign" against Tūhoe, which was characterized by one contemporary account as an "extermination." Finlayson acknowledged that during the Crown's assault on Tūhoe, "villages and crops [were] burned; families [were] killed and men [were] executed." Even conservative New Zealand prime minister John Key characterized the settlement as "the first serious attempt to change the relationship [between Tūhoe and the Crown] from a largely negative one to a distinctly positive one" (TVNZ 2013). Finlayson proclaimed: "Ngāi Tūhoe, it's your day. The relationship between Tūhoe and the Crown, which should have been defined by honour and respect, was instead disgraced by many injustices including indiscriminate raupatu [confiscations], wrongful killings, and years of scorched-earth warfare. The Crown apologises for its unjust and excessive behaviour and the burden carried by generations of Tūhoe who suffer greatly and carry the pain of their ancestors" (cited in Fox 2014). Along with this historic apology, Tūhoe received a treaty settlement of NZ$170 million and the return of Te Urewera, which is no longer a national park and whose *legal personhood* is now enshrined in New Zealand law. Iti (2015) has pronounced that "we finally got respect and understanding from the Crown," which has been refigured in the media as an agent of colonial violence, as "incivility" is disarticulated from Iti and rearticulated to the settler state. A review of early media interviews with Iti suggests that he never expected Māori to achieve as much as they have (see *Keskidee Aroha* 1980). The post-settlement terrain for Tūhoe is a radically changed one full of hopes for the future, new opportunities, and a renewed sense of struggle for the recognition of Tūhoe sovereignty. According to Iti, the challenge for Tūhoe now is to rebuild their nation, to organize their own spatial planning strategies, and to reach through their own media to all Tūhoe who are living outside the *iwi*'s traditional lands (interview with authors, July 2015). In other words, the conjuncture demands new and different kinds of struggle.

While Indigenous media may generally operate on the margins of national mediascapes that produce neocolonial and imperializing discourses and representations, we reject the idea of a fixed geometry of power that structures relations between mainstream and Indigenous media, and wish to foreground the hybrid spatialities that coloniality and its resistances inevitably produce. Kevin Bruyneel (2007) suggests in a U.S. context that Indigenous populations have developed ways of occupying a third space of sovereignty that "refuses to conform to the binaries and boundaries that frame dualistic choices for Indigenous politics, such as assimilation-secession, inside-outside, modernity-traditionalism, and so on, and in so doing refuses to be divided by settler-state boundaries" (21). From this third space of sovereignty, Native Americans demand "rights and resources from the liberal democratic settler-state while also challenging the imposition of colonial rule on their lives" (xvii). This spatiotemporal boundary-confounding strategy of Indigenous struggle emerges as a mode of opposition to forms of colonial imposition that are themselves ambivalent. Both American and New Zealand coloniality are based upon a simultaneous reverence for and rejection of Indigenous peoples, who are thus deemed to at once belong and not belong to the nation-state, which acts as both their conqueror and their guardian. By both "expressing power against and drawing power from Indigenous people" (14), colonial rule becomes inconsistent in its application and is thus characterized by *colonial ambivalence*. Such colonial ambivalence facilitated both the actions of the New Zealand police in Ruatoki in 2007 and the media discourses of Tame Iti as a terrorizing and insurrectionary Indian, even as New Zealand celebrifies Iti and strives to figure itself as a bicultural nation engaged in postcolonial redress. Bruyneel acknowledges that Indigenous peoples are harmed by this ambivalence but calls attention to the ways in which its contingencies can be exploited by Indigenous actors who work across boundaries, struggling both within the postcolonial political system to attain benefits while simultaneously working to promote and defend their own sovereignty. It is perhaps unsurprising that the structural ambivalence of colonialism itself should demand an ambivalent politics in response.

Bruyneel's conception of colonial ambivalence bears some comparison to Stallybrass and White's (1986) influential discussion of abjection, whereby dominant social orders seek to expel their "low-Others," only to learn that they are not only in many ways dependent upon but also deeply fascinated by and drawn to them. As they write, "the result is a mobile, conflictual fusion of power, fear and desire," whereby "the low-Other is despised and denied at the level of political organization and social being whilst it is instrumentally constitutive of the shared imaginary repertoires of the dominant culture" (Stallybrass and White 1986: 5–6). This analysis helps, perhaps, to explain the celebritization of Indigenous activism, and creates permanent cultural and therefore political instabilities that are, as Stallybrass and White show, mapped onto bodies, geographical spaces, and whole social formations, and through which the "low-Other" repeatedly disturbs the hierarchies and binaries that differentiate it from the "high"/dominant.

Whakaata Māori broadcasters and Māori political actors such as Tame Iti have been able to exploit colonial ambivalence and instabilities to enact their own modes of resistance. The boundaries between mainstream media and Whakaata

Māori, like those between Indigenous and Pākehā ways of knowing, are not impermeable barriers but rather contact zones or "sites of co-constitutive interaction" (Bruyneel 2007: xix) through which epistemological and ontological orientations and differences collide dialogically. The spatial and discursive politics of Whakaata Māori and the digital media technologies and communities that surround it are beginning to reconfigure the landscape of New Zealand media in ways that carry a clear decolonizing potential. While stigmatizing and problematic representations of Māori persist, what comes across to us most clearly is an unsettled and anxious mainstream media that is attempting to come to terms with New Zealand's violent colonial past in more inclusive ways. The discursive flows and dynamics of both Māori and mainstream media are then not so much separate and parallel as hybrid and entangled.

Anderson and Hokowhitu (2021: 157) write that "celebrity events involving Indigenous peoples must always be read via a colonial genealogical method" that is sensitive to "the production of Indigenous bodies through discourse." Conjuncturalism inflects genealogical analysis by attuning it to the dynamics of discursive struggle, the instabilities, and the shifting balance of forces at work in postcolonial contexts such as Aotearoa New Zealand and in the wider contemporary world. Manuel Castells (2009) writes that "the network society" is comprised of "multimodal, diversified and pervasive communication networks" whereby "social movements and insurgent politics" gain historically unprecedented opportunities "to enter the public space from multiple sources" and to deploy "*both horizontal communication networks and mainstream media to convey their images and messages* . . . even if they start from a subordinate position in institutional power, financial resources, or symbolic legitimacy" (302, emphasis in original). In Aotearoa New Zealand, Whakaata Māori is putting stories and debates onto the political agenda, while relationships between Māori and mainstream media seem increasingly horizontal rather than vertical, as the latter look to the former for guidance in their treatment of Māori issues. The production of reciprocal and horizontal relationships between Whakaata Māori and mainstream media disrupts the forms of vertical social classification associated with coloniality (see Maldonado-Torres 2007: 244), the persistence of which facilitated the actions of the police terror raiders. In the current conjuncture defined by neoliberalism, securitization, and the resurgence of Indigenous politics, both imperializing power (Fiske 2016b) and decoloniality find new ways to reinvent themselves. Mainstream media continues to be a space of epistemic violence, and Indigenous actors continue to work at the margins of systems of coloniality that are largely alienating and disabling. But the sites in which Māori can speak back to epistemic and other forms of colonial violence are proliferating across geographical space and enabling marginal discourses to gain traction as they cross media platforms. As Indigenous communicators assert their presence within a rapidly changing and unstable media environment, we increasingly encounter the problematization of coloniality itself.

Part IV

Mediated Struggles for Democratization, Decolonization, and Cultural Citizenship in Central America

7
Authoritarianism and Participatory Cultures

Central American Conjunctures and Histories of the Present

As we noted at the end of chapter 6, the new media environment has produced expanded spaces for the circulation of the voices of Indigenous peoples in sites of decolonial struggle like Aotearoa New Zealand. In this chapter and the next, we will extend this analysis by returning to Central America, whose new media environments share many of the characteristics of those we have explored in previous chapters (and indeed the digital expansion of the global mediasphere has meant that these localized media environments share overlapping spaces and interact dialogically with others in significant ways), but are built upon different histories of coloniality, mediation, and struggles for democratization and decoloniality. Our shared engagement with these processes and histories began a decade and a half ago, when we took advantage of an opportunity to combine our respective long-term research interests. Kevin had developed an interest in Indigenous media, especially Māori television in Aotearoa New Zealand. Julie had been working in Nicaragua for many years on neoliberal politics, gender, revolution, and disaster. She was working on the Caribbean Coast of Nicaragua with Miskito survivors of Hurricane Felix in 2007 when she learned of the recent development of an intercultural community television channel, then called BilwiVision, which was created to center Black Creole and Indigenous voices and perspectives. We saw this as an opportunity to develop new collaborative research on Indigenous media and returned together in early 2008 to the port city of Bilwi (also known as Puerto Cabezas, or in Creole English simply as "Port") on Nicaragua's Caribbean Coast, where we worked closely with the Black Creole Costeño academic and civil society leader, Dixie Lee. Bilwi was still dealing with the aftermath of Hurricane Felix, and during our first joint visit, Dixie invited us to a meeting of the Black Creole community, where we witnessed a group of disaster survivors expressing their outrage over the uneven distribution of aid after the hurricane. Over the sound of a constantly whirring diesel generator (as the meeting time coincided with a power cut), the participants, who spoke not in Spanish but in Creole English, were demanding zinc roofs to fix their hurricane-damaged homes, and condemning what they saw as an unfair and corrupt system of aid distribution. Noting that some people had received two sheets of zinc while they had received none, and that much donated material had ended up for sale in local markets, many at the meeting believed they had been excluded because of anti-Black racism and a state that was hostile to Black Creole interests. We soon learned that while there was much shared grievance, solidarity, and common struggle between Indigenous and Afrodescendant groups in Nicaragua, there were also important tensions between them that had deep historical roots. We also realized that our focus on local media cultures would need to be inclusive of the other groups on the Coast, especially the Black Creole/Afrodescendant population that was, like the Indigenous one, harnessing the power of participatory media cultures in support of autonomy and political rights. The deep historical, cultural, and familial connections between the Black Creole population in Nicaragua and those elsewhere in the Caribbean region led us to expand our work further into the Creole Nation and thus to work with mediamakers on the Caribbean Coast of Costa Rica and eventually on the islands of San Andrés and Providence.

This chapter and the next extend our analysis of the decolonial and Indigenous (geo)politics of the new media environment and draw upon in-depth fieldwork we conducted in Nicaragua and Costa Rica between 2007 and 2019, where we worked in the towns and cities of Bilwi, Bluefields, Pearl Lagoon, Limón, Cahuita, Puerto Viejo, and Bribri. We explore how convergent media cultures have developed and been mobilized by Nicaraguan and Costa Rican mediamakers, activists, and community members. Part IV includes a discussion of the emergence and expansion of Indigenous and Afrodescendant media outlets (including TV and radio) in the region, and outlines how Indigenous, Afrodescendant and mestizo broadcasters, media activists and consumers are appropriating digital and other media resources to form intercultural solidarities and to challenge erasure, marginalization, racism, political authoritarianism, environmental destruction, and governmental indifference. We outline how, amid a context of political violence and growing authoritarianism, there is an inspirational politics of life at work that struggles to construct a different kind of modernity. Nicaraguans and Costa Ricans, especially those who are Indigenous or Afrodescendant, understand the failure of Eurocentric efforts to assimilate them, and while their identities, cultures, and knowledges have been threatened, marginalized, and undermined by coloniality, they continue to rearticulate and reassert them in creative and affirmative ways. A range of transmedia resources are harnessed in the production of this life politics.

The Central American isthmus has a shared colonial and postcolonial history that has relegated it to a peripheral status on the world stage. All the countries of the region have had to negotiate the presence of European powers on their soil from the sixteenth century onward, a presence that decimated Indigenous populations, brought African slaves to work on plantations, and established export-oriented commodity trade as the dominant development model. This exploitative model is driven by racist ideologies and established entrenched patterns of underdevelopment that have proven difficult to dismantle. Prior to the arrival of Europeans, there were many Indigenous groups in the region, but the current forms of native identification have consolidated in the colonial and postcolonial eras, in part through interaction with many outsiders: the traders, settlers, escaped slaves, buccaneers, missionaries, and capitalists who came to the region in search of prosperity or livelihoods, or to evangelize.

Most of Central America was colonized by Spain, but there were places where Spanish colonization failed to penetrate. There was a lengthy British colonial presence in the Caribbean parts of Nicaragua and elsewhere that worked in conjunction with Indigenous resistance to prevent the Spanish from colonizing the region known as the Mosquitia. While the British were of course focused on exploitation of the region's resources and on gaining the upper hand in their fierce rivalry with Spain, the Miskito developed alliances with Britons to engage in mutually beneficial trading practices, as well as to keep the Spanish at bay (Helms 1971; Hale 2004; Pineda 2006). As a result of these alliances, the Miskito rose to prominence and pushed the Mayangna and other Indigenous groups inland from the Caribbean Coast. Indeed, the region has a long history of creative cultural borrowing and exchange (Glynn and Cupples 2011). Both Miskito and Creole populations developed a strong appreciation for first British and later U.S. culture, which Charles Hale (1994) calls an "Anglo affinity." Indeed, in the early seventeenth century, Miskito chiefs, whose territory lies in both Honduras and Nicaragua, adopted British names, clothing, and monarchical practices, in addition to acquiring their weapons. As Mary Helms (1988: 197) writes, the Miskito people "gloried in titles such as 'governor', 'admiral', and 'king' bestowed along with commissions at formal coronation ceremonies held by English authorities in Jamaica or Belize ... accompanied by appropriate, brightly colored British officers' uniforms and royal scepters." Some Miskito also engaged in slave-raiding practices for the British.

Anglo affinity was further fortified by the Protestant churches and missionaries who came to the region. The Moravian Church in Nicaragua (and the Baptist Church in Costa Rica) became important providers of education for Black populations and thus filled gaps created by extreme state neglect. While the

Moravian Church has been slow to admit the validity of Miskito cosmologies, knowledges, and cultural perspectives, over time the U.S. missionaries were replaced by Miskito and Black Creole pastors, and by the 1980s, the Moravian Church had become a key defender of Indigenous rights (Hale 1994; García 1996). Miskito and Black Creole forms of spirituality and traditional healing practices have thus survived evangelization and remain strong. While the people of the Nicaraguan Caribbean have frequently embraced external foreign elements such as Christian religions, they have, as noted (and like other Indigenous peoples of Latin America), inflected these with Indigenizing accents and elements, and have in general fiercely resisted Hispanicization. In 1860, Britain and Nicaragua signed the Treaty of Managua, whereby Britain recognized Nicaragua's claim over the region, but whereby Nicaragua also acknowledged Miskito and Black Creole inhabitants' autonomy in what remained of the Mosquito Kingdom. There thus persisted a considerable degree of autonomy in the Mosquito Reserve, which heavily restricted Nicaragua's ability to extract natural resources or control trade in the region. In 1894, however, the region was traumatically and violently annexed by Nicaragua (Pineda 2006). The passages quoted below were sent by a correspondent to the U.S. State Department in 1894 (United States Department of State 1894); the act of aggression described in this document laid down a pattern of internal colonialism that has continued to this day and remains a key source of political contestation that is central to collective memory in the region:

> Allow me to draw the attention of your readers to an act of aggression on the part of Nicaragua. She violently took possession of the Mosquito Reservation on the morning of the 12th instant, invading its capital, the town of Bluefields, with an armed force of soldiers when all its inhabitants were fast asleep, breaking open the Government buildings, and placing them under a strong guard, temporarily arresting those who might have escaped to raise an alarm, forcing open the gaols and letting loose all the prisoners, hoisting her flag on the Mosquito flagstaff, and declaring the natives Nicaraguan citizens. By these measures the Nicaraguans have deprived the chief, Robert Henry Clarence, of his authority as president of the council, dismissed the members of that body, removed the judges of the supreme court, the magistrates, and every government official in the service of his excellency the chief. They have also appropriated moneys, and roughly handled a British subject, the customhouse collector, to obtain the keys of the safe. Up to the present date we have been tinder martial law, which was proclaimed on the 12th instant.
>
> In this way Nicaragua has used force and intimidation to deprive the Mosquitos of their rights. She has also offered bribes to many influential persons to agree and consent to this when the final settlement comes. The natives are opposed to any closer relation with Nicaragua, with whom they have no sympathy, their customs, manners, and character being so much at

variance. The Mosquitos have a great liking for England; they were happy and contented while under her protectorate from the latter part of the seventeenth century to 1800, and a pang went through the whole of the tribes when the best part of their territory was handed over to Honduras and Nicaragua. However, they were pacified by having a portion set apart for their use and at being free to govern themselves without any interference from the supreme Government; and they implicitly believed that England would see that all the stipulations of the treaty of Managua made between Her Britannic Majesty and the Republic of Nicaragua in 1800 were carried out.[1] So far they have done their best to comply with all the stipulations of this treaty, and have respected the rights of the sovereign power.

While African slavery in Central America occurred on a smaller scale than elsewhere across the Americas, there were thousands of African slaves working on British plantations in the region, and many Black Costeños bear the surnames of their ancestors' masters. While the brutality of the transatlantic slave trade and forced labor in mines and on plantations destroyed African lives and cultures, many slaves and their descendants not only survived but went on to decisively shape the cultures, politics, and development of their new homes. They maintained their ancestral knowledges, spiritual practices, and modes of governance, creatively resisted the subordination imposed upon them, and thus generated in the process new shared languages (such as Creole English), identities, and collectivities. The Afrodescendant population of Central America expanded dramatically after the abolition of slavery, when Black migrants travelled from Jamaica, Trinidad, and even the southern United States to work on the railroad and in banana production in Costa Rica, on the construction of the Panama Canal, and in lumber, mining, banana, and fishing companies in Nicaragua. Consequently, many of the Black populations who live in Central America today are descendants of free Black populations who migrated from elsewhere. Garífuna people from St. Vincent and Honduras also settled in Nicaragua. Since the colonial era, Black, Indigenous, and mestizo populations have interacted and intermarried, and many Costeños thus have mixed ancestry and have engaged in historically shifting practices of multiethnic identification (see Pineda 2006). The Caribbean Coast of both Nicaragua and Costa Rica developed enclave economies dominated by the United Fruit Company (UFCO) and other U.S. businesses. In Costa Rica, it took eighty years for the Black populations that had migrated there in the 1870s (until after the civil war of 1949) to gain citizenship (Monestel 2013).

After Mexico and most nations to its south gained independence in the nineteenth century, hierarchically racializing discourses of *mestizaje* (racial mixing) began to circulate in Central and South America. It was at this time, as Walter Mignolo (2005) outlines, that "Latin America" emerged as a concept that worked in part to differentiate the region on identitarian grounds from the imperialist

United States. But the concept of Latin America was also adopted by the criollo elites of the Americas to exclude Black and Indigenous populations, who often do not identify with the "*Latin*" in "Latin America" in the same way mestizo populations do, from the standpoint of the region's nation-building projects.[2] These Euro-descended criollo elites have historically understood both Indigenous and Afrodescendant populations, along with their cultures and knowledges, as obstacles to national progress and therefore began, after the establishment of "Latin America" as a hegemonic element of common sensemaking throughout the region, to generate policies designed to assimilate these populations into Eurocentric ways of knowing and being. As Mignolo (2005: 56–57) writes, "the history of "Latin" America after independence is the variegated history of the local elite, willingly or not, embracing "modernity" while Indigenous, Afro, and poor mestizo/a peoples get poorer and more marginalized. The "idea" of Latin America is that sad one of the elites celebrating their dreams of becoming modern while they slide deeper and deeper into the logic of coloniality." Like all hegemonic formations, though, the Eurocentric elite's approach to the problem of difference was contested from the moment of its conception. The liberatory thought of Cuban intellectual José Martí (1977 [1891]), for example, posited *Nuestra América* (Our America) in opposition to the cultural values of the United States, which he understood to be rooted in racist ideologies. Furthermore, the political consequences of the successful Haitian slave insurrection and revolution (1790–1804) continued to reverberate throughout the continent and the world, as both Black and Indigenous peoples asserted their intellectuality and engaged in political rebellion rooted in non-Eurocentric ways of knowing and non-Christian cosmologies and spiritualities, albeit from positions of extreme marginality. Their struggles notwithstanding, *mestizaje* became, as noted, a hegemonic ideology that underpinned state-led efforts to assimilate Black and Indigenous populations and that continued to reproduce hierarchized categories of racial difference (Hale 2004).

While both Afrodescendant and Indigenous peoples are thus subject to racism in Latin America, the hegemonic ideologies of *mestizaje* tend to exacerbate Afro-erasure and invisibilization more than they do those of Indigenous populations; indeed, the primary impact of these ideologies has been to include Indigenous ancestry in an assimilated and temporally transmuted form, while denying and invisibilizing Blackness. Nicaraguan author Sergio Ramírez (2007) says that although Black people lived throughout Nicaragua during the colonial era, Nicaragua's Black heritage is something that people do not talk about, to the extent that many mestizo Nicaraguans do not think that there is such a thing as a Black Nicaraguan or that Nicaragua is an English-speaking country as well as a Spanish-speaking one (see Vílchez 2017; Pineda 2006; Romero Vargas 1993).[3] Yet Creole-English-speaking Black Central Americans have established vibrant communities and contributed massively to the economic and cultural development of the region, however much their contributions remain largely overlooked. Black Creoles in Central America have been subject to various kinds of everyday and institutional racism that continue to this day. Both Black and Indigenous peoples continue to be essentialized and Othered by racializing discourses that ascribe to them lower intelligence, greater laziness, and higher predispositions to criminality than mestizo populations. Nevertheless, while both Blackness and Indigeneity are often exoticized and folkloricized, Indigeneity is, albeit in Eurocentrically romanticized forms, indispensable to the region's hegemonic ideologies of *mestizaje* in a way that Blackness is not. Moreover, the region's hegemonic racial discourses ascribe to formerly enslaved Black Creoles an essential diasporicity that always already strips them of opportunities to claim lands rights on the same basis as Indigenous populations can and do. Of course, neither the importance of a mythicized Indigeneity to Eurocentric ideologies of *mestizaje* nor Indigenous people's access to land rights claims prevents Indigenous dispossession from taking place throughout Latin America, as we shall see. Nevertheless, Afrodescendant Latin Americans are subject to more extreme forms of exclusion than other racialized groups, a state of affairs that Black Creole political theorist Juliet Hooker (2005a) describes as "Indigenous inclusion and Black exclusion." As Afro–Costa Rican television presenter Nayiba Witinia put it, when Afro–Costa Ricans from the Caribbean Coast travel to the capital city to attend university, "we meet people that see us as strange," which makes one feel "like a foreigner in your own country." Some Black Central Americans have begun to reidentify as Indigenous in order to evade the controlling power exerted through the region's hegemonic racial discourses (Gordon 1998). It should be noted as well that racial and ethnic identities and identifications on the Caribbean Coast have for many centuries been unstable, flexible, fluid, shifting, and not infrequently reconstituted as wider conjunctural forces have been reconfigured over time (see Pineda 2006; Glynn and Cupples 2011).

While Latin American nation-states organized around the ideologies of *mestizaje* became stronger during the twentieth century, Black and Indigenous populations continued to practice their own forms of governance and economic activities. In Nicaragua, the geographic isolation of and state neglect toward the Caribbean region afforded Costeños a degree of political autonomy despite their official annexation, and many there continued to identify with Britain rather than with Spanish-speaking Nicaragua; to this day they often refer to Pacific Nicaraguans as "Spaniards," a practice they share with Black Creoles who live elsewhere in the Anglophone Caribbean. The Black Creole and Raizal populations of Costa Rica and the San Andrés archipelago (which sits just off the Caribbean Coast of Nicaragua but officially belongs to Colombia) also refer to Spanish-speaking Costa Ricans and mainland Colombians as "Spaniards" or "*paña* people." Indeed, this part of the Caribbean has been characterized by constant migratory flows of Black Creoles who have long exchanged goods and cultural practices with each other. The Anglophonic Caribbean regions of

Nicaragua, Costa Rica, and Panama are indeed built on these migrations. As Philippe Bourgois (1989: 46) writes, during the first half of the twentieth century, Black immigrants traveled from "country to country" and "from company to company," so that, generally speaking, "the same individual who planted bananas in Bocas del Toro, had previously shoveled dirt on the Panama Canal, and later went on to harvest cacao in Limón, only to end up ultimately emigrating to New York to work as an orderly in a hospital."

Across the region, Black populations displayed a high degree of cosmopolitanism. In Costa Rica, this can be attributed in part to the fact that Black populations were avid readers of the Bible and consequently had higher degrees of literacy than others (Monestel 2003). This cosmopolitanism was also advanced by other linguistic, as well as political and economic factors. While all low-income and poor Nicaraguans suffered during the brutal Somoza dictatorship (1936–1979) and some Costeños joined the revolutionary struggle to help bring about its demise, it is probably fair to say that inhabitants of the Caribbean region (which had by then been renamed Zelaya, after the president responsible for its annexation) experienced less repression than those of the Pacific region, and support for the revolutionary struggle was therefore much lower in the former than the latter. Indeed, in the early twentieth century, the Anglo affinity that had developed during the colonial era through interaction with the British began to extend to U.S. culture, as both Miskito and Black Creole Costeños had a level of receptivity to external cultural elements, such as country and western music, from English-speaking places (see Glynn and Cupples 2011). For the Black Creole population in particular, the Somoza dictatorship was also understood as a time of prosperity and consumption rather than one of repression. In the early twentieth century, Bilwi/Puerto Cabezas became a U.S. company town that provided a base for North American lumber, mining, banana, and fishing operations, so the period from 1920 until the triumph of the Sandinista Revolution in 1979 is known in Port as "company time" (Pineda 2006). While the presence of these companies transformed the lives of all the inhabitants of the Northern Caribbean and helped to generate a discernible cosmopolitanism and consumer culture, Pineda (2006) explains how it also gave rise to racially unequal employment practices that were recognized and resented by Miskito people, as employers tended to prefer Black workers, some of whom were local and others, recent migrants from the U.S. South, Jamaica, and the Panama canal zone, in large measure because they spoke English. These workers were often paid in script (coupons redeemable at company stores, which were full of goods imported from the United States) and thus grew dependent on U.S. wheat, vegetables, meat, newspapers, and magazines shipped from New Orleans. In the process, they grew to love U.S. popular culture, including country music, basketball, and baseball. The triumph of the revolution and the U.S. embargo imposed by President Reagan led to the departure of U.S. companies from Nicaragua, and the products people had consumed routinely thus disappeared from local shelves.

The U.S. companies left behind a legacy of serious environmental destruction, but the employment they brought and consumption they facilitated meant that many Costeños did not share the anti-imperialist philosophy of the Sandinista Revolution. Furthermore, the revolutionary triumph led not only to a decline in Costeño living standards, but also brought an end to the de facto autonomy that had been in place since the time of the Mosquito Reserve (Jarquín 2016).

Other cultural and ideological sources of ambivalence regarding the triumph of the Sandinista Revolution were also active in the Caribbean region of Nicaragua. The Sandinistas' vision of vanguard politics and of large state farms did not sit easily with the communal modes of land tenure and agriculture predominant on the coast. Tensions between the Eurocentric and modernist Marxist-Leninist ideologies that underpinned the Nicaraguan Revolution and Black and Indigenous cultures and cosmologies did not take long to emerge. The new revolutionary government tried to include the coast in its political vision and created an organization called MISURATA (Miskitos, Sumos, Ramas and Sandinistas) in order to work together for change, but the urban mestizo political leaders lacked the cultural competence to engage horizontally with Black and Indigenous knowledges and ways of being, and struggled to comprehend a part of Nicaragua where the inhabitants were neither Catholic nor spoke Spanish. Furthermore, for the mestizo Sandinistas, Anglo affinity was a source of suspicion that was too readily articulated to U.S. imperialism (Hooker 2005b; Pineda 2006). Moreover, the Sandinistas largely failed to understand the collective trauma that was experienced on the Caribbean Coast as a consequence of its 1894 annexation—a trauma that was still deeply embedded in the region's historical memory and blocked the regional development of a commitment to the project of national liberation that was central to the Sandinista Revolution. Indeed, the revolution revealed just how ill-equipped Sandinista leaders were to engage with the cultures of the coast, and it did not take long for their cultural incompetence and racism to produce tragic consequences. Many Miskitos joined the Contra forces in Honduras to oppose the new revolutionary government. Then, in December 1981, the FSLN (Sandinista Front for National Liberation) government forcibly relocated thousands of Miskito people who lived near the border with Honduras to a new settlement known as Tasba Pri; many died during this forced relocation, which came to be known as *Navidad Roja* (Red Christmas) because of the blood that was spilled.

In 1988, just over a half-decade after Red Christmas, two Miskito Contra leaders formed a new political party, YATAMA (Yapti Tasba Masraka Nanih Asla Takanka; the Organization of the Peoples of the Mother Earth), and thus embarked on a struggle for Indigenous autonomy. As the 1980s progressed with no military triumph of the Sandinista army over the Contra forces, the leaders of the revolutionary government began tentatively to recognize the political errors they had made in their dealings with the Caribbean Coast and to acknowledge that the resolution of the war would require them to accept the clamors for autonomy coming from the region. As Miguel González (2016) shows, there were divergent visions of autonomy at work; while YATAMA struggled for Indigenous-based territorial autonomy, the Sandinista government advanced a regional multiethnic model of autonomy capable of including all the people on the Coast. The latter approach was more acceptable to the Afrodescendant people who were also fighting for autonomy, though they felt the Sandinistas' proposal would cede too much power to the numerically larger mestizo populations, whose numbers were still growing due to migration from the Pacific region. Despite these differences, substantial progress was made. Autonomy for the region was enshrined in the 1987 constitution and in the 1987 autonomy law, *Ley* 28 (Law 28). Two new autonomous regions, the Región Autónoma del Atlántico Norte (RAAN; Autonomous Region of the North Atlantic) and Región Autónoma del Atlántico Sur (RAAS; Autonomous Region of the South Atlantic) were formed; they have now been renamed the Región Autónoma de la Costa Caribe Norte (RACCN; Autonomous Region of the North Caribbean Coast), and the Región Autónoma de la Costa Caribe Sur (RACCS; Autonomous Region of the South Caribbean Coast).

The autonomy process has created tensions between ethnic groups on the Coast. It has complicated the position of long-established Costeño mestizos, who can claim neither Black nor Indigenous identity but whose families have lived on the Coast for many years and thus differ from recent mestizo migrants and illegal settlers from the Pacific (about whom we will say more in chapter 8). Furthermore, the fact that Black populations were able to access a higher standard of living during company time was a source of Indigenous resentment and, indeed, we were told by a Miskito politician who had been elected to the regional government that this was now *their* time of ascendancy, just as the Black Creole population had experienced in the twentieth century. The autonomy law that was passed to rectify the cultural insensitivity that had been shown by the leaders of the revolutionary government belongs to all Costeños, but is often seen as a form of distinctively pro-Indigenous legislation. Nonetheless, the passage of Law 28 in 1987 was a historic moment for all the people of the Coast, though another sixteen years would pass before this legislation was ratified and the process of granting ancestral land titles could thus commence. The 2003 ratification of Law 28 by Law 445 (the Law of the Communal Property Regime of the Indigenous Peoples and Ethnic Communities of the Autonomous Regions of the Atlantic Coast of Nicaragua and of the Bocay, Coco, Indio and Maíz Rivers) took place two years after the Mayangna people of Awas Tingni had successfully defended their own collective land rights in an international court in defiance of a destructive, state-endorsed concession for commercial logging activities (Grossman 2001; Hale 2005). In its ruling, the Inter-American Court held that the Nicaraguan state must pass a law to establish the processes necessary for the demarcation, titling, and thus protection of the communal lands that were formally recognized by Law 28.

Law 445 was administered by an entity called CONADETI, the National Commission for Demarcation and Titling, which planned to complete this work by 2011 (Acosta 2010), but at the time of this writing in 2024 has still not done so. Law 445 received a boost from a very short-lived electoral alliance between YATAMA and the FSLN that was put in place for the 2006 national elections (Finley-Brook 2011). The FSLN was in the opposition for sixteen years after its defeat in the 1990 elections by a U.S.-backed coalition, but returned to power in 2006. The passage of Law 445 took place in a conjuncture marked by the global ascendancy and enshrinement in international law of Indigenous rights. In 2007 Nicaragua voted in favor of the UN Declaration of Indigenous Rights and in 2010 ratified International Labour Organization Convention 169, which established the principle of Free, Prior and Informed Consent (FPIC) and meant, as one Black Creole leader put it, that in the case of any proposed development, "the community, [who are] the owners of the land, have to be consulted and the consultation has to be free, prior and informed." While the FSLN government was and is officially in favor of the Caribbean autonomy process, it has, as we note below, been a thoroughly obstructive force in relation to efforts to secure Afro-Indigenous rights, and has failed to respect the principles of FPIC. Indeed, the FSLN government mobilizes the rhetoric of support for Caribbean autonomy while ceaselessly working to contain struggles for its achievement within a nationalistic discursive regime, and has frequently removed territorial leaders who were elected by their own communities from office. Furthermore, as we discuss below, since their return to power in 2006, the FSLN government has become increasingly authoritarian and violent, and has taken brutal action against struggles for decolonization and democratization throughout the country. Moreover, the FSLN has taken control of all four branches of government and the security services, engaged in electoral fraud, violated both the constitution and the rule of law, undermined women's rights, used riot police to quash public protests, shut down hundreds of NGOs and civil society organizations, and assassinated, criminalized, forced into exile, and imprisoned hundreds of opposition leaders and activists, including a number of our own close friends and research collaborators. Until recently, the FSLN, with the backing of Chinese capital investment, was planning to build a new shipping canal from the Caribbean to the Pacific and thereby displace thousands of people (including Afrodescendant and Indigenous communities) and wreak widespread environmental destruction. In 2021 Nicaragua became the world's most dangerous country (in per capita terms) in which to be an environmental defender (Global Witness 2021).

In addition to the racializing impacts of the ideologies of *mestizaje*, all countries of the region have experienced the deleterious consequences of the neoliberal structural adjustment policies that were widely implemented after the 1980s Latin American debt crisis and, to some extent, of twenty-first-century neoextractivist practices. In Nicaragua, structural adjustment was enacted after the electoral defeat of the Sandinistas in 1990, which brought rapid trade liberalization that hit small and subsistence farmers and fishers hard. For several years in the 1990s, prior to the institution of the Heavily Indebted Poor Countries Initiative by the International Monetary Fund and the World Bank in 1996, Nicaragua spent more to service external debt than on health care and education.

Despite shared histories and political similarities, there are key conjunctural differences between the northern countries of Central America, Nicaragua, Honduras, El Salvador, and Guatemala—which experienced military governments, brutal civil wars, and U.S. intervention on a devastating scale in the twentieth century and have been experiencing growing repression, authoritarianism and, de-democratization for much of the twenty-first century—and the southern countries, Costa Rica and Panama—which have not escaped the regional consequences of these processes, but have managed to retain something of a democratic polity whose citizens enjoy higher standards of living, but where poverty, inequality and racism are persistent too, as they are in the northern countries of the isthmus.

Nevertheless, it is clear that despite the brutalities of conquest and subsequent forms of internal colonialism and ongoing coloniality, the multiethnic and multilinguistic populations of the Caribbean Coasts of Nicaragua and Costa Rica have defended and developed their own distinctive cultural and historical memories, narratives, and practices. In Nicaragua and Costa Rica, there are important Indigenous (Miskito, Mayangna, Rama, and Bribri) and Afrodescendant (Black Creole and Garífuna) groups that actively perpetuate and reinvent, often through their appropriations and innovations of new media technologies and forms, their own traditions and languages. Bilwi also has a well-established Chinese population that works in commerce, local government, and the Moravian Church, and there are many Chinese surnames such as Lau, Lee, Siu, and Sujo among the region's populations (Pineda 2001). There is also an important Chinese presence in Port Limón, Costa Rica. Of the seven ethnic groups that live on the Caribbean Coast of Nicaragua, it is the Rama community in the South Caribbean, with a population of around just two thousand, that is at the highest risk of extinction; most Rama people today speak Creole English or Rama-Kriol, but a small group of Rama elders continue working to transmit the Rama language to the next generation, and their Indigenous perspectives and cosmologies remain strong. There are more than 200,000 speakers of Miskitu spread between Nicaragua and Honduras, around 20,000 Mayangna speakers, and Creole English is commonly heard on the streets of the main Nicaraguan and Costa Rican Caribbean coastal cities and towns, including Bilwi, Bluefields, Limón, and Puerto Viejo, as well as on their radio stations. The Afrodescendant people of the Caribbean Coasts of Costa Rica (Limón) and Nicaragua (Bilwi and Bluefields) do, however, inhabit a linguistic world that is dominated and threatened by the Spanish language, which is eroding the use of Creole English, particularly among younger people who are exposed to Spanish in schools, universities, and workplaces, and who thus tend to speak Creole primarily when they are with parents or grandparents, but not among generational peers. Due to the power of coloniality, Creole English is often dismissed as a (mere) dialect or an inferior form of so-called standard English, rather than understood as a remarkable, transgenerational achievement of enslaved populations who managed against the odds to create a shared, dynamic, living language that is similar to English but has its own grammar and distinctive African influences (though as we shall see, the important and resurgent traditions of calypso music constitute one transmedia cultural site where a Creole English renaissance is actively under way).

While a number of distinct ethnic groups inhabit Nicaragua's Caribbean regions, their members all identify collectively as Costeños and are generally of mixed heritage and bi- or trilingual. Our collaborator Dixie Lee identifies as Black Creole but also has Miskito and Chinese ancestry and is fluent in Spanish, Creole English, and Miskitu. Ethnic identification usually stems from the community one grew up in, the school or church one belonged to, and the language spoken, but it can vary. One of our collaborators who has a Miskito father and Black Creole mother told us she identified primarily as Black Creole, while her two sisters identified primarily as Miskito. The Miskitu language is heavily influenced by Creole English and by Spanish to a lesser degree, while the Creole English vocabulary also draws creatively on Spanish linguistic resources.

As we discussed in chapter 1, the post-9/11 geopolitical world and the new media environment have produced one another in complex ways. While the nations of Latin America were not affected by the 9/11 attacks in the same way as the United States, the conjunctural ramifications of these attacks have both been global and taken geographically specific forms. In Latin America, as John Beverley (2011: 5) writes, the post-9/11 world coincides with and inflects a sense of the failure of modernity and of "the need to reimagine Latin American nation-states, societies, cultural identity, and politics at a moment in which not only communism but also a capitalist-neoliberal model of modernization have entered into crisis." Starting in 1998 with the election of Hugo Chávez in Venezuela, but accelerating after 2002 and throughout the following decade, we saw the fall of the first group of democratically elected governments that embraced neoliberal structural adjustment policies and their replacement by leaders who campaigned against the Washington Consensus. Dubbed the "pink tide" (and also known as the Latin American "turn to the left") for their moderation and skepticism toward, rather than wholesale rejection of, neoliberal policies, these governments represented an important shift, despite significant colonial continuities and contradictions that remained fairly well intact in most nations. Many of the pink tide governments continued to promote extractivist practices, such as the production of oil and natural gas (although these were nationalized and resulting profits were often invested in social programs to tackle hunger or improve housing), and developed trading relations with China that were not necessarily any better for local people and environments than those in place with the United

States (see Cupples 2022). The post-9/11 world in Latin America is one in which neoliberal capitalism has been deeply interrogated and significantly moderated but continues to persist, especially through extractivism that continues to expand and accelerate (while it still can). The conjunctural crisis of neoliberalism takes different forms in different parts of Latin America but has produced ongoing contestation and racialized violence that has been harmful to people and destructive of environments. While it is crucial to analyze racial violence and other colonial legacies, we must not, as Beverley (2011: 6) warns, represent Latin America as "essentially violent and ungovernable," or suggest that Black and Indigenous populations should be defined solely by oppression or their experiences of colonialism and coloniality (Tuck 2009; Liboiron and Lepawsky 2022).

In Nicaragua, the Sandinista government that has been in power since 2006 is not part of the pink tide, but often identifies with and receives support from pink tide governments in Bolivia and Venezuela. While it continues to mobilize a left-wing, anti-imperialist rhetoric drawn from the Nicaraguan Revolution, it makes sweetheart deals with big business and has criminalized social movements, including struggles for racial, gender, and sexual liberation.

Participatory Cultures of the New Central American Media Environment

While our interest here is in the participatory cultures of the new media environment and the ways in which the latter creates space for the development of Afrodescendant, Indigenous, and other subaltern media practices, it is important to recognize that convergent media activity with a liberatory and decolonial ethos in Latin America long predates the new media environment. The pathbreaking work of Latin American–based cultural studies scholars such as Néstor García Canclini (1990) and Jesús Martín-Barbero (1993, 2004a) revealed the complexity and creativity of bottom-up sensemaking and hybridizing cultural, including media, practices. In the context of the failure of development and the exclusion of ordinary people from the spaces of decision-making, this scholarship has demonstrated the importance of popular and "mainstream" media consumption for the construction of belonging and cultural citizenship, and for the articulation of development aspirations. Furthermore, it has challenged the paternalism often displayed by development practitioners who are critical of the media consumption practices of the poor, whom they criticize for seeming to prioritize satellite dishes over food and clothing; such critics fail to understand that subordinated populations use media to constitute themselves as citizens (García Canclini 1995; see also Cupples 2015). As Pablo Alabarces (2018: 50) puts it, "popular cultures always signaled—and continue to signal—the dimensions in which the possibility of a democratic culture is discussed, negotiated and disputed" in Latin America. For Alarbaces, there is no dividing line between political culture and popular culture, and subordinated populations have always managed to mobilize popular cultural forms to challenge state power, corruption, and political violence and to engage in democratizing and decolonizing practices. Consequently, convergent and participatory media cultures in the present are drawing on long-established practices rooted in a desire for democratization and liberation. The brutality of slavery, colonialism, and extractivism and the ongoing epistemic violence wrought by Eurocentrism notwithstanding, there have always been social groups in Latin America who are able to imagine otherwise and to evade, modify, and rearticulate hegemonic ways of knowing; media and popular culture have long been central to these endeavors.

Popular and contemporary media cultures have thus been crucial to the contestation of the "development industry" that rose to prominence in the post–World War II era. As Arturo Escobar (1995) writes, the post-war settlement established "development" as a key mode of geopolitical intervention in the world. Escobar showed how development, as it was promoted and materialized by practitioners, experts, and academics based in multilateral and government aid agencies, NGOs, universities, and think tanks, rested on the idea that the so-called third world was "underdeveloped," but with western help, knowledge, and technology could "catch up." As we noted in chapter 5, colonial media organizations and practices also reproduced, recirculated, promoted, and legitimated hegemonic colonial discourses, such as those formed around Eurocentric notions of "underdevelopment" and "modernization." In the geographical imaginaries and hegemonic geopolitical discourses of the Global North, the "inferior," perpetually "lacking," politically unstable, and ostensibly disease-ridden Global South was an appropriate site for western intervention and development (see Fiske 2016b: 143–159). But such imaginaries and discourses were rapidly contested by Marxist dependency theorists, who produced an alternative, anti-imperialist account of the causes of underdevelopment (Kay 2019). They were also contested by Afrodescendant, Indigenous, *campesino*, and poor mestizo organic intellectuals who continued to engage in a politics of liberation, often through cultural practices that asserted spiritual connections to land and place, and maintained noncapitalist economic relations rooted in reciprocity. Landlessness, socioeconomic inequality, political violence, and cultural exclusion were nevertheless cruelly and painfully persistent. Latin American activists and organic intellectuals have engaged in what Gramscians call wars of position and in interstitial or marginal popular practices and tactics that have subverted or (at least temporarily) evaded the techniques of top-down, controlling forms of dominating power (see Cupples, Glynn, and Larios 2007). Media technologies became key tools in these popular wars of position and were appropriated by groups like the Zapatistas to expose oppression, raise awareness, and build solidarities with wider audiences and publics. Earlier instances of such media appropriation and activism include the practices of the mothers of those disappeared by the Dirty War in Argentina, and the survivors of the 1985 Mexico City earthquake, who both expressed their grievances while the cameras of the global mainstream media were turned toward them during the World Cup soccer championships in Buenos Aires and in the Mexican capital in 1978 and 1986, respectively. Nonetheless, while mainstream media can be appropriated to make interventions in the political realm, many groups have also established and operated their own autonomous media organizations, which have opened and occupy key spaces within the contemporary fragmented and convergent media environment.

As noted above, we started this component of our research in 2007 on the Caribbean Coast of Nicaragua after the creation there of a community television channel that was explicitly aimed at defending and enhancing regional autonomy and at promoting local Indigenous and Afrodescendant perspectives, interculturality, and development needs. BilwiVision (which was later renamed Canal 5) was created in 2005 by the local intercultural university URACCAN (Universidad de las Regiones Autónomas de la Costa Caribe Nicaragüense / University of the Autonomous Regions of the Nicaraguan Caribbean Coast) (see Cupples and Glynn 2014; Glynn and Cupples 2011). BilwiVision came into being just over a decade after cable television was first made available in Nicaragua's Northern Caribbean region, and only five years or so after broadcast programming from the Pacific part of Nicaragua became available there via cable.[4] While the internet was already quite widely available (albeit not always affordably) in the Pacific part of Nicaragua by 2007, very few people on the Caribbean Coast had cell phones or internet access at home, social media platforms like Facebook and YouTube were new, and struggles for Indigenous and Afrodescendant liberation were intensifying. With limited financial resources, but tremendous cultural commitment, BilwiVision began to broadcast a range of homemade media content in local languages, and filled the remaining airtime with imported shows.

Prior to the creation of these important televisual spaces, however, and even before the internet became widely available there, people in places like Bilwi, Bluefields (in Southern Caribbean Nicaragua), and Limón (in Caribbean Costa Rica) already had vibrant and quite well-established participatory media cultures and so were substantially competent in their uses of media. First, there were clearly critical discourses circulating in these regions regarding the representational practices of mainstream national media, which generated deeply racialized popular geopolitical imaginaries that stigmatized and exoticized the Caribbean as a disaster-prone site of drug trafficking and backwardness. Moreover, long before local Indigenous and Afrodescendant people had access to smartphones and the internet, they made quite creative uses of community radio stations. Many stations had long offered open mike sessions, for instance, where all people could come to speak out on air regarding important political matters they cared about. Local citizens frequently used this airtime to express their grievances to politicians and other authorities who might be listening, especially when efforts made through more formal (or informal) channels had fallen on deaf ears or been otherwise unsuccessful. Rural Miskito communities often pooled their resources to send a community member to the regional capital to denounce failures by authorities to resolve this or that issue. In many cases, such publicly aired grievances forced politicians to respond on air in an effort to retain their legitimacy. As the director of the now defunct Kabu Yula radio station told us: "We put up Kabu Yula so that anyone in the vicinity of Puerto Cabezas and the villages around Puerto Cabezas that has something to say to the government and their word can't go through different channels, Kabu Yula is there for that. They will come here, we will offer them, you know, some time on the radio, we'll give it to them and their word can be heard in this way, and it has worked. It has worked a lot."

Such participatory radio practices still exist in the region, but the ubiquity of cell phones means that travel to the station just to get one's voice on the air is no longer necessary. If you walk around any Miskito village today, you will hear local radio stations broadcasting in the Miskitu language and featuring phone-in participation by locals who have grievances to air or other opinions to share. Community radio has also enabled local people to practice important forms of Black and Indigenous leadership. One Black Creole broadcaster and former drug dealer from Bluefields, Dalila Josefina Marquinez Garth, who is known locally as "La Popó," gained a substantial radio following after she displayed an extraordinary set of negotiating skills and managed to diffuse a prison riot that the police could not bring under control in 2011. She saw her role as solving people's problems, and although she worked on one of the government radio stations, she subverted top-down efforts to control the station's content. She told us:

> I am a blessed Black woman and a Christ-believer and it is a great opportunity for me to get on this radio station probably through [Bluefields] Stereo. You could get it on the 96.5 FM and if you have Internet you could get it on the caribedigital.com media.... First when I begin, I was told that I going be there on the radio station to give the information about the things, them that the Government is doing for our people. But one day I went to work and I say, "wait, let me see if I could make this program different, more dynamic and instead of just coming out and reading out what the government do....
> Because I start to thinking that you have people out there that are very frustrated. Having different problems, don't know who to come to share their problems with. So, then I put my program as an open program, which I named it "Take a Look Around." That's the name of my program: "Take a Look Around." I begin from 8:30 until 10:30.... I had been working in the different neighborhoods, trying to help people with their problems. You have some people with their jurisdiction problems, and they don't know where to go. They don't know which office to visit. Then I have the facility to visit these offices and talk with the judges and the lawyers and the fiscals [tax authorities].

Popó went on to describe how she used her platform to help get people out on bail, to provide funds for travel to the Pacific region for urgent medical treatment, to acquire schoolbooks and uniforms for children whose parents cannot afford them, and to obtain a wheelchair for a baseball player who had become disabled. Her program was highly interactive. For instance, listeners would post comments on Facebook during the broadcast, and Popó would read and incorporate these comments into her show. The program was broadcast in Creole English, and Popó identified the threats to the language and to Creole identification from encroaching Hispanicization as among the most significant challenges facing Black Creole people.

> Well, definitely we have a lot of ups and down being Creole, because some accept they is Creole, and some no accept they is Creole. Some say they are not Creole, them don't speak Creole. Well, as for me, my language is—I am a Black woman, and I speak proper English when I have to. But for me [my language] is Creole. And as Creole, I think we trampling, and I think that we should be more united as Creole to develop our language, to develop our culture, to rescue back a lot of our culture. I think we lose our interest in our Creole communities by adapting another man's language, which is the Spanish. We have a lot of Creole people that love to express themselves more in Spanish than our normal language, and I think that is one of the big problems that we have here in our in our community.

Former Miskito Contra leader, Osorno Coleman, who also hosted a community radio show in the Miskitu language from Bilwi, described how his work in the media began clandestinely in the mountains, but operated in the most difficult of circumstances, and with a need for high political and technical capacity and mobility.

> So the radio itself was born in the mountains, in the 1980s during the war and its purpose was to let Indigenous communities know what going on, to explain the situation of the war, the situation of the refugees who were in Honduras and Costa Rica, and the communities that were being persecuted by the Sandinista Popular Army. So, it played a role in denouncing the abuses of the Sandinista Front at that time. At the same time, it also used to report on the progress of the Indigenous struggle. And that is how the radio started in 1982. In July that year, we managed to get a transmitter, and it was installed clandestinely. At that time, the radio broadcast on shortwave, on frequency 5770, and it had a wide range. It entered as far as Europe and South America. So, the station had a lot of power, but it was also mobile. It was not a fixed station. One moment it could be in one place, but if there was danger we could leave and move it somewhere else. That was how we started.

When we interviewed him in 2014, Osorno described the aims of his station as focused on "the Indigenous struggle, the rights of Indigenous communities, with respect to land rights," and on raising awareness about natural resources, deforestation, and pollution. He was particularly concerned about the existential threat to his people posed by the invasion of mestizo settlers from the Pacific region on ancestral Indigenous lands: "An Indigenous people without land will cease to exist." This concern motivated much of the on-air discussion involving Osorno's listeners, who phoned in frequently to share their views.

By the time community television came to the Coast in 2005, then, the region was already home to established popular participatory media networks, cultures, traditions, and practices for the use of broadcasting as a local political advocacy tool, and TV was quickly appropriated for similar practices. As one Black Creole mediamaker told us, locals came "to view media as a kind of tribunal which can both appeal and raise awareness," so these people "come to us, to get us to publicize their problem. They get us to travel to their community, and take some shots, and then we broadcast to the rest of the region and to the authorities so that people can see what is really going on in the communities" (Glynn and Cupples 2011). To further support this goal, BilwiVision developed an ethnographic show called *La comunidad en su casa* (The community in your home), described by the then-director, Aracely Duarte, as a means to "bring the everyday lives of our communities to the screen." In the process, the people of the region developed new visual imaginaries for presenting themselves and their communities to others, which both transformed the conditions of possibility for dialogical exchange and intercultural understanding, and, as Aracely noted, potentially served the economic development purpose of boosting their capacities to imagine new activities for improving local living conditions, such as the development of strategies for the promotion of tourist visitation opportunities (Glynn and Cupples 2011). Our collaborators, Shaun Bush and Dixie Lee, began to broadcast a weekly Black Creole program on the channel that dealt with issues specific to the Black community of Bilwi. It had quite a rustic and low-budget feel in comparison to the international cable TV offerings that were also available in the region, but attracted a large local audience as it was the only program that dealt specifically with the issues facing the Black population of Bilwi. Indeed, the show's hosts often took the opportunity to highlight the local relevance of global issues like the United Nations' International Decade for People of African Descent, and to encourage surrounding communities to engage with such international developments.

In Costa Rica, too, media that is controlled by Black and Indigenous populations is seen as central to cultural survival. Community radio was brought to the Bribri community in southern Costa Rica in the 1970s by German Catholic priests as a literacy-promoting tool, but is now run and controlled by local Indigenous mediamakers with a broader vision. While it is a financial struggle to stay on air, and radio workers do not earn a living wage, the radio is understood to be vital for community survival. As the board member of a Bribri community radio station, Danilo León, stated: "On the other hand, radio was brought here to sustain our culture, so that our culture wouldn't be lost, so that people can understand that culture is our source of wealth. It is what we live off every day. It is the development of a people. The people have to understand via the radio, that our culture, the strength of this people is culture. . . . The idea is that: that people understand that values and wealth are right here." For Danilo, this radio project is posited as one that can at once facilitate tourism, artisanal entrepreneurship, and organic agricultural production, protect the Bribri language, raise awareness of the dangers of deforestation and the presence of invasive fish species, and prevent Bribri youth from falling into drug addiction by encouraging them to play sports. The project is also focused on "human values of brotherhood" rather than consumption or material gain. Danilo described it as "the first cultural radio station in Costa Rica," and its thirty-six-year history is for him undeniably a source of pride. Its convergence with the internet has enhanced and strengthened the Bribri station in important ways, but because their equipment is outdated and website hosting prohibitively expensive, their online presence is mediated by Facebook. While there are important criticisms of the forms of algorithmic exploitation utilized by social media, including Facebook, the latter has proven to be a widely useful and affordable means of dissemination that extends the reach of Bribri radio and other Indigenous media projects in Latin America. There was an urgency in Danilo's voice as he outlined for us the challenges facing the Bribri community that their radio project seeks to address:

> Let me tell you how it is. We are in a moment of agony, that is why I'm talking about the need to rescue our culture, to rescue our cultural values. Why? Because we are in agony. I am not going to hide from you what I cannot hide. Whoever says that this is a lie would be lying to you. But we are at a critical moment with culture, and culture is not only about life in our homes. It is also about our language, and the language is collapsing. If we do not get our act together, 20 years from now, we will have lost everything.[5]

Danilo went on to express fear that the Bribri ritual of stone pulling (*jala de piedra*)—an old community tradition that involves carrying a heavy stone used for grinding cocoa, corn, and coffee over large distances—is currently under threat as a quotidian spiritual and domestic practice and risks reduction to a tourist spectacle.

Many of the Black and Indigenous media operations that we have engaged with operate cautiously in the new media environment. Osorno Coleman said they would never play *narcocorridos*, the Mexican songs that glorify the drug trade and cartels, in spite of their popularity, and we were told that, in the early days of BilwiVision/Canal 5, the station deliberately avoided the use of violent images, including sensationalistic accounts of local accidents, crimes, and disasters, because of the ideological work such images perform by stigmatizing the Afrodescendant and Indigenous Caribbean Coast as a site of disorder in

Hispanicized Pacific mediascapes. Nevertheless, some younger Black and Indigenous mediamakers at BilwiVision found this environment to be too restrictive in its exclusion of even coverage of groups that have taken up arms to defend Indigenous rights like the Zapatistas in Mexico, so they left to create their own intercultural channel, TV7, which is cablecast locally. Both TV7 and Canal 5 have survived and continue to broadcast, but have suffered immensely as a result of growing authoritarianism, as we discuss below. Furthermore, although it took a bit longer to achieve, the Afrodescendant community of Costa Rica also began production of a Black-oriented show for distribution on a local cable TV channel, LimónTV, as we also discuss further below.

Danilo, our Bribri participant, expressed concern about the proliferation within the region of cell phones and satellite dishes that enabled people to access a range of national and international channels. He said he was not a great fan of these developments, that he lives in "another world"—in his "natural world"—and that he prefers to avoid news media because he finds it so depressing (he added, however, that he procured a cable TV subscription once so he could watch the World Cup). Later, he reflected that while technological change can be damaging, such consequences were not inevitable, and he hoped that Bribri people were using cell phones, computers, and television to "improve their harmony with nature" and "their harmony with other people."

At a time when media and political spaces for Black and Indigenous empowerment were beginning to open up in Costa Rica, Nicaragua was descending into authoritarianism and repression. While Black and Indigenous Central American media operations are welcomed and celebrated by many, the Nicaraguan Sandinista government led by President Daniel Ortega (once a left-wing revolutionary who played a leading role in the struggle to overthrow the Somoza dictatorship in the 1970s, but who has, since his return to power in 2006, increasingly emulated Somoza's dictatorial practices with ever-intensifying brutality) and his wife and vice president, Rosario Murillo, often views these operations as a threat to its power and control. The Sandinistas have made sweeping efforts to shut down spaces of dissent, democratic action, and media that lie outside their ownership and control. Ortega-Murillo have repeatedly violated laws and the Nicaraguan constitution, rigged elections, gained control of all branches of the state, deployed violent mobs to beat or shoot public protestors, transferred aid from the Venezuelan government into private hands (including their own), used clientelism to win strategic support, expelled dissidents from the government, shrunken women's rights, and, as we noted earlier, plotted with Chinese capitalists to build a new interoceanic shipping canal that would destroy the territories and livelihoods of a large number of Indigenous and Afrodescendant people, poor *campesinos*, and the biodiversity of wider ecosystems. They have subverted press freedoms by acquiring ownership and control of media companies, attacking independent journalists, and squelching critical commentary and oppositional discourses. Our informants in Nicaragua have told us that Ortega and Murillo have cultivated an "ideological brigade" of digitally savvy young online pro-Sandinista dissident surveillance and disruption agents. Additionally, the Sandinista government developed systems and protocols for the centralized vertical dissemination of official communications by Rosario Murillo, who daily uses state television, radio, and internet channels to exclaim how wonderfully the nation is running. The Ortega-Murillo regime has also transformed urban landscapes through hypersecuritization (particularly around the presidential palace in El Carmen), the adornment of Managua's streets with dozens of metallic trees erected at a cost of millions of dollars (but which have become popular targets for anti-Ortega dissidents), and the erection of billboards and other forms of publicity on vehicles, lampposts, and small businesses showcasing the images of *el presidente y la vicepresidenta*, Daniel Ortega and Rosario Murillo (see figure 7.1).

In response to these concerted assaults on democracy and dissent, human rights defenders, independent mediamakers, and ordinary citizens have found creative ways to make use of alternative and social media spaces to challenge the Ortega-Murillo regime. Consequently, by 2015, the Sandinista government was facing serious political opposition from environmentalists, anti-canal *campesinos*, Indigenous and Afro-leaders, what was left of the independent media sector, NGOs, and feminist activists. Our participants frequently described trying to make independent media in this climate of hostility and intimidation. A Bluefields radio program entitled *Demarcation Now* that aimed to support the land

FIGURE 7.1 "We bless you, Daniel!" (Source: Photograph by Julie Cupples.)

titling process by exploring Black Creole history was taken off the air as a result of government pressure on the owner of the radio station. A Miskito freelance journalist who was broadcasting a program about Indigenous rights on TV7 called *Tawan Inangka* (The clamor of the people) started getting death threats. The station, too, was threatened with closure. To save her own life and the channel, the journalist stopped making and broadcasting the show. Another Miskito radio journalist whose life was also threatened by anonymous phone callers was assaulted by pro-government thugs during a shopping trip. Ángel Gahona, a Bluefields-based journalist and director of the local television channel *El Meridiano*, broadcast a program that captured and circulated the voices of people whose land was at risk of being eliminated by the construction of Ortega-Murrillo's pet interoceanic canal project. He told us, "The program hadn't finished when people who are part of the government who were watching it started calling me and sending me messages. I had to sincerely apologize out of fear they would close my company. I live off this. I look after my family with it and employ people. And if I as a media operator have this fear, you can imagine how afraid ordinary people are. There is fear in the population, especially among those who live along the canal route." As we note in the next chapter, Angel would indeed go on to lose his life while reporting in Bluefields during the violent government repression of 2018. Indeed, since 2014, it has become apparent to many that Nicaraguan Indigenous and Afrodescendant mediamakers are an endangered population that would have to develop new and creative transmedia practices that could not be so easily attacked and undermined by the Ortega-Murrillo regime if they are to successfully defend their land and other rights. The next chapter discusses how these activities have challenged the authoritarian political violence of the Sandinistas.

8

Transmediation and New Central American Digital Activisms

Indigenous Media: Defending Lives and Territories

As we noted in chapter 7, Law 445 contains the legal potential to satisfactorily complete the communal land titling process and, as such, is a crucial piece of legislation for Indigenous and Afrodescendant Costeños in Nicaragua. The law is supposed to "guarantee the Indigenous peoples and ethnic communities the full recognition of their communal property rights, use, administration, management of their traditional lands and natural resources through the demarcation and titling of their lands" (República de Nicaragua 2003). One of the biggest threats to the regional autonomy necessary for the fulfilment of these rights and practices is the presence of illegal settlers, known as *colonos* or *terceros*, on ancestral lands in the Northern Caribbean region. While the first four stages of the process specified by and required under Law 445 (namely, the submission of applications, the settlement of disputes, and the measurement, demarcation, and titling of lands) have been completed in twenty-two of the region's twenty-three communities, the fifth and final stage, *saneamiento*, which acknowledges the need to find a legal solution to the problem of *colonos* who are living illegally on titled communal lands, has not been completed anywhere. Indeed, the Sandinista-YATAMA electoral alliance created in 2006 collapsed as the land titling process was gaining momentum, and as the illegal and often violent and environmentally destructive invasion of Indigenous and Afrodescendant ancestral lands in the Caribbean region by settlers or *colonos* from the Pacific region was accelerating. These *colonos* cleared forests, illegally sold the valuable timber, brought in cattle, built homes, and engaged in unlawful land trades supported by falsified documents.

Complaints about these invasions presented by the territorial governments were simply ignored by the police. The Sandinista government also turned a blind eye to the illegal incursions, and to the serious security situation that had developed in the Northern Caribbean region. The resulting environmental damage has been staggering: more than half of the Bosawás Forest, which is a designated UNESCO Biosphere Reserve, has been lost since 1997, and no government reforestation program has yet been enacted (Silva 2015). The loss of habitat has also reduced the populations of animals that have traditionally been important sources of bushmeat, including *guardatinajas* (pacas) and *guatusas* (agoutis). The willful destruction of the Bosawás Forest led to the creation of an active environmental movement and organizations such as Misión Bosawás and Bacanalnica, which have used Facebook and other social media extensively to raise awareness of the situation. These mediated interventions often draw attention to the Sandinista government's failure to protect Nicaragua's forests and to plant live trees, rather than merely pouring millions of dollars into the erection of decorative metallic tree sculptures in the capital city of Managua.

In this chapter, we provide a detailed account of mediated popular struggles to defend Miskito and Mayangna land rights from illegal settlers in the Northern Caribbean region, and Rama-Kriol cultures and ways of life from the proposed (and now abandoned) Nicaraguan interoceanic canal in the Southern Caribbean region. We also explore how regional calypso music and culture draw upon diverse media resources to reconstitute and revivify Afrodescendant identities and to produce vibrant transmedia spaces that cut across and include different generations of Afro–Costa Ricans in the assertion of cultural, historical, and territorial rights and claims. We end with a discussion of the creative forms of online and offline activism mobilized during the 2018 popular uprisings against authoritarianism in Nicaragua. This chapter draws on media produced by Indigenous (Miskito, Mayangna, and Rama Kriol) and Black Creole Nicaraguans and Costa Ricans, as well as by young activists of mestizo descent, who are building new forms and practices of cultural citizenship and ways of doing democratic and decolonial politics.

By 2015, tensions over illegal settlement in the RACCN had escalated, especially in the communities around Waspam. The well-armed *colonos* were engaging in acts of intensifying violence, destroying Indigenous homes and crops, and displacing people from their own lands. Fifteen Indigenous people had been murdered by *colonos* and many more were injured while trying to reach or defend their communal territories. On 3 October 2015, the Centro por la Justicia y Derechos Humanos de la Costa Atlántica Nicaragua (CEJUDHCAN: the Center for Justice and Human Rights on the Atlantic Coast of Nicaragua) took the case of Waspam to the Inter-American Commission on Human Rights. The Commission acknowledged the gravity and urgency of the situation and granted cautious measures in favor of four communities: Esperanza, Santa Clara, Wisconsin, and Francia Sirpi, all of which belong to the Indigenous territory of Wangki Twi Tasba Raya (CEJIL 2015). In addition to using national and international law to defend their rights, CEJUDHCAN and their supporters began to make innovative use of the media resources that were available to them.

Given the urgency of the situation, territorial and communal leaders and human rights defenders were anxious to complete the land demarcation and titling process. As Law 445 did not specify how the final stage (*saneamiento*) of this process was to be carried out, activists appealed to the authorities in Managua to come to the negotiating table in the hope of reaching an agreement on these matters. Their efforts were, however, met with silence from the Sandinista government. In the face of this silence, CEJUDHCAN and community leaders produced a manual with an accompanying popular version that recommended a workable process. They then travelled to Managua to present their proposal to the relevant authorities. In the face of the Sandinistas' consistent and repeated non-responses, Black and Indigenous leaders used video cameras to document the latest phase of their struggle and uploaded the footage to YouTube. The result is a fourteen-minute film that captures the situation that confronted them. When the presidents of the twenty-three Black and Indigenous territories travelled by bus with their supporters along the arduous, two-day unpaved jungle route from Caribbean Nicaragua to the capital to meet with government officials at the Crowne Plaza hotel, the Managua-based officials failed to materialize. So, the Black and Indigenous leaders posted a video depicting a room full of empty chairs bearing the names of the members of the Nicaraguan government who refused to appear (Cejudhcan derechos humanos 2015a); in place of the absent Sandinistas is an explanation of Law 445, including the section that states that the central government must work with territorial leaders to complete the demarcation and titling of communal lands. Those Black and Indigenous leaders who have shown up to negotiate with the Sandinista government over the invasions of their ancestral territories tell the camera of the urgency of their situation, of the deepening threats to their ways of life, and of the serious environmental destruction enacted through the ever-intensifying presence of illegal settlers on their terrain. They then denounce the situation to the national media. The video thus draws attention to the Black and Indigenous leaders' failed attempts to engage in a horizontal and inter-epistemic dialogue with government authorities, and reveals that Nicaragua is not a space of democracy and social justice in which autonomy is flourishing, but rather is one in which Black and Indigenous rights, and even attempts at dialogue, are denied. The activist filmmakers conclude the video with footage of a march for justice in which their banners articulate the presence of the *colonos*, the government's failure to address the issue, and the problem of the proposed canal, thus casting all three as products of a common matrix of coloniality.

As a result of this video, the missing bodies of Nicaraguan government officials who may wish to communicate nothing at all, are instead made to communicate rather a lot about their attitudes toward Caribbean Coast autonomy and about the acceptability to the subordinated of these attitudes. The number of witnesses to this failed attempt to engage in peaceful dialogue was numerically expanded and spatially extended, moreover, once the video footage of the event was shared on YouTube. Hence, the event became spatially unbound and available for articulation (in the sense of linkage) to other places. In the process, the place meanings of Nicaragua as a site of democracy, which the government attempts routinely to stabilize, are similarly rearticulated (in the sense of resignification) to express (and oppose) the denial of Black and Indigenous rights and attempts at dialogue. As John Fiske (2016a: 230) writes, "making visible... is a form of counter-power, and the knowledge it produces and circulates works to construct and validate a counter-reality."

CEJUDHCAN went on to make several more videos that also produced knowledges that the Sandinistas were seeking to consign to the category of the unknown, including one with English voice-over and subtitles that strives to circulate these knowledges as a means of generating new transnational solidarities (Cejudhcan derechos humanos 2015b). For example, in July 2015, fifty community members from the territory of Wangki Twi Tasba Raya embarked on a field trip with members of CEJUDHCAN to determine the number of *terceros* present in their territory and to produce videographic documentation of the extent of ongoing natural resource destruction there. Their video (Cejudhcan derechos humanos 2015c) reveals the tragic felling of huge quantities of trees, the presence of cattle, and the pollution of rivers. A CEJUDHCAN technician explains in the film that this visibly rampant forest clearance was done not with machetes and axes, but with chain saws, thus indicating either that the *colonos* are not impoverished *campesinos*, or that if they are, they have been provided with expensive machinery by others in support of their efforts to colonize these indigenous communal lands. During filming, community members encounter a *colono* who tells them that he purchased one hundred manzanas (seventy hectares) of land for C$300,000 (or about US$8,000), and had already completely clear-felled forty-five of these. In this way, these filmmakers use cameras to bring into knowledge that which would otherwise go unseen and thus unknown: compelling evidence of illegal sales of their lands, and of extreme environmental and biodiversity destruction. What is unknown cannot be acted upon, so the production of knowledge is a source of mobilization.

Inspired perhaps by the new media visibility that CEJUDHCAN has brought to the conflict, a group of young Miskito men from the community of Francia Sirpi wrote, performed, and filmed a song about "the territorial invasion by the *colonos*" and their struggle for justice (Cejudhcan derechos humanos

2015d). These performers are shown gathered on their ancestral lands and singing about the "many problems and situations" that afflicted Francia Sirpi in 2015, including the inability to farm or safely cross the river, the disappearance of wildlife, and the widespread deforestation of cedar and mahogany trees. Their song describes an encounter with a *colono* who flees into the mountains in fear when confronted and entreats the "authorities" to "support us, support us." The song appropriates the language of Nicaragua's revolutionary past in its appeal to an imagined "*Comandante*: brave man, where are you?" The singers thus implicitly reject the mestizo masculinism of Daniel Ortega's latest incarnation as a counterrevolutionary strongman (*caudillo*) who calls upon the nation's revolutionary history only to serve his own narrow interests. In this way, these singers engage in a struggle for the meanings of Nicaraguan revolution and seek to extend those meanings to include and to advance their own struggles for Indigenous land rights against an illegal colonial invasion. When they call "where are you?" these Miskito singers indict the mestizo state for its failures to implement the law and uphold security, and they subvert the mestizo norm against which the Indigenous/Creole identity is repeatedly marked as other. The boys' appeal to Nicaragua's revolutionary past is encoded in what Fiske (2016b: 138) calls the "videolow" mode of a cell phone recording: a "low-technicity" that is "low in clarity but high in authenticity," for it stems from "the videolow's apparently continuous or metonymic relationship with the experiential truths (or 'true' experiences) of the socially disempowered." This sense of videographic authenticity is both enhanced by and reinforces the boys' evocations of Nicaragua's revolutionary history and tradition.

Starting in 2016 and 2017, the president of CEJUDHCAN, Lottie Cunningham, and other staff began to receive death threats via text messages as well as CEJUDHCAN's Facebook page, which suggests that their work was indeed drawing attention to the state's failure to protect life and territory in the North Caribbean. In March 2017, the threats to Lottie's life became the subject of an urgent appeal by the Dublin-based human rights organization Front Line Defenders, whereby they urged the Nicaraguan authorities to "carry out an immediate, thorough and impartial investigation into the threats against CEJUDHCAN's staff and other human rights defenders in Nicaragua, with a view to publishing the results and bringing those responsible to justice in accordance with international standards."

Local intercultural television channels such as TV7 also began to upload their broadcast content on the *colonos* to YouTube and Facebook to increase its circulation and its potential for transmediation across technologies and platforms. These social media platforms attract many more viewers than those who watch the original broadcasts. In this way, Nicaraguan media activists work to fulfil Michael Strangelove's (2015: 223) observation that "as states renege on their responsibility to provide information systems that promote democratic accountability, the internet appears well placed to revive the role of local news and an independent and critical press." In comparison with mainstream national media coverage, these reports that are produced by Indigenous and Black Creole broadcasters provide more context to the conflict with the *colonos*, give extended voice to the Miskito community members that are directly affected, inflect the broader narrative with Indigenous "accents" and ways of knowing, and advocate explicitly for Indigenous perspectives and positions. What we see is feisty Indigenous women and men fighting for their territorial rights with remarkably high levels of both legal and media literacy. In one such video, entitled "Conflict between miskitos and *colonos*" (Funez 2015), the reporter's voiceover says, "the Miskitos are tired of being trampled on by the *colonos* in their own home and they are ready to give their lives for Mother Earth. The laws are clear: these lands cannot be confiscated, sold or transferred. Nevertheless, there are corrupt people who are dealing in these transactions and getting rich, the consequences of which must be paid for." The video cuts to an upset and angry female community member who tells the reporter:

> We are ready to die defending our lands. They came to invade us, and they won't let us go to work. They have killed all the wild animals. Right now there is no peace for the Atlantic Coast. The Atlantic Coast has become a disaster. We don't have the right to live on our own land. This is our own land that our grandparents left to us more than 500 years ago, and they cared for it for their grandchildren, for the next generations. Those that come from the Pacific have no reason to come here.

Other community members go on to remind viewers that these are titled Indigenous lands and that the land ownership is enshrined in Nicaraguan law and the Constitution, and that it is the responsibility of the government to provide security and investigate human rights abuses.

Innovative media production notwithstanding, the situation in the Northern Caribbean region continued to deteriorate. As Mittel and Mayer (2020) document, the Ortega-Murillo government has made Nicaraguan ancestral lands available for mining and forestry concessions (and have shared in the profits generated thereby); these operations have continued to attract *colonos* to the region. Meanwhile, the Sandinista government acts repressively against those who oppose the illegal and environmentally destructive expansion of mining, forestry, and internal colonization. In January 2020, a Mayangna community was attacked by eighty armed men who killed four people and burned sixteen homes to the ground. This attack was followed by another on the Miskito community of Santa Clara in February 2020. In August 2021, nine Miskitos and three Mayangnas were massacred by *colonos* in the Bosawás Forest and their bodies were left hanging from a tree (Associated Press 2021). On 11 March 2023, in the remote Mayangna community of Wilu in the Bosawás, a group of heavily armed men murdered five members of a single family and burned sixteen homes to the ground, forcing their inhabitants to flee and take refuge in Musawas, a five-hour walk away. At the time of this writing, the situation in the North Caribbean remains extraordinarily challenging and the demand for *saneamiento* remains.

The Rama-Kriol community of Bangkukuk Taik in the South Caribbean was facing imminent destruction as a result of the proposed interoceanic canal. The community members worked with the Legal Assistance Centre for Indigenous Peoples (CALPI), a Nicaraguan NGO (now stripped of its legal status by the regime), to document the failure of the government to consult with them about the proposed canal and have demonstrated how it would destroy their culture and way of life. Their twenty-minute YouTube film (Bangkukuk Taik 2015) is analytically rich and contributes to the production and circulation of counter-knowledges that defy and challenge the government's colonial practices, including through its interrogation of apparent government lies about why a "tide marker" was placed in their community, of the Sandinistas' failure to either inform or consult with the people about the proposed canal, and of the state's efforts to deliver forms of development that are incompatible with the survival of Rama cultures. In the video, the villagers respond from an alternative epistemology that is rooted in a rich history and a self-sufficient economy that lies beyond and outside of the state. They offer an anticapitalist rejection of money and a sense of responsibility instead to land, water, flora, and fauna, whereby the elders transmit cultural practices and the Rama language to the children, and wherein time is understood to be nonlinear, as posterity and future well-being for Rama depends on conserving the efforts of ancestors. The film projects the beauty of everyday life, where food is abundant, culture is vibrant, children are free to swim and play baseball, and a sense of place and well-being are palpable. In response to the idea that the canal will bring development, the community pastor, Roberto Wilson says, "So I told them, I don't need money because we don't live by money. We live by the earth and the water that Jesus gave us in our territory and in our country. I don't need any money. I tell them, money is not good." The community treasurer, Kathelin Alvarado, says, "In here, we don't buy nothing, we get pretty fresh fish, we plant and we eat *tranquilo* [peacefully]. Nobody bothers us." The communal president of the neighboring community, Monkey Point, states that Law 840, which establishes the Sandinista government's right to dig a new interoceanic canal, "was created with one objective: to make the government could make the project without consulting anyone from Nicaragua. He [Ortega] just take the decision and do it how he wants and do what he wants in the territory. Use the land, the property where he wants to use it without having to consult with no one." The communal president's smooth shift of subject from "the government" to "he" here signals his rejection of the pretense of Nicaraguan democracy and his recognition and criticism of Ortega's authoritarian *caudillismo*. Similarly, the communal president of Bangkukuk Taik, Carlos Bilis, asserts that "we don't live by the government. Sorry to tell him but we don't live by the government." Bilis aligns the canal project with colonialism in his declaration that it aims to make the people of his community into the "slaves" of the mestizos. Nevertheless, Bilis defiantly asserts the rights of the Rama community under the law: "We have the last word about the issue of the canal because the land belongs to the Indigenous people." He thus occupies what Enrique Dussel describes as "the place of affirmation within which the negation in the negation of the system can take place" (quoted in Sáenz 2000: 214).

Rama-Kriol efforts to defend their communities, culture, and way of life is not antimodern but constitutes rather a multifrontal struggle for a particular form of Indigenous modernity. Indeed, the Rama-Kriol pursue this struggle and defend their rights and interests at a variety of scales and in a range of different institutional locations: in the Nicaraguan capital of Managua, at the United Nations, on YouTube and elsewhere on the internet (including through sites such as Avaaz and IndieGogo), in their interactions with international journalists, and in sites where they conducted detailed research into the canal proposal and developed appropriate forms of legal literacy necessary for the defense of their communities. They vociferously assert that the canal project, were it to proceed, would constitute epistemicide and culturecide, as well as the destruction of an ecosystem. The proposal to build a canal in their territory would threaten the Rama-Kriol's "collective right to survival as an organised people, with control over their habitat as a necessary condition for the reproduction of their culture, for their own development and to carry out their life aspirations"; this right was established in a 2005 Inter-American Commission on Human Rights ruling in the case of Ya Kye Axa Indigenous Community v. Paraguay (cited in Lenzerini 2014: 178–179). By positioning the canal as a hypermodern project embedded in modernist development discourses that can only look forward, the Rama-Kriol YouTube film powerfully imagines and asserts an alternative Indigenous modernity that struggles against the hegemonic one whose completion relies upon the continued production of coloniality (Mignolo 2005: xv).

In addition to issuing press releases to independent media operations, the Rama-Kriol people intensified their use of social media to denounce Ortega-Murillo's plans to build the canal and to confirm that they had neither been consulted about nor consented to the use of their lands in this way (see Onda Local 2016a, 2016b, 2016c). Thus, in July 2016, for example, a new twenty-four-minute Rama-Kriol video challenging the legitimacy of claims of communal consent to the canal project was posted on Vimeo and other social media sites (Bangkukuk Taik 2016). The film begins with subtitles that explain the significance of Law 445 (which ensures Rama-Kriol land rights) and Law 840 (which allows for the construction of the canal), displayed over images of everyday life in the Rama-Kriol communities of the Southern Caribbean Coast of Nicaragua. The video then cuts to a story that was broadcast on Sandinista TV in May 2016, and which reports on a purported "historic" agreement between the Rama-Kriol Territorial Government (GTRK) and the Nicaraguan Interoceanic Grand Canal

Commission, whereby, according to the report, the GTRK granted the consent of the nine Rama-Kriol communities to the construction of the canal. The remainder of the video travels through these Caribbean communities documenting the refusal of the people to accept the claims for their supposed consent to this agreement, and thus countering the narrative circulated by Sandinista TV. In community after community, people gather to state for the cameras and for the record that they were given no opportunity for free, prior, and informed consultation with regard to the proposed canal project, nor any chance to object on the basis of the devastating impacts it would have on their territories. Community members state that they were promised great wealth if they would sign, but nevertheless refused to do so. One community leader explains that "money never fools me. . . . Right now, we have a little fish. We have a little lobster. We have a little turtle. Maybe have one animal [per family]. We have a little land. But if that project come here now, we're going to have nothing. We're going to lose everything." In Bangkukuk Taik, citizens were told that they would be removed from their territory if the canal proceeds, and they protest that the first they have heard of such an outcome is from the makers of the video, despite Sandinista claims that they have been fully informed and have freely consented to the project. In Rama Cay, an impassioned woman proclaims that "money is temporary, but our territory is for eternity. We have to think, money will be spent, but our territory will always be here, and we have to defend it." In the video we see the Rama-Kriol people adding their signatures to a document that announces their rejection of the assertion that they have given their free, prior, and informed consent to the canal project.

The Rama-Kriol rejection of neoliberal and neocolonial globalization and environmentally and culturally destructive development, in tandem with their use of global online media platforms to assert their rights both as Rama and as indigenous peoples, and to connect with international law and global solidarity campaigns, can be understood in terms of what de Sousa Santos (2004: 240, emphasis in original) calls "the *ecology of trans-scale*," which recovers those elements of the local that are "not the result of hegemonic globalisation," and which therefore leads toward "the de-globalisation of the local and its eventual counter-hegemonic re-globalisation." The visual media activism of Rama-Kriol is one of the ways in which their diverse everyday ecologies are made visible to themselves and the world. These ecologies are pro-environment, pro-children, pro-linguistic protection, and based on a deep sense of place forged through horizontal community logics. Nicholas Mirzoeff (2015: 293) argues that the contemporary expansion of visual activism around the world stems from a widespread sense that "*they* do not represent *us*" (in multiple senses of the term "represent"). Hence, "a desire to live otherwise lies behind the worldwide surge in participatory media, from YouTube channels to Snapchatting, and performance" (295, emphasis added). "Visual activism" such as that undertaken by Rama-Kriol, and which Mirzoeff (297) defines as "the interactions of pixels and actions to make change," is oriented toward the production of "new ways to see and be seen, and new ways to see the world." Furthermore, Costeño-made media differ sharply from Sandinista-controlled news sources, which have not reported on the conflicts and present Caribbean autonomy as a Sandinista success story. Thus, "as states renege on their responsibility to provide information systems that promote democratic accountability" (Strangelove 2015: 223), activist Costeño video makers are emerging as members of a Central American digital vanguard and "an agenda-setting force" that is challenging official media narratives and authority (221).

Media activism on the Coast is not confined to those with the skills or support to make, edit, and upload their own films to YouTube. Many Costeños who are perhaps unable to engage in community media or online video production, are nevertheless extremely active on Facebook, where they share material about the conflicts and form solidarities with Indigenous groups elsewhere, especially in Panama and Honduras. Facebook pages run by Miskito and YATAMA activists frequently circulate memes and other graphical forms that critique the political forces and situations confronting them. This includes serious and humorous criticism of Miskito politicians who have been co-opted by the Sandinistas. Memes are central to convergence culture as they involve the reworking of dominant meanings through the disarticulation and rearticulation of disparate materials. They also pose an interesting challenge to the government's attempts to produce ignorance around key issues and events, as memes depend on "gaps and inconsistencies" that encourage creators to insert their own meanings (Shifman 2013: 199). Memes thus play a role in the process whereby popular discourses and knowledges participate in "filling the knowledge vacuums created by official silence," and thus intervening "into the epistemic void" such silence produces (Glynn 2000: 179).

As the power bloc has intensified its struggles to exert control while seeking to conceal its activities, grassroots media production, distribution, and visibility have become key practices of opposition and important modes of countersurveillance (Fiske 1998; see also Thompson 2005; Goldsmith 2010). The use of YouTube and Facebook to advance decolonial struggles is not, however, straightforward or without its contradictions and complications. Both are highly profitable commercial companies that algorithmically track users' viewing preferences and search terms. Yet they are platforms that are "both industry and user-driven" (Snickars and Vonderau 2009: 11) and can therefore be very useful to grassroots struggles and for "transmedia mobilization," whereby activists deploy "any and all available media channels to share their messages" (Jenkins 2016: 17).

YouTube is an active node in the convergent media environment where content constantly migrates to and from other parts of the internet and other mainstream media. It is routinely viewed on PCs, smartphones, tablets, and television sets. Having gained sufficient access to the technological tools and skill sets required to make, edit, and upload videos, the challenge for Costeños is to produce videos that are viewed, shared, and hopefully acted upon politically.

Costeños need "to be seen and heard" and "make others hear and see" (Thompson 2005: 49), though this is a potential that will not necessarily be realized, as the ongoing political violence perhaps attests. On the other hand, YouTube is also an archive (see, for example, Gehl 2009), and the YouTube channels created by Costeños, therefore, remain available to those who are not yet but in the near future will be digitally connected. While YouTube as an entity has turned into an "accidental and disordered public archive" (Burgess and Green 2009: 88), parts of it are becoming quite deliberately curated archives in which human rights abuses can be more systematically documented and accessed. Furthermore, mediated interventions accumulate and can at specific moments of crisis result in significant conjunctural shifts. Indeed, the situation in Nicaragua intensified in April 2018, as we discuss below.

Resisting Erasure: Afro-Costa Rican Identities

Kendall Cayasso Dixon is an Afrodescendant teacher, community leader, musician, and important role model to young Afro–Costa Ricans in the Caribbean city of Limón. He was inspired in part by his mother's long history of engagement in cultural activism within the area. When we first met Kendall in 2015, he was organizing an event in the Baptist church and wore long dreadlocks, which he attributed partly to his desire to de-stigmatize this hairstyle, as many who wear it are widely assumed to be drug addicts or criminals, rather than teachers or community leaders. Kendall described himself to us as a follower of Marcus Garvey, the famed Jamaican intellectual, journalist, and activist who travelled around the world in the early twentieth century promoting Black self-determination. Garvey founded the United Negro Improvement Association (UNIA) along with its shipping and transportation arm, the Black Star Line. The Black Star Line was a key part of Garvey's aspirations to spur a large-scale return to Africa by the descendants of formerly enslaved peoples, but both the shipping line (which was infiltrated by U.S. federal agents) and the twentieth-century incarnation of a Garvey-backed Back-to-Africa movement failed. Nevertheless, the UNIA, which is dedicated to Black improvement through education, hard work, and economic entrepreneurship, has gained a significant presence in many parts of the world, and Kendall is active in its Limón branch, which was created in 1919. Kendall is also the CEO of Townbook Limón, a multimedia communication project that aims "to empower our Afrodescendant youth" in the city "with the usage of technology and information and communication to rescue and project the different expression; cultural expressions of the Afrodescendant culture in Limon, Costa Rica."

Townbook Limón boasts the Garveyite slogan: "You need to know where you come from to know exactly where you're going to. Respect Limon." Their project involves working across community radio, television, and social media platforms, and they have developed a deliberately broad, dynamic, and transmediated approach that aims to get young Afro–Costa Rican people involved in a grassroots audiovisual process of cultural recovery. Townbook Limón has a particularly strong emphasis on music (reggae, calypso, and hip-hop) but has also expanded into many forms of Afrodescendant entrepreneurship, including tourism and gastronomy, UN initiatives such as the Decade for People of African Descent (2015–2024), graffiti art, and work in jails that together combine to create spaces in which young people of African descent can express themselves and encounter others doing the same. Their focus is also transnational and aims to both connect Afrodescendants throughout the Americas and project the cultures of Limón to the wider world in ways that challenge forms of anti-Black racism, such as those that have often been characteristic of mainstream national Costa Rican media. Kendall collaborates with a wide range of cultural workers in the region, who engage savvily with the contemporary convergent media environment that traverses radio, local television, YouTube, Facebook, TikTok, and other social media platforms. Their work is deeply embedded in the urban fabric of Limón, including via its presence in schools and other sites of education, such as the American Corner (a U.S.-government funded initiative that promotes English learning in the Limón central library), at music and film festivals, and in local businesses led by Afrodescendants.

By 2019, Kendall was broadcasting a weekly program on Limón cable TV that showcases the social, cultural, and economic contributions made by Afro cultures to Limón, a project he described as "a dream come true." Another local Afrodescendant cultural worker and artist, Glenda Halgarson Brown, who has combined her passion for Afro–Costa Rican gastronomy and music with a multimedia initiative dedicated to the recovery and maintenance of collective memory, draws on the struggles waged by older generations to provide cultural and economic resources for future generations of Afro–Costa Ricans. Speaking to us from the Marcus Garvey Liberty Hall in Puerto Viejo, she told us:

> So, the rich culture and the inheritance [my parents] had about the living, as we say in our projects, the living of a Caribbean soul, what they learn on the journey, they apply it. From Africa, from British, or from everywhere. They basically, mainly with their African roots but with a lot of knowledge they start to achieve working for other peoples, and keeping their traditions alive during the journey. It's amazing because it's a multicultural community, you know. We have our local English, Creole, some say broken, some call it Patois and then we become a very globalized community where we have to share with people around the world, not just as tourists but citizens or inhabitants of Puerto Viejo, the South Caribbean. In the middle of this transformation and evolution we started to work, like five years ago on a project where we were declared a cultural interest by the Ministry of Culture.... We developed a cultural center, but a center of culture with a sustainable economical perspective for development. Like from culture how can we really be a community

that can use the riches of our culture to translate it into economic incomes. And to do that we need to recuperate our memories, we need to recuperate our values. We need to look back and recognize in the work of our ancestors. We need to research and see what they did to have this place for so long and how they approached the resources we have in the area. Our work involves exposing [exhibiting] old pictures. Recovering memories. Making events where the kids can be influenced by the knowledge and the traditions and culture of our ancestors. With the school. With the neighbors. With the tourists. From here: from the cultural house. . . . This is the Branch 301 [of the Marcus Garvey Liberty Hall], Puerto Viejo. It started very small and it was a space for the Black people to meet to get strength, ideas and propose projects for development. You know, Marcus Garvey ideas was so clear that they should not have a slave mentality and they have the potential to be successful in business, in education and other skills that he also was an example for in his communities. So, three years ago, the house, a lot of it was abandoned and so forth. So, that is a little bit of my work, like, restoring. I work, like, developing projects, not only to restore the infrastructure but to restore the memories. First, we start by motivating the people to make use of the space. And making events, when it wasn't, like, renewed, like now. It is very nice for us now. And after we start that process, two areas: restoration of the building, and then the restoration of the memories. And I start to work on this. Like we start exposing pictures and making drama with the kids about the old days, so much and so forth.

Calypso as Transmedia

One of the most exciting transmedia initiatives that has developed in Costa Rica in recent years has been around the cultural tradition of calypso. As a result of the efforts of a new generation of calypsonians and activists that draw on and extend its rich cultural traditions, calypso is becoming a kind of connective tissue that is capable of articulating multiple transgenerational elements of Afrodescendant struggle and being, and this tissue is increasingly projected and extended through the networked assemblages of the new media environment. Much of the history of Costa Rican calypso is captured in a 2021 documentary, *The Calypsonians of Today/Los Calypsonianos de Hoy*, which was directed by Afro–Costa Rican musician, audiovisual artist, and anthropologist Ramón Morales-Garro, was screened in 2022 on Kendall's Afrodescendant LimónTV show and on which we draw extensively (along with material from our own interviews) in the analysis that follows.[1] The film examines the roots and evolution of the genre, and how it is gaining new relevance in the contemporary media environment as an agent of Afro–Costa Rican cultural revival, assertion, and self-determination. Morales-Garro, with the support of the Limón Association for Art, Race and Culture (Asociación Limonense de Arte, Raíz y Cultura), has also completed a four-part YouTube series on calypso. Academic research on calypso within Costa Rica has been gaining momentum as well.

Calypso is a musical genre with Angolan origins that became established in many parts of the Anglophone Caribbean. It was brought to Costa Rica's Caribbean Coast by Black immigrant workers who travelled there from Jamaica in search of employment. It is likely that in the evenings as early as the 1920s, banana and cacao plantation workers were singing and reworking old Jamaican mento songs enjoyed by their parents and grandparents into a Costa Rican calypso vernacular (Morales-Garro 2022). While calypso is important in other Caribbean countries, including Panama and Trinidad, limonense calypso has its own distinctive style. Its key influence is undoubtedly Jamaican mento, though it also draws on cumbia, guaracha, cuadrilla, and reggae. Over time the genre has creatively incorporated new elements. The original conga drum and guitar were replaced by banjos, ukuleles, clarinets, maracas, and box drums. The calypsonians also modified and popularized older songs from Jamaica or Nicaragua (Monestel 2003) and paid little attention to Euromodern notions of textual fixity, individual authorship, or intellectual property. For example, "Launch Turn Over" is about a shipwreck off the island of Uvita near Limón, but originally commemorated a shipwreck off the coast of Bluefields, Nicaragua. Most Costa Rican calypso songs nevertheless originate in Limón or Cahuita. Limonense calypso also incorporates elements of Rastafarianism and the spirit of Jah. For instance, calypsonians "take pauses to breathe" and make references to Babylon (*The Calypsonians of Today* 2021; Monestel 2003). The Caribbean Coast of Costa Rica is home to many famous Calypsonians, including Walter "Gavitt" Ferguson, who died at the age of 103 in February 2023, having composed more than 200 songs and deeply influenced younger generations of calypso performers. Some call him the Bob Marley of Costa Rica.[2]

Calypso has long involved grassroots and participatory forms of mediation and dissemination. In his youth, Ferguson could barely afford train fare to travel the twenty-five miles from his home in Cahuita to Limón to perform; he recorded thousands of cassettes of his music that he sold to people, including tourists who visited the region, for a few *colones* to help support himself. His son, Peck recounts that "if somebody wanted a tape, he would send one of us to the store to get a blank cassette and he would fill it up with song. And each time somebody came, he would need to sing and record again," so that each tape was a unique record of a different performance. Ferguson did not record a CD with a record company until 2002 (MacLeod, 2019). Calypso also involves a great deal of social and political commentary, as well as improvisational, agonistic, and combative traditions that gave rise to a vibrant cultural dynamic of *call and response* that has helped to generate a competitive ethos between calypsonians throughout the Caribbean. In her account of the emergence of calypso in nineteenth-century Trinidad, Gail-Ann Greaves (1998: 326) writes that the medium "provided slaves with an opportunity to assemble socially and to communicate" by singing "about their ancestors and gods, about injustices perpetrated by slave masters, about oppressive social conditions, about those brave enough to resist their masters, and about how they would rebel. Thus emerged the initial form of the calypso of political commentary, which interpreted, evaluated, judged, and satirized policies and actions of the European government and ruling class." On the Caribbean Coast of Costa Rica more than a century later, Walter Ferguson displayed so much talent as a calypsonian lyricist that he was urged to participate in a lyrical fight or "sing-off" with the Panamanian calypsonian, Lord Cobra. Although this event never actually got off the ground, such musical challenges and "duels" were commonplace. As Morales-Garro (2022: 7–8, our translation) writes, "a calypsonian had to be mentally prepared to create eloquent rhymes and think up jokes in seconds, to mock his opponent and entertain the audience." Calypso had thus appeared as a key idiomatic form in the genealogy of agonistic African diasporic musical and linguistic practices that would ultimately include "playing the dozens," "signifyin'," and jazz improvisation, all of which required, promoted and developed "performative skills" and a "sheer wit" that, as Kobena Mercer (1987: 46) notes, "defied the idea that Black English was a degraded 'version' of the master language" by "systematically subverting" the "white master code" and "voice of authority." This linguistic bravado has also been a key ingredient in the emergence and development of "Black Twitter," as scholars of the new media environment have argued (see Florini 2014; Brock 2020). André Brock (2020: 82) notes the importance of "signifyin'" (see Smitherman 1977; Gates 1983) as a key "marker of Black cultural identity" that is crucial for the distinctiveness of Black Twitter and argues that "it is the articulation of a shared worldview, where recognition of the forms plus participation in the wordplay signals membership in the Black community. From this perspective, Black discourse moves from a bland information transfer to a communal commentary on political and personal realities."

Like Black Twitter, calypso is a crucial site for the performative production of communal identities, political commentaries, and solidarities within the Black Atlantic (Gilroy 1993), as well as an element in a genealogy of the remix culture we discussed in chapter 1, in part for its participatory blurring of boundaries between composition, performance, and reception. Manuel Monestel (2003) observes that calypso involves the creative promotion of two distinct identities, a dualism that captures the spirit of Anancy, a cunning trickster spider figure that was brought to the Caribbean from Ghana with the transatlantic slave trade and is central to Caribbean folklore and storytelling. The calypsonian endures a marginal socioeconomic status, but his ability to master song makes him powerful and gives him the capacity like Anancy, to creatively find his way out of any difficult situation he may be in. Furthermore, calypso facilitates the adoption of a range of distinct identities that can be put on and taken off; the calypsonian might self-deprecate (the calypsonian *pobrecito* or "one pant man") or, alternatively, overvalue his own abilities (the "king of calypso").[3] Calypso lyrics have historically drawn attention to the marginal status of Black Costa Rican people, their exclusion from the mestizo nation-building project, and their struggle for recognition and land rights. One of Walter Ferguson's best-known songs, "Cabin in the Wata," tells the story of a Black man named Bato, who was displaced by the creation of the National Park in Cahuita and so forced to build his cabin in the water (Monestel 2013). The song tells of the dispute between Bato and the Director of the National Park in Cahuita:

> Now they came to a big dispute
> Bato said me born in Costa Rica
> You could have born in Ethiopia
> Me no want no cabin in the wata

In the 1940s and 1950s, calypso was performed without amplification, mostly in private homes, at picnics, or on the beach, although it was also sometimes played in the Limón Black Star Line building. The genre was popular on the Caribbean Coast of both Panama and Costa Rica but was not known in San José (Monestel 2003). The performers were not able to make a living from their music and often worked in construction or other sectors in order to survive economically. Some, however, started to perform in the street to earn money. *The Calypsonians of Today* describes how El Combo Alegre started playing in a San José restaurant, Los Lechones, where, as the calypso singer Ulysses Grant notes, it was received by the people of San José as an exotic musical form that had not originated in Costa Rica. Over time, the genre's popularity grew in the capital city, San José, as well as on the Caribbean Coast, and some calypsonians, especially Walter Ferguson, but also Alfonso "Gianty" Goulbourne, Herbert Glinton "Lenky," Papa Tún, Ulysses Grant, Manuel Monestel, Cyril Sylvan, and Rafael Zapata, became household names. They are now joined by younger calypso bands such as Caribbean Calypso, Changó, Leche de Coco, Di Gud Frenz, and Shanty y su Calypso.

Alfonso "Gianty" Goulbourne notes that by the 1960s and 1970s calypso had become a well-established media form such that, "like the newspaper, through calypso everyone knew what was happening in town." Similarly, calypso scholar Haydee Jimenez told Morales-Garro (2022: 12) that calypso was the main source of news on Costa Rica's Caribbean Coast at a time when the people of Puerto Viejo had no radio, television, or internet: "Someone who came on the bus told something that happened to the president and with that information an improvised song appeared. So that story tells us that calypso is the reporter of the people, that calypso tells anecdotes, that it gives us a summary of what is happening. That is something that I lived in Puerto Viejo." Jimenez described how she would arrive in the national capital, San José, some 137 miles from her home, having already learned from calypso the stories that were circulating in the press there. Famous calypso songs often tell the stories of disasters and other social challenges, including earthquakes ("Terremoto Coming"), hurricanes ("Hurricane Joan"), shipwrecks ("Launch Turn Over"), malaria ("Zancudo"), class struggle ("Retribution"), and fungal infestations that devastated the cacao crop ("Monilia"). As Monestel (2003: 32–33, our translation) writes, "the dynamic social history of Limón and its constant ups and downs serve as the framework for cultural expressions like the Limón calypso, which follows Limón's rhythms and emerges as a song genre with a versatility and malleability that has no comparison in other Costa Rican musical genres. Calypso *limonense* is somehow heir to this rich and sinuous history, which it captures in its lyrics, its rhythm and its melodies. The rhythmic and thematic nuances of the songs seem to follow the steps and the setbacks that Limón has faced since its origins."

By the 1980s, however, calypso was clearly in decline across the region and was widely seen as a musical genre that belonged to old people and offered little if anything of interest to Afrodescendant youth. While reggae remained popular across the region at this time, calypso was being displaced by newer genres such as hip-hop and reggaeton. In recent years, however, thanks to the commitments of a new generation of musicians, including Kendall and his collaborator, Mike Joseph, as well as that of veteran musician and researcher, Manuel Monestel, and their creative harnessing of transmedia technologies, capacities, and competencies, calypso is now gaining a new status and enhanced visibility. Mike Joseph describes how he and Kendall were inspired by a calypso performance at the 2015 Cahuita festival, where they saw calypsonian Junior Alvarez performing with his young son, Danny, and disrupting the notion that passion for this music was confined to elderly men. Mike Joseph then began to think seriously about calypso as a genre that is rich with cultural and political possibility for the twenty-first century and started to perform with a band called Leche de Coco. He and Kendall subsequently formed Di Gud Frenz and now perform calypso fused with reggae at live shows on Costa Rica's Caribbean Coast for audiences of all ages. These performances, furthermore, connect not only different generations but online and offline cultural and political spaces as well. Di Gud Frendz circulate their live performances on Facebook and other social media sites where they gain additional audiences (see figure 8.1).[4] As activists, Kendall and Mike have promoted an expanding cultural reevaluation and reenergization of calypso that has given the genre renewed visibility, a growing audience, and enhanced recognition and status in official political spaces. In 2012, Costa Rican Executive Decree No. 37418-C gave "special recognition" to calypso as a key element of "national patrimony" and cultural identity (Tico Times 2012). In 2018, a bill originally introduced by Epsy Campbell Barr, the Vice-President of Costa Rica and the first woman of African descent to serve as the vice-president of any Latin American nation, declared Walter Ferguson a "distinguished citizen," and declared that 7 May, his birthday, shall be observed every year as the National Day of the Costa Rican Calypso (*AM Costa Rica* 2021). In 2020, in conjunction with the "Historic Month of Afrodescendants in Costa Rica," Ferguson was "immortalized" in a

FIGURE 8.1 Di Gud Frendz in the studio. (Source: Di Gud Frenz, reproduced with permission.)

postmark featuring a line drawing of him singing into a microphone, thus ensuring that his face would travel around the world as an icon of calypso's "intangible cultural heritage," as Campbell Barr put it (*TCRN* 2020).

Calypso in Costa Rica is thus achieving renewed levels of visibility, status, and engagement among a generation of Black Costa Ricans who are harnessing new media technologies articulated to the reenergization of participatory Afrodescendant political cultures and are rediscovering the genre's rich traditions and historical links to (trans)regional identities and struggles. Mike Joseph, for example, embraces the traditional notion of calypso as information and news media and says that performing this music makes him feel like a journalist communicating about important events and life experiences, searching for information and putting it out there (*buscan una información y la exponen*), and challenging mainstream coverage that depicts Afro Costa Rica as a site of violence (*The Calypsonians of Today* 2021). While some express concerns about the commercialization or commodification of calypso,[5] Kendall and Mike situate its performance (and that of other Afro–Costa Rican music) within struggles for Afrodescendant livelihoods and insist that calypsonians and other Afrodescendant cultural workers must be able to earn a living from their labor. As Kendall told us, it is crucial to dismantle the idea that Afro culture is something that can be freely consumed without regard for whether its producers are compensated for their work. For Mike, calypso means "travelling with positive vibes, feeling proud to be from Limón and honoring what our ancestors did here." But he also stresses that calypso must be commercially viable enough to ensure that musicians can live with dignity while they use this music to subvert the hegemonic ideologies of *mestizaje* that stigmatize Limón, the Caribbean Coast, and its inhabitants. The rise of the new transmedia environment has become one of the conditions of possibility for the commercial viability of the work of a new generation of young calypsonians.

An additional important benefit stems from calypso's role in the maintenance of Creole English, which is increasingly marginalized by Spanish language dominance in the region. Indeed, calypso's participatory lyric formation and creative uses of Creole English, Creole French, and African vernacular expressions provide a powerful "platform for the renovation" of limonense identities in the face of the serious threat posed by Hispanicization throughout the Caribbean Coast (Herzfeld and Moskowitz 2004: 260). As Monestel (2013: 70, our translation) emphasizes, "the Limón calypso is a bastion of the persistent struggle for the preservation of Afro-Caribbean culture and heritage in the province of Limón, in a Costa Rican historical context plagued by segregation, invisibilization, persecution, and open and latent racism." In recent years, Afro–Costa Rican activists have begun to activate transmedia, translinguistic, transgenerational, and transgeneric properties of calypso and are providing a source of Afrodescendant affirmation, pride, and income, while also intervening in the formal political sphere and energizing the politics of antiracism within the region. But while cultural and political spaces that support Afrodescendant life and well-being have been creatively expanding in Costa Rica, Nicaraguans are struggling with intensified political repression that requires a different kind of transmedia response.

Digital Activism and the 2018 Nicaraguan Uprisings

In 2018, the growing authoritarianism in Nicaragua that we outlined in chapter 7 descended into violent, state-led repression. As noted, the FSLN government was faced with serious and expanding political opposition from environmentalists, anti-canal *campesinos*, Indigenous and Afrodescendant leaders, independent (including Indigenous) media sectors, NGOs, human rights defenders, and feminist activists, and as these oppositional factions accumulated, they began to merge, fuse, and explode in April 2018. This situation gave rise to a dramatic expansion, then, of social movement activism led especially by digitally connected and media-savvy students and other young people who erupted onto the streets of the capital and in many other towns and cities. These self-organizing grassroots movements (*autoconvocados*) started demanding Ortega's removal from power and the democratization of the country. Nicaraguan police and paramilitary forces, in turn, responded with violence and killed hundreds, while many more were taken as political prisoners. Over the course of 2018 and 2019, these uprisings benefited from a proliferating array of digital activisms characterized by viral and spreadable spontaneity, hashtag creativity, digital artwork production, and meme generation. Moreover, these digital activisms drew on and honored Nicaragua's revolutionary history by disarticulating radical slogans from their links with the FSLN and rearticulating them with the current emergent moment of uprising and political possibility. In this section, we assess the significance of these uprisings within the wider context of the convergent media environment and explore the role of everyday media platforms such as Facebook and Twitter in the production of spaces for the generation and facilitation of a heterogeneous multiplicity of revolutionary subjectivities and identities. Our analysis is rooted in debates about media convergence that emphasize both continuities with and transformations of the "old" media environment, and through which we trace digital activists' practices of discursive circulation across multiple media platforms and technologies, as well as their practices of articulation, disarticulation, and rearticulation, which worked to shift and expand the conditions of political possibility on the ground.

As noted, political antagonisms in Nicaragua escalated dramatically in April 2018, when popular struggles against the increasingly authoritarian government gave rise to full-blown street protests that took place in all the country's major cities and towns. There were two main triggers: a fire that the government allowed to burn out of control in the Indio Maíz Reserve and neoliberal pension reforms announced by the Sandinista government that would increase workers' contributions while reducing their benefits. Widespread protests against these two developments converged on 18 April and drew a violent response from the police and Sandinista mobs. On the next day, protestors began occupations at several university campuses in the capital city of Managua and launched other actions in the towns and cities of Monimbó, Masaya, León, Matagalpa, Granada, Carazo, Boaco, Rivas, and Estelí, many of which are sites with important revolutionary histories. While the protestors relied on homemade mortars and stones, police and paramilitary forces were heavily armed. Several independent media channels were forced to close while Daniel Ortega's wife and vice president, Rosario Murillo, flooded the airwaves with official denunciations of the protestors as "right-wing vandals," "bloodthirsty vampires," and "tiny groups" of "mediocre beings" with "mean souls." Ortega-Murillo simultaneously began to establish a sweeping, "cross-governmental" network of digital surveillance operations and "troll farms" designed to target and undermine critics of their regime (Davis 2021; Diaz 2021; 100% Noticias 2021). Moreover, Ortega-Murillo foreshadowed the justificatory formula Vladimir Putin would use after his invasion of Ukraine three years later when they excused Nicaraguan state violence by calling the Nicaraguan uprisings an attempted right-wing coup orchestrated by the forces of U.S. imperialism.

The next few days and weeks were characterized by dramatic street protests, organized opposition marches, and very heavy-handed government repression. Masked paramilitaries in Hilux trucks (which some organizations have called "parapolice") began arbitrarily detaining and killing protestors. The Bluefields community television journalist Ángel Gahona, who was one of our research participants whom we quoted in chapter 7, was shot and killed while delivering a Facebook Live report on these events.[6] In response, protestors began to tear down Ortega-Murillo's metallic trees, hold candlelit vigils, and, in scenes reminiscent of the revolutionary struggle of the 1970s, erect barricades in the streets. Formal and less formal civil society movements began to emerge, including the Civic Alliance for Justice and Democracy, the Madres de Abril (made up of mothers of children and young people killed by government forces as the state-led violence intensified), and the Movimiento Universitario 19 de Abril. Across social media, a proliferation of pages, groups, hashtags, and accounts with names that reference the April uprising began to emerge and grow. This proliferation drew in a heterogeneous collection of actors, including students, women, LGBTQ+ activists, *campesinos*, and Indigenous and Afrodescendant leaders who have all united in their opposition to Ortega-Murillo.

At a multisectoral dialogue that was convened by the Catholic Church, televised, and livestreamed on Facebook, student leaders Lesther Alemán and Madelaine Caracas galvanized the nation by speaking directly and defiantly to Daniel Ortega about the violence and reading out the names of all those killed by Sandinista forces. These interventions, which were widely shared and spread through social media, seriously undermined the government's attempts to restore the status quo. Nevertheless, the dialogue failed after a few days, and government paramilitaries continued their attacks on protestors. The barricades were bulldozed by the state, more than 300 people were killed, and many thousands were injured. In the Carlos Marx barrio in Managua, regime forces set fire to the home of a family that had refused snipers the use of their roof to target dissidents and activists; the fire killed six members of the Velázquez Pavón family, including a three-year-old child and a four-month-old baby. This deadly act of political arson has been characterized by both the Organization of American States and the Inter-American Court of Human Rights as a crime against humanity that remains unpunished (Havana Times 2023). In addition, more than 700 people were taken into custody and held as political prisoners, and more than 50,000 Nicaraguans were driven into exile. Moreover, numerous international human rights organizations, including Amnesty International and the Organization of American States Group of Interdisciplinary Independent Experts (GIEI), issued reports condemning the severity of state-led human rights abuses that have been carried out by police and parapolice forces, including the use of threats, torture, intimidation, and arbitrary detention (Amnesty International 2018; GIEI 2018).

Over the next few months, digital activism and urban rebellion converged in important ways. We reject essentializing and sometimes technologically deterministic approaches that substitute sweeping techno-utopian or techno-pessimistic discourses for engagement with what activists actually do with social media tools and resources (cf. Gerbaudo 2012). As Grant Bollmer (2018: 28, emphasis added) writes, social media do not "inherently democratize the means of communication" and thus "directly *cause* democratic revolutions." Nevertheless, the forms of connectivity, spreadability, and other affordances associated with media digitalization, miniaturization, distributed networking, and mobility have been enlisted to advance grounded political struggles and produce profound material consequences. For several months, digital activism undertaken in conjunction with the ongoing political uprisings was widespread, diverse, and highly creative. Digital activists and ordinary Nicaraguan citizens have been using their cellphones along with Facebook, Twitter, and YouTube, sometimes openly and sometimes anonymously, to document their rebellion, share images of police and parapolice brutality, contest the official discourses of the regime, and generate solidarities. Some of the films and photos of state-led brutality on social media contained scenes of very graphic violence that the regime would prefer did not circulate. Social media were used to raise awareness of kidnappings and detentions by the government, to make visible the many funerals of those killed by the regime, to spread handwritten letters composed by political prisoners seeking to document their inhumane treatment at the hands of the state, and to circulate a vast trove of artistic works created by painters, graphic designers, cartoonists, sculptors, poets, and musicians inspired by the rebellion. Those who the regime attempted to silence in the most dramatic fashion found ways to speak, their voices amplified and spatially extended by ordinary people's sharing practices. The mobilization of cellphones and other devices as noted above is important, not least for its challenge to the state's ability to exert control over the images and narratives used to produce a socially effective sense of events (Faris and Meier 2013).

The bottom-up mediation of the rebellion produced a number of viral and shareable moments as Twitter and other social media platforms have become central sites of discursive contestation between the regime and grassroots movements. The rebellion's practices of remixing, rearticulating, and recirculating helped to produce a number of new iconic figures and leaders among a largely horizontal and self-organizing movement. For instance, in April 2018, a red-hatted protestor's angry denunciation of Ortega in the revolutionary community of Monimbó in Masaya was captured on a cellphone, spread quickly across the convergent mediascape and a variety of urban landscapes, and thus gave rise to *"Comandante Caperucita Roja"* (Commander Little Red Riding Hood). Similarly, in September 2018, cellphone users captured the violent arrest of seventy-eight-year-old water seller Doña Coquita for giving free water to protestors. Like Caperucita Roja, Coquita soon became an iconic national symbol of protest as T-shirts bearing her image appeared throughout the country, dissidents rushed to take selfies with her, and the legendary Nicaraguan revolutionary folk singer Carlos Mejía Godoy (who has been in exile in the United States for years) dedicated a song to her.[7]

Throughout the uprising, the mobilization of a horizontally- and self-organized urban opposition via the deployment of barricades, marches, vigils, and graffiti was met with consistently brutal state violence and repression. In response, a massive outpouring of grassroots digital activism raised awareness of this brutality and circulated counternarratives of the Ortega-Murillo regime. Urban uprising in the streets and digital activism online have thus been mutually constitutive and reinforcing phenomena in Nicaragua. The brutality faced there by opponents of the regime included the violent removal of their barricades by Sandinista bulldozers and the unconstitutional criminalization of peaceful protest and assembly; these repressive measures have made organization of the rebellion in urban spaces increasingly difficult and eventually brought them to an end. Nevertheless, the forms of urban resistance we have witnessed to date continue to have a mobilizing effect and continue to generate a collective sense of solidarity and determination to topple the government. As scholars writing on the 2006 Oaxaca uprising have asserted, barricades produce forms of "barricade sociality" (Dzenovska and Arenas 2012) that persist in collective popular imaginaries long after these barricades have been physically removed (see also Magaña 2016). Online artwork and other forms of digital activism have also persisted (Nísia 2019) and contributed to the production and maintenance of a vital, dissident barricade sociality in Nicaragua (see figures 8.2 and 8.3).[8] One feminist-inspired video created by Olga Valle and Madelaine Caracas, narrated by Alicia Henriquez, and released in May 2021 describes how the violence of April 2018 has become quotidian.[9] While popular memories of April 2018 invoke fears of repression, of government agents shooting at peaceful protesters, of university courses that could not be finished, and of homes under siege, they also work to rekindle the memory of hope, of newly forged solidarities, of dissident companionships, of resistance unleashed, and of struggles for human rights, liberty, and justice. This underscores how the crisis and its digitalization have given rise to the emergence and circulation of a broader analysis of conjunctural linkages between the feminization, racialization, and precaritization of human bodies and the power bloc's attacks on wider environments and biodiversity.

We have identified four interconnected strategies of discursive articulation, disarticulation, and rearticulation that were mobilized by the rebellion to engage in transmedia activism that produces and sustains oppositional forms of barricade sociality. The first involves the disarticulation of radical slogans from their links with the FSLN and their rearticulation with the current uprisings in a way that honors and renews Nicaragua's revolutionary history. For more than a decade

FIGURE 8.2 "We've always fought with the conviction that this revolution will either be inclusive or it will not *be*." This artwork calls for an inclusive and pro-LGBTQ+ rebellion. (Source: Artwork by Clausunk and Suprime. Retrieved from Nísia 2019.)

now, Daniel Ortega's regime has been compared with the Somoza dictatorship that Ortega helped to overthrow, and many of Ortega's former revolutionary comrades differentiate between *Sandinismo* and *Danielismo* or *Orteguismo* (that is, support for the historical Sandinista movement rather than support for the leadership of Daniel Ortega) to designate Ortega's betrayal of the core principles of the Sandinista revolution. The use of revolutionary rhetoric to oppose Ortega did not originate with the April uprising but was deeply intensified by it. The movement appropriated a number of slogans from the Sandinista revolution, including "*Que se rinda tu madre*" (literally, "Let your mother surrender," which were the final words yelled by the revolutionary poet Leonel Rugama at Somoza's National Guard in 1970 when they demanded his surrender from the safe house in which he was hiding); "*Nicaragua volverá a ser República*" ("Nicaragua will be a republic again," which was a pronouncement made by newspaper editor Pedro Joaquín Chamorro, whose assassination by Somoza's national guard was instrumental in generating broad popular support for the Revolution); and "*Patria Libre para Vivir*" ("Free country in order to live," a modification of "*Patria Libre o Morir*," "Free country or death"). Similarly, the 2018 rebellion reappropriated and rearticulated the "motherist" discourses of the Sandinista revolution, which honored mothers who had sacrificed their sons and daughters to the revolutionary struggle against Somoza and the U.S.-backed Contra, and who were thus highly revered as the "Mothers of Heroes and Martyrs."[10] Today, one of the most prominent and vocal opposition groups to

FIGURE 8.3 *Guegüense* in rebellion. This image deploys the Indigenous theatrical trickster figure of the *Guegüense*. (Source: Artwork by Noland Castellón Pineda. Retrieved from Nísia 2019.)

emerge has been the Madres de Abril (the Mothers of April), who are, as noted previously, the mothers of the young people killed by the government in 2018. The movement has thus drawn on Nicaragua's revolutionary past as a key critical resource through which to challenge not only the state's repressive brutality and violations of human rights, but also its betrayal of the principles of the revolution, for which its own current leader once fought, and its recidivistic verticalism and corrupt *caudillismo*.

The second digital activist strategy involves the satirical reappropriation and rearticulation of the statements and utterances of the current government, especially those of vice president Rosario Murillo, in a manner that deprives them of their seriousness and discursive power. For instance, many protestors have in their social media profiles and elsewhere ironically embraced or reclaimed the terms of derogation that Rosario Murillo generated to refer insultingly to them. They have thus converted terms like *"vandálicos"* (vandals) *"golpistas"* (coup plotters) and *"minúsculos"* (insignificant little people) into sources of oppositional identity and pride, and they have otherwise mocked and parodied the regime's discourses of legitimation and self-authorization.

The third strategy involves the resignification of signs of the nation. Rita Segato (2016) notes that totalitarian regimes rely on nationalistic and primordialist discourses to constitute loyalty to the state and maintain narrative control within the social and political realms. All the rebellion's marches, barricades, vigils, and international solidarity events have made use of blue and white Nicaraguan national flags and balloons. In October 2018, forty different opposition movements formed the Blue and White Alliance (Alianza Azul y Blanco) to present a united front against *Orteguismo*. These practices of resignification have proven so threatening to the regime that protestors have been arrested simply for carrying a Nicaraguan flag or blue and white balloons. Consequently, the term *"azul y blanco"* became synonymous with the rebellion and people started to daub walls, benches, and other spaces with blue and white paint or stickers as a way to *"retomar las calles"* (retake the streets). Other protestors drew upon elements of popular culture that are central to Nicaraguan national identity, such as the Indigenous theatrical trickster figure of the *Güegüense*, which has been used in social media to resignify images of police brutality through folkloric tactics of anti-coloniality, just as the original figure of the *Güegüense* was used for centuries by Indigenous peoples to subvert Nicaragua's imposed colonial order. This is not the first time that the *Güegüense* has been mobilized against the FSLN; it was also drawn upon by popular sectors in the 2006 electoral campaign to question the FSLN electoral strategy (see Cupples 2009b).

The fourth strategy is the articulation of the Nicaraguan struggle to other Latin American progressive movements in order to forge international alliances and solidarities, especially by using Twitter hashtags such as #SOSNicaragua and #NosEstánMatando. While these movement-generated hashtags are often quite specific to Nicaragua, some of them also connect with broader struggles across Latin America, and particularly with events in Venezuela, but also with hashtags used in Colombia and elsewhere to denounce femicides and the murders of human rights and environmental defenders (e.g., #NosEstanMatando and #NiUnaMenos). By the same token, the hashtag #MeDueleRespirar ("it hurts me to breathe") refers to the words uttered by fifteen-year-old Alvaro Conrado after he was shot by *Orteguista* paramilitaries on 20 April 2018, and also to the Black Lives Matter #ICan'tBreathe hashtag.

The new Nicaraguan mediascape thus became an important terrain of ongoing struggle over the future of *Orteguismo*. In a context where the state controls much of the mainstream media and relentlessly attacks independent journalism and journalists, ordinary Nicaraguans have turned to digital activism, using their cellphones and Facebook, Twitter, and YouTube accounts to circulate images of police and parapolice violence and to capture and spread the spirit of rebellion present in marches, jails, and elsewhere on the streets. Their user-generated images and videos became key constituents of national and international mainstream media coverage and of emergent solidarities, as well as important sources for those investigating human rights abuses in Nicaragua. As David Faris and Patrick Meier (2013: 198) write, social media do not simply add extra implements to the toolkits of activists, for they can "fundamentally alter certain types of interaction between authoritarian governments and their opponents." Nicaragua's digital activists have intervened in and disrupted the regime's ability to mobilize and turn the discursive repertoire of the Sandinista revolution toward the defense of authoritarianism and have reappropriated the signs and discourses of Nicaraguan nationhood and its popular revolutionary cultures. This left the regime cornered and its strategies of communication, legitimation, and self-authorization seriously damaged to the extent that it decided it had no choice but to release a large group of political prisoners in 2019. Nevertheless, in 2020 and 2021, state-led repression escalated again as the regime passed new laws under which opposition activists could be convicted as enemies of the state for treason or for undermining national integrity. In 2021, the regime began rounding up a new wave of political prisoners, including each and every one of the potential presidential candidates who were planning to run for office against Ortega in elections to be held later that year. The regime's violence against and criminalization of protest and peaceful assembly, along with the fact that many of its opponents were driven into exile in Costa Rica or elsewhere, thus led to a decline in street-level activism of the sort that erupted in 2018, while transmedia contestation remains widespread and continues to sustain a spirit of anti-authoritarianism.

As well as incarcerating many opposition activists, including some of our own close friends and collaborators, the regime began to close down and seize the assets (including workplaces, vehicles, documents, and computers) of hundreds of NGOs and civil society organizations, including CEJUDHCAN. In February 2022, the death of political prisoner and former Sandinista guerrilla fighter Hugo Torres while in custody caused international outrage. In 1974, Hugo Torres risked his life to free Daniel Ortega and others from the jail of the Somoza dictatorship where they were being held. The regime had refused to reveal Torres's place of imprisonment and had not disclosed his deteriorating state of health to his family. August 2022 brought a new Sandinista attack on the Catholic Church in Nicaragua and the arrest of the bishop of Matagalpa, Rolando Alvarez, along with a number of other priests and seminarians. More than 2,000 NGOs and civil society organizations have been shuttered by the state, including organizations with whom we have close and long-term collaborations, such as INGES (Instituto de Investigación y Gestión Social), Puntos de Encuentro, and Colectivo de Mujeres de Matagalpa.

In February 2023, the regime released 222 political prisoners, whom they deported to the United States and stripped of their Nicaraguan citizenship, their homes and assets, and their pensions and qualifications. Bishop Alvarez refused to leave and remained in jail in Managua. A further ninety-four Nicaraguans, including internationally known Nicaraguan authors Gioconda Belli and Sergio Ramírez, were stripped of their Nicaraguan nationalities. In October 2023, twelve priests (not including Alvarez) were deported to the Vatican. In December 2023 and January 2024, another fourteen priests were detained, including some for asking their congregations during Christmas services to pray for Bishop Alvarez. The opposition movement gained a little mediated boost in November 2023, when twenty-three-year-old Nicaraguan model Sheynnis Palacios was crowned Miss Universe. Many Nicaraguans celebrated this news by taking to the streets of Nicaragua with blue and white flags. This display of national pride posed the regime with an extreme dilemma, not only because of the way the Nicaraguan flag had been resignified by the 2018 protests, but also because Palacios had herself participated in those very protests. Prior to the Miss Universe pageant, Palacios had been heavily criticized in Sandinista official media, which had referred to her as "Miss Tranquera" (Miss Barricader) and "Miss Buñuelos" (in reference to her humble origins as a street seller of traditional Nicaraguan dough fritters). After she won, Ortega and Murillo attempted heavy-handedly to repress all popular expressions of joy by, for instance, ordering that a colorful new mural created in Palacios's honor be painted over (see figure 8.4), and preventing the director of the Miss Nicaragua organization and her daughter from reentering the country when they tried to return home from the Miss Universe pageant (Graham 2023).[11] In her characteristic style, Rosario Murillo attacked those celebrating the victory, accusing them of engaging in a form of "evil terrorist communication that is trying to turn a beautiful and well-deserved moment of Pride and Celebration [sic] into destructive coup-mongering."[12] However, international geographies of transmediation lit up in response with stories that put Nicaraguan state-led political violence back into the global spotlight, including in coverage by the *New York Times*, the *Guardian*, *Le Monde*, and *El País*, the last of which characterized the state of the Ortega regime as one of "repressive delirium" (*El País* 2023; also see, for example, Graham 2023; Montoya 2023; Wagner 2023). On 14 January, in a surprise move which perhaps had something to do with the way Ortega-Murillo botched their response to the Miss Universe contest, the Nicaraguan government released two imprisoned bishops, including Alvarez, along with fifteen priests and two seminarians and deported them to the Vatican (Redacción Confidencial 2024). At the time of this writing, more than ninety political prisoners remain in Nicaragua, and activists are using all official and non-official means possible to restore democracy there.

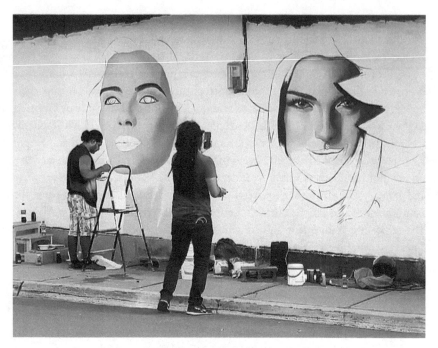

FIGURE 8.4 A mural dedicated to the dissident Nicaraguan winner of Miss Universe 2023, Sheynnis Palacios, is painted over on orders from the regime. (Source: Anonymous, printed in the *La Prensa* and *Divergentes*.)

Current forms of (transmediated) activism are not in themselves sufficient to bring an end to the Ortega-Murillo regime in the way that many former Sandinista revolutionaries and young progressives alike have both predicted and hoped for, particularly given Nicaragua's peripheral global status and increasingly brutal authoritarian state. Nevertheless, the newly released prisoners and other Nicaraguans in exile are working hard to raise awareness of the inhumane conditions under which they are living, as are independent journalists such as Carlos Fernando Chamorro, who broadcasts his current affairs show, *Esta Semana*, from Costa Rica. But digital activism can no longer catalyze, mobilize, orchestrate, and help direct street-level protests as it did in 2018, however significant highly mediated moments such as the Miss Universe victory may be. Digital and offline spaces of dissidence, opposition, and struggle no longer produce one another as generatively and prolifically as was possible prior to the escalation of authoritarianism under Ortega-Murillo. Nonetheless, there are important moments of transmedia practice through which opposition to and critiques of Daniel Ortega's growing authoritarianism are inserted into new spaces and reach new audiences. For example, the families and allies of political prisoners have creatively extended mediascapes of dissidence. An organization called Se Humano (Be Human) began to circulate dramatic before-and-after images of political prisoners that contrasted their appearance prior to their arrests with computer-generated images of how they would look after: thin, gaunt, and with signs of torture and trauma on their faces. Political prisoners held in *Orteguista* cells have reported that the quality and quantity of food they received began to improve after these images were circulated. Tamara Dávila, a political prisoner who was arrested in June 2021 in front of her five-year-old daughter, whom she had not seen for more than a year by the summer of 2022, started a hunger strike that coincided with family members and supporters circulating a video about the mother and child's plight. Five days later, the regime allowed Tamara's daughter to visit her in prison. Tamara's late grandmother, Pinita Gurdián (whose oldest child, Ana Margarita Vijil, was also a political prisoner), previously broadcast cooking shows on television and used her media exposure to denounce the regime until she died in August 2023; her interventions were widely circulated across social media terrains. Tamara and Ana Margarita were both released and deported in February 2023, and Tamara's testimony to the Permanent Council of the Organization of American States on 29 March of that year, in which she outlined the forms of psychological and physical torture and violence to which she had been subjected and in which she stressed that "banishment, expatriation and exile" do not constitute "freedom," was widely shared on Twitter, YouTube, and Facebook, and through WhatsApp and Signal groups.[13] Her ability to address the Council was accorded by Chile. This is only the second time in history that a Nicaraguan has occupied the chair of another country to denounce human rights violations; the first time was in 1979, when Sandinista liberation theologian Miguel D'Escoto held the chair of Panama to denounce the Somoza dictatorship and thus accelerate its downfall.

While such videos spread rapidly among Nicaragua's opposition activists and their allies in exile, there are moments when they enter other locations and open new kinds of political spaces. In September 2021, visibility of the situation in Nicaragua shot up across global transmediascapes when the regime arrested seventy-six-year-old Francisco Aguirre-Sacasa, the former Nicaraguan ambassador to the United States, for "alleged crimes against national sovereignty" (Medrano 2022). The ambassador's son, Roberto Aguirre-Sacasa, is the creator of the cultish, genre-bending teen-TV drama *Riverdale* (on the CW and Netflix), and so the show's entire cast appeared in a social media video about the arrest, thus spreading awareness of Nicaraguan authoritarianism among new generations of TV viewers and streamers.[14] Not only was the video widely shared on Twitter and Facebook, but the story (and the story of the story) made several mainstream news sites in the United States and beyond (Brito 2021; Hirwani 2021; Madhani 2021; Soares 2021), as well as in the trade and entertainment press (Cordero, 2021; Seddon, 2021). Roberto Aguirre-Sacasa (2021) was then invited to write about his family's situation in *Time* magazine, and the issue attracted public attention from and condemnation of the Nicaraguan regime by Democratic senators Michael Bennet, James Coleman, and Bob Menendez, in addition to the U.S. Department of State. In a tweet, Menendez, who chairs the Senate Foreign Relations Committee, expressed his gratitude to the *Riverdale* cast for "shining a light on the Ortega regime's abuses, including the kidnapping and jailing of Francisco Aguirre-Sacasa and others speaking out against unrestrained assaults on democracy in Nicaragua," and called for an end to *Orteguista* violence against citizens struggling for human rights, social justice, and democratization.[15] Back in Nicaragua, the alternative media organization Bacanalnica (2021) published an article entitled "Look out, Daniel Ortega, Archie [the *Riverdale* protagonist] is coming to get you!" which noted that "it's one thing for the international community and civilized countries to recognize you as a dictator, as someone who commits crimes against humanity and massacres children. It is another, very different thing when Hollywood does so too" (Ampie 2021, our translation).

Francisco Aguirre-Sacasa was convicted of "conspiracy to undermine national integrity" on 9 February 2022 and sentenced to eight years in jail (Medrano 2022). Instead of being sent to prison like so many others in Nicaragua, Aguirre-Sacasa was placed under house arrest ten days after his conviction on grounds of ill health; the regime subsequently reversed this decision and reincarcerated him. He was released and deported with the other Nicaraguan political prisoners in February 2023. This example shows how a violent regime that seeks to clamp down on any form of dissent by incarcerating and silencing its critics cannot control the informational, circulatory, sensemaking, re-articulatory, and rhizomatic properties and practices of convergent media environments. The tiny actions undertaken within and around Nicaraguan authoritarianism are accumulating, connecting, and unpredictably forming and extending new rhizomatic networks that continue to sustain hope within and beyond the country for an eventual end to the current dictatorship, just as Ortega's Sandinista guerrillas managed over time and against all odds, with widespread popular support, to topple the Somoza regime in 1979. As Deleuze and Guattari (1987: 7) note, "a rhizome ceaselessly establishes connections between semiotic chains, organizations of power, and circumstances relative to the arts, sciences, and social struggles."

Conclusion

Struggles over Modernity and the New Media Environment

In early 2024, as we were putting the finishing touches on this book, a four-episode TV drama about an ongoing real-life scandal aired in the United Kingdom and instantly became a major national media event that forced the Conservative government to respond rapidly with promises and actions designed to correct decades of legal errors, injustices, and coverups that had resulted in the wrongful convictions of hundreds of Britons. *Mr. Bates vs. The Post Office* dramatized the harrowing experiences of a large number of sub-postmasters and -postmistresses: ordinary people who had run post offices in British cities, towns, and villages, and had been accused of fraud, theft, and false accounting over a period of more than two decades due to a deeply flawed Fujitsu computer system known as "Horizon." Many hundreds of these postmasters lost their livelihoods, homes, pensions, and reputations. More than 900 were convicted; many of these were imprisoned, several either took their own lives or tried to do so, and at least sixty died before they could receive any sort of compensation or apology (Harrison 2024). The TV miniseries captures their frequent and often desperate calls to a Horizon helpline that was unable and unwilling to provide help. Although the Horizon-generated cash shortfalls that led to the convictions of postmasters began to appear as early as 1999, not one employee of either the Japanese computing megacorporation or the U.K. Post Office has as yet "been held to account over the scandal, much less faced criminal investigation" (Mitchell 2024), despite the fact that a December 2019 British High Court ruling established that Fujitsu's faulty software was responsible for the postmasters' purported cash shortfalls. In fact, Paula Vennells, who was CEO of the Post Office from 2012 to 2019—while the organization persistently and strenuously denied any fault in the Horizon system and innocent postmasters were actively and falsely being accused and convicted—was awarded a CBE (one of the United Kingdom's highest state honors) for "services to the Post Office" (Rawlinson 2024; Sweney 2024), while the outgoing boss of Fujitsu, Duncan Tait, received a golden parachute worth £2.6 million in 2019 (Davies 2024a).

Mr. Bates vs. The Post Office aired at the start of the new year in 2024 and within just eight days had been watched or streamed by more than 16 million viewers. The series, which starred a host of actors who were household names in the United Kingdom, told the real-life stories of eight postmasters (chosen from the many hundreds who were affected). The show engagingly depicted the heartbreaking treatment these postmasters had endured and their arduous long-term struggles for compensation in the wake of traumatic losses of lives, livelihoods, liberties, and reputations. After decades of coverups, denials, and ongoing investigations, the United Kingdom's prime minister, Rishi Sunak, and the government minister responsible for the Post Office, Kevin Hollinrake, were forced by a TV drama that had captured the attention of the nation to offer immediate promises of urgent legislation to quash the postmasters' criminal convictions and deliver timely financial compensation. Paula Vennells even returned the CBE she had been awarded after more than a million people signed a petition demanding that she do so (Stacey, Mason, and Boffey 2024).

The Post Office scandal did not come to government attention as a result of a TV drama. Everybody in the House of Commons knew about it. A small number of Members of Parliament (MPs) on both sides of the House had supported postmasters in their struggle for justice. Some (inadequate and bureaucratically complex) compensation schemes had already been established (although what compensation had been paid was largely swallowed up by legal costs and did not even begin to match the losses incurred by the wrongly accused and convicted postmasters). A public inquiry was already well underway. The scandal had been covered in different media by journalists, including an excellent, in-depth BBC Radio 4 series, an hour-long episode of the long-running investigative BBC TV show *Panorama*, and frequent coverage in the news and by outlets such as the satirical current affairs magazine *Private Eye* and the trade magazine *Computer Weekly*. The government *knew* that ordinary people's lives had been ruined and could have committed to delivering justice at any point in the past decade, but had chosen not to do so. In fact, as the *Financial Times* reported, knowing about the deep flaws in the Horizon system, coverups, and miscarriages of justice did not prevent the British government from continuing to award lucrative contracts to Fujitsu, which amounted to some £4.9 billion *after* the 2019 High Court ruling against the Post Office, £2.6 billion of which was awarded during Sunak's time as Chancellor of the Exchequer (head of the U.K. Treasury) and as prime minister (Uddin, Fisher, and Gross 2024).[1]

In the days and weeks after the drama aired, the story dominated news cycle after news cycle and proliferated widely across media platforms. The convergent media environment kicked into overdrive as the scandal trended heavily on social media and provided reporters, hosts, and talking-head commentators, as well as computer experts, activists, and indignant ordinary people, with a proliferating array of new angles and lines of inquiry that were highly spreadable, including tales of the many obstacles to justice that had been deployed to obstruct the official public inquiry into the Horizon scandal over a period of years (Davies 2024b), as well as information about the close working relationship between the firm Infosys, which is owned by prime minister Sunak's father-in-law, and Fujitsu (Infosys 2023). The real victims were invited to share their stories across many different media platforms, while many of the actors who had played the postmasters in the drama became activists themselves and demanded in frequent TV and radio appearances that justice be served. Those in government during previous phases of the postmasters' struggle who had the power to do something about the miscarriages of justice, but failed to act, including Vince Cable and Ed Davey, were called to account. Public inquiries rarely constitute riveting viewing, but thousands tuned in to watch the Horizon hearings online after the drama had aired (Crace 2024).[2] In the days and weeks following the conclusion of *Mr. Bates vs. the Post Office*, the ongoing spectacle of protestations and grandstanding performed on media screens around the country by real-life Conservative party politicians and Post Office investigators alike have played like further episodes in a still-unfolding miniseries (Adams 2024).

Understanding why and how a powerfully crafted TV drama touched the nerve of the British nation and forced a series of desperate maneuvers by a government that had for many years responded only half-heartedly and inadequately at best requires a conjunctural analysis, an approach that deeply informs our project. Gramscian conjunctural analysis, as pioneered and developed by Stuart Hall and others associated with the Birmingham School of Cultural Studies, is particularly useful for avoiding some of the theoretical and analytical pitfalls of other approaches, including a tendency of some to overlook geographical and historical specificities, or to see the media as dangerously monolithic and necessarily reproductive of existing economic and other relations of power and inequality. As we noted in chapter 6, this approach grasps conjuncturally related events not through mechanistic or scientific conceptions of cause and effect but rather as mutually determinative of one another via their colocation within a particular historical and geographical conjuncture (see Hall 1996). And as we have seen throughout this book, media events, television dramas, and political practices have, in our contemporary convergent mediascapes, often become thoroughly intertwined and co-constitutive terrains of struggle. The transmedia events and popular geopolitical dramas of the new media environment should be understood, as we argued in chapters 1 and 2, as sites of discursive and affective activity, maximal turbulence, and competing bids and counterbids for meaning and knowledge. They are capable of resonating powerfully with a culture's deepest fears, desires, and anxieties, and may therefore lead to significant shifts in a culture's overall structure of feeling. In the case of *Mr. Bates vs. the Post Office*, it appears that this shift of feeling might be characterized as one of extreme national indignation. As John Crace (2024) wrote, "the country is seized with indignation. An indignation all the more righteous for most of us having taken our eyes off the ball. People want those responsible for perpetuating one of the worst miscarriages of justice over a period of 25 years to be named and shamed. They are now watching every move."

As we have seen, the contemporary media environment is central to the forms of political polarization, contestation, and struggle that are at work in a number of different parts of the world, where the boundaries between expert and popular knowledges, and between Eurocentric and Black or Indigenous knowledges, appear to be in constant states of multiplication, conflict, and flux. At times, power blocs lose control of key narratives and must invest in reasserting or rearticulating their discursive positions within perpetually shifting ideological terrains. The same discourses and forms of articulation, disarticulation, and rearticulation can of course be deployed for different purposes, whether reactionary, centrist, or progressive (nor do these relational directionals have fixed and stable coordinates). These political dynamics unfold in geographically specific ways and in sites where local colonial and postcolonial pasts and presents shape the balance of forces, and determine which discursive and technological resources are available at any given time, though our continually expanding webs and technologies of transmediation seem to make more of both available to ever more people all the time (albeit on socially and spatially unequal terms). As we have asserted throughout this book, within the hybridizing and indeterminate logics of the new media environment, possibilities always remain for surprising outcomes, as when, despite the forced closure of independent media operations by the Ortega-Murillo regime, the grassroots digital practices of dissident Nicaraguans are taken up by the cast members of a cultish Hollywood teen drama and spread to new generations of young viewers. Or when the outcomes of a beauty pageant often ignored by many people become global news and a means to tell a story of government repression. Or when the politicized calypso traditions forged by enslaved Trinidadians and transformed by Afro–Costa Ricans are rearticulated with reggaeton and recirculated through YouTube and Facebook. As we saw in our discussions of 9/11 Truthers, Māori mediamakers, and post-Katrina dissidents in previous chapters, the official knowledges and racialized currencies that have long been central to much mainstream media content can be weakened, undermined, disarticulated, and rearticulated when alternative narratives and discourses gain traction through new media networks and practices that defy strategies for their containment.

With respect to *Mr. Bates vs. The Post Office*, then, it is not just that the drama was well written and casted, nor that it was screened at a time when many people were on leave and at home, nor that 2024 is an election year for a government that has been tanking in the polls for many months, although these are all elements that contributed to the miniseries' surprising impacts and helped give rise to the myriad indignant, desperate, and grandstanding responses to it. The show resonated deeply with ordinary people, many of whom have been affected by one or more of the scandals, injustices, cruelties, and necropolitical agendas that have become familiar elements of late neoliberalism in the United Kingdom in general, and of Tory rule since 2010 in particular. The miniseries' widespread resonances facilitated and propelled the story's rapid transmediation and ongoing rearticulations across multiple intertwined platforms and geographies of everyday life. This mediatized movement revealed how the social contract that is expected (in the Global North, at least) to protect and compensate the innocent has been stretched to the breaking point in late-neoliberal modernity, especially in the United Kingdom, as Tory cuts to legal aid budgets have made routes to justice unaffordable for those on low incomes. During the depths of the COVID-19 crisis, the Conservative government managed to find billions of pounds to pay major Tory Party donors and cronies to deliver defective (and therefore unusable) personal protective equipment (PPE, to the tune of £15 billion wasted; see Cameron-Chilesque 2023; Conn 2022, 2023) and to set up infrastructures that did not work and were abandoned, such as the U.K. government's failed "Test and Trace" program (to the tune of £36 billion wasted; see U.K. Parliament 2021). Meanwhile, pay rises in line with inflation for essential public sector and public service employees such as nurses, teachers, and railway workers have been deemed unaffordable by the government, and growing numbers of young adults earn too little to pay rent, let alone contemplate buying their own homes. Struggles for justice, compensation, and official recognition of suffering have been devastating not only for postmasters, but also for stigmatized and sanctioned welfare recipients (see Cupples and Glynn 2016), for care home residents and their loved ones during the waves of deaths that swept these places during the early phase of the COVID-19 pandemic, for the members of the Windrush generation who were victimized (and mostly still not yet compensated) by the deportation scandals of the 2010s (see Gentleman 2022; Rawlinson, Badshah, and Weaver 2022), for the victims of the infected blood scandal (see Siddique 2024), for migrants and asylum seekers, and for the inhabitants of Grenfell Tower, who, just a couple days before *Mr. Bates vs. the Post Office* went to air, lashed out against Tory government inaction and delays throughout the nearly seven years since seventy-two people lost their lives there (see Ungoed-Thomas 2023). In all these cases, people have died or had their lives ruined as a direct result of top-down neglect, incompetence, and apparent indifference, and in all these cases political redress has been desperately slow in coming. Indeed, after *Mr. Bates* aired, the show's producers began to receive email communications from viewers asking them to make a TV drama about their own failed struggles for justice (Adams 2024), thus revealing the extent to which the miniseries tapped into a collective trauma and widespread social anxiety about living in what is increasingly understood as "broken Britain," where being on hold on a helpline that is "experiencing exceptionally high call volumes" is now part of everyday life.

This example underscores the storytelling power of TV drama and the continuing importance—indeed centrality—of television in the contemporary media environment. It also suggests that television drama is capable of promoting affective engagement among audiences in ways that more conventional forms of news and current affairs programming often struggle to match (though in chapter 4, we encountered an affectively powerful example of the latter in *Campell Live*). *Mr. Bates*, like some of the other TV shows we have mentioned or examined closely in this book, including *Geraldo at Large* (chapter 1), *Homeland* (chapter 2), *Treme* (chapter 3), *Campbell Live* (chapter 4), *Songs from the Inside* (chapter 5), *3rd Degree* (chapter 6), *La comunidad en su casa* (chapter 7), and *Riverdale* (chapter 8), also reveals that the convergent media environment sometimes operates in highly unpredictable and surprising ways in relation to political struggles for change. In the case of *Mr. Bates*, a televisual text built upon, condensed, and concentrated a variety of the many forms of political and media intervention that the Post Office's victims and their supporters had engaged in for the previous two decades, while power blocs allowed grievances to build. While these grievances were contested across a range of mediatized and institutional spaces, U.K. power blocs have generally relied upon socially and economically subordinated people's insufficient access to resources to prevent them from mounting insurmountable challenges to their long-term hegemony, and from adequately recruiting others who were not directly impacted by the scandal from joining their cause in a counter-hegemonic alliance. But no power bloc can prevent the prospect that mediated and mediating events might trigger the formation of new solidarities and a sudden collective reckoning with grievances that have accumulated over time. In Chile in 2019, the hiking of subway fares unleashed a major rebellion that led to the formation of a powerful movement for the adoption of a new constitution, as well as intensified and expanded struggles against both neoliberalism and gender-based violence. During these rebellions, protestors took to the streets to perform a song called "A Rapist in Your Path," which they had written for the occasion and which articulated gendered violence to neoliberal economic exploitation; this song spread rapidly around the world through social media networks and TV news coverage, and was mobilized by activists in other countries who were inspired by the Chileans (see Cupples 2022). In Nicaragua in 2018, it was the combination of the government's decision to allow the officially protected Indio Maíz reserve to burn uncontrollably and to simultaneously propose cuts to people's pensions that sparked the popular uprisings we discussed in chapter 8. These uprisings decisively opposed the many injustices and harms inflicted upon older Nicaraguans, forests, non-human animals, Indigenous people, Afrodescendants, LGBTQ+ people, and leaders of NGOs and other civil society institutions and organizations. As we have seen in part IV, Ortega-Murillo are still in power, but collective indignation against the regime has spread globally, continues to gain traction, and has already done serious damage to the legitimacy of the dictatorial couple.

At moments of tumult and crisis like these, various power blocs struggle to control narratives, other social and cultural forces, and power relations in the hope of restoring an unsettled equilibrium, for they find all around them the political fracture lines and other signs of potentially deep conjunctural shifts in the making. Robert F. Carley (2021: 2) notes that a conjuncture is a moment when "things begin to converge in entirely unforeseen ways." While he uses the term "moment," conjunctures are "problem-space[s]" (Grossberg 2010: 58) of indeterminate and variable scale and temporal duration.[3] Carley (2021: 2) suggests the metaphor of the "quick onset of a storm on an otherwise mild day" to characterize conjunctural crises and shifts as "chaotic mixture[s]" of forces that "can neither be controlled nor contained by politics as usual." Already existing elements come "together in new ways," thus potentially giving rise to "strange formations." A conjuncture, therefore, is this convergence of social forces in particular ways to produce distinctive impacts, possibilities, and opportunities. Conjunctural *analysis*, in turn, seeks to identify, interpret, and strategically mobilize these elements in ways that might "harness" them toward the production of particular political transformations (Carley 2021: 2–3). As Grossberg (2010: 58) writes, the "various crises and contradictions" that are always at work in a conjuncture must be illuminated through analyses that enable us to grasp "the contingency of the present" and so better understand how it might most effectively be transformed and reconstituted.

As we noted in chapter 5, struggles to establish new spaces of Māori mediamaking and to expand the visibility and audibility of Indigenous perspectives across the mediascapes of Aotearoa New Zealand were very protracted and involved many different actors working across a variety of media, *marae* (traditional tribal Māori meeting houses), and other places and spaces to chip away at the unbearable and resilient coloniality that has long been active within New Zealand. And as we have seen in chapters 5 and 6, it is significant that these decolonial struggles in Aotearoa New Zealand had ensconced a courageous Indigenous television channel within the country's mediascapes to the extent that, when the government terror raids were conducted in 2007, it quickly became clear that colonial business as usual would no longer be possible. A new rightwing government elected in Aotearoa New Zealand in 2023 is at the time of this writing trying to roll back many of the gains that Māori have achieved, but the conjuncture has shifted: Tame Iti has a mainstream media platform and his major contributions to the project of making a better world for Tūhoe and other Māori is now abundantly recognized, and Whakaata Māori has become a well-established part of New Zealand mediascapes and is watched and enjoyed by New Zealanders of all races and ethnicities. It would appear that these developments have placed substantial political and cultural limits on projects for colonial revanchism in Aotearoa New Zealand, at least in the short-term, though we recognize the dangers of the ongoing expansion of racist authoritarian nationalism in many parts of the world even as we write these words.

There are many clear colonial continuities that persist in the world and especially in the United States, Central America, and Aotearoa New Zealand, where decolonization remains incomplete, democracy precarious, and racist ideologies and knowledges persistent; active forces of coloniality thus work continuously to marginalize non-Eurocentric and anti-capitalist ways of knowing and being. But many people, and especially Indigenous, Afrodescendant, and subordinated mestizo ones are devising and deploying creative ways to appropriate the resources and networks of the new media environment to disrupt and contest repressive, racist, and environmentally destructive practices, and to (re)imagine, reassert, and reenact alternative ways of living. In Central America, the activities of mainstream and expanding state-controlled media continue to reproduce and re-entrench "commonsense" hegemonic ideologies of *mestizaje* through practices that attach racializing and "Othering" meanings to the peoples and places of the Caribbean Coast, which are thereby signified as sites of traitorous and insubordinate opposition to and subversion of the nation. Meanwhile, the bottom-up, participatory cultures and media activities harnessed by those struggling against coloniality, racial subordination, and political repression are actively producing new connectivities and spaces of contestation over, and interrogation of, twenty-first-century authoritarianism and other forms of contemporary, racialized domination.

These are messy processes. At times, those in Latin America who are circulating counterhegemonic narratives draw on global discourses of Indigenous rights that have expanded there in the wake of the 9/11 attacks, which brought neoliberalism into deep interrogation and crisis throughout the region (see Beverley 2011). These activists also both draw upon and contribute to the ongoing development of global environmental discourses and political projects. Their practices of appropriation and rearticulation have in some ways enhanced the impacts of counterhegemonic narratives in the region at certain times of authoritarian, colonial, environmental, and other crises and disasters (as we have also seen in our discussions of the mediation of disastrous events in Aotearoa New Zealand and the United States). At other times, the sheer fragmentation of the new media environment means that the community media forms and practices that sometimes best address the local concerns and needs of Indigenous and Afrodescendant peoples of the Caribbean Coasts of Central America or the Māori people of the Tūhoe nation must compete for attention with global celebrity culture, high-budget telenovelas, CNN, Hollywood movies, professional sports, and streaming services such as Netflix. Moreover, the growing authoritarianism of many states around the world has led to intensified data collection, surveillance, and "trolling" practices of the sort used to undermine, persecute, and imprison Nicaraguan dissidents, as we have noted in part IV. But the media production and consumption practices of subordinated and marginalized people do, as noted above and throughout this book, sometimes possess the capacity to challenge oppressions.

We have seen that the new media environment, like the broader processes and formations of contemporary, neoliberal globalization of which it forms a part, is constituted and mobilized differently across many different sites. It has in this way become central to current struggles over the cultural politics of modernity and modernization. The spaces that both produce and are produced by and through the new media environment increasingly constitute a primary terrain in the broader conjuncture defined by Lawrence Grossberg (2010: 3–4) as that "problem space" where modernity is both "the site and object of struggle"—of struggles over "what other modernities—as well as alternatives to modernity—are possible" (294). Contemporary and deeply racialized forms of, and movements both for and against, political authoritarianism constitute one node of these conjunctural struggles that can be observed across our field sites and beyond. When an armed mob of white nationalist insurrectionists deployed contemporary transmedia networks to organize and orchestrate their attempts (see, e.g., Marantz 2021) to overturn and displace U.S. institutionalized democracy (such as it is) on 6 January 2021, they were, like the Indigenous and Afrodescendant Nicaraguans, Māori activists, and mediamakers we have discussed, also engaged in this major and ongoing struggle over modernity. And like those struggling against authoritarianism in Nicaragua or coloniality in Aotearoa New Zealand, those struggling for it in the United States during the 6 January insurrection were both reliant on and further elaborating a plexus woven through a very old live broadcast medium, and in particular the Salem talk radio network, which had by then established itself as arguably the most far-reaching and important source of news and commentary among right-wing Christians across the nation. Salem Radio and social media (along with the Fox News cable TV channel) thus formed key elements of a rhizomatic transmedia network that was crucial in promoting, encouraging, and enabling the insurrection during the months (and years) prior to its enactment (see Nelson 2019; Stone 2021; Wilson-Hartgrove 2021; Piore 2020). Hence, just as live broadcast radio has been a key foundation and core element in popular transmedia struggles against authoritarianism in Central America and for struggles for Māori sovereignty in Aotearoa, so has it also been central to contemporary struggles *against* democracy in the United States and beyond. Indeed, we saw that the followers of a former Brazilian president who is openly nostalgic for that country's bygone military dictatorship were also engaged in contemporary conjunctural struggles over modernity when they attacked Brazil's institutions of democracy on 8 January 2023 in their efforts to ignite a new coup d'état. As Jem Bartholomew (2023) has recently written in the *Columbia Journalism Review*, the new media environment has facilitated the emergence of an amorphous, online alt-right "swamp" where "tactics, strategies, narratives and organizing tips" spill across national borders and increasingly interconnected (trans)media platforms, so that TV commentators were prepared well in advance of votes being cast to report that the winning Brazilian candidate, Lula da Silva, had delivered what was, as then Fox News host Tucker Carlson put it, "very clearly a rigged election" (also see Leloup 2023). The many Ukrainians whose mobilization of rhizomatic transmedia assemblages (see, e.g., Specia 2022) has been central in their efforts to win and sustain the attention of viewers around the world are also engaged in transmediated conjunctural struggles over modernity. These Ukrainians are struggling to retain their territorial integrity and to repel the rapacious authoritarian onslaught driven by Vladimir Putin's efforts to establish effective counternarratives and redrawn borders, and thus to restore a purportedly rogue, breakaway corner of a bygone Russian Empire. The Ukrainians, like Indigenous and Afrodescendant peoples of the Americas, are exploiting the fact that these rhizomatic transmedia assemblages traverse the so-called first, third, and fourth worlds. And so too, therefore, has our analysis.

Like Ortega-Murillo in Nicaragua, Putin has captured and contained most of Russia's media companies within a state-run authoritarian enclosure (see Myers 2022; Inskeep and Maynes 2022), and has established a vast "surveillance and censorship system" that the Russian state deploys "to find and track opponents, squash dissent and suppress independent information even in the country's furthest reaches" (Mozur et al. 2022; also see Litvinova 2023). Putin's struggles over modernity in Ukraine can be understood as extensions of not only his regime's prior history of imperializing invasions and carpet-bombing endeavors in places like Chechnya, Syria, and Crimea, but also of their hacking and digital tampering with democratic processes and systems in the 2016 U.K. Brexit referendum (see U.K. Parliament 2018; U.S. Senate 2018; Cadwalladr and Graham-Harrison 2018; U.K. Information Commissioner 2018; Sabbagh, Harding, and Roth 2020) and recent U.S. presidential elections (see, e.g., Lipton, Sanger, and Shane 2016; Greenberg 2017; O'Connor and Schneider 2017; Sanger and Edmondson 2019; Herb et al. 2020; CNN 2022). These are, as Grossberg (2010: 289) reminds us, struggles that span "multipolar, multitemporal, and multiscalar webs of connectivity, relationality, and difference," and that are "driving the creation of contemporary geo-economic, political, and cultural formations and spaces," as well as the "new subjectivities and collectivities" emerging "within and across them." As people's encounters with various and expanding sites and types of disaster around the world escalate (see Glynn and Cupples 2024), and as the contemporary media environment continues to develop, particularly under the shadow of neoliberal, authoritarian, neoliberal-authoritarian, or, as Clara Mattei (2022) conceives it, authoritarian austerity capitalism, we might expect contemporary mediated struggles over modernity to intensify, produce new spaces of contestation, and take on new forms and dimensions. In recent years, efforts to devise new modalities of AI capable of generating and operating an increasingly effective range of automated weapons and citizen/consumer surveillance systems have intensified (see, e.g., Leetaru 2019; Woods 2018), and journalists have noted the widespread transnational exportation of AI-driven Chinese facial recognition software (Yang and Murgia 2019). Such automated systems offer military and governmental leaders the prospect of extending the distance between drone operators and their targets, for example (which *Homeland* brought to our attention, as we saw in chapter 2), and of fighting back against and curtailing oppositional political mobilization in other ways (as we have noted in part IV). But the new media environment, as we have seen, also includes many spaces for the assertion of alterity and difference. Last Moyo (2020: 23) notes that "the Global South still endures the psycho-cultural trauma of the legacies of slavery, colonialism, apartheid, and the vagaries of neocolonialism and new racisms that are dehumanizing" and undermining of "the people's collective agency," and that "a dehumanized people with no cultural and mental universes of their own cannot be a community." Moyo argues, therefore, that the Global South does not "need technology or money to pick themselves up and develop, they need culture," and that "this means the creation of robust media systems to radiate their cultures into the multiverse thus creating a sense of global cultural diversity. Indeed, if technology and economy are the hardware of social and economic development, then culture is the software." Hence, we argued in chapter 3 that Mardi Gras is as important for the recovery of post-Katrina New Orleans and the prevention of further disasters as are well-engineered levees.

Both the forces of expanding authoritarianism, on one hand, and, on the other, those of democratization and of the decolonial preservation, regeneration, rearticulation, and (re)assertion of different ways of knowing and being, continue to develop ways of utilizing, mobilizing, and exploiting the affordances of the new, expanding, and evolving global transmedia environment. The 9/11 Truth movement with which we began part I has been joined by new digital-political subcultures and transmedia networks associated with the likes of Alex Jones, QAnon, and exponents of the many variants of "great replacement" conspiratorialism (see, e.g., "Great Replacement," n.d.), along with a spectacular array of anti-vaxxer groups, claims, and discourses that have come into focus since the disastrous COVID-19 pandemic unleashed itself on the world (see, e.g., Birchall and Knight 2023; Klein 2023; Tuters and Willaert 2022). As conspiracy theories are stories about power and secrecy (see Fenster 2008), it should not surprise us that they often feature centrally on our screens in an age of transmediated conjunctural struggles over many aspects of modernity at a time when disaster, the forces of authoritarianism, and technological systems of connectivity and surveillance all seem to be gaining ground all around us. Nor should it surprise us that it is through these same transmedia digital systems of connectivity (and sometimes of countersurveillance, "cop-watching," and "digital drag"; see, e.g., Canella 2018; Kornstein 2019) that people around the world who are struggling for democratization forge new ways of engaging in and expanding their practices of cultural citizenship. We have seen in part II that such practices include the appropriation of a variety of digital media tools to forge new connectivities that promote decoloniality, to amplify the voices of the marginalized that contest hegemonic discourses and representations of disaster events, and to assert the perspectives of Indigenous and other racialized communities. Such perspectives have had notable impacts through their transmedial spreadability from social media across mainstream television formats and outlets, including via TV dramas such as *Treme* and *Hope and Wire*, and current affairs shows such as *Campbell Live*. In part III, we examined the impacts that a state-funded, dedicated Indigenous people's broadcaster, Whakaata Māori, can have in relation to the post-9/11 emergence of discourses of "terrorism" in the face of struggles for decoloniality and historical redress in fourth world contexts such as Aotearoa New Zealand. Transmediated struggles for decoloniality within Aotearoa have had demonstrable impacts on the wider media and cultural environment there, as we have shown in particular with regard to such issues as the representation of Māori activism and criminalization. It is through the appropriation of the tools of the new media environment, contemporary weapons of the weak as well as of the powerful, that struggles abide. ¡*La lucha continúa!*

Notes

Introduction

1. The "fourth world" is a common term for the terrain occupied by formerly colonized Indigenous peoples. We conceive of authoritarian post-democracy as a crisis of democracy, not as its supersession, not least because many people around the world struggle ardently for democratization of various realms of practice across a wide array of sites and scales.
2. "Aotearoa" is the Māori name for New Zealand.
3. Half a decade before Trump's campaign began, and with what might now be read as prescience, Lawrence Grossberg (2010: 223) wrote that, despite the "explosion" of scholarly work on reality TV, this "category does not describe a genre, since its formal structures are so variable; and it does not describe a specific discursive formation, precisely because its affective possibilities are too multiple and dispersed.... But much of 'reality tv' (including parts of specific programs), along with other cultural events and affective regimes, as well as certain social and political regimes, participate in a discursive formation that I might call a 'humiliation machine'. I believe this is in fact an important emerging, if not already dominant, structure of feeling in the contemporary United States."
4. Cultural studies has drawn upon Gramsci to theorize hegemony as a multifaceted and multifrontal "war of maneuver," within which cultural processes and practices play a central role in power bloc alliances' efforts to win popular consent for the ways of understanding and feeling these alliances promote as commonsensical (see, e.g., Hall 1996). Cultural studies has thus theorized hegemonic social formations structured in dominance as "moving equilibria" in constant search of stabilities (cf., e.g., Hebdige 1979: 26–27; Grossberg 2010).
5. Trump's first official actions as president included slashing funding for UN programs that provide reproductive healthcare to women in hundreds of countries, giving the green light for the highly controversial Keystone XL and Dakota Access oil pipelines to operate across Indigenous people's territories in the face of active Native American opposition, suspending visas for citizens of majority Muslim countries, reinstating the torture of terror suspects, and ordering construction of a wall along the U.S.-Mexico border. Sites of transmediated parodic and satirical

reaction to Trump's first presidential initiatives included *Saturday Night Live, The Daily Show, Full Frontal with Samantha Bee, The Onion, The Poke, The New Yorker,* @Art_Mofo's Trump-Toon, @minismitty's parody of *The Office,* and *Zondag met Lubach,* a weekly Dutch TV political satire whose material went viral in the early days of the Trump administration (see, e.g., Zondag met Lubach's "The Netherlands welcomes Trump in his own words" at https://www.youtube.com/watch?v=y4cc4Y7E7u0).

6   See https://www.youtube.com/watch?v=CnG4fEqH-pg. For Latin Americans, America/América names the entire continent of 35 nations, not just the United States. Uruguayan journalist and novelist Eduardo Galeano (1997: 2) famously wrote that as a result of U.S. imperialism, "we [Latin Americans] have even lost the right to call ourselves Americans."

7   "¡Viva América! Somos más que un país, somos un continente y no un país que se cree dueño del mundo puede separarnos. No es el país en sí, son los políticos los que nos dividen y sus ideologías de superioridad. Todos somos iguales y todos podemos ayudarnos. Los que nos puede destruir, también nos puede salvar y el orgullo, la soberbia y el despotismo tendrán una larga y justa caída. América para los americanos y no solo para los Estadounidenses ¡Viva América!" Retrieved from https://www.youtube.com/watch?v=CnG4fEqH-pg. This response begins with the following declaration: "Un comercial que estremece. Feliz de ser Americano y bendecido por ser Mexicano. ¡Viva México! ¡Viva Canadá! ¡Viva Guatemala! ¡Viva Honduras! ¡Viva Perú! ¡Viva Argentina! ¡Viva Chile! ¡Viva Ecuador! ¡Viva Belice! ¡Viva Uruguay! ¡Viva Jamaica! ¡Viva Haití! ¡Viva Costa Rica! ¡Viva Panamá! ¡Viva Brasil! ¡Viva Cuba! ¡Viva Venezuela! ¡Viva Guayana! ¡Viva Antigua y Barbuda! ¡Viva República Dominicana! ¡Viva Dominica! ¡Viva Surinam! ¡Viva Bahamas! ¡Viva Trinidad y Tobago! ¡Viva San Cristóbal y Nieves! ¡Viva San Vicente y Granadinas! ¡Viva Santa Lucía! ¡Viva El Salvador!" ("A commercial that makes you tremble [shake with emotion]. Happy to be American and blessed to be Mexican. Long live Mexico! Long live Canada! Long live Guatemala! Long live Honduras! Long live Peru! Long live Argentina! Long live Chile! Long live Ecuador! Long live Belize! Long live Uruguay! Long live Jamaica! Long live Haiti! Long live Costa Rica! Long live Panama! Long live Brazil! Long live Cuba! Long live Venezuela! Long live Guyana! Long live Antigua and Barbuda! Long live the Dominican Republic! Long live Dominica! Long live Suriname! Long live Bahamas! Long live Trinidad and Tobago! Long live Saint Kitts and Nevis! Long live Saint Vincent and the Grenadines! Long live Saint Lucia! Long live El Salvador!") Other responses include the following: "Soy Costarricense y debo decir que este video me enorgullece como parte de esta gran familia americana!!!!! Gracias Mexico excelente!!!!" ("I am Costa Rican and I have to say that this video makes me feel proud to be part of this great American family!!!!! Thanks Mexico excellent!!!!") "Somos 35 estados unidos que conforman américa, incluso (y no sólo) los estadounidenses, Qué viva a México, Brasil, Argentina, Paraguay, Panamá y a todos los demás países de este gran continente. Felicitaciones a los creadores de este anúncio." ("We are 35 united states that make up America, including and not only U.S. Americans. Long live Mexico, Brazil, Argentina, Paraguay, Panama, and all the other countries of this great continent. Congratulations to the creators of this advert.") "Hermosa publicidad, América somos todos los que vivimos desde Alaska hasta Tierra del fuego, no es solamente EEUU. Esto es así. Somos un continente gigante con gente pujante y luchadora, abrazo gigante a mis hermanos Mexicanos desde Argentina." ("Beautiful advert. We are all America those that

live from Alaska down to Tierra del Fuego, it's not just the United States. This is how it is. We are a gigantic continent with brave and fighting people, big hug to my Mexican brothers and sisters from Argentina.")

8   See https://www.youtube.com/watch?v=-8vDwiwlnmI; https://www.youtube.com/watch?v=2DLpK5pARwc.

9   As David Gauntlett (2009: 39) writes: "Wikipedia embodies the essence of 'Web 2.0', and is a quintessentially 'Web 2.0' project."

10 We regard to neoliberalism as a contested hegemonic political project rather than as, say, a coherent economic philosophy (see, e.g., Cupples and Glynn 2016; Glynn and Cupples 2022). The period of neoliberal hegemony of the past forty years or so has often entailed the imposition of brutal market forces upon racially and economically subordinated populations, combined with socialist-style state subsidies for economic elites, as during the "welfare reforms" of the 1980s and 1990s in the United States and the United Kingdom, for instance, or amid the state bailouts of major corporations after the global financial crisis of 2007–2008. Like all hegemonies, neoliberalism in different parts of the world, such as Latin America and Aotearoa New Zealand, share some similarities and linkages with their North Atlantic counterparts, but are also marked by significant differences and place specificities. For instance, the Latin American debt crisis of the 1980s was crucial to the imposition, via the institutions of global governance associated with the Washington Consensus, of rapid privatization and trade liberalization across most of Latin America during that decade, with varying degrees of complicity or accommodation on the part of economic elites in different countries (see Cupples 2022).

11 For similar reasons, critical scholars of disaster have for decades rejected the concept of "natural disasters," in favor of the idea that disasters are fundamentally products of the economic, social, and (geo)political orders within which they appear. See, for example, N. Smith (2006).

12 As Shohat and Stam (2014: 369) write, contemporary globalization is deeply anchored in "1492 and the *conquista* of the Americas as the event which installed the first truly global era of what Walter Mignolo and others call 'coloniality/modernity'. In fact, for many indigenous groups the *conquista* is occurring in the present, whether in the case of groups just now being 'contacted' in the Amazon region, or just now being threatened with the loss of their land due to squatters, miners, or transnational corporations. . . . The contemporary globalized world is still being shaped by Columbus and the *conquista*."

13 As we note in chapter 1, some "9/11 Truthers" allege that elements within the Bush administration deliberately failed to act on U.S. state intelligence that indicated al-Qaeda's plans to attack the World Trade Center with airplanes after Bush took office, thus enabling the Bush administration to reap a variety of sought-after military opportunities and advantages after the attacks. More than twenty years later, such claims were notably echoed (Damon 2023) after the *New York Times* (Bergman and Goldman 2023) reported that the Israeli state learned in strikingly precise detail of the planned Hamas raids more than a year before they were undertaken, yet chose to do nothing about them until after the events of 7 October 2023 were actually carried out.

14 Also see Andrejevic (2004), for an analysis of the entanglements between reality TV and the wider new media environment that emphasizes the political economies of interactivity and emergent practices and ideologies of expanding apparatuses of surveillance. And see Ouellette and Hay (2008), which analyzes reality

TV's connections to the wider convergent new media environment in relation to neoliberalism and Foucauldian accounts of governmentality. Finally, Jenkins (2008) also discusses two major examples of reality TV as key constituents of convergence culture.

Chapter 1   Transmediation, 9/11, and Popular Counterknowledges

1 We intend "articulation" in the theoretical sense that this term has acquired within cultural studies, where the simultaneity and conjoint productivity of its dual meanings (*contingent linkage* and *expression*) are given emphasis. When signifying elements or agents are contingently linked (articulated) to one another, this linkage generates particular meaning effects (articulations) and mobilizes particular actions and agents (to which these meaning effects are in turn articulated or contingently linked). See Grossberg (1996).

2 For Baudrillard (1988), "obscenity" is a condition of total transparency/visibility that obtains in late-modern media-saturated societies: "Obscenity begins when there is . . . no more illusion, when everything becomes immediately transparent, visible, exposed in the raw and inexorable light of information and communication. . . . It is no longer the obscenity of the hidden, the repressed, the obscure, but that of the visible, the all-too-visible, the more-visible-than-visible; it is the obscenity of that which no longer contains a secret and is entirely soluble in information and communication" (26–27).

3 Arva (2020) writes that the impact of the instantaneous global spread of "live televised images of extreme violence" (237) on 9/11 was so profound that it "marked a turning point in the overall discourse on the effect of images on the viewers' consciousness, screen trauma, and vicarious traumatization" (240).

4 The CNN footage containing figure 1.1 is available at http://www.youtube.com/watch?v=k3nLbc_8wfM. A similar famous, widely circulated image was taken by photojournalist Mark Phillips and appeared on the front pages of many newspapers and across other media (cf. Phillips 2011).

5 Available at http://www.guardianangel.in/ga/268-D-Obituary-Images-of-the-World-Trade-Center-fire-reveal-the-face-of-Satan.html.

6 Andrejevic (2011: 616) observes that Fox News, for example, "relies on the mobilization of intensities that congeal in various contexts into fear, anger, indignation, patriotism, pride and so on." We would suggest that such mobilizations of intensities also help us to grasp the televisual presences and affectivities/effectivities of the likes of Jon Stewart and Stephen Colbert during the first two decades of the new millennium, though the latter clearly mobilized these intensities in ways that carried very different political valences from those that Fox News strives to orchestrate (see Glynn 2009a).

7 These allegations of complicity by elements within the Bush administration are typically categorized as either "MIHOP" (they "made it happen on purpose"; i.e., participated actively in one way or another in the 9/11 attacks) or "LIHOP" (they "let it happen on purpose"; i.e., they ignored the large body of U.S. state intelligence that had been gathered for years on Al-Qaeda's plans to conduct a second, more destructive attack on the World Trade Center than the Al-Qaeda-connected 1993 World Trade Center bombing had been; see, e.g., Tobin 2007; Bratich 2008; Jones 2012).

8 Operation Northwoods was designed to involve terrorist attacks by the U.S. government on major U.S. cities and the false attribution of the attacks to Cuba as a

pretext for the invasion of that country; the operation was approved by the Joint Chiefs of Staff in 1962, but rejected by JFK. See http://en.wikipedia.org/wiki/Operation_Northwoods.

9 For work by academics associated with the 9/11 Truth movement, see, e.g., Benjamin 2017; Griffin and Scott 2006; Griffin 2004a, 2004b, 2006, 2007, 2010, 2011a, 2011b, 2018; Harrit et al. 2009; Hughes 2020; Truscello 2011.

10 Avery was originally writing a fiction film in 2002 about some friends who inadvertently learn that the 9/11 attacks were the product of a U.S. government conspiracy, but the more time Avery spent researching his script, the more he came to believe that his fictional premise was indeed most likely factual (McDermott 2020). In this regard, his story is similar to that of David Ray Griffin, a professor of religion and theology at the Claremont Graduate School in California, who set out in 2002 to write a scathing critique of a book that claims the U.S. government was involved in the 9/11 attacks, but his research ultimately led him not only to agree with the book's claims (Voltaire Network 2022), but to spend the next fifteen years producing his own string of books in support of them (including Griffin 2004a, 2004b, 2006, 2007, 2010, 2011a, 2011b, 2018; Griffin and Scott 2006). Mos Def, Immortal Technique, and Eminem are hip-hop artists; "Bin Laden" is available at https://www.youtube.com/watch?v=RJ4iZE2yoLk. *Fahrenheit 9/11* is a film by Michael Moore that won the Palme d'Or at the 2004 Cannes Film Festival and went on to become the highest-grossing documentary of all time.

11 See http://www.loosechange911.com/about/faq/.

12 "Vidding" involves the production of music videos through the appropriation of material from media sources such as TV shows and news reports. By recontextualizing music and media images in this way, vidders comment on the music, the imagery, or both. Vidding (the production of "vids") has become a common practice within contemporary fan cultures and has had an influence on practices of political remix videomaking—the appropriation and recontextualization of media source material to make political or critical arguments.

13 For an analysis of the 1990s "Blackstream Knowledge" of the HIV pandemic as a product of genocidal whiteness, see Fiske 2016a: chap. 4.

14 de Zeeuw and Tuters (2020) develop an additional dimension to this geography of the contemporary transmedia landscape in their analysis of the differentiations between the "mask cultures" of the "deep vernacular web" (DVW) (which includes the "chan cultures" of anonymous imageboards) and the "face cultures" of the "mainstream surface web," which are made up predominantly of megacorporate data-mining platforms such as Facebook and similar social media sites. Their analysis suggests a further reason for the importance of the "medium visibility" of the likes of Fox News, as we have suggested, for de Zeeuw and Tuters argue that alt-right appropriations of DVW subcultural practices risk running aground in the mire of ambiguity created by the refusal of any and all seriousness and earnestness that defines the transgressive practices of the DVW, which insists on a refusal of the commercial "authenticity" that corporate data-mining by Meta and others requires.

15 See, for example, Richard Gage on Fox TV affiliate KMPH's breakfast show (May 2009), available at http://www.youtube.com/watch?v=oO2yTouBQbM.

16 Footage of this interview is available at http://www.youtube.com/watch?feature=player_embedded&v=pFPobKeSzKQ.

17 These were arguably the two key moments of high media spectacle in the United States in 2008. Obama's speech at Mile High Stadium on 28 August was delivered to

an estimated crowd of 84,000 people in attendance, and his 4 November electoral victory speech was delivered to a Grant Park audience estimated at 240,000. Millions around the world watched both events on TV.

Chapter 2 The Gendered Geopolitics of Post-9/11 TV Drama

1. In fact, both concepts, "gender" and "genre," are expressed by the same word in Spanish: *género*.
2. Available at https://www.youtube.com/watch?v=CewNhrRhOtM.
3. Available at http://www.imdb.com/title/tt0701989/reviews.
4. See, for example, the mistakes identified in season 4, episode 1 by viewers at http://www.imdb.com/title/tt3284012/goofs.

Chapter 3 Decoloniality, Disaster, and the New Media Environment

1. The August 2014 police killing of eighteen-year-old African American Michael Brown in Ferguson, Missouri, led to uprisings against racialized police violence that, along with numerous other racialized police killings that took place both before and after the Brown shooting, helped give rise to the emergence of the Black Lives Matter movement.
2. Escobar (2010: 9) differentiates between Western modernity's dualist ontologies, which produce a "world as universe," and the non-modern, relational ontologies that produce a "world as pluriverse." The former establishes and sustains "the primacy of humans over non-humans (separation of nature and culture) and of some humans over others (the colonial divide between us and them); the idea of the autonomous individual separated from community; the belief in objective knowledge, reason, and science as the only valid modes of knowing; and the cultural construction of 'the economy' as an independent realm of social practice, with 'the market' as a self-regulating entity outside of social relations." The latter, a pluriversal social order, by sharp contrast, emphasizes "relationality and reciprocity; the continuity between the natural, the human and the supernatural . . . ; the embeddedness of the economy in social life and the restricted character of the market; and a deeply relational worldview that shapes the notions of personhood, community, economy, and politics."
3. Bilwi is also known by its Spanish name, Puerto Cabezas. An autonomy law passed in 1987 created two autonomous zones, the Autonomous Region of the North Atlantic (RAAN) and the Autonomous Region of the South Atlantic (RAAS), later renamed the RACCN (Autonomous Region of the North Caribbean Coast) and the RACCS (Autonomous Region of the South Caribbean Coast). Bilwi/Puerto Cabezas is part of the RACCN. The Caribbean Coast, which was never colonized by Spain, is quite ethnically and linguistically distinct from Nicaragua's Pacific region.
4. There are also important cultural similarities between the two sites, observed for example in the use of the term "Creole." As Nederveen Pieterse (1994: 170) writes, Creolization has different meanings in different parts of the continent. In the United States, Canada, and the Caribbean, it means a fusion of European and African, while in most of Latin America it refers to people of European heritage who were born in Latin America. In Bilwi, however, the Caribbean rather than the Latin American meaning holds sway, as Creole refers to the English-speaking Afrodescendant population. In New Orleans, the celebration of All Saints Day is

closely aligned with Mesoamerican festivals such as the Mexican Day of the Dead. It can be said that Bilwi finds many of its cultural references by looking north toward New Orleans, while New Orleans does so by looking south toward the Caribbean and Latin America.

5   While valuing the insights that come from the denaturalization of disaster, Nigel Clark (2010; see also Clark, Chhotray, and Few 2013) urges us not to lose sight of the fact that the planet is also home to autonomous geotectonic, atmospheric, and biological processes that operate according to a set of temporalities inaccessible to human experience and that are indifferent to human agency. Humans can make other humans less vulnerable through their actions, but cannot control the movement of tectonic plates.

6   "Brownie" was Bush's nickname for Michael Brown, a grossly underqualified crony appointed by Bush to head the Federal Emergency Management Agency (FEMA). Brown was removed from his post-Katrina duties (and resigned as FEMA head days later) after his poor performance in New Orleans (and Bush's public praise for him in the face of that performance) provoked national outrage, particularly among African Americans (see Bumiller 2005).

7   After she visited survivors in the Astrodome, Barbara Bush said, "And so many of the people in the arena here, you know, were underprivileged anyway, so this is working very well for them."

8   MR-GO refers to the Mississippi River–Gulf Outlet Canal, a channel (inadequately) constructed by the U.S. Army Corps of Engineers in the mid-twentieth century. It was the failure of MR-GO that led to the flooding of New Orleans during Hurricane Katrina.

9   Until they were hit by Hurricane Felix, the Miskito Keys, located about forty kilometers or three hours by boat from the RACCN capital of Bilwi, were sites of important economic activity for both Miskito and Creole men and women. Men worked mostly as lobster divers for industrial boats, while women worked as local traders or *piquineras*, selling beer, biscuits, chicken, and other goods to divers and using the profits to buy lobsters, which they sold on their return to the mainland. Prior to the hurricane, the divers and *piquineras* lived in the Keys in self-help houses built on stilts (for more detail, see Cupples 2012b). In the years since Felix struck, some of these workers have managed to rebuild and return to work in the Keys.

10 See http://www.youtube.com/watch?v=AXIBfAd-oYw.

11 Davis McAlary is based on local New Orleans musician Davis Rogan, and this song is based on one written by Rogan that was lost in the storm and subsequently recreated for *Treme*.

12 A version of the original blog by Morris can be found at http://ashleymorris.type pad.com/ashley_morris_the_blog/2005/11/fuck_you_you_fu.html.

13 See http://www.youtube.com/watch?v=S68ksghDNg4.

14 See, for example, http://www.youtube.com/watch?v=IblL_rXpdu8.

15 See http://www.youtube.com/watch?v=_AMDMEdZY_c.

Chapter 4 The Transmediation of Disaster Down Under

1   The ensuing debacle involved what has been a long-running story in New Zealand since it underwent a neoliberal revolution during the 1980s that was inspired by Thatcherism and Reaganism: the privatization of profits and nationalization of losses. Just as the U.S. government bailed out the Wall Street investment banks that gave the world the great recession several years earlier, the New Zealand

government had no choice but to bail out AMI, the second-largest private provider of residential insurance in the country when the Christchurch earthquakes hit (see Van den Bergh and Kay 2011). Underspending on reinsurance by private insurers in the hope that a substantial disaster will not strike and profits will therefore be much greater than would otherwise be possible is apparently a "surprisingly typical" (see *Artemis* 2011) way of embracing and leveraging excessive risk in the industry. Indeed, a high threshold for discomfort with routine risk-taking has become a heavily valued attribute of neoliberal masculinities during the past forty years and is sometimes used to explain the persistence of the "glass ceiling" (see, e.g., Sundheim 2013).
2 The others were 26 December 2010 (4.9), two on 13 June 2011 (5.9 and 6.4), and 23 December 2011 (6.2).
3 See http://www.heritage.org.nz/the-list/lost-heritage/canterbury-earthquakes for a catalog of the heritage lost as a result of the quakes.
4 See sundaythefilm.com/about, retrieved 7 April 2020.
5 The forces of coloniality have since brought about the restoration and reinstatement of all three statues in prominent central city locations.
6 The story of "the first four ships" full of British settlers sent from England by the Canterbury Association has been heavily mythologized by Christchurch's colonial descendants and is often repeated around kitchen tables and at well-appointed dinner parties in the city's affluent suburbs. These ships arrived near Christchurch in December 1850.
7 In the wake of both the Christchurch earthquakes and the COVID-19 pandemic, Whakaata Māori gave notable emphasis to perspectives and approaches to Indigenous caring.
8 This slide show is available at https://www.twinkl.co.uk/resource/nz-mfl-180-ruaumoko-the-god-of-earthquakes-and-volcanoes-powerpoint-te-reo-maori-english?

Chapter 5 Coloniality, Criminalization, and the New Media Environment

1 African American "pirate radio" in the United States might be understood in this sense as a precursor to or an emergent instance of the new media environment. See, e.g., Fiske 2016a, chaps. 2–5, and 2016b, part 4: "White Power, Black Power," on Black Liberation Radio.
2 *Tohunga* are experts of Māori knowledge.
3 New Zealand and three other former British colonies (the United States, Canada and Australia) were the only nations to vote against the UN Declaration on the Rights of Indigenous Peoples when it was formally adopted in 2007 after decades of struggle and debate. However, in 2010, New Zealand publicly announced its support for the Declaration.
4 New Zealand's previous prime minister provides an illustrative example of the Pākehā tendency to gloss over the pain, brutality, and violence of colonialism. In 2008, just before he became prime minister, John Key described New Zealand as follows: "We're not a country that's come about as a result of civil war or where there's been a lot of fighting internally, we're a country which peacefully came together" (New Zealand Government 2008). The new right-wing coalition government elected in 2023 led by Christopher Luxon has committed to rolling back Treaty rights (*NZ Herald* 2023).
5 By 2010, Māori Television's audience had grown every year since the station's inauguration and was comprised of more than two million individuals per year, 83 percent of whom were not Māori (Turner 2011).

6 According to Gilmore (2007), the prison population in California increased by 500 percent between 1982 and 1990, even as crime rates declined, with African Americans and Latinos making up two-thirds of all prisoners. She also observes a positive correlation between an increase in incarceration and an increase in crime, or a decrease in incarceration and a decrease in crime, contrary to what one would expect if prison succeeds in doing what it is meant to do. In her words, the "places that spare the cage are calmer than the places that use imprisonment more aggressively" (16). Cunneen (2013) cites Treasury figures from New Zealand that show the Māori prison population increasing from 150 per 100,000 in 1999 to 195 in 2009.

7 The Tūhoe are a Māori *iwi* whose territory covers the Bay of Plenty and Ureweras on the east coast of the North Island of Aotearoa New Zealand. The Tūhoe declined to sign the Treaty of Waitangi and thus never formally acceded to the British settlement of Aotearoa.

8 This tendency has intensified since 9/11 but predates it. For example, in 1999, *Military Review: The Professional Journal of the U.S. Army* published a special issue on "Emerging Threats." A section of this issue headed "Emerging Threats, Ominous Horizons" included a paper entitled "Insurgencies, terrorist groups and Indigenous movements" (Gato 1999). For a post-9/11 example, the Indigenous Bolivian scholar Waskar Ari (2014: xii) discusses the protracted struggle that was necessary for him to procure a visa in the wake of 9/11 so he could take up an academic position in the United States.

9 This point was made in the mainstream news media on 16 October 2007 by both Iti's partner, Maria Steens, and also by Māori Party MP Te Ururoa Flavell, who said: "The fact is in order to teach them about being Tūhoe in the Tūhoe nation, they need to know about weaponry."

10 According to the online Māori dictionary available at http://www.maoridictionary.co.nz/, "mana" is "a supernatural force in a person, place or object" that conveys a sense of "prestige, authority, control, power, influence, status, spiritual power, [and] charisma."

11 As Maldonado-Torres (2007: 243) writes, "coloniality is different from colonialism." Coloniality is what remains when formal colonialism has ended and is maintained through a range of political, cultural and institutional practices, and it is something that "we breathe . . . all the time and everyday."

12 Tariana Turia told ONE News on 16 October the following: "It's not the first time Māori have been targeted as terrorists. We know some years ago when Māori people went to Cuba, they were accused of terrorism then. Nobody's been blown up since then."

Chapter 6   Indigeneity and Celebrity

1 Marcos is not actually Indigenous but is a mestizo intellectual from Mexico City who has been part of the Zapatista struggle since the early 1990s.

2 We have been interacting with Tame Iti in person and by email since 2015. In July 2015 we spent four days in the Tūhoe Nation interviewing Tame, visiting his painting studio, and spending time with him and other Tūhoe. We also spent three days with Tame in Dunedin, Aotearoa New Zealand, in May 2016.

3 Waitangi Day is an annual national holiday that commemorates the signing of the Treaty of Waitangi and has in recent decades been a day of widespread Māori protests.

4 See https://maoridictionary.co.nz/search?idiom=&phrase=&proverb=&loan=&histLoanWords=&keywords=Muru.
5 In 2014, Te Urewera National Park was redefined by an act of the New Zealand Parliament as "a legal entity" possessing "all the rights, powers, duties, and liabilities of a legal person." Te Urewera is thus no longer owned by the Crown. The 2014 legislation defines Te Urewera as a "place of spiritual value with its own mana and *mauri*" (which the online Māori dictionary, available at http://www.maoridictionary.co.nz, defines as the "vital essence," "special nature," or "essential quality and vitality of a being or entity"). Te Urewera is managed by a board consisting of six members appointed by Tūhoe and three members appointed by the Crown. The board is obliged to act in accordance with customary Tūhoe values and principles (Ruru 2014a). Jacinta Ruru (2014b) avers that the 2014 legislation "demonstrates a new bi-cultural way of understanding the importance of place."
6 Available at https://suite.co.nz/exhibitions/223/.
7 On Māori Television's current affairs show *Native Affairs*, presenter Mihingarangi Forbes asked the police commissioner why nobody had been called to account and suggests that this fact makes the commissioner's apology seem "inadequate and defensive" (Māori Television 2013).

Chapter 7 Authoritarianism and Participatory Cultures

1 The Treaty of Managua was signed in 1860, as we have noted, and not in 1800, as stated in this correspondence.
2 The term "criollo/Creole" means different things in different parts of Latin America. Here we use the Spanish term "criollo" to refer to people of European descent who were born in Latin America, while we use the English terms "Creole" and "Black Creole" to refer to the Afrodescendant populations in Costa Rica and Nicaragua who live mostly but not exclusively in the Caribbean region and speak Creole English as well as or instead of Spanish.
3 Romero Vargas (1993, quoted in Pineda 2006: 47) writes that ever since the appearance in the nineteenth century of "the myth that *mestizaje* occurred only between the Spanish and the Indians," Nicaraguans have "tried to hide and disguise" the deep significance of Afrodescendants throughout their nation and to "conceal the African elements of Nicaraguan social formation" in the Hispanicized Pacific region (despite its widespread recognition in the country's Caribbean region).
4 The Pacific and Caribbean regions of Nicaraguan are separated by a dense jungle, so broadcast signals from the former could not generally be received in the latter.
5 "Hasta el momento les cuento algo estamos en un momento de agonía, por eso yo le decía los rescates culturales, el rescate de valores culturales ¿Por qué? porque estamos en agonía. Yo no le voy a esconder a usted lo que no puedo esconder, el que diga que eso es mentira pues estaría mintiéndote, pero nosotros estamos en un momento crítico con la cultura y la cultura no solamente es al vida en nuestras casas también es el lenguaje principalmente y el lenguaje se está viniendo al suelo. Nosotros aquí en 20 años mucho si no nos ponemos las pilas perdemos todo, entonces esa es la lucha también, vea la jalada de piedras se había perdido esa parte de la cultura."

Chapter 8   Transmediation and New Central American Digital Activisms

1. In addition to the YouTube URL given in our references, this film can also be accessed via the LimónTV Facebook page here: https://www.facebook.com/townbook.limon/videos/319695243328515.
2. See, e.g., the film *Walter Ferguson: The Father of Calypso* (Carlos Zúñiga Lossio, 2017), available here: https://www.youtube.com/watch?v=_PebdJc73rg.
3. Walter Ferguson's "One Pant Man" endures on YouTube here: https://www.youtube.com/watch?v=q08s6zoX6r8, and his "I Am the King of Calypso" has been digitized from an old cassette tape here: https://www.youtube.com/watch?v=_L30OQG7pqw.
4. See, e.g., "Pañaman or Black?" at the start of the nationally televised Costa Rican concert available here: https://www.youtube.com/watch?v=klTIe3i1EZg. "Paña people" is a Creole language designation for Spanish-speaking mestizo Latin Americans.
5. Calypsonian Ulysses Grant, for example, believes that commodification destroys calypso's artisanal form (*The Calypsonians of Today*, 2021).
6. His report can be viewed at https://www.youtube.com/watch?v=H2akcSLNO6s.
7. The song "*Doña Coquita Matus*" is available on YouTube here: https://www.youtube.com/watch?v=ccDrIDJ5Jy0.
8. The online graphic activism shown in figures 8.2 and 8.3 began to circulate online in 2018 and 2019. These and other images like them were developed on the basis of "microstories" sent by student protestors to artists Clausunk and Suprime.
9. The video can be viewed here: https://nadaestaolvidado.com/#voces.
10. The Contra were a U.S.-backed counterrevolutionary military organization that waged a decade-long war against the revolutionary Sandinista government.
11. The image depicted in figure 8.4 appeared in the independent Nicaraguan media outlets, *La Prensa* and *Divergentes*, which have both given their permission for us to reproduce the photo. But they acknowledge that it is not their photo, as they are both reporting on what is happening in Nicaragua in exile. For reasons of safety, the actual photographer, who is still in Nicaragua, cannot be named as it would put them at risk of imprisonment or harassment by the regime. As the director of *La Prensa* (in exile) commented to us: "I think it is very difficult to find a more 'exact' example of what is happening in Nicaragua. Do you know that the artist was taken to prison and the mural was erased? Imagine what could happen to the photographer." The photo can be found here: https://www.laprensani.com/2023/11/21/vida/3241777-impiden-a-artistas-pintar-mural-en-homenaje-a-miss-universo-sheynnis-palacios-en-esteli.
12. Murillo's original words were: "En estas horas y en estos días de Nuevas Victorias vemos el aprovechamiento grosero, y la tosca y malvada comunicación terrorista, que pretende convertir un lindo y merecido momento de Orgullo y Celebración, en golpismo destructivo, o en un retorno, por supuesto imposible, a las nefastas prácticas, egoístas y criminales, de quienes, como vampiros y vividores, se han servido del Pueblo, de los Bienes del Pueblo, de los Patrimonios Naturales, Culturales, legítimos Patrimonios del Pueblo nicaragüense" (Murillo 2023). See Divergentes (2023) for more detail.
13. Tamara's testimony is available at https://www.youtube.com/watch?v=e8tsdpUc9Qw&ab_channel=LaPrensaNicaragua.
14. The Riverdale cast video can be seen here: https://twitter.com/WriterRAS/status/1435634270568022017?s=20&t=f9OGAYK5TYi6WM1oz0MP4A.
15. See https://twitter.com/SFRCdems/status/1435744646244839426?s=20&t=f9OGAYK5TYi6WM1oz0MP4A.

Conclusion

1 The 2019 High Court ruling found that Fujitsu's Horizon system contained "bugs, errors and defects," despite the Post Office's persistent, "cult"-like protestations that the software was reliable and "fit for purpose" (Flinders 2023).
2 Perhaps one exception is the U.K. COVID-19 inquiry, which has attracted substantial public attention and also began after a Channel 4 drama, *Partygate*, examined the frequent parties that took place in government offices and the prime minister's home on Downing Street during lockdowns, when the wider public was required to forego social contact and people were unable to go to hospitals or care homes to visit or say goodbye to dying loved ones.
3 Stuart Hall (1996: 422) noted that unresolved conjunctural crises can take decades of struggle to develop, and wrote in the late-1980s that successive U.K. conjunctures had by that time "been in a deep social crisis for most of the 20th century" (Hall 1987: 20).

References

Abel, S. (2008). Tūhoe and "terrorism" on television news. In D. Keenan (Ed.), *Terror in Our Midst? Searching for Terror in Aotearoa New Zealand* (pp. 113–128). Wellington: Huia.
———. (2011). The racial political economy of Māori Television. *Australian Journal of Communication* 38(3): 125–138.
———. (2013). Māori Television, its Pākehā audience and issues of decolonialization. *Studies in Australasian Cinema* 7(2–3): 111–121.
———. (2016). Māori, media and politics. In G. Kemp, B. Bahador, K. McMillan, and C. Rudd (Eds.), *Politics and the Media* (2nd ed., pp. 310–325). Auckland: Auckland University Press.
Acosta, M. L. (2010). Los retos del proceso de titulación y saneamiento como protección a la propiedad indígena. *Wani* 60: 5–17.
Adams, M. (2011). Is family a moral capital resource for female politicians? The case of ABC's *Commander in Chief. Media Culture and Society* 33(2): 223–241.
Adams, T. (2024) "The timing was impeccable": Why it took a TV series to bring the Post Office scandal to light. *Guardian*, 13 January. Retrieved 15 January 2024 from https://www.theguardian.com/uk-news/2024/jan/13/mr-bates-vs-the-post-office-why-it-took-a-tv-series-to-bring-the-post-office-scandal-to-light.
Agamben, G. (2005). *State of Exception* (K. Attell, Trans.). Chicago: University of Chicago Press.
Aguirre-Sacasa, R. (2021). My father was a vocal critic of Nicaragua's president. Now he's a political prisoner. *Time*, 21 September. Retrieved 13 June 2024 from https://time.com/6099978/francisco-aguirre-sacasa-nicaragua-political-prisoner/.
Akass, K., and McCabe, J. (2005). *Reading Six Feet Under: TV to Die for*. London: I. B. Tauris.
Alabarces, P. (2018). The popular culture turn. In J. Poblete (Ed.), *New Approaches to Latin American Studies: Culture and Power* (pp. 50–64). New York: Routledge.
A'Lee Frost, A. (2016). The necessity of political vulgarity. *Current Affairs: A Magazine of Politics and Culture*, 25 August. Retrieved 30 May 2020 from https://www.currentaffairs.org/2016/05/the-necessity-of-political-vulgarity.

AM Costa Rica. (2021). Costa Rica celebrates National Calypso Day. *AM Costa Rica*, 7 May. Retrieved 19 February 2023 from https://amcostarica.com/Costa%20 Rica%20celebrates%20National%20Calypso%20Day.html.

Amnesty International. (2018). *Instilling Terror: From Lethal Force to Persecution in Nicaragua*. London: Amnesty International.

Ampie, J. C. (2021). Alistate, Daniel Ortega . . . ¡Archie viene por vos! #SOSNicaragua. Bacanalnica, 21 September. Retrieved 9 September 2022 from https://www.bacanal nica.com/alistate-daniel-ortega-archie-viene-por-vos-sosnicaragua/.

Anderson, B. (2006). *Imagined Communities: Reflections on the Origin and Spread of Nationalism*. Rev. ed. London: Verso.

Anderson, K., and Hokowhitu, B. (2021). "Pretty Boy" Trudeau versus the "Algonquin Agitator": Hitting the ropes of Canadian colonialist masculinities. In J. Adese and R. A. Innes (Eds.), *Indigenous Celebrity: Entanglements with Fame* (pp. 146–162). Winnipeg: University of Manitoba Press.

Anderson, M. D. (2009). *Black and Indigenous: Garífuna Activism and Consumer Culture in Honduras*. Minneapolis: University of Minnesota Press.

Andrejevic, M. (2004). *Reality TV: The Work of Being Watched*. Lanham, MD: Rowman and Littlefield.

———. (2007). *iSpy: Surveillance and Power in the Interactive Era*. Lawrence: University Press of Kansas.

———. (2011). The work that affective economics does. *Cultural Studies* 25(4–5): 604–620.

———. (2013). *Infoglut: How Too Much Information is Changing the Way We Think and Know*. New York: Routledge.

Andrews, R., and Graham, J. (2014). *Te Hīkoi a Rūaumoko/Rūaumoko's Walk*. Napier: Hawkes Bay Emergency Management Group. Retrieved 11 January 2024 from https://www.hbemergency.govt.nz/ruaumokos-walk-ebook/ruaumoko_sc1.html.

Arellano, J. (2016). Introduction: Comparative media studies in Latin America. *Revista de Estudios Hispánicos* 50(2): 281–291.

Ari, W. (2014). *Earth Politics: Religion, Decolonization, and Bolivia's Indigenous Intellectuals*. Durham, NC: Duke University Press.

Artemis. (2011). NZ government to bail out insurer without enough reinsurance. *Artemis*, 7 April. Retrieved 9 February 2023 from https://www.artemis.bm/news/nz -government-to-bail-out-insurer-without-enough-reinsurance/.

Arva, E. (2020). The analogical legacy of ground zero: Magical realism in post-9/11 literary and filmic trauma narratives. In R. Perez and V. A. Chevalier (Eds.), *The Palgrave Handbook of Magical Realism in the Twenty-First Century* (pp. 237–262). Cham, Switzerland: Palgrave Macmillan.

Asaro, P. (2017). The labor of surveillance and bureaucratized killing: New subjectivities of military drone operators. In L. Parks and C. Kaplan (Eds.), *Life in the Age of Drone Warfare* (pp. 282–314). Durham, NC: Duke University Press.

Associated Press. (2021). 12 Dead after attacks on Indigenous communities in Nicaragua. AP News, 26 August. Retrieved 8 September 2022 from https://apnews.com /article/caribbean-nicaragua-2640a440b9b45e86ead03ae87623e511.

Austrin, T., and Farnsworth, J. (2012). Upheaval: Seismic, social and media mash-ups after the Christchurch earthquakes. *New Zealand Journal of Media Studies* 13(2): 78–94.

Auyero, J. (2012). *Patients of the State: The Politics of Waiting in Argentina*. Durham, NC: Duke University Press.

Baker1000. (2015). Lostpedia is 10 years old. *Lostpedia* (blog), 22 September. Retrieved 20 February 2018 from http://lostpedia.wikia.com/wiki/User_blog:Baker1000 /Lostpedia_is_10_years_old.

Bangkukuk Taik. (2015). Bangkukuk Taik[,] an indigenous Rama community and the Nicaraguan interoceanic grand canal [YouTube]. Retrieved 25 November 2015 from https://www.youtube.com/watch?v=IIM-D-2lb4.

———. (2016). We do not consent! The indigenous struggle against the Grand Canal of Nicaragua [Vimeo]. Retrieved 6 December 2016 from https://vimeo.com/174291184.

Barclay, B. (2003). Celebrating Fourth Cinema. *Illusions* 35: 7–11.

Barrett, K. (2005). Griffin seals case for 9/11 WTC demolition, calls on *NY Times* to end coverup. *Indymedia UK*, 19 October. Retrieved 14 December 2022 from https://www.indymedia.org.uk/en/2005/10/326074.html.

Bartholomew, J. (2023). "Mosquitoes from the same swamp": How the digital media landscape birthed the internationalist far right. *Columbia Journalism Review*, 13 February. Retrieved 8 March 2023 from https://www.cjr.org/tow_center/brazil-insurrection.php.

Baudrillard, J. (1983). The ecstasy of communication. In H. Foster (Ed.), *The Anti-Aesthetic: Essays on Postmodern Culture* (pp. 126–134). Port Townsend, WA: Bay Press.

———. (1988). *The Ecstasy of Communication* (S. Lotringer, Ed., B. Schutze and C. Schutze, Trans.). New York: Semiotext(e).

———. (2003). *The Spirit of Terrorism* (C. Turner, Trans.). London: Verso.

Beltrán, M. C. (2002). The Hollywood Latina body as site of social struggle: Media constructions of stardom and Jennifer Lopez's "cross-over butt." *Quarterly Review of Film and Video* 19(1): 71–86.

Benjamin, A. B. (2017). 9/11 as false flag: Why international law must dare to care. *African Journal of International and Comparative Law* 25(3): 371–392.

Benjamin, W. (1999). *The Arcades Project* (H. Eiland and K. McLaughlin, Trans.). Cambridge, MA: Belknap Press of Harvard University Press.

Bennett, J. (2011). Introduction: Television as digital media. In J. Bennett and N. Strange (Eds.), *Television as Digital Media* (pp. 1–27). Durham, NC: Duke University Press.

Bergman, R., and Goldman, A. (2023). Israel knew Hamas's attack plan more than a year ago. *New York Times*, 30 November. Retrieved 28 December 2023 from https://www.nytimes.com/2023/11/30/world/middleeast/israel-hamas-attack-intelligence.html.

Bevan, A. (2015). The national body, women, and mental health in *Homeland*. *Cinema Journal* 54(4): 145–151.

Beverley, J. (2011). *Latinamericanism after 9/11*. Durham, NC: Duke University Press.

Bhattacharyya, G. (2014). Narrative pleasure in *Homeland*: The competing femininities of "rogue agents" and "terror wives." In C. Carter, L. Steiner, and L. McLaughlin (Eds.), *The Routledge Companion to Media and Gender* (pp. 374–383). London: Routledge.

Binney, J. (2010). *Stories without End: Essays 1975–2010*. Wellington: Bridget Williams Books.

Birchall, C. (2006). *Knowledge Goes Pop: From Conspiracy Theory to Gossip*. Oxford: Berg.

Birchall, C., and Knight, P. (2023). *Conspiracy Theories in the Time of COVID-19*. London: Routledge.

Blundell, S. (2014). Resisting erasure. In B. Bennett, J. Dann, E. Johnson, and R. Reynolds (Eds.), *Once in a Lifetime: City-Building after Disaster in Christchurch* (pp. 45–51). Christchurch: Freerange Press.

Boal, I., Clark, T. J., Matthews, J., and Watts, M. (2005). *Afflicted Powers: Capital and Spectacle in a New Age of War*. London: Verso.

Bobo, J. (2009). Impact of grassroots activism. *Journal of Visual Culture* 8(2): 158–160.

Bollmer, G. (2018). *Theorizing Digital Cultures*. London: Sage.

Bolter, J. D., and Grusin, R. (1999). *Remediation: Understanding New Media*. Cambridge, MA: MIT Press.

Bonilla, Y. (2020). The coloniality of disaster: Race, empire, and the temporal logics of emergency in Puerto Rico, USA. *Political Geography* 78: 1–12.

Bourdieu, P. (2000). *Pascalian Meditations*. Cambridge: Polity Press.

Bourgois, P. (1989). *Ethnicity at Work: Divided Labor on a Central American Banana Plantation*. Baltimore, MD: John Hopkins University Press.

Bowron, J. (2013). *Campbell* becoming last court of appeal. *Dominion Post*, 2 June. Retrieved 25 July 2020 from http://www.stuff.co.nz/dominion-post/culture/television/8744912/Campbell-becoming-last-court-of-appeal.

Braddock, J. (2003). New Zealand policeman acquitted in private prosecution for murder. *World Socialist Web Site*, 28 January. Retrieved 31 March 2023 from https://www.wsws.org/en/articles/2003/01/newz-j28.html.

Bragman, W., and Kotch, A. (2021). How the Koch network hijacked the war on Covid. *Exposed by CMD: Investigating Power, The Center for Media and Democracy*, 22 December. Retrieved 9 February 2023 from https://www.exposedbycmd.org/2021/12/22/how-the-koch-network-hijacked-the-war-on-covid/.

Bratich, J. Z. (2008). *Conspiracy Panics: Political Rationality and Popular Culture*. Albany: State University of New York Press.

Brebner, P. (2022). "I Will Not Speak Māori": Tame Iti's provocative new artwork creates a splash. *Stuff*, 26 August. Retrieved 28 March 2023 from https://www.stuff.co.nz/pou-tiaki/129683587/i-will-not-speak-mori-tame-itis-provocative-new-artwork-creates-a-splash.

Brito, C. (2021). "Riverdale" creator pleads for release of father, who is a political prisoner in Nicaragua: "We have no idea how this ends." *CBS News*, 7 October. Retrieved 9 September 2022 from https://www.cbsnews.com/news/riverdale-roberto-aguirre-sacasa-father-prisoner-nicaragua.

Brock, A. (2020). *Distributed Blackness: African American Cybercultures*. New York: New York University Press.

Brockington, D. (2009). *Celebrity and the Environment: Fame, Wealth and Power in Conservation*. London: Zed Books.

———. (2014). *Celebrity Advocacy and International Development*. London: Routledge.

Brockington, D., and Henson, S. (2015). Signifying the public: Celebrity advocacy and post-democratic politics. *International Journal of Cultural Studies* 18(4): 431–448.

Brodine, M. T. (2011). Post-Katrina citizen media: Speaking NOLA. *Invisible Culture* 16: 88–102.

Bronner, M. (2006). 9/11 live: The NORAD tapes. *Vanity Fair*, 17 October. Retrieved 27 August 2020 from https://www.vanityfair.com/news/2006/08/norad200608.

Broughton, C. (2020). Christchurch statues staying put despite low regard from local iwi. *Stuff*, 12 June. Retrieved 11 February 2023 from https://www.stuff.co.nz/national/300033885/christchurch-statues-staying-put-despite-low-regard-from-local-iwi.

Brun, C. (2015). Active waiting and changing hopes: Towards a time perspective on protracted displacement. *Social Analysis* 59(1): 19–37.

Bruns, A. (2008). *Blogs, Wikipedia, Second Life and Beyond: From Production to Produsage*. New York: Peter Lang.

Bruyneel, K. (2007). *The Third Space of Sovereignty: The Postcolonial Politics of US-Indigenous Relations*. Minneapolis: University of Minnesota Press.

Bumiller, E. (2005). Casualty of firestorm. *New York Times*, 10 September. Retrieved 1 August 2020 from http://www.nytimes.com/2005/09/10/national/nationalspecial/10crisis.html?pagewanted=print.

Burgess, J., and Green, J. (2009). *YouTube: Online Video and Participatory Culture*. Cambridge, MA: Polity Press.

Butler, J. (2010). Torture and the ethics of photography. In F. Macdonald, R. Hughes, and K. Dodds (Eds.), *Observant States: Geopolitics and Visual Culture* (pp. 41–64). London: I. B. Tauris.

Cadwalladr, C., and Graham-Harrison, E. (2018). Cambridge Analytica: Links to Moscow oil firm and St Petersburg university. *Guardian*, 17 March. Retrieved 22 February 2023 from https://www.theguardian.com/news/2018/mar/17/cambridge-academic-trawling-facebook-had-links-to-russian-university.

Caldwell, J. T. (2003). Second-shift media aesthetics: Programming, interactivity, and user flows. In A. Everett and J. T. Caldwell (Eds.), *New Media: Theories and Practices of Digitextuality* (pp. 127–144). New York: Routledge.

The Calypsonians of Today/Los Calypsonianos de Hoy. (2021). Directed by Ramón Morales-Garro [television documentary]. Retrieved 15 February 2023 from https://www.youtube.com/watch?v=aGaDx2ilfJU.

Cameron-Chilesque, J. (2023). Nearly £15bn wasted on Covid PPE, says UK spending watchdog. *Financial Times*, 26 January. Retrieved 15 January 2024 from https://www.ft.com/content/15c3630a-b31a-425a-935b-e07d180a8b58.

Canella, G. (2018). Racialized surveillance: Activist media and the policing of Black bodies. *Communication Culture and Critique* 11: 378–398.

Carley, R. F. (2021). *Cultural Studies Methodology and Political Strategy: Metaconjuncture*. Cham, Switzerland: Palgrave Macmillan.

Castells, M. (2009). *Communication Power*. Oxford: Oxford University Press.

Castonguay, J. (2015). Fictions of terror: Complexity, complicity and insecurity in *Homeland*. *Cinema Journal* 54(4): 139–145.

CEJIL. (2015). Comisión Interamericana de Derechos Humanos exige a Nicaragua la protección de los miskitos de la Costa Caribe Norte. [Press release], 17 October. Retrieved 29 November 2015 from https://cejil.org/comunicados/ comision-inter americana-de-derechos-humanos-exige-a-nicaragua-la-proteccion-de-los-miski.

Cejudhcan derechos humanos. (2015a). Documental CEJUDHCAN. Retrieved 19 February 2023 from https://www.youtube.com/watch?v=uSiByOazZ9Y.

———. (2015b). Deadly conditions on the Miskito Coast. Retrieved 19 February 2023 from https://www.youtube.com/watch?v=jDMdPHQ-Jdo.

———. (2015c). Situación del territorio indígena Wangki Twi Tasba Raya. Retrieved 19 February 2023 from https://www.youtube.com/watch?v=lG4D9HF1KXo.

———. (2015d). Adolescentes indígenas piden ayuda a través de su canto ante la invasión de colonos. Retrieved 19 February 2023 from https://www.youtube.com/watch?v=fbi6Qk8rUIo.

Chaudhuri, A. (2016). The real meaning of Rhodes Must Fall. *Guardian*, 16 March. Retrieved 11 February 2023 from https://www.theguardian.com/uk-news/2016/mar/16/the-real-meaning-of-rhodes-must-fall.

Chouliaraki, L. (2013). *The Ironic Spectator: Solidarity in the Age of Post-Humanitarianism* (Kindle version). Cambridge: Polity Press.

Christian, A. J. (2016). Video stars: Marketing queer performance in networked television. In S. U. Noble and B. M. Tynes (Eds.), *The Intersectional Internet: Race, Sex, Class, and Culture Online* (pp. 95–113). New York: Peter Lang.

Clark, N. (2010). *Inhuman Nature: Sociable Life on a Dynamic Planet*. London: Sage.

Clark, N., Chhotray, V., and Few, R. (2013). Global justice and disasters. *The Geographical Journal* 179(2): 105–113.

Clarke, M. J. (2013). *Transmedia Television: New Trends in Network Serial Production*. New York: Bloomsbury.

Cloke, P., Dickenson, S., and Tupper, S. (2017). The Christchurch earthquakes 2010, 2011: Geographies of an event. *New Zealand Geographer* 73(2): 69–80.

Clough, P. T. (2000). *Autoaffection: Unconscious Thought in the Age of Teletechnology*. Minneapolis: University of Minnesota Press.

CNN. (2022). 2016 presidential campaign hacking fast facts. CNN, 20 October. Retrieved 22 February 2023 from https://edition.cnn.com/2016/12/26/us/2016-presidential-campaign-hacking-fast-facts/index.html.

Cogburn, D. L., and Espinoza-Vasquez, F. K. (2011). From networked nominee to networked nation: Examining the impact of Web 2.0 and social media on political participation and civic engagement in the 2008 Obama campaign. *Journal of Political Marketing* 10(1–2): 189–213.

Cohen, M. (2013). *Homeland* isn't just bad TV, it peddles the worst lies about US foreign policy. *Guardian*, 16 December. Retrieved 16 August 2020 from https://www.theguardian.com/commentisfree/2013/dec/16/homeland-worst-lies-us-power-foreign-policy.

Conn, D. (2022). Revealed: Tory peer Michelle Mone secretly received £29m from "VIP lane" PPE firm. *Guardian*, 23 November. Retrieved 16 January 2024 from https://www.theguardian.com/uk-news/2022/nov/23/revealed-tory-peer-michelle-mone-secretly-received-29m-from-vip-lane-ppe-firm.

———. (2023). Michelle Mone admits she lied to media over links to PPE firm. *Guardian*, 17 December. Retrieved 16 January 2024 from https://www.theguardian.com/uk-news/2023/dec/17/michelle-mone-admits-she-stands-to-benefit-from-60m-pounds-ppe-profit?ref=mc.news.

Cooper, A. F. (2007). *Celebrity Diplomacy*. Abingdon, UK: Routledge.

Cordero, R. (2021). "Riverdale" cast support EP Roberto Aguirre-Sacasa as he decries father's treason charge in Nicaragua. *Deadline*, 8 September. Retrieved 9 September 2022 from https://deadline.com/2021/09/riverdale-cast-support-roberto-aguirre-sacasa-father-treason-charge-nicaragua-1234828636.

Couldry, N. (2010). *Why Voice Matters: Culture and Politics after Neoliberalism*. Los Angeles: Sage.

———. (2011). More sociology, more culture, more politics. *Cultural Studies* 25(4–5): 487–501.

Couldry, N., and Markham, T. (2007). Celebrity culture and public connection: Bridge or chasm? *International Journal of Cultural Studies* 10(4): 403–422.

Couzens, G. (2017). Spanish language content removed from White House website after Trump inauguration. *Express*, 23 January. Retrieved 30 July 2022 from https://www.express.co.uk/news/world/757904/Spanish-language-White-House-website-Donald-Trump.

Crace, J. (2024). The Post Office is now box office as inquiry resumes with righteous fury. *Guardian*, 11 January. Retrieved 16 January 2024 from https://www.theguardian.com/politics/2024/jan/11/the-post-office-is-now-box-office-as-inquiry-resumes-with-righteous-fury.

Cram, F. (2021). Mahi aroha: Māori work in times of trouble and disaster as an expression of a love for the people. *Kōtuitui: New Zealand Journal of Social Sciences* 16(2): 356–370.

Crawford, N. C. (2012). "Targeted" drones strikes and magical thinking. *Huffpost*, 23 September. Retrieved 11 March 2018 from https://www.huffingtonpost.com/neta-crawford/drones-civilian-casualties_b_1907597.html.

Creeber, G. (2004). *Serial Television: Big Drama on the Small Screen*. London: BFI Publishing.

Creeber, G., and Martin, R. (2009). Introduction. In G. Creeber and R. Martin (Eds.), *Digital Cultures: Understanding New Media* (pp. 1–10). Maidenhead, UK: Open University Press.

Cultural Survival. (2012). Human rights violations in Guatemala: Hearing Indigenous voices. *Cultural Survival Quarterly Magazine*, June. Retrieved 22 February 2017 from https://www.culturalsurvival.org/publications/cultural-survival-quarterly/human-rights-violations-guatemala-hearing-indigenous.

Cunneen, C. (2013). Colonial processes, Indigenous peoples, and criminal justice systems. In S. M. Bucerius and T. Michael (Eds.), *The Oxford Handbook of Ethnicity, Crime and Immigration* (pp. 386–407). Oxford: Oxford University Press.

Cupples, J. (2009a). Remaking the Anglophilic city: Visual spectacles in suburbia. *New Zealand Geographer* 65(1): 23–34.

———. (2009b). Rethinking electoral geography: Spaces and practices of democracy in Nicaragua. *Transactions of the Institute of British Geographers* 34(1): 110–124.

———. (2012a). Boundary crossings and new striations: When disaster hits a neoliberalising campus. *Transactions of the Institute of British Geographers* 37(3): 337–341.

———. (2012b). Wild globalization: The biopolitics of climate change and global capitalism on Nicaragua's Mosquito Coast. *Antipode: A Journal of Radical Geography* 44(1): 10–30.

———. (2015). Development communication, popular pleasure and media convergence. In S. Mains, J. Cupples, and C. Lukinbeal (Eds.), *Mediated Geographies and Geographies of Media* (pp. 351–366). Dordrecht, Netherlands: Springer.

———. (2022). *Development and Decolonization in Latin America*. 2nd ed. London: Routledge.

Cupples, J., and Glynn, K. (2009). Editorial: Counter-cartographies: New (Zealand) cultural studies/geographies and the city. *New Zealand Geographer* 65(1): 1–5.

———. (2013). Postdevelopment television? Cultural citizenship and the mediation of Africa in contemporary TV drama. *Annals of the Association of American Geographers* 103 (4): 1003–1021.

———. (2014). Indigenizing and decolonizing higher education on Nicaragua's Atlantic Coast. *Singapore Journal of Tropical Geography* 35(1): 56–71.

———. (2016). Neoliberalism, surveillance and media convergence. In S. Springer, K. Birch, and J. MacLeavy (Eds.), *The Handbook of Neoliberalism* (pp. 175–189). New York: Routledge.

Cupples, J., Glynn, K., and Larios, I. (2007). Hybrid cultures of postdevelopment: The struggle for popular hegemony in rural Nicaragua. *Annals of the Association of American Geographers* 97(4): 786–801.

Cupples, J., and Harrison, J. (2001). Disruptive voices and boundaries of respectability in Christchurch, New Zealand. *Gender, Place and Culture* 8(2): 189–204.

Curran, J., and Park, M. (2000). Beyond globalization theory. In J. Curran and M. Park (Eds.), *De-Westernizing Media Studies* (pp. 2–15). London: Routledge.

Dally, J. (2012). Brownlee apologises to Christchurch residents. *Stuff*, 12 September. Retrieved 15 June 2020 from http://www.stuff.co.nz/national/7662481/Brownlee-apologises-to-Christchurch-residents.

Damon, A. (2023). Documents expose Israeli conspiracy to facilitate October 7 attack. *World Socialist Website*, 2 December. Retrieved 28 December 2023 from https://www.wsws.org/en/articles/2023/12/02/klox-d02.html.

Davies, H., McKernan, B., and Sabbagh, D. (2023). "The Gospel": How Israel uses AI to select bombing targets in Gaza. *Guardian*, 1 December. Retrieved 28 December 2023 from https://www.theguardian.com/world/2023/dec/01/the-gospel-how-israel-uses-ai-to-select-bombing-targets.

Davies, R. (2024a) Fujitsu gave £2.6m payoff to its former UK boss, filings suggest. *Guardian*, 11 January. Retrieved 16 January 2024 from https://www.theguardian.com/business/2024/jan/11/fujitsu-gave-26m-payoff-to-former-uk-boss-in-2020-filings-suggest.

———. (2024b). Lost emails and last-ditch finds: How the Post Office inquiry was delayed. *Guardian*, 11 January. Retrieved 16 January 2024 from https://www.theguardian.com/uk-news/2024/jan/11/lost-emails-and-last-ditch-finds-how-the-post-office-inquiry-was-delayed.

Davis, C. R. (2021). Facebook says it just uncovered one of the largest troll farms ever—run by the government of Nicaragua. *Business Insider*, 1 November. Retrieved 30 December 2023 from https://markets.businessinsider.com/news/stocks/facebook-said-uncovered-troll-farm-run-by-nicaraguan-government-2021-11.

Dayan, D. (2009). Sharing and showing: Television as monstration. *Annals of the American Academy of Political and Social Science* 625(1): 19–31.

Dean, A. (2015). *Ruth, Roger and Me: Debts and Legacies*. Wellington: Bridget Williams Books.

Dean, J. (2002). *Publicity's Secret: How Technoculture Capitalizes on Democracy*. Ithaca, NY: Cornell University Press.

———. (2009). *Democracy and Other Neoliberal Fantasies: Communicative Capitalism and Left Politics*. Durham, NC: Duke University Press.

De Certeau, M. (1984) *The Practice of Everyday Life* (S. Rendall, Trans.). Berkeley: University of California Press.

Deleuze, G., and Guattari, F. (1987). *A Thousand Plateaus: Capitalism and Schizophrenia* (B. Massumi, Trans.). Minneapolis: University of Minnesota Press.

Dennis, P. A. (2004). *The Miskitu People of Awastara*. Austin: University of Texas Press.

Desinformémonos. (2014). Subcomandante Marcos is no more. *Upside Down World*, 26 May. Retrieved 1 August 2020 from http://upsidedownworld.org/news-briefs/news-briefs-news- briefs/subcomandante-marcos-is-no-more.

Devadas, V. (2013). Governing indigenous sovereignty: Biopolitics and the "terror raids" in New Zealand. In B. Hokowhitu and V. Devadas (Eds.), *The Fourth Eye: Māori Media in Aotearoa New Zealand* (pp. 3–24). Minneapolis: University of Minnesota Press.

De Zeeuw, D., and Tuters, M. (2020). Teh [sic] Internet is serious business: On the deep vernacular web and its discontents. *Cultural Politics* 16(2): 214–232.

Diaz, M. (2021). Facebook y Twitter hicieron una redada en TELCOR (adios trolls sandinistas). Bacanalnica, 1 November. Retrieved 30 December 2023 from https://www.bacanalnica.com/facebook-y-twitter-hicieron-una-redada-en-telcor-adios-trolls-sandinistas/?fbclid=IwAR04OYp6Wbo_5T5ObMBIVJwIoCH2twQ7ygHzhVK3qThytd8VOFiiGw-Oi-Q.

di Piramo, D. (2010). *Political Leadership in Zapatista Mexico: Marcos, Celebrity, and Charismatic Authority*. Boulder, CO: First Forum Press.

Divergentes. (2023). El doble discurso del régimen sobre Sheynnis Palacios. *Divergentes*, 22 November. Retrieved 11 January 2024 from https://www.divergentes.com/el-doble-discurso-del-regimen-sobre-sheynnis-palacios.

Dowd, M. (2003). Walk this way. *New York Times*, 21 May. Retrieved 1 December 2013 from http://www.nytimes.com/2003/05/21/opinion/21DOWD.htm.

Driessens, O. (2012). The celebritization of society and culture: Understanding the structural dynamics of celebrity culture. *International Journal of Cultural Studies* 16(6): 641–657.

Du Bois, W.E.B. (1903). *The Souls of Black Folk: Essays and Sketches*. Chicago: A. C. McClurg.

Duncan, S. (2013). Consume or be consumed: Targeting Māori consumers in print media. In B. Hokowhitu and V. Devadas (Eds.), *The Fourth Eye: Māori Media in Aotearoa New Zealand* (pp. 76–97). Minneapolis: University of Minnesota Press.

Dunleavy, T. (2018). *Complex Serial Drama and Multiplatform Television*. New York: Routledge.

Durkay, L. (2014). "Homeland" is the most bigoted show on television. *Washington Post*, 2 October. Retrieved 6 March 2018 from https://www.washingtonpost.com/posteverything/wp/2014/10/02/homeland-is-the-most-bigoted-show-on-television/?utm_term=.f862a7882e21.

Dussel, E. (1995). Eurocentrism and modernity (introduction to the Frankfurt lectures). In J. Beverley, J. Ovieda, and M Aronna (Eds.), *The Postmodernism Debate in Latin America* (pp. 65–76). Durham, NC: Duke University Press.

———. (2002). World-system and "trans"-modernity. *Nepantla: Views from the South* 3(2): 221–244.

Dyson, M. E. (2006). *Come Hell or High Water: Hurricane Katrina and the Color of Disaster*. New York: Basic Civitas.

Dzenovska, D., and Arenas, I. (2012). Don't fence me in: Barricade sociality and political struggles in Mexico and Latvia. *Comparative Studies in Society and History* 54(3): 644–678.

Edmonds, P. (2015). Tame Iti at the confiscation line: Contesting the consensus politics of the Treaty of Waitangi in Aotearoa New Zealand. In K. Darian-Smith and P. Edmonds (Eds.), *Conciliation on Colonial Frontiers: Conflict, Performance and Commemoration in Australia and the Pacific Rim* (pp. 171–192). New York: Routledge.

Elers, S., and Elers, P. (2018). Tāme Iti and Twitter: A voice from prison. *Media International Australia* 169(1): 74–83.

Elliot, J. (2010). Life preservers: The neoliberal enterprise of Hurricane Katrina survival in *Trouble the Water, House MD* and *When the Levees Broke*. In D. Negra (Ed.), *Old and New Media after Katrina* (pp. 89–112). New York: Palgrave Macmillan.

Ellis, J. (1999). Television as working-through. In J. Gripsrud (Ed.), *Television and Common Knowledge* (pp. 55–70). London: Routledge.

El País. (2023). Repressive delirium in Nicaragua. *El País*, 28 November. Retrieved 11 January 2024 from https://english.elpais.com/opinion/2023-11-28/repressive-delirium-in-nicaragua.html.

Emmerson, R. (2011). A message from the heartland. *New Zealand Herald*, 16 April.

Enarson, E., and Morrow, B. H. (1998). Why gender? Why women? An introduction to women and disaster. In E. Enarson and B. H. Morrow (Eds.), *The Gendered Terrain of Disaster: Through Women's Eyes* (pp. 1–10). Westport, CT: Praeger.

Escobar, A. (1995). *Encountering Development: The Making and Unmaking of the Third World*. Princeton, NJ: Princeton University Press.

———. (2007). Worlds and knowledges otherwise: The Latin American modernity/coloniality research program. *Cultural Studies* 21(2–3): 179–210.

———. (2008). *Territories of Difference: Place, Movements, Life, Redes*. Durham, NC: Duke University Press.

———. (2010). Latin America at a crossroads. *Cultural Studies* 24(1): 1–65.
Everett, A. (2009). The Afrogeek-in-chief: Obama and our new media ecology. *Journal of Visual Culture* 8(2): 193–196.
Fagoth, R., Gioanetto, F., and Silva, A. (1998). *Wan Kaina Kulkaia/Armonizando con Nuestro Entorno*. Managua: Imprimatur Artes Gráficas.
Faris, D., and Meier, P. M. (2013) Digital activism in authoritarian countries. In A. A. Delwiche and J. Jacobs Henderson (Eds.), *The Participatory Cultures Handbook* (pp. 197–205). London: Routledge.
Fenster, M. (2008). *Conspiracy Theories: Secrecy and Power in American Culture*. Revised and updated ed. Minneapolis: University of Minnesota Press.
Finley-Brook, M. (2011). "We are the owners": Autonomy and natural resources in Northeastern Nicaragua. In L. Baracco (Ed.), *National Integration and Contested Autonomy: The Caribbean Coast of Nicaragua* (pp. 302–332). New York: Algora.
Fisher, K. (2015). Seismic energy and symbolic exchange in *When A City Falls*. In A. Wright (Ed.), *Film on the Faultline* (pp. 163–179). Bristol, UK: Intellect.
Fiske, J. (1992). British cultural studies and television. In R. C. Allen (Ed.), *Channels of Discourse, Reassembled: Television and Contemporary Criticism* (2nd ed., pp. 214–245). New York: Routledge.
———. (1998). Surveilling the city: Whiteness, the black man and democratic totalitarianism. *Theory, Culture and Society* 15(2): 66–88.
———. (2011). *Television Culture*. 2nd ed. London: Routledge.
———. (2016a). *Media Matters: Race and Gender in U.S. Politics*. 2nd ed. London: Routledge.
———. (2016b). *Power Plays Power Works*. 2nd ed. London: Routledge.
Flinders, K. (2023). Paula Vennells' email fuelled Post Office Horizon cult, inquiry told. *Computer Weekly*, 29 November. Retrieved 16 January 2024 from https://www.computerweekly.com/news/366561493/Paulla-Vennells-email-fuelled-Post-Office-Horizon-cult-inquiry-told.
Florini, S. (2014). Tweets, Tweeps, and Signifyin': Communication and Cultural Performance on "Black Twitter." *Television and New Media* 15(3): 223–237.
Foucault, M. (1978). *The History of Sexuality*. Vol. 1: *An Introduction* (R. Hurley, Trans.). New York: Pantheon.
———. (1979). *Discipline and Punish: The Birth of the Prison* (A. Sheridan, Trans.). New York: Vintage.
Fox, D. T. (1993). Honouring the Treaty: Indigenous television in Aotearoa. In T. Dowmunt (Ed.), *Channels of Resistance: Global Television and Local Empowerment* (pp. 126–137). London: British Film Institute.
Fox, M. (2014). Crown makes historic apology to Tūhoe. *Waikato Times*, 22 August. Retrieved 10 April 2020 from http://www.stuff.co.nz/national/politics/10412354/Crown-makes-historic-apology-to-Tuhoe.
Frankenberg, R. (1993). *White Women, Race Matters: The Social Construction of Whiteness*. Minneapolis: University of Minnesota Press.
Freedberg, D. (1991). *The Power of Images: Studies in the History and Theory of Response*. Chicago: University of Chicago Press.
Freeman, M. (2017). Funding and management in the media convergence era: Introduction. *International Journal on Media Management* 19(2): 103–107.
Freeman, M., and Proctor, W. (2018). Introduction: Conceptualizing national and cultural transmediality. In M. Freeman and W. Proctor (Eds.), *Global Convergence Cultures: Transmedia Earth* (pp. 1–16). New York: Routledge.

Fuqua, J. V. (2010). The Big Apple and the Big Easy: Proximity and home in (old and) new media. In D. Negra (Ed.), *Old and New Media after Katrina* (pp. 1–22). New York: Palgrave Macmillan.

Funez, S. (2015). Conflicto entre miskitos y colonos. [YouTube,] 7 September. Retrieved 23 November 2015 from https://www.youtube.com/watch?v=5js3h2bINO4.

Galeano, E. (1997). *Open Veins of Latin America: Five Centuries of the Pillage of a Continent*. 25th anniversary ed. (C. Belfrage, Trans.). New York: Monthly Review Press.

García, C. (1996). *The Making of the Miskitu People of Nicaragua: The Social Construction of Ethnic Identity*. Uppsala, Sweden: Uppsala University.

García Canclini, N. (1990). *Culturas híbridas: Estrategias para entrar y salir de la modernidad*. Mexico City: Grijalbo.

———. (1995). *Consumidores y ciudadanos: Conflictos multiculturales de la globalización*. Mexico City: Grijalbo.

Gardiner, W. (1996). *Return to Sender: What Really Happened at the Fiscal Envelope Hui*. Auckland: Reed Books.

Gates, C. (2017). Christchurch ranked as a global street art capital in new *Lonely Planet* book. *Stuff*, 12 March. Retrieved 9 February 2023 from https://www.stuff.co.nz/travel/90284773/christchurch-ranked-as-a-global-street-art-capital-in-new-lonely-planet-book.

Gates, H. L. (1983). The blackness of Blackness: A critique of the sign and the signifying monkey. *Critical Inquiry* 9(4): 685–723.

Gato, G. (1999). Insurgencies, terrorist groups and indigenous movements: An annotated bibliography. *Military Review* 79(4): 72–82.

Gauntlett, D. (2009). Case study: Wikipedia. In G. Creeber and R. Martin (Eds.), *Digital Cultures: Understanding New Media* (pp. 39–45). Maidenhead, UK: Open University Press.

Gehl, R. (2009). YouTube as archive: Who will curate this digital Wunderkammer? *International Journal of Cultural Studies* 12(1): 43–60.

Gentleman, A. (2022). Windrush scandal caused by "30 years of racist immigration laws"—report. *Guardian*, 29 May. Retrieved 17 January 2024 from https://www.theguardian.com/uk-news/2022/may/29/windrush-scandal-caused-by-30-years-of-racist-immigration-laws-report.

Gerbaudo, P. (2012). *Tweets and the Streets: Social Media and Contemporary Activism*. London: Pluto Press.

GIEI. (2018). *Report on the Violent Events That Took Place in Nicaragua between April 18th and May 30th*. Washington, DC: Organization of American States/Interdisciplinary Group of Independent Experts. Retrieved 10 January 2023 from https://www.oas.org/es/cidh/actividades/giei-nicaragua/GIEI_INFORME-en.pdf.

Gilmore, R. W. (2007). *Golden Gulag: Prisons, Surplus, Crisis and Opposition in Globalizing California*. Berkeley: University of California Press.

Gilroy, P. (1993). *The Black Atlantic: Modernity and Double Consciousness*. Cambridge, MA: Harvard University Press.

Ginn, F. (2009). Colonial transformations: Nature, progress and science in the Christchurch Botanic Gardens. *New Zealand Geographer* 65(1): 35–47.

Ginsburg, F. (2002). Screen memories: Resignifying the traditional in Indigenous media. In F. Ginsburg, L. Abu-Lughod, and B. Larkin (Eds.), *Media Worlds: Anthropology on New Terrain* (pp. 39–57). Berkeley: University of California Press.

Gledhill, C. (1988). Pleasurable negotiations. In E. Deirdre Pribam (Ed.), *Female Spectators: Looking at Film and Television* (pp. 64–89). London: Verso.

Global Witness. (2021). *The Last Line of Defence: The Industries Causing the Climate Crisis and Attacks against Land and Environmental Defenders*. Retrieved 21 October 2021 from www.globalwitness.org/documents/20191/Last_line_of_defence_-_high_res_-_September_2021.pdf.

Glynn, K. (2000). *Tabloid Culture: Trash Taste, Popular Power, and the Transformation of American Television*. Durham, NC: Duke University Press.

———. (2003). Challenging disenchantment: The discreet charm of occult TV. *Comparative American Studies: An International Journal* 1(4): 421–447.

———. (2008). And postmodern justice for all: The tabloidization of O.J. Simpson. In A. Biressi and H. Nunn (Eds.), *The Tabloid Culture Reader* (pp. 176–190). Maidenhead, UK: Open University Press.

———. (2009a). The 2004 election did not take place: Bush, spectacle, and the media nonevent. *Television and New Media* 10(2): 216–245.

———. (2009b). Contested land and mediascapes: The visuality of the postcolonial city. *New Zealand Geographer* 65(1): 6–22.

Glynn, K., and Cupples, J. (2011). Indigenous mediaspace and the production of (trans)locality on Nicaragua's Mosquito Coast. *Television and New Media* 12(2): 101–135.

———. (2024). Stories of decolonial resilience. *Cultural Studies* 38(4): 537–566.

Glynn, K., and Tyson, A. F. (2007). Indigeneity, media and cultural globalization: The case of *Mataku*, or the Maori *X-Files*. *International Journal of Cultural Studies* 10(2): 205–224.

Goldsmith, A. J. (2010). Policing's new visibility. *British Journal of Criminology* 50: 914–934.

Gonçalves, D. (2012). September 11 and the disruption of singularity. In C. Meiner and K. Veel (Eds.), *The Cultural Life of Catastrophes and Crises* (pp. 213–222). Berlin: De Gruyter.

González, G. (2005). "War on terror" has Latin American indigenous people in its sight. *Inter Press Service*, 6 June. Retrieved 24 August 2020 from http://www.ipsnews.net/2005/06/latin-america-war-on-terror-has-indigenous-people-in-its-sights.

González, M. (2016). The unmaking of self-determination: Twenty-five years of regional autonomy in Nicaragua. *Bulletin of Latin American Research* 35(3): 306–321.

Gordon, E. T. (1998). *Disparate Diasporas: Identity and Politics in an African Nicaraguan Community*. Austin: University of Texas Press.

Graham, T. (2023). Nicaragua's Miss Universe emerges as symbol of defiance against Ortega regime. *Guardian*, 2 December. Retrieved 2 December 2023 from https://www.theguardian.com/world/2023/dec/02/nicaragua-miss-universe-sheynnis-palacios-ortega?CMP=Share_AndroidApp_Other.

Gray, H. (2012). Recovered, reinvented, reimagined: *Treme*, television studies and writing New Orleans. *Television and New Media* 13(3): 268–278.

Gray, J. (2006). *Watching with* The Simpsons: *Television, Parody and Intertextuality*. London: Routledge.

———. (2008). *Entertainment Television*. London: Routledge.

———. (2010). *Show Sold Separately: Promos, Spoilers, and Other Media Paratexts*. New York: New York University Press.

"Great Replacement." (n.d.) *Wikipedia*. Retrieved 21 March 2023 from https://en.wikipedia.org/wiki/Great_Replacement#.

Greaves, G.-A. (1998). Call-response in selected calypsoes of political commentary from the Republic of Trinidad and Tobago. *Journal of Black Studies* 29(1): 34–50.

Greenberg, A. (2017). Everything we know about Russia's election-hacking playbook: A brief history of Russia's digital meddling in foreign elections shows disturbing progress. *Wired*, 9 June. Retrieved 22 February 2023 from https://www.wired.com/story/russia-election-hacking-playbook.

Greenwald, G. (2013). NSA collecting phone records of millions of Verizon customers daily. *Guardian*, 6 June. Retrieved 30 December 2023 from https://www.theguardian.com/world/2013/jun/06/nsa-phone-records-verizon-court-order.

Gregory, D. (2004). *The Colonial Present*. Malden, MA: Blackwell.

———. (2011). From a view to a kill: Drones and late modern war. *Theory, Culture and Society* 28(7–8): 188–215.

———. (2017). Drones and death in the borderlands. In L. Parks and C. Kaplan (Eds.), *Life in the Age of Drone Warfare* (pp. 25–58). Durham, NC: Duke University Press.

Grey, J. (2020). Bristol George Floyd protest: Colston statue toppled. BBC News, 7 June. Retrieved 11 February 2023 from https://www.bbc.co.uk/news/uk-england-bristol-52955868.

Griffin, D. R. (2004a). *The 9/11 Commission Report: Omissions and Distortions*. Northampton, MA: Olive Branch Press.

———. (2004b). *The New Pearl Harbor: Disturbing Questions about the Bush Administration and 9/11*. Northampton, MA: Olive Branch Press.

———. (2006). *Christian Faith and the Truth behind 9/11: A Call to Reflection and Action*. Louisville, KY: Westminster John Knox Press.

———. (2007). *Debunking 9/11: An Answer to the Defenders of the Official Conspiracy Theory*. Northampton, MA: Olive Branch Press.

———. (2010). *The Mysterious Collapse of World Trade Center 7*. Northampton, MA: Olive Branch Press.

———. (2011a). *9/11 10 Years On: When State Crimes against Democracy Succeed*. London: Haus Publishing.

———. (2011b). *Cognitive Infiltration: An Obama Appointee's Plan to Undermine the 9/11 Conspiracy Theory*. Northampton, MA: Olive Branch Press.

———. (2018). *Bush and Cheney: How They Ruined America and the World*. Northampton, MA: Olive Branch Press.

Griffin, D. R., and Scott, P. D. (Eds.). (2006). *9/11 and American Empire: Intellectuals Speak Out*. Northampton, MA: Olive Branch Press.

Grossberg, L. (1996). On postmodernism and articulation: An interview with Stuart Hall. In D. Morley and K. Chen (Eds.), *Stuart Hall: Critical Dialogues in Cultural Studies* (pp. 131–150). London: Routledge.

———. (2010). *Cultural Studies in the Future Tense*. Durham, NC: Duke University Press.

Grossman, C. (2001). Awas Tingni v. Nicaragua: A landmark case for the Inter-American system. *Human Rights Brief* 8(3): 2–4, 8.

Grusin, R. (2010). *Premediation: Affect and Mediality after 9/11*. New York: Palgrave Macmillan.

Gwenllian-Jones, S., and Pearson, R. E. (Eds.). (2004). *Cult Television*. Minneapolis: University of Minnesota Press.

Hall, C. (2024). Fox News finally surrenders to Trump with subservient town hall. *Mediaite*, 11 January. Retrieved 12 January 2024 from https://www.mediaite.com/opinion/fox-news-finally-surrenders-to-trump-with-subservient-town-hall.

Hale, C. R. (1994). *Resistance and Contradiction: Miskitu Indians and the Nicaraguan State*. Stanford, CA: Stanford University Press.

———. (2004). Rethinking indigenous politics in the era of the "indio permitido." *NACLA Report on the Americas*, September/October: 16–20.

———. (2005). Neoliberal multiculturalism: The remaking of cultural rights and racial dominance in Central America. *PoLAR: Political and Legal Anthropology Review* 28(1): 1–28.

———. (2006). *Más que un indio: Racial Ambivalence and Neoliberal Multiculturalism in Guatemala*. Santa Fe, NM: School of American Research Press.

Hale, C. R., and Millamán, R. (2006). Cultural agency and political struggle in the era of the *Indio permitido*. In D. Sommer (Ed.), *Cultural Agency in the Americas* (pp. 281–304). Durham, NC: Duke University Press.

Hall, S. (1981). The whites of their eyes: Racist ideologies and the media. In G. Bridges and R. Brunt (Eds.), *Silver Linings: Some Strategies for the Eighties* (pp. 28–52). London: Lawrence and Wishart.

———. (1987) Gramsci and us. *Marxism Today*, June: 16–21.

———. (1996). Gramsci's relevance for the study of race and ethnicity. In D. Morley and K. H. Chen (Eds.), *Stuart Hall: Critical Dialogues in Cultural Studies* (pp. 411–440). London: Routledge.

———. (2011). The neo-liberal revolution. *Cultural Studies* 25(6): 705–728.

———. (2019). Notes on deconstructing "the popular." In D. Morley (Ed.), *Stuart Hall, Essential Essays*, vol. 1: *Foundations of Cultural Studies* (pp. 347–361). Durham, NC: Duke University Press.

Hall, S., Critcher, C., Jefferson, T., Clarke, J., and Roberts, B. (2013). *Policing the Crisis: Mugging, the State and Law and Order*. 2nd ed. Houndmills, UK: Palgrave Macmillan.

Han, L. C. (2007). Is the United States *really* ready for a woman president? In L. C. Han and C. Heldman (Eds.), *Rethinking Madam President: Are We Ready for a Woman in the White House?* (pp. 1–16). Boulder, CO: Lynne Rienner.

Harris, H. E., Moffitt, K. R., and Squires, C. R. (Eds.). (2010). *The Obama Effect: Multidisciplinary Renderings of the 2008 Campaign*. Albany: State University of New York Press.

Harrison, E. (2024). "We all secretly think they're spinning it out so everyone dies before they get their money": Inside Mr Bates vs the Post Office. *Independent*, 1 January. Retrieved 15 January 2024 from https://www.independent.co.uk/arts-entertainment/tv/features/mr-bates-vs-the-post-office-itv-b2465992.html.

Harrit, N. H., Farrer, J., Jones, S. E., Ryan, K. R., Legge, F. M., Farnsworth, D., Roberts, G., Gourley, J. R., and Larsen, B. R. (2009). Active thermitic material discovered in dust from the 9/11 World Trade Center catastrophe. *The Open Chemical Physics Journal* 2: 7–31.

Hartley, J. (2004). Television, nation, and Indigenous media. *Television and New Media* 5(1): 7–25.

Hartocollis, A., and Alcindor, Y. (2021). Women's march highlights as huge crowds protest Trump: "We're not going away." *New York Times*, 21 January.

Hasian, M. A. (2016). *Humanitarian Aid and the Impoverished Rhetoric of Celebrity Advocacy*. New York: Peter Lang.

Havana Times. (2023). Five years ago a horrendous crime took place in Managua. *Havana Times*, 16 June. Retrieved 11 January 2024 from https://havanatimes.org/features/five-years-ago-a-horrendous-crime-took-place-in-managua.

Hayward, M. (2018). Seven years on: Seven challenges for post-quake Christchurch. *The Press*, 22 February. Retrieved 9 February 2023 from https://www.stuff.co.nz/the-press/business/the-rebuild/101478063/seven-years-on-seven-challenges-for-post-quake-christchurch.

Hebdige, D. (1979). *Subculture: The Meaning of Style*. London: Methuen.

———. (1988). *Hiding in the Light: On Images and Things*. London: Routledge.

Heidegger, M. (1977). *The Question Concerning Technology and Other Essays* (Trans. and intro. W. Lovitt). New York: Harper Torchbooks.

Heldman, C. (2007). Cultural barriers to a female president in the United States. In L. C. Han and C. Heldman (Eds.), *Rethinking Madam President: Are We Ready for a Woman in the White House?* (pp. 17–42). Boulder, CO: Lynne Rienner.

Helms, M. (1971). *Asang: Adaptations to Culture Contact in a Miskito Community*. Gainesville: University of Florida Press.

———. (1988). *Ulysses' Sail: An Ethnographic Odyssey of Power, Knowledge, and Geographical Distance*. Princeton, NJ: Princeton University Press.

Herb, J., Fung, B., Hansler, J., and Cohen, Z. (2020). Russian hackers targeting state and local governments have stolen data, US officials say. *CNN Politics*, 23 October. Retrieved 22 February 2023 from https://edition.cnn.com/2020/10/22/politics/russian-hackers-election-data/index.html.

Hermes, J. (2005). *Re-reading Popular Culture*. Malden, MA: Blackwell.

Herzfeld, A., and Moskowitz, D. (2004). The Limonese calypso as an identity marker. In G. Escure and A. Schwegler (Eds.), *Creoles, Contact, and Language Change: Linguistic and Social Implications* (pp. 259–284). Amsterdam: John Benjamins.

Hesketh, M., and Morton, D. A. (2014). Subcomandante Marcos dies, Galeano lives, the Zapatistas continue. *For the Desk Drawer* (blog). Retrieved 10 February 2017 from http://adamdavidmorton.com/2014/05/subcomandante-marcos-dies-galeano-lives-the-zapatistas-continue.

Hewitt, K. (1995). Excluded perspectives in the social construction of disaster. *International Journal of Mass Emergencies and Disasters* 13(3): 317–339.

Hill, R. (2008). Māori, police and coercion in New Zealand history. In D. Keenan (Ed.), *Terror in Our Midst? Searching for Terror in Aotearoa New Zealand* (pp. 39–61). Wellington: Huia.

Hilmes, M. (2009). Digital television: High definitions. In G. Creeber and R. Martin (Eds.), *Digital Cultures: Understanding New Media* (pp. 46–54). Maidenhead, UK: Open University Press.

Hinchliffe, S. (2004). Living with risk: The unnatural geography of environmental crises. In S. Hinchliffe and K. Woodward (Eds.), *The Natural and the Social: Uncertainty, Risk, Change* (2nd ed., pp. 115–151). London: Routledge/Open University.

Hirwani, P. (2021). Riverdale cast calls for Nicaragua government to release showrunner's activist father. *Independent*, 9 September. Retrieved 9 September 2022 from https://www.independent.co.uk/arts-entertainment/tv/news/riverdale-cast-nicaragua-aguirre-sacasa-b1916834.html.

Hoffman, S. M. (1999). The regenesis of traditional gender patterns in the wake of disaster. In A. O. Smith and S. M. Hoffman (Eds.), *The Angry Earth: Disaster in Anthropological Perspective* (pp. 174–191). London: Routledge.

Hokowhitu, B., and Devadas, V. (Eds.). (2013a). *The Fourth Eye: Māori Media in Aotearoa New Zealand*. Minneapolis: University of Minnesota Press.

———. (2013b). Introduction: Fourth eye: The Indigenous mediascape in Aotearoa New Zealand. In B. Hokowhitu and V. Devadas (Eds.), *The Fourth Eye: Māori Media in Aotearoa New Zealand* (pp. xv–l). Minneapolis: University of Minnesota Press.

Holm, I. W. (2012). The cultural analysis of disaster. In C. Meiner and K. Veel (Eds.), *The Cultural Life of Catastrophes and Crises* (pp. 15–32). Berlin: De Gruyter.

Hooker, J. (2005a). Indigenous inclusion/black exclusion: Race, ethnicity and multicultural citizenship in Latin America. *Journal of Latin American Studies* 37: 1–26.

———. (2005b). "Beloved enemies": Race and official mestizo nationalism in Nicaragua. *Latin American Research Review* 40(3): 14–39.

Hughes, D. A. (2020). 9/11 truth and the silence of the IR discipline. *Alternatives: Global, Local, Political* 45(2): 55–82.

Hunt, E. (2021). "Joy and agony": Christchurch earthquake survivors ten years on. *Guardian*, 19 February. Retrieved 11 February 2023 from https://www.theguardian.com/world/2021/feb/20/trauma-and-transformation-christchurch-earthquake-survivors-ten-years-on.

Hynes, W. J. (1993a). Mapping the characteristics of mythic tricksters: A heuristic guide. In W. J. Hynes and W. G. Doty (Eds.), *Mythical Trickster Figures: Contours, Contexts, and Criticisms* (pp. 33–45). Tuscaloosa: University of Alabama Press.

———. (1993b). Inconclusive conclusions: Tricksters—metaplayers and revealers. In W. J. Hynes and W. G. Doty (Eds.), *Mythical Trickster Figures: Contours, Contexts, and Criticisms* (pp. 202–217). Tuscaloosa: University of Alabama Press.

Ihaka, J. (2014). Apology over Urewera raids. *NZ Herald*, 27 July. Retrieved 24 August 2020 from https://www.nzherald.co.nz/nz/apology-over-urewera-raids/7TJD7NLSHV2IADFRUL3FJK36EY/.

Infosys. (2023). Infosys partners with Fujitsu to enhance functionality of product suite. Press release, 17 October. Retrieved 16 January 2024 from https://www.infosys.com/newsroom/press-releases/2003/partners-fujitsu.html.

Inskeep, S., and Maynes, C. (2022). Russia has reasserted state control over the country's major media companies. NPR, 7 March. Retrieved 18 March 2023 from https://www.npr.org/2022/03/07/1084870797/russia-has-reasserted-state-control-over-the-country-s-major-media-companies.

IPCA. (2013). *Operation Eight: The Report of the Independent Police Conduct Authority*. Wellington: IPCA.

Irwin, M. (2022). "Activist, artist, terrorist and cyclist" Tame Iti named Arts Foundation Laureate. *Ocula Magazine*, 9 September. Retrieved 28 December 2023 from https://ocula.com/magazine/art-news/tame-iti-named-arts-foundation-laureate.

Iti, T. (2015). Mana: The power in knowing who you are. *Tedx Talks*, 17 June. Retrieved 25 August 2020 from https://www.youtube.com/watch?v=qeK3SkxrZRI.

Jack, A. (2023). Tame Iti on his early *Celebrity Treasure Island* exit: "I couldn't carry on." *Stuff*, 27 September. Retrieved 28 December 2023 from https://www.stuff.co.nz/entertainment/tv-radio/300978290/tme-iti-on-his-early-celebrity-treasure-island-exit-i-couldnt-carry-on.

Jackson, M. (1987). *Maori and the Criminal Justice System: A New Perspective He Whaipaanga Hou, Part One*. Wellington: Ministry of Justice.

———. (1988). *Maori and the Criminal Justice System: A New Perspective He Whaipaanga Hou, Part Two*. Wellington: Ministry of Justice.

———. (1998). Research and the colonisation of Māori knowledge. *He Pukenga Kōrero* 4(1): 69–84.

———. (2008). Preface: The constancy of terror. In D. Keenan (Ed.), *Terror in Our Midst? Searching for Terror in Aotearoa New Zealand* (pp. 1–10). Wellington: Huia.

Jameson, F. (1979). Reification and utopia in mass culture. *Social Text* 1(1): 130–148.

———. (1992). *Postmodernism, or, The Cultural Logic of Late Capitalism*. Durham, NC: Duke University Press.

Jamieson, M. (2009). Contracts with Satan: Relations with "spirit owners" and apprehensions of the economy among the coastal Miskitu of Nicaragua. *Durham Anthropology Journal* 16(2): 44–53.

Jansson, A., and Lindell, J. (2015). News media consumption in the transmedia age: Amalgamations, orientations and geo-social structuration. *Journalism Studies* 16(1): 79–96.

Jarquín, M. (2016). Navidad Roja: La historia de la violencia en el Caribe. *Confidencial*, 13 October. Retrieved 9 January 2023 from https://www.confidencial.digital/opinion/navidad-roja-la-historia-la-violencia-caribe.

Jaschik, S. (2007). A flood of censure. *Inside Higher Ed*, 11 June. Retrieved 9 February 2023 from https://www.tulanelink.com/tulanelink/floodofcensure_box.htm.

Jauhola, M., and Pedersen, J. (2010). Who might we become? An interview with Cynthia Weber. *International Feminist Journal of Politics* 12(1): 105–115.

Jay, M. (1993). *Downcast Eyes: The Denigration of Vision in Twentieth-Century French Thought*. Berkeley: University of California Press.

Jedlowski, A. (2016). Studying media "from" the South: African media studies and global perspectives. *Black Camera: An International Film Journal* 7(2): 174–193.

Jenkins, H. (2008). *Convergence Culture: Where Old and New Media Collide*. Rev. ed. New York: New York University Press.

———. (2016). Youth voice, media, and political engagement: Introducing the core concepts. In H. Jenkins, S. Shresthova, L. Gamber-Thompson, N. Kligler-Vilenchik, and A. Zimmerman (Eds.), *By Any Media Necessary: The New Youth Activism* (pp. 1–60). New York: New York University Press.

Jenkins, H., Ford, S., and Green, J. (2013). *Spreadable Media: Creating Value and Meaning in a Networked Culture*. New York: New York University Press.

Johnston, J., Sears, C., and Wilcox, L. (2012). Neoliberalism unshaken: A report from the disaster zone. *Excursions* 3(1): 1–26.

Jones, L. (2012). The commonplace geopolitics of conspiracy. *Geography Compass* 6(1): 44–59.

Jordan, J. (2004). Afro-Colombia: A case for pan-African analysis. *Souls* 6(2): 19–30.

Just Speak. (2012). *Māori and the Criminal Justice System: A Youth Perspective*. Wellington: Just Speak.

Kackman, M., Binfield, M., Payne, M. T., Perlman, A., and Sebok, B. (2011a). The convergent experience: Viewing practices across media forms. In M. Kackman, M. Binfield, M. T. Payne, A. Perlman, and B. Sebok (Eds.), *Flow TV: Television in the Age of Media Convergence* (pp. 11–12). New York: Routledge.

———. (2011b). *Flow TV: Television in the Age of Media Convergence*. New York: Routledge.

Kapoor, I. (2013). *Celebrity Humanitarianism: The Ideology of Global Charity*. London: Routledge.

Kay, C. (2019). Modernization and dependency theory. In J. Cupples, M. Palomino-Schalsha, and M. Prieto (Eds.), *Routledge Handbook of Latin American Development* (pp. 15–28). London: Routledge.

Keegan, B. (2020). An encyclopedia with breaking news. In J. Reagle and J. Koerner (Eds.), *Wikipedia @ 20: Stories of an Incomplete Revolution* (pp. 55–70). Cambridge, MA: MIT Press.

Keenan, D. (2008). Autonomy as fiction: The Urewera Native District Reserve Act 1896. In D. Keenan (Ed.), *Terror in Our Midst? Searching for Terror in Aotearoa New Zealand* (pp. 79–92). Wellington: Huia.

Kellner, D. (2003). *Media Spectacle*. London: Routledge.

———. (2007). The Katrina hurricane spectacle and crisis of the Bush presidency. *Cultural Studies ↔ Critical Methodologies* 7(2): 222–234.

———. (2016). *American Nightmare: Donald Trump, Media Spectacle, and Authoritarian Populism*. Rotterdam, Netherlands: Sense Publishers.

Keskidee Aroha. (1980). Directed by Merata Mita and Martyn Sanderson [documentary film]. Auckland: New Zealand Broadcasting Corporation.

King, A. (2009). Relative justice: Indigenous families in Australian lifestyle media. *Australian Journal of Communication* 36(2): 17–33.

King, G. (2005). "Just like a movie"? 9/11 and Hollywood spectacle. In G. King (Ed.), *The Spectacle of the Real: From Hollywood to "Reality" TV and Beyond* (pp. 47–57). Bristol, UK: Intellect.

Kirshenblatt-Gimblett, B. (2003). Kodak moments, flashbulb memories: Reflections on 9/11. *The Drama Review* 47(1): 11–48.

Klein, N. (2005). The threat of hope in Latin America. *The Nation*, 21 November. Retrieved 24 August 2020 from www.thenation.com/article/threat-hope-latin-america.

———. (2007). *The Shock Doctrine: The Rise of Disaster Capitalism*. New York: Metropolitan Books/Henry Holt.

———. (2023). *Doppelganger: A Trip into the Mirror World*. London: Penguin.

Kobayashi, A. (2009). "Here we go again": Christchurch's antiracism rally as a discursive crisis. *New Zealand Geographer* 65(1): 59–72.

Kornstein, H. (2019). Under her eye: Digital drag as obfuscation and countersurveillance. *Surveillance and Society* 17(5): 681–698.

Koti, T. (2017). Māori programming wins big at 2017 NZTV Awards. *Te Ao: Māori News*, 30 November. Retrieved 18 January 2024 from https://www.teaonews.co.nz/2017/11/30/maori-programming-wins-big-at-2017-nztv-awards.

Krøvel, R. (2011). Fighting superior military power in Chiapas, Mexico: Celebrity activism and its limitations. In L. Tsaliki, C. A. Frangonikolopoulos, and A. Huliaris (Eds.), *Transnational Celebrity Activism in Global Politics: Changing the World?* (pp. 122–138). Bristol, UK: Intellect.

Kuletz, V. (1998). *The Tainted Desert: Environmental and Social Ruin in the American West*. New York: Routledge.

Kusch, R. (1975). *La negación en el pensamiento popular*. Buenos Aires: Editorial Cimarrón.

———. (2010 [1970]). *Indigenous and Popular Thinking in América*. Durham, NC: Duke University Press.

LaCapria, K. (2015). After birth abortion. *Snopes*, 29 July. Retrieved 12 January 2024 from https://www.snopes.com/fact-check/after-birth-abortion.

———. (2016). "Abortionist" strangled baby born alive. *Snopes*, 11 April. Retrieved 12 January 2024 from https://www.snopes.com/fact-check/abortionist-strangled-baby-born-alive.

Lakhani, N. (2020). *Who Killed Berta Cáceres: Dams, Death Squads, and an Indigenous Defender's Battle for the Planet*. London: Verso.

Lao-Montes, A. (2007). Decolonial moves: Trans-locating African diaspora space. *Cultural Studies* 21(2–3): 309–338.

Larner, W. (2003). Guest editorial: Neoliberalism? *Environment and Planning D: Society and Space* 21(5): 509–512.

Leetaru, K. (2019). AI package delivery drones are just killer robots in waiting. *Forbes*, 19 April.

Leland, J. (2009). This is America: New Orleans post-Katrina, post-urban, post-national. *Safundi: The Journal of South African and American Studies* 10(2): 121–131.

Leloup, D. (2023). Riots in Brazil: An attempted insurrection openly organized on social media. *Le Monde*, 10 January. Retrieved 8 March 2023 from https://www.lemonde.fr/en/international/article/2023/01/10/riots-in-brazil-an-attempted-insurrection-organized-openly-on-social-media_6010980_4.html.

Lenzerini, F. (2014). *The Culturalization of Human Rights Law*. Oxford: Oxford University Press.

Levin, B. (2020). Texas Lt. governor: Old people should volunteer to die to save the economy. *Vanity Fair*, 24 March. Retrieved 9 February 2023 from https://www.vanityfair.com/news/2020/03/dan-patrick-coronavirus-grandparents.

Lévy, P. (1997). *Collective Intelligence: Mankind's Emerging World in Cyberspace* (R. Bononno, Trans.). Cambridge, MA: Perseus.

Leyda, J. (2012). "This Complicated, Colossal Failure": The Abjection of Creighton Bernette in HBO's *Treme*. *Television and New Media* 13(3): 243–260.

Liboiron, M., and Lepawsky, J. (2022). *Discard Studies: Wasting, Systems, and Power.* Cambridge, MA: MIT Press.

Lipsitz, G. (1988). Mardi Gras Indians: Carnival and counter-narrative in New Orleans. *Cultural Critique* 10: 99–121.

Lipton, E., Sanger, D. E., and Shane, S. (2016). The perfect weapon: How Russian cyberpower invaded the U.S. *New York Times*, 13 December.

Litvinova, D. (2023). "Total digital surveillance": How Russia tracks, censors and controls its citizens. *Los Angeles Times*, 23 May. Retrieved 30 December 2023 from https://www.latimes.com/world-nation/story/2023-05-23/russia-digital-surveillance-censors-controls-citizens.

Longhurst, R. (2008). *Maternities: Gender, Bodies and Space*. New York: Routledge.

López, A. M. (2014). Calling for intermediality: Latin American mediascapes. *Cinema Journal* 54(1): 135–141.

López, F. (2007). Quieren volver a Cayos Miskitos. *El Nuevo Diario*, 16 September.

Lotz, A. D. (2007). *The Television Will Be Revolutionized*. New York: New York University Press.

———. (2014). *The Television Will Be Revolutionized*. 2nd ed. New York: New York University Press.

Lyotard, J. (1984). *The Postmodern Condition: A Report on Knowledge* (G. Bennington and B. Massumi, Trans.; foreword by F. Jameson). Minneapolis: University of Minnesota Press.

Lysaght, R. (2010). Teanga and tikanga: A comparative study of national broadcasting in a minority language on Māori Television and Teilifís na Gaeilge. PhD thesis, University of Auckland, New Zealand.

Macdonald, F., Hughes, R., and Dodds, K. (2010). Introduction: Envisioning geopolitics. In F. Macdonald, R. Hughes, and K. Dodds (Eds.), *Observant States: Geopolitics and Visual Culture* (pp. 1–19). London: I. B. Tauris.

MacLeod, E. (2019). Calypso calamity! Hunt for the lost tapes of 100-year-old Walter Ferguson. *Guardian*, 29 October. Retrieved 29 March 2023 from https://www.theguardian.com/music/2019/oct/29/calypso-walter-ferguson-limon-costa-rica.

Madhani, D. (2021). "Riverdale" cast calls for Nicaraguan government to release showrunner's father. NBC News, 9 September. Retrieved 9 September 2022 from https://www.nbcnews.com/news/world/riverdale-cast-calls-showrunner-s-father-be-released-nicaraguan-government-n1278739.

Magaña, M. R. (2016). Spaces of resistance, everyday activism, and belonging: Youth reimagining and reconfiguring the city in Oaxaca, Mexico. *Journal of Latin American and Caribbean Anthropology* 22(2): 215–234.

Maldonado-Torres, N. (2003). Imperio y colonialidad del ser. Paper presented at the XXIV International Congress, Latin American Studies Association, Dallas, 27–29 March.

———. (2007). On the coloniality of being. *Cultural Studies* 21(2–3): 240–270.

———. (2008). La descolonización y el giro descolonial. *Tabula Rasa* 9: 61–72.

Māori Television. (2007). Guerrillas in the mist? *Native Affairs* [current affairs program]. First broadcast 23 October.
Marantz, A. (2021). How social media made the Trump insurrection a reality. *New Yorker*, 7 January. Retrieved 22 February 2023 from https://www.newyorker.com/news/daily-comment/how-social-media-made-the-trump-insurrection-a-reality.
Marenco, E. (2007). Ortega ataca a EU y olvida a víctimas del Félix. *El Nuevo Diario*, 25 September.
Markham, T. (2015). Celebrity advocacy and public engagement: The divergent uses of celebrity. *International Journal of Cultural Studies* 18(4): 467–480.
Martí, J. (1977 [1891]). Our America. In P. S. Foner (Ed.), *Our America by José Martí: Writings on Latin America and the Struggle for Cuban Independence* (pp. 84–94). New York: Monthly Review Press.
Martín-Barbero, J. (1993). *Communication, Culture and Hegemony: From the Media to Mediations* (E. Fox and R. A. White, Trans.). London: Sage.
———. (2004a). *De los medios a las mediaciones: Comunicación, cultura y hegemonía*. Barcelona: Editorial Gustavo Gili.
———. (2004b). A nocturnal map to explore a new field. In A. del Sarto, A. Ríos, and A. Trigo (Eds.), *The Latin American Cultural Studies Reader* (pp. 310–328). Durham, NC: Duke University Press.
———. (2011). From Latin America: Diversity, globalization and convergence. *Westminster Papers in Communication and Culture* 8(1): 39–64.
Mattei, C. E. (2022). *The Capital Order: How Economists Invented Austerity and Paved the Way to Fascism*. Chicago: University of Chicago Press.
Matthews, P. (2012). Corporate culture choking the creative? *The Press*, 5 May. Retrieved 28 July 2020 from http://www.stuff.co.nz/the-press/news/6865088/Corporate-culture-choking-the-creative.
Maxwell, R., and Miller, T. (2012). *Greening the Media*. New York: Oxford University Press.
Mayerle, J. (2015). WCCO's Jennifer Mayerle shares unforgettable story of Katrina survivor. WCCO CBS Minnesota, 27 August. Retrieved 20 August 2020 from https://minnesota.cbslocal.com/2015/08/27/wccos-jennifer-mayerle-shares-unforgettable-story-of-katrina-survivor.
McCarthy, J., and Prudham, S. (2004). Neoliberal nature and the nature of neoliberalism. *Geoforum* 35: 275–283.
McCurdy, P. (2013). Conceptualising celebrity activists: The case of Tamsin Omond. *Celebrity Studies* 4(3): 311–324.
McDermott, J. (2020). A comprehensive history of *Loose Change*—and the seeds it planted in our politics. *Esquire*, 10 September. Retrieved 14 December 2022 from https://www.esquire.com/news-politics/a33971104/loose-change-9-11-conspiracy-documentary-history-interview.
McHugh, R. (2016). Anarchism and informal *informal* pedagogy: "Gangs," difference, deference. In S. Springer, M. Lopes de Souza, and R. J. White (Eds.), *The Radicalization of Pedagogy: Anarchism, Geography, and the Spirit of Revolt* (pp. 147–170). London: Rowman and Littlefield.
McInnis, K. J. (2012). How "Homeland" undercuts real women in government. *The Atlantic*, 16 November. Retrieved 6 March 2018 from https://www.theatlantic.com/sexes/archive/2012/11/how-homeland-undercuts-real-women-in-government/265242.
McKee, A. (1999) Love affair against the odds: Ernie Dingo and reconciliation. *Australian Studies* 14(1–2): 189–208.

McNaughton, H. (2009). Re-inscribing the urban abject: Ngai Tahu and the Gothic Revival. *New Zealand Geographer* 65(1): 48–58.

Media Matters Staff. (2024). Angelo Carusone: Fox News' Donald Trump town hall proves the network has surrendered and will lead the right-wing echo chamber. Media Matters for America, 11 January. Retrieved 12 January 2024 from https://www.mediamatters.org/msnbc/angelo-carusone-fox-news-donald-trump-town-hall-proves-network-has-surrendered-and-will-lead.

Medrano, M. (2022). Nicaragua finds former foreign minister and journalist guilty of conspiracy. CNN, 9 February. Retrieved 14 December 2022 from https://edition.cnn.com/2022/02/09/americas/nicaragua-foreign-minister-journalist-conspiracy-intl/index.html.

Meek, A. G. (2013). Postcolonial trauma: Child abuse, genocide and journalism in New Zealand. In B. Hokowhitu and V. Devadas (Eds.), *The Fourth Eye: Māori Media in Aotearoa New Zealand* (pp. 25–41). Minneapolis: University of Minnesota Press.

Meet the Prick. (2005). Directed by Ilya Ruppeldt [television documentary]. Auckland: Golem Productions.

Meikle, G., and Young, S. (2012). *Media Convergence: Networked Digital Media in Everyday Life*. Houndmills, UK: Palgrave Macmillan.

Meiner, C., and Veel, K. (2012). Introduction. In C. Meiner and K. Veel (Eds.), *The Cultural Life of Catastrophes and Crises* (pp. 1–12). Berlin: De Gruyter.

Mercer, K. (1987). Black hair/style politics. *New Formations* 3: 33–54.

Mignolo, W. D. (2000). *Local Histories/Global Designs: Coloniality, Subaltern Knowledges and Border Thinking*. Princeton, NJ: Princeton University Press.

———. (2005). *The Idea of Latin America*. Malden, MA: Blackwell.

———. (2007). Introduction: Coloniality of power and decolonial thinking. *Cultural Studies* 21(2–3): 155–167.

———. (2010). Introduction: Immigrant consciousness. In R. Kusch, *Indigenous and Popular Thinking in América* (M. Lugones and J. M. Price, Trans., pp. xiii–liv). Durham, NC: Duke University Press.

———. (2018). Decoloniality and phenomenology: The geopolitics of knowing and epistemic/ontological colonial differences. *Journal of Speculative Philosophy* 32(3): 360–387.

Mihaka, T.R.M., and Prince, D. P. (1984). *Whakapohane: I na tuohu koe me mea hei maunga tei tei*. Porirua, NZ: Ruatara Publications.

Mikkelson, D. (2005). Fishing trip: Photographs show President Bush engaged in various recreational activities in flooded New Orleans? *Snopes*, 16 September. Retrieved 15 February 2024 from https://www.snopes.com/fact-check/fishing-trip.

Mirzoeff, N. (1999). *An Introduction to Visual Culture*. London: Routledge.

———. (2005). *Watching Babylon: The War in Iraq and Global Visual Culture*. New York: Routledge.

———. (2006). Invisible empire: Visual culture, embodied spectacle, and Abu Ghraib. *Radical History Review* 95: 21–44.

———. (2015). *How to See the World*. London: Pelican.

Mitchell, A. (2024). Postmasters prosecuted by CPS while Keir Starmer was in charge. *Independent*, 11 January. Retrieved 15 January 2024 from https://www.independent.co.uk/news/uk/politics/post-office-scandal-keir-starmer-b2476524.html.

Mitchell, W.J.T. (2009). Obama as icon. *Journal of Visual Culture* 8(2): 125–129.

Mittel, A., and Mayer, J. (2020). *Nicaragua's Failed Revolution: The Indigenous Struggle for Saneamiento*. Oakland, CA: Oakland Institute.

Mittell, J. (2006). Narrative complexity in contemporary American television. *The Velvet Light Trap* 58: 29–40.

———. (2015a). *Complex TV: The Poetics of Contemporary Television Storytelling*. New York: New York University Press.

———. (2015b). Why has TV storytelling become so complex? *The Conversation*, 27 March. Retrieved 5 March 2017 from https://theconversation.com/why-has-tv-storytelling-become-so-complex-37442.

Molina-Guzmán, I. (2010). *Dangerous Curves: Latina Bodies in the Media*. New York: New York University Press.

Monestel, M. (2003). Ritmo, cancion e identidad: El calypso limonense (1920–2020). Unpublished master's dissertation, Universidad de Costa Rica.

———. (2013). Negritud, resistencia cultural y ciudadanía en letras de calypsos limonenses. *Ístmica: Revista de La Facultad de Filosofía y Letras* 16: 69–75.

Montoya, A. (2023). Au Nicaragua, le régime de Daniel Ortega embarrassé par Miss Univers. *Le Monde*, 30 November. Retrieved 11 January 2024 from https://www.lemonde.fr/international/article/2023/11/30/au-nicaragua-le-regime-de-daniel-ortega-embarrasse-par-miss-univers_6203217_3210.html.

Morales-Garro, R. (2022). Procesos históricos de conformación del calypso costarricense. *Temas de Nuestra América* 38(72): 1–14.

Moran, J. (2003). Benjamin and boredom. *Critical Quarterly* 45(1–2): 168–181.

Morris, P. (2020). As monuments fall, how does the world reckon with a racist past? *National Geographic*, 29 June. Retrieved 11 February 2023 from https://www.nationalgeographic.com/history/article/confederate-monuments-fall-question-how-rewrite-history.

Morse, V. (2008). The New Zealand terror raids. *Counterpunch*, 19 February. Retrieved 25 August 2020 from http://www.counterpunch.org/2008/02/19/the-new-zealand-terror-raids.

———. (2010). Introduction. In V. Morse (Ed.), *The Day the Raids Came: Stories of Survival and Resistance to the State Terror Raids* (pp. 11–18). Wellington: Rebel Press.

Mountz, A. (2011). Where asylum-seekers wait: Feminist counter-topographies of sites between states. *Gender, Place and Culture* 18(3): 381–399.

Moyo, L. (2020). *The Decolonial Turn in Media Studies in Africa and the Global South*. Cham, Switzerland: Palgrave Macmillan.

Mozur, P., Satariano, A., Krolik, A., and Aufrichtig, A. (2022). "They are watching": Inside Russia's vast surveillance state. *New York Times*, 22 September. Retrieved 30 December 2023 from https://www.nytimes.com/interactive/2022/09/22/technology/russia-putin-surveillance-spying.html.

Murillo, R. (2023). Nicaragua tiene Paz . . . Tiene Amor, y Dignidad. Más claro, cantamos y celebramos. *El 19 Digital*, 22 November. Retrieved 11 January 2024 from https://www.el19digital.com/articulos/ver/titulo:146794-nicaragua-tiene-paztiene-amor-y-dignidad-mas-claro-cantamos-y-celebramos.

Muru. (2022). Directed by Tearepa Kahi [feature film]. Auckland: Jawbone Pictures and Wheke Group.

Myers, S. L. (2022). With new limits on media, Putin closes a door on Russia's "openness." *New York Times*, 7 March.

Nairn, R., Moewaka Barnes, A., Borell, B., Rankine, J., Gregory, A., and McCreanor, T. (2012). Māori news is bad news: That's certainly so on television. *MAI Journal* 1(1): 39–49.

Nederveen Pieterse, J. (1994). Globalization as hybridization. *International Sociology* 9(2): 161–184.

Negra, D. (2010). Introduction: Old and new media after Katrina. In D. Negra (Ed.), *Old and New Media after Katrina* (pp. 1–22). New York: Palgrave Macmillan.

Negra, D., and Lagerwey, J. (2015). Analyzing *Homeland*: Introduction. *Cinema Journal* 54(4): 126–131.

Nelson, A. (2019). *Shadow Network: Media, Money, and the Secret Hub of the Radical Right*. New York: Bloomsbury.

Newcombe, H., and Hirsch, P. (1983). Television as a cultural forum: Implications for research. *Quarterly Review of Film Studies* 8(3): 45–55.

Newman, M., and Levine, E. (2011). *Legitimating Television: Media Convergence and Cultural Status*. New York: Routledge.

New Zealand Drug Foundation. (2009). Once were gardeners—Moana Jackson on the scientific method and the "warrior gene" [video]. Retrieved 24 August 2020 from https://www.youtube.com/watch?v=HfAe3Zvgui4.

New Zealand Government. (2008). Key needs to be honest on New Zealand's history. [Press release], 26 June. Retrieved 24 August 2020 from www.scoop.co.nz/stories/PA0806/S00425.htm.

New Zealand Māori Council and Hall, D. M. (1999). Restorative justice: A Māori perspective. In H. Bowen and J. Consedine (Eds.), *Restorative Justice: Contemporary Themes and Practice* (pp. 25–35). Lyttelton, NZ: Ploughshares Publishers.

Ngā Tamatoa: 40 Years On. (2012). Directed by Kim Webby [television documentary]. Auckland: Tūmanako Productions.

Nísia. (2019). Talentos en demanda de justicia y democracia. *Onda Local*, 1 February. Retrieved 29 March 2023 from https://ondalocalni.com/especiales/590-talentos-en-demanda-de-justicia-y-democracia.

Norman, E. (2015). Tame Iti film fires-up social media. *Wairarapa Times-Age*, 11 September. Retrieved 24 August 2020 from https://www.nzherald.co.nz/nz/tame-iti-film-fires-up-social-media/PLMFYRLOHZZSUSOJSG5FKXE7BY/#google_vignette.

NZ Herald. (2023). Tukoroirangi Morgan: We will mobilise against "racist" policies of incoming government. *New Zealand Herald*, 27 November. Retrieved 11 January 2024 from https://www.nzherald.co.nz/kahu/tukoroirangi-morgan-we-will-mobilise-against-racist-policies-of-incoming-government/2O3YYWKSQBBNLMUVN5H2V3FPRY.

O'Connor, G., and Schneider, A. (2017). How Russian Twitter bots pumped out fake news during the 2016 election. NPR: All Tech Considered, 3 April. Retrieved 22 February 2023 from https://www.npr.org/sections/alltechconsidered/2017/04/03/522503844/how-russian-twitter-bots-pumped-out-fake-news-during-the-2016-election.

October 15: After the Raids. (2010). Directed by Kim Webby [television documentary]. New Zealand: NZ On Air. First broadcast on Māori Television, 7 August.

Offen, K. (2002). The Sambu and Tawira Miskitu: The colonial origins of intra-Miskitu differentiation in Eastern Nicaragua and Honduras. *Ethnohistory* 49(2): 328–333.

OHCHR (Office of the High Commissioner for Human Rights). (2018) *Report of the Special Rapporteur on the Rights of Indigenous Peoples*. Report to the UN General Assembly. Retrieved 9 June 2019 from http://ap.ohchr.org/documents/dpage_e.aspx?si=A/HRC/39/17.

O'Keefe, P., Westgate, K., and Wisner, B. (1976). Taking the naturalness out of natural disasters. *Nature* 260: 566–567.

Oliver-Smith, A. (1986). *The Martyred City: Death and Rebirth in the Andes*. Albuquerque: University of New Mexico Press.

Onda Local. (2016a). Carlos Wilson Billis, 6 May. Retrieved 9 June 2016 from https://www.youtube.com/watch?v=ny-mbVj_9ZU.

———. (2016b). Monkey Point Allen Clair, 17 May. Retrieved 9 June 2016 from https://www.youtube.com/ watch?v=R2Y6VzRN8eQ.

———. (2016c). Bankukuk Taik Comunitarios, 17 May. Retrieved 9 June 2016 from https://www.youtube.com/ watch?v=104uSBFj34I.

100% Noticias. (2021). "Trolls" de Rosario Murillo operan en Correos de Nicaragua. *100% Noticias*, 21 April. Retrieved 30 December 2023 from https://100noticias.com.ni/nacionales/106265-rosario-murillo-trolls-redes-sociales-telcor.

Operation 8. (2011). Directed by Abi King-Jones and Errol Wright [television documentary]. Wellington: CUTCUTCUT Films. First broadcast on Māori Television, 30 October.

Ouellette, L., and Hay, J. (2008). *Better Living Through Reality TV: Television and Post-welfare Citizenship*. Malden, MA: Blackwell.

Ouellette, L., and Murray, S. (2009). Introduction. In S. Murray and L. Ouellette (Eds.), *Reality TV: Remaking Television Culture* (2nd ed., pp. 1–20). New York: New York University Press.

Palast, G. (2006). *Armed Madhouse*. New York: Dutton.

Parks, L. (2005). *Cultures in Orbit: Satellites and the Televisual*. Durham, NC: Duke University Press.

———. (2017). Drone media: Grounded dimensions of the US drone war in Pakistan. In C. Marvin and S. Hong (Eds.), *Place, Space and Mediated Communication* (pp. 13–28). London: Routledge.

Paton, S. (2020). Cummings: Protect the economy and if some pensioners die, "too bad." *The National*, 22 March. Retrieved 9 February 2023 from https://www.thenational.scot/news/18325353.cummings-protect-economy-pensioners-die-too-bad.

Pears, L. (2016). Ask the audience: Television, security and *Homeland*. *Critical Studies on Terrorism* 9(1): 76–96.

Pearson, R. (2011). Cult television as digital television's cutting edge. In J. Bennett and N. Strange (Eds.), *Television as Digital Media* (pp. 105–131). Durham, NC: Duke University Press.

Pearson, R., and Smith, A. N. (Eds.). (2015). *Storytelling in the Media Convergence Age: Exploring Screen Narratives*. Houndmills, UK: Palgrave Macmillan.

Peck, J. (2006). Liberating the city: Between New York and New Orleans. *Urban Geography* 27(8): 681–713.

———. (2012). Renormalizing neoliberalism. Paper presented to the In, Against and Beyond Neoliberalism conference, University of Glasgow, 22 March.

Peters, M. (2004). Gerry! Tame! Both say cheese! *New Zealand Listener*, 8 May.

Phillips, M. (2011). *Satan in the Smoke? A Photojournalist's 9/11 Story*. Brooklyn, NY: South Brooklyn Internet.

Phipps, C. (2015). "Homeland is racist": Artists sneak subversive graffiti on to TV show. *Guardian*, 15 October. Retrieved 6 March 2018 from https://www.theguardian.com/tv-and-radio/2015/oct/15/homeland-is-racist-artists-subversive-graffiti-tv-show.

Pickles, K. (2016). *Christchurch Ruptures*. Wellington: Bridget Williams Books.

Pineda, B. (2001). The Chinese Creoles of Nicaragua: Identity, economy, and revolution in a Caribbean port city. *Journal of Asian American Studies* 4(3): 209–233.

———. (2006). *Shipwrecked Identities: Navigating Race on Nicaragua's Mosquito Coast*. New Brunswick, NJ: Rutgers University Press.

Piore, A. (2020). The sin spinners: The Salem Media empire preaches morality and Donald Trump. *Columbia Journalism Review*, 3 February. Retrieved 16 March 2023 from https://www.cjr.org/special_report/salem-media-group.php.

Poata-Smith, E. (1996). He pokeke uenuku i tu ai: The evolution of contemporary Māori protest. In P. Spoonley, D. Pearson, and C. Macpherson (Eds.), *Nga Patai: Racism and Ethnic Relations in Aotearoa/New Zealand* (pp. 97–116). Palmerston North, NZ: Dunmore Press.

Poniatowska, E. (1995) *Nothing, Nobody: The Voices of the Mexico City Earthquake*. Philadelphia: Temple University Press.

Potter, T., and Marshall, C. W. (Eds.). (2008). *Cylons in America: Critical Studies in Battlestar Galactica*. New York: Continuum.

Pratt, J. (1992). *Punishment in a Perfect Society: The New Zealand Penal System, 1840–1939*. Wellington: Victoria University Press.

Punathambekar, A. (2017). Globalization. In L. Ouellette and J. Gray (Eds.), *Keywords for Media Studies* (pp. 84–87). New York: New York University Press.

Quijano, A. (2005). The challenge of the "Indigenous movement" in Latin America. *Socialism and Democracy* 19(3): 55–78.

———. (2007). Coloniality and modernity/rationality. *Cultural Studies* 21(2–3): 168–178.

Quilliam, R. (2013). Police acted "unlawfully" during Urewera raids. *New Zealand Herald*, 22 May.

Radcliffe, S. A. (2007). Latin American indigenous geographies of fear: Living in the shadow of racism, lack of development, and antiterror measures. *Annals of the Association of American Geographers* 97(2): 385–397.

Rafferty, J. P. (n.d.). Women's march: Worldwide protest [2017]. *Britannica*. Retrieved 30 July 2022 from https://www.britannica.com/event/Womens-March-2017.

Ramírez, S. (2007). *Tambor Olvidado*. San José, Costa Rica: Aguilar.

Rawlinson, K. (2024). Post Office scandal: More than 1m sign petition to strip ex-boss of CBE. *Guardian*, 8 January. Retrieved 16 January 2024 from https://www.theguardian.com/business/2024/jan/08/post-office-horizon-scandal-petition-cbe-paula-vennells.

Rawlinson, K., Badshah, N., and Weaver, M. (2022). Windrush scandal: Timeline of key events. *Guardian*, 31 March. Retrieved 17 January 2024 from https://www.theguardian.com/uk-news/2018/apr/16/windrush-era-citizens-row-timeline-of-key-events.

Redacción Confidencial. (2024). Dictadura destierra a monseñor Rolando Alvarez y a otross 18 religiosos presos politicos al Vaticano. *Confidencial*, 14 January. Retrieved 15 January 2024 from https://confidencial.digital/nacion/dictadura-destierra-a-monsenor-rolando-alvarez-y-a-otros-17-religiosos-presos-politicos-al-vaticano/?utm_source=Telegram&utm_medium=Telegram&utm_id=Telegram.

Redfield, M. (2009). *The Rhetoric of Terror: Reflections on 9/11 and the War on Terror*. New York: Fordham University Press.

Reeves, J. L., Rodgers, M. C., and Epstein, M. (1996). Rewriting popularity: The cult files. In D. Lavery, A. Hague, and M. Cartwright (Eds.), *Deny All Knowledge: Reading the* X-Files (pp. 22–35). London: Faber and Faber.

Renner, E. (2017). "Homeland" recap: Babysitting gone wrong. *Baltimore Sun*, 21 February. Retrieved 7 August 2020 from http://www.baltimoresun.com/entertainment/tv/tv-lust/bal-homeland-recap-season-6-episode-5-20170221-story.html.

República de Nicaragua. (2003). *Ley 445: Ley del regimen de propiedad comunal de los pueblos indígenas y comunidades étnicas de las Regiones Autonomas de la Costa Atlántica de Nicaragua y de los Ríos Bocay, Coco, Indio y Maíz*. Managua: Gaceta Oficial Asamblea Nacional.

Richey, L. A., and Ponte, S. (2008). Better (red)™ than dead? Celebrities, consumption and international aid. *Third World Quarterly* 29(4): 711–729.

RNZ. (2020). Ngāi Tahu, Christchurch council commit to colonial monuments discussion. *RNZ*, 12 June. Retrieved 11 February 2023 from https://www.rnz.co.nz/news/te-manu-korihi/418893/ngai-tahu-christchurch-council-commit-to-colonial-monuments-discussion.

———. (2022). Tame Iti: "It's time to put that aside." *Saturday Morning with Kim Hill*, 3 September. Retrieved 28 March 2023 from https://www.rnz.co.nz/national/programmes/saturday/audio/2018857292/tame-iti-it-s-time-to-put-that-aside.

Robinson, C. J. (1983). *Black Marxism: The Making of the Black Radical Tradition*. Chapel Hill: University of North Carolina Press.

Robinson, W. I. (2014). *Global Capitalism and the Crisis of Humanity*. Cambridge: Cambridge University Press.

Rogin, M. (1987). *Ronald Reagan, the Movie, and Other Episodes in Political Demonology*. Berkeley: University of California Press.

Rojek, C. (2001). *Celebrity*. London: Reaktion Books.

Romero Vargas, G. (1993). La población de origen Africano en Nicaragua. In L. M. Martínez Montiel (Ed.), *Presencia Africana en Centroamérica* (pp. 151–198). Mexico City: Consejo Nacional para la Cultura y las Artes.

Ruru, J. (2014a). Te Urewera Act 2014. *Māori Law Review: A Monthly Review of Law Affecting Māori*, October.

———. (2014b). Troubled space: Tensions in Indigenous and colonial notions of national space. Keynote address delivered at Space, Race, Bodies: Geocorpographies of the City, Nation, Empire, 8–10 December, University of Otago, Dunedin, Aotearoa New Zealand.

Sabbagh, D., Harding, L., and Roth, A. (2020). Russia report reveals UK government failed to investigate Kremlin interference. *Guardian*, 21 July. Retrieved 22 February 2023 from https://www.theguardian.com/world/2020/jul/21/russia-report-reveals-uk-government-failed-to-address-kremlin-interference-scottish-referendum-brexit.

Sáenz, M. (2000). Dussel on Marx: Living labor and the materiality of life. In L. M. Alcoff and L. Mendieta (Eds.), *Thinking from the Underside of History: Enrique Dussel's Philosophy of Liberation* (pp. 213–248). Lanham, MD: Rowman and Littlefield.

Saldaña-Portillo, M. J. (2007). From the borderlands to the transnational? Critiquing empire in the twenty-first century. In J. Flores and R. Rosaldo (Eds.), *A Companion to Latina/o Studies* (pp. 502–512). Malden, MA: Wiley-Blackwell.

Sanger, D. E., and Edmondson, C. (2019). Russia targeted election systems in all 50 states, report finds. *New York Times*, 25 July.

Saunders, R. A. (2019). Small screen IR: A tentative typology of geopolitical television. *Geopolitics* 24(3): 691–727.

Scheible, J. (2010). From Mr. Pregnant to Mr. President: Prepositioning Katrina online. In D. Negra (Ed.), *Old and New Media after Katrina* (pp. 203–229). New York: Palgrave Macmillan.

Schilling, V. (2017). White House website removes Native American, LGBT, climate change, healthcare and civil rights web pages. *ICT*, 21 January. Retrieved 30 July 2022 from https://indiancountrytoday.com/archive/white-house-website-removes-native-american-lgbt-climate-change-healthcare-civil-rights-web-pages.

Schiwy, F. (2003). Decolonizing the frame. *Framework* 44(1): 116–132.

Schram, J. (2014). Pakistani officials furious over "Homeland." *New York Post*, 27 December. Retrieved 16 August 2020 from https://nypost.com/2014/12/27/pakistani-officials-furious-over-countrys-portrayal-in-homeland.

Schwartz, B. (1974). Waiting, exchange, and power: The distribution of time in social systems. *American Journal of Sociology* 79: 841–870.

Sconce, J. (2004). What if? Charting television's new textual boundaries. In L. Spigel and J. Olsson (Eds.), *Television after TV: Essays on a Medium in Transition* (pp. 93–112). Durham, NC: Duke University Press.

Seddon, D. (2021). Riverdale boss publicly asks for information about missing father. *Digital Spy*, 8 August. Retrieved 9 September 2022 from https://www.digitalspy.com/showbiz/a37252645/riverdales-robert-aguirre-sacasa-missing-father-plea.

Segato, R. (2016). *La guerra contra las mujeres*. Madrid: Traficantes de Sueños.

Sharp, J. (2000a). Remasculinising geo(-)politics? Comments on Gearóid Ó Tuathail's Critical Geopolitics. *Political Geography* 19(3): 361–364.

———. (2000b). *Condensing the Cold War:* Reader's Digest *and American Identity*. Minneapolis: University of Minnesota Press.

Shifman, L. (2013). *Memes in Digital Culture*. Cambridge, MA: MIT Press.

Shohat, E., and Stam, R. (2014). *Unthinking Eurocentrism: Multiculturalism and the Media*. 2nd ed. London: Routledge.

Siddique, H. (2024). Infected blood scandal: Victims' families call for action amid Post Office injustice. *Guardian*, 10 January. Retrieved 17 January 2024 from https://www.theguardian.com/uk-news/2024/jan/10/infected-blood-scandal-victims-families-call-for-action-amid-post-office-injustice.

Silva, J. A. (2015). Claves para entender el conflicto en el Caribe Norte. *La Prensa*, 17 September. Retrieved 20 January 2023 from https://www.laprensani.com/2015/09/17/reportajes-especiales/1903452-claves-para-entender-el-conflicto-en-el-caribe-norte.

Smith, J. (2006). Parallel quotidian flows: Māori Television on air. *New Zealand Journal of Media Studies* 9(2): 27–35.

———. (2016). *Māori Television: The First Ten Years*. Auckland: Auckland University Press.

Smith, J., and Abel, S. (2015). Ka whawhai tonu mātou: Indigenous television in Aotearoa/New Zealand. In W. G. Pearson and S. Knabe (Eds.), *Reverse Shots: Indigenous Film and Media in an International Context* (pp. 175–188). Waterloo, Ontario: Wilfrid Laurier University Press.

Smith, J., and de Bruin, J. (2012). *Survivor*-styled indigeneity in two reality television programmes from *Aotearoa*/New Zealand. *Australasian Journal of Popular Culture* 1(3): 297–311.

Smith, L. T. (2012). *Decolonizing Methodologies: Research and Indigenous Peoples*. 2nd ed. London: Zed Books.

Smith, N. (2006). There's no such thing as a natural disaster. *Items: Insights from the Social Sciences*, 11 June. Retrieved 12 April 2020 from https://items.ssrc.org/understanding-katrina/theres-no-such-thing-as-a-natural-disaster.

Smitherman, G. (1977). *Talkin and Testifyin: The Language of Black America*. Detroit: Wayne State University Press.

Snickars, P., and Vonderau, P. (2009). Introduction. In P. Snickars and P. Vonderau (Eds.), *The YouTube Reader* (pp. 9–21). Stockholm: National Library of Sweden.

Soares, I. (2021). Padre de creador de "Riverdale," uno de los políticos presos antes de las elecciones en Nicaragua. CNN en Español, 22 October. Retrieved 9 September 2022 from https://cnnespanol.cnn.com/video/elecciones-nicaragua-arresto-creador-riverdale-roberto-aguirre-daniel-ortega-inhs-pkg-isa-soares.

Solnit, R. (2010). *A Paradise Built in Hell: The Extraordinary Communities That Arise in Disasters*. New York: Viking.

Sontag, S. (2004 [1965]). The imagination of disaster. In G. Rickman (Ed.), *The Science Fiction Film Reader* (pp. 98–113). New York: Limelight Editions.

Specia, M. (2022). "Like a weapon": Ukrainians use social media to stir resistance. *New York Times*, 25 March. Retrieved 22 February 2023 from https://www.nytimes.com/2022/03/25/world/europe/ukraine-war-social-media.html.

Spicer, R. (2010). The Obama mass: Barack Obama, image, and fear of the crowd. In H. E. Harris, K. R. Moffitt, and C. R. Squires (Eds.), *The Obama Effect: Multidisciplinary Renderings of the 2008 Campaign* (pp. 190–208). Albany: State University of New York Press.

Spigel, L. (2004). Entertainment wars: Television culture after 9/11. *American Quarterly* 56(2): 235–270.

———. (2015). TV and the spaces of everyday life. In S. Mains, J. Cupples, and C. Lukinbeal (Eds.), *Mediated Geographies and Geographies of Media* (pp. 37–63). Dordrecht, Netherlands: Springer.

Stacey, K., Mason, R., and Boffey, D. (2024). Former Post Office chief hands back CBE as Horizon scandal intensifies. *Guardian*, 9 January. Retrieved 16 January 2024 from https://www.theguardian.com/uk-news/2024/jan/09/former-post-office-boss-paula-vennells-to-return-cbe-amid-horizon-scandal.

Stadler, J. (2009). Stigma and stardom: Nelson Mandela, celebrity identification and social activism. In R. Clarke (Ed.), *Celebrity Colonialism: Fame, Power and Representation in Colonial and Postcolonial Cultures* (pp. 309–325). Newcastle upon Tyne, UK: Cambridge Scholars.

Stallybrass, P., and White, A. (1986). *The Politics and Poetics of Transgression*. Ithaca, NY: Cornell University Press.

Steenberg, L. (2010). Uncovering the Bones: Forensic approaches to Hurricane Katrina on crime television. In D. Negra (Ed.), *Old and New Media after Katrina* (pp. 23–40). New York: Palgrave Macmillan.

Stone, P. (2021). Money and misinformation: How Turning Point USA became a formidable pro-Trump force. *Guardian*, 23 October. Retrieved 16 March 2023 from https://www.theguardian.com/us-news/2021/oct/23/turning-point-rightwing-youth-group-critics-tactics.

Strangelove, M. (2015). *Post-TV: Piracy, Cord-Cutting, and the Future of Television*. Toronto: University of Toronto Press.

Strauss, E. (2014). Call me a bitch, call me a slut, just don't call me crazy. *Elle*, 3 October. Retrieved 16 August 2020 from https://www.elle.com/life-love/a14808/just-dont-call-me-crazy.

Stubblefield, T. (2014). *9/11 and the Visual Culture of Disaster*. Bloomington: Indiana University Press.

Sturken, M. (2007). *Tourists of History: Memory, Kitsch and Consumerism from Oklahoma City to Ground Zero*. Durham, NC: Duke University Press.

Sundheim, D. (2013). Do women take as many risks as men? *Harvard Business Review*, 27 February. Retrieved 9 February 2023 from https://hbr.org/2013/02/do-women-take-as-many-risks-as.

Sutton, R. (2014). A blank canvas for new beginnings. In B. Bennett, J. Dann, E. Johnson, and R. Reynolds (Eds.), *Once in a Lifetime: City-Building after Disaster in Christchurch* (pp. 52–58). Christchurch, NZ: Freerange Press.

Sweney, M. (2024). Paula Vennells to Ed Davey: The people with questions to answer on the Post Office scandal. *Guardian*, 8 January. Retrieved 16 January 2024 from https://www.theguardian.com/uk-news/2024/jan/08/paula-vennells-to-ed-davey-the-people-with-questions-to-answer-on-the-post-office-scandal.

Taffel, S. (2019). *Digital Media Ecologies: Entanglements of Content, Code and Hardware*. New York: Bloomsbury Academic.
Takacs, S. (2010). The contemporary politics of the Western form: Bush, *Saving Jessica Lynch* and *Deadwood*. In J. Birkenstein, A. Froula, and K. Randell (Eds.), *Reframing 9/11: Film, Popular Culture and the "War on Terror"* (pp. 153–165). New York: Continuum.
———. (2012). *Terrorism TV: Popular Entertainment in Post-9/11 America*. Lawrence: University of Kansas Press.
Tame Iti: The Man behind the Moko. (2005). Directed by Chelsea Winstanley [television documentary]. Auckland: KIWA Media. First broadcast on Māori Television 30 November.
Tay, J., and Turner, G. (2008). What is television? Comparing media systems in the post-broadcast era. *Media International Australia* 126: 71–81.
TCRN. (2020). Father of Costa Rican calypso Wálter Ferguson will be immortalized in a new postmark. *TCRN: The Costa Rica News*, 2 September. Retrieved 19 February 2023 from https://thecostaricanews.com/father-of-costa-rican-calypso-walter-ferguson-will-be-immortalized-in-a-new-postmark.
Thompson, J. (2005). The new visibility. *Theory, Culture and Society* 22: 31–51.
Thorby, A. (2012). Urewera 4 trial: Day 17—waiting for a bit of land. *Scoop*, 9 March. Retrieved 25 August 2020 from http://www.scoop.co.nz/stories/HL1203/S00079/urewera-4-trial-day-17-waiting-for-a-bit-of-land.htm.
Thussu, D. K. (2009a). Introduction. In D. K. Thussu (Ed.), *Internationalizing Media Studies* (pp. 1–10). London: Routledge.
———. (2009b). Why internationalize media studies and how? In D. K. Thussu (Ed.), *Internationalizing Media Studies* (pp. 13–31). London: Routledge.
Tico Times. (2012). Costa Rica declares calypso music "national patrimony." *Tico Times*, 17 December. Retrieved 19 February 2023 from https://ticotimes.net/2012/12/17/costa-rica-declares-calypso-music-national-patrimony.
Timutimu, R. (2016). Tamariki Māori use culture to cope with earthquakes. *Te Ao Māori News*, 18 February. Retrieved 11 February 2023 from https://www.teaomaori.news/tamariki-maori-use-culture-cope-earthquakes.
Tobin, H. (2007). Big events, big causes: MIHOPs, LIHOPs and the "truth" behind September 11. *Institute of Public Affairs Review*, March: 44–47.
Todd, K. (2020). EQC poorly prepared for Canterbury earthquakes—inquiry. *RNZ*, 9 April. Retrieved 27 August 2020 from https://www.rnz.co.nz/news/national/413860/eqc-poorly-prepared-for-canterbury-earthquakes-inquiry.
Truscello, M. (2011). The response of cultural studies to 9/11 skepticism in American popular culture. *Anarchist Developments in Cultural Studies* 1: 27–77.
Tsaliki, L., Frangonikolopoulos, C. A., and Huliaras, A. (Eds.). (2011). *Transnational Celebrity Activism in Global Politics: Changing the World?* Bristol, UK: Intellect.
Tuck, E. (2009). Suspending damage: A letter to communities. *Harvard Educational Review* 79(3): 409–428.
Tuggle, L. (2011). Encrypting Katrina: Traumatic inscription and the architecture of amnesia. *Invisible Culture* 16: 65–87.
Turner, G. (2004). *Understanding Celebrity*. London: Sage.
———. (2016). *Re-inventing the Media*. London: Routledge.
Turner, R. J. (2011). Non-Māori viewing of Māori Television: An empirical analysis of the New Zealand broadcast system. MA thesis, Massey University, New Zealand.
Tuters, M., and Willaert, T. (2022). Deep state phobia: Narrative convergence in coronavirus conspiracism on Instagram. *Convergence: The International Journal of Research into New Media Technologies* 28(4): 1214–1238.

TVNZ. (2010). Māori activist Tame Iti. *Waka Huia* [television program], first broadcast 24 October.

———. (2013). Tūhoe settlement marks a "new beginning"—Finlayson. *ONE News*. Retrieved 2 April 2014 from http://tvnz.co.nz/national-news/tuhoe-settlement-marks-new-beginning-finlayson-5454757.

———. (2022) "I will not speak Maori." *Seven Sharp* [television program]. Retrieved 28 March 2023 from https://www.tvnz.co.nz/shows/seven-sharp/clips/i-will-not-speak-maori.

Tyler, I. (2013). *Revolting Subjects: Social Abjection and Resistance in Neoliberal Britain*. London: Zed Books.

Uddin, R., Fisher, L., and Gross, A. (2024). Fujitsu won contracts on Sunak's watch despite Post Office scandal. *Financial Times*, 9 January. Retrieved 15 January 2024 from https://www.ft.com/content/c38044f3-05cb-45a2-abbd-bc1b03551d9d?sharetype=blocked.

U.K. Information Commissioner. (2018). Investigation into the use of data analytics in political campaigns, 11 July. Retrieved 22 February 2023 from https://ico.org.uk/media/action-weve-taken/2259371/investigation-into-data-analytics-for-political-purposes-update.pdf.

U.K. Parliament. (2018). Select Committee on Culture, Media and Sport interim report on disinformation and "fake news," part 5: Russian influence in political campaigns. 29 July. Retrieved 22 February 2023 from https://publications.parliament.uk/pa/cm201719/cmselect/cmcumeds/363/36308.htm#_idTextAnchor033.

———. (2021). "Unimaginable" cost of Test & Trace failed to deliver central promise of averting another lockdown. *Public Accounts Committee*, 10 March. Retrieved 15 January 2024 from https://committees.parliament.uk/committee/127/public-accounts-committee/news/150988/unimaginable-cost-of-test-trace-failed-to-deliver-central-promise-of-averting-another-lockdown.

Ungoed-Thomas, J. (2023). Grenfell families "left in limbo" lash out at delays to decision on demolition. *Guardian*, 31 December. Retrieved 17 January 2024 from https://www.theguardian.com/uk-news/2023/dec/31/grenfell-families-in-limbo-delays-decision-demolition-fire-72-lives.

United States Department of State. (1894). *Foreign Relations of the United States, 1894, Nicaragua (Mosquito Territory)*, document no. 23, the Nicaraguan attach [sic] on Bluefields. Retrieved 19 February 2023 from https://history.state.gov/historicaldocuments/frus1894Nicaragua/d23.

U.S. Senate. (2018). Committee on Foreign Relations minority staff report on Putin's asymmetric assault on democracy in Russia and Europe: Implications for U.S. national security. 10 January. Retrieved 22 February 2023 from https://www.foreign.senate.gov/imo/media/doc/FinalRR.pdf.

Van den Bergh, R., and Kay, M. (2011). Government announces $500m bailout for insurer AMI. *Dominion Post*, 7 April. Retrieved 9 February 2023 from https://www.stuff.co.nz/dominion-post/4858410/Government-announces-500m-bailout-for-insurer-AMI.

Vann, B. (2003). White House bans coverage of coffins returning from Iraq. World Socialist Web Site, 23 October. Retrieved 20 August 2020 from https://www.wsws.org/en/articles/2003/10/bush-o23.html.

Vílchez, D. (2017). Juliet Hooker: "No pensamos que el nicaragüense puede ser negro." *Confidencial/ Niú*, 17 July. Retrieved 10 January 2023 from https://niu.com.ni/juliet-hooker-no-pensamos-que-el-nicaraguense-puede-ser-negro.

Voltaire Network. (2022). Death of David Ray Griffin. 2 December. Retrieved 14 December 2022 from https://www.voltairenet.org/article218471.html.
Wadi, R. (2011). Living under the oppression of democracy: The Mapuche people of Chile. Upside Down World, 31 January. Retrieved 24 August 2020 from http://upsidedownworld.org/main/chile-archives-34/2887-living-under-the-oppression-of-democracy-the-mapuc-he-people-of-chile.
Wagner, J. (2023). She was crowned Miss Universe. Then her government cracked down. *New York Times*, 16 December. Retrieved 11 January 2024 from https://www.nytimes.com/2023/12/16/world/americas/nicaragua-miss-universe.html.
Walker, R. (2002). Māori news is bad news. In J. McGregor and M. Comrie (Eds.), *What's News: Reclaiming Journalism in New Zealand* (pp. 215–232). Palmerston North, New Zealand: Dunmore.
———. (2004). *Ka Whawhai Tonu Matou: Struggle without End*. Auckland: Penguin.
Walsh, C. (2007). Shifting the geopolitics of critical knowledge: Decolonial thought and cultural studies "others" in the Andes. *Cultural Studies* 21(2–3): 224–239.
Walzer, J. (2009). Yes, Ms. President? *Dissent* (Winter): 101–104.
Webby, K. (2015). Telling the story of the Urewera "terrorists." *E-Tangata: A Māori and Pasifika Sunday Magazine*, 29 November. Retrieved 25 August 2020 from http://e-tangata.co.nz/news/kim-webby-telling-the-story-of-the-urewera-terrorists.
Weber, B. R. (2010). In desperate need (of a makeover): The neoliberal project, the design expert and the post-Katrina social body in distress. In D. Negra (Ed.), *Old and New Media after Katrina* (pp. 175–201). New York: Palgrave Macmillan.
Weber, C. (1999). *Faking It: U.S. Hegemony in a "Post-phallic" Era*. Minneapolis: University of Minnesota Press.
Wellington City Council. (2022). Tame Iti's "I Will Not Speak Māori" installation happening in Odlin's Plaza. *Tō Tātou Pōneke Our Wellington*, 26 August. Retrieved 28 March 2023 from https://wellington.govt.nz/news-and-events/news-and-information/our-wellington/2022/08/tame-iti-exhibition.
White, A. (1983). The dismal sacred word: Academic language and the social reproduction of seriousness. *Journal of Literature Teaching Politics* 2: 4–15.
Wichtel, D. (2012). John Campbell: The woo-hoo man. *New Zealand Listener*, 10 November.
Williams, R. (1977). *Marxism and Literature*. Oxford: Oxford University Press.
Wilson-Hartgrove, J. (2021). Christian nationalism's role in the insurrection was four decades in the making. TPM, 3 February. Retrieved 16 March 2023 from https://talkingpointsmemo.com/cafe/without-help-christian-nationalism-decades-making-might-not-been-insurrection.
Woods, H. S. (2018). Asking more of Siri and Alexa: Feminine persona in service of surveillance capitalism. *Critical Studies in Media Communication* 35(4): 334–349.
Wu, J. C. (2012). Cultural citizenship at the intersection of television and new media. *Television and New Media* 14(5): 402–420.
Yang, Y., and Murgia, M. (2019). How China cornered the facial recognition surveillance market. *Los Angeles Times*, 9 December. Retrieved 30 December 2023 from https://www.latimes.com/business/story/2019-12-09/china-facial-recognition-surveillance.
York, L. (2016). Celebrity and the cultivation of indigenous publics in Canada. In K. Lee and L. York (Eds.), *Celebrity Cultures in Canada* (pp. 93–110). Waterloo, ON: Wilfred Laurier University Press.

Zibechi, R. (2011). Ecuador: The construction of a new model of domination. Upside Down World, 5 August. Retrieved 24 August 2020 from http://upsidedownworld.org/main/ecuador-archives-49/3152-ecuador-the-construction-of-a-new-model-of-domination.

Žižek, S. (2002a). Welcome to the desert of the real. *The Symptom: Online Journal for Lacan*. Retrieved 25 August 2020 from http://www.lacan.com/thesymptom.htm.

———. (2002b). *Welcome to the Desert of the Real! Five Essays on September 11 and Related Dates*. London: Verso.

Index

Aboriginals, 112, 132, 137
activism, 2, 9, 27, 93, 99, 115, 134–135, 139, 144, 147–148, 188, 206; Afrodescendant activism, 164, 190, 198, 214; digital activism, 186–187, 196–208, 231n8; feminist activism, 176, 196, 200, 214; Indigenous activism, 110, 112–113, 124, 132–137, 139, 148–149, 151, 214, 220; LGBTQ+ activism, 198, 201, 214
Aeroméxico, 4
Afghanistan, 48–50, 54, 123
African Americans: disaster and, 74, 79, 227n6; elections and, 23; equality and, 47; incarceration and, 113, 229n6; marginalization and, 16; media and, 228n1; police brutality and, 107, 226n1; social movements and, 64, 69–70
aftershocks, 84–85, 88
Aguirre-Sacasa, Francisco, 207–208
Aguirre-Sacasa, Roberto, 207–208
AI (artificial intelligence), 6, 218
Alemán, Lesther, 198
algorithms, 5, 187
Al-Qaeda, 23, 25, 32, 42, 50, 52–54, 131, 223n13, 224n7
Alvarez, Junior, 194
Alvarez, Rolando, 204–205
ambivalence, 142, 151, 163
American exceptionalism, 32, 41, 44, 47–48, 100
America's Most Wanted (TV show), 74

Amnesty International, 198–199
Anancy, 192
Angel at My Table, An (film), 85
anti-racism, 3, 124, 131
Aotearoa New Zealand. *See* New Zealand
apartheid, 136–137, 219
Apprentice, The (TV show), 2
Arahanga, Julian, 117, 119, 121, 123
Argentina, 93, 169, 222–223n7
Army Corps of Engineers, 75, 227n8
articulation/disarticulation/rearticulation, 15, 31, 37, 104, 135–136, 163, 168–169, 187; Black Twitter and, 192; calypso and, 190, 195; coloniality and, 109, 115, 125, 149–150, 157, 216, 219; conjunctural analysis and, 212–214; cultural studies and, 224n1; disasters and, 62, 65, 68, 78–80, 87, 90; Indigenous media and, 7, 111–112, 118–121, 131, 140–145, 180–181; Nicaraguan activism and, 97, 199–201, 203, 208; 9/11 and, 22–27, 29; postdisaster waiting and, 92, 96, 99
artificial intelligence. *See* AI (artificial intelligence)
Auckland, 117, 139
audiences: calypso and, 194; *Campbell Live* and, 97; Creole television and, 173; Donald Trump and, 32; elections and, 49, 226; engagement and, 35, 42, 53, 56, 76, 100–101, 214; fiscal envelope and, 138; imagination and, 55; Māori Television

265

audiences (cont.)
  and, 110, 118–123, 147, 228n5; media figures and, 135; new media environment and, 1–2, 7, 22, 31, 34, 36, 65, 206; 9/11 and, 14, 18; radio and, 139; reception and, 34, 45–46, 52; sensemaking and, 37, 134; solidarity and, 149, 169; storytelling and, 103
Australia, 112, 113, 132, 137, 228n3
Autonomous Region of the North Caribbean Coast (RACCN), 70, 72, 164, 179, 182–184, 226n3, 227n9
Autonomous Region of the South Caribbean Coast (RACCS), 164, 170, 184–186, 226n3
autonomy, 156, 158, 161, 163–165, 178, 180–181, 187, 226n3
Avery, Dylan, 27–28, 225n10

Bacanalnica, 179, 208
Bangkukuk Taik, 184–186
Barclay, Barry, 118, 120
barricades, 67, 198, 200, 203, 205
baseball, 46, 162, 172, 184
basketball, 162
Battlestar Galactica (TV show), 39–40
BBC, 210
Beehive, the (New Zealand Parliament building), 141–142
Belize, 157, 222n7
Belli, Gioconda, 205
Big Uneasy, The (film), 74, 79, 81
Biloxi, Mississippi, 77, 100
Bilwi, 81; ethnic composition of, 166; Hurricane Felix and, 64, 73, 75, 78; history of, 70–72, 156, 162, 226n3, 226–227n4; media and, 170, 172
BilwiVision (TV channel), 155, 170, 173–175
"Bin Laden" (song), 27–28, 29, 225n10
bin Laden, Osama, 23, 131
Birmingham School of Cultural Studies, 211. *See also* cultural studies
Black Liberation Radio, 228n1
Black Lives Matter, 125, 142, 203, 226n1
Black Panthers, 136
Black Star Line, 188
blogs, 31, 36, 65–66, 73, 75–76, 79–80, 101–102 104, 227n12
Bluefields, 156, 158, 166, 170, 171, 177, 191, 198
Bolivia, 69, 168, 229n8
Bones (TV show), 74

border thinking, 69, 72
boredom, 93–94
Bosawás Forest, 179, 183
Boston Legal (TV show), 39–41, 74
Bourdain, Anthony, 80
Brazil, 112, 132, 217, 218, 222n7
Brexit, 218
Bribri (people), 156, 166, 173–175
Broad, Howard, 126, 131
Brothers and Sisters (TV show), 39–40
Brown, Michael (African American killed in Missouri), 226n1
Brown, Michael (FEMA chief), 227n6
Brownlee, Gerry, 91, 99, 139
Bush, Barbara, 74, 79, 227n7
Bush, George W., 23, 63; Hurricane Katrina and, 73–74, 78, 84, 227n6; 9/11 and, 25, 26–29, 32–33, 48, 223n18, 224n7; war on terror and, 38–41, 43–45
Bush, Jeb, 23
Bush, Mike, 150

Cable, Vince, 211
Cáceres, Berta, 132–133
Cahuita, 156, 191, 193
calypso, 9, 167, 179, 189–196, 212
Calypsonians of Today, The (film), 190–191
Campbell, John, 90–100
Campbell Barr, Epsy, 194–195
Campbell Live (TV show), 90–100, 214
campesinos, 175, 181, 196, 198
Cam's Kai (TV show), 118
Canada, 14, 69, 112, 129, 222n7, 226n4, 228n3
Canal 5 (TV channel). *See* BilwiVision
Canterbury, New Zealand, 83–84, 91, 94, 98–99
capitalism, 62–63, 101, 113, 134–135, 168, 218. *See also* disaster capitalism
Caracas, Madelaine, 198, 200
Caravan of Complaint, 95, 98
Caribbean Calypso, 193
Carlson, Tucker, 218
Catholic Church, 173, 198, 204
Cayasso Dixon, Kendall, 188–190, 194–196
celebrification, 8, 133–135, 142, 147
celebritization, 132–136, 144, 148, 151
celebrity, 2, 28, 131–134, 143, 148, 152
Celebrity Treasure Island (TV show), 148
cellphones, 54, 199, 204. *See also* smartphones

Chamorro, Carlos Fernando, 206
Chamorro, Pedro Joaquín, 201
Changó, 193
Channel 4 (U.K.), 232n2
Chávez, Hugo, 167
Chechnya, 218
Checkpoint (radio program), 99–100
Cheney, Dick, 23, 25–27, 32, 40–41, 44
Chicago, 32, 80
Chile, 124, 207, 214, 222n7
China, 42, 44, 45, 48, 137, 167
Christchurch, 83–92, 94–102, 117, 228n1, 228nn6–7
Christchurch Dilemmas (web series), 88
Christchurch earthquakes (2010–2011), 83–92, 95–101, 139, 228n1, 228n3, 228nn7–8
CIA, 42, 50, 52–53, 56
Clark, Helen, 126
Clinton, Hillary, 43
CNN, 20, 28, 31, 73, 216, 224n4
Coca-Cola, 4
Colbert, Stephen, 224n6
Cold War, 2, 14, 43
Colectivo de Mujeres de Matagalpa, 205
Colombia, 49, 65, 124, 161, 203
colonial ambivalence, 151
colonialism, 123, 125, 134, 169; in Christchurch, 84, 86, 89–90, 228n6; colonial attitudes, 112, 113; colonial discourses, 118, 169; colonial divide, 226n2; colonial media, 118, 169; colonial present, 124; colonial violence, 130, 136, 138, 140, 144; criminal justice system and, 107, 112–115, 119, 121, 141; Indigenous peoples and, 111, 114, 118, 168; internal colonialism, 70–71, 76, 158, 166; legacies of, 167, 168, 219; in New Orleans, 64, 70, 75–76; in New Zealand, 108–110, 113, 115, 121, 126, 138–141, 145, 147–152, 215, 228n4 (*see also* coloniality: in New Zealand); in Nicaragua, 64, 159, 185–186 (*see also* coloniality: in Nicaragua)
coloniality, 2, 5–8, 72, 82, 94, 99, 101, 212, 215–216; as concept, 68–69, 160, 223n12, 229n11; in Costa Rica, 157, 166; in New Zealand, 6–7, 100, 109, 113, 115, 120, 128, 138–142, 144, 147, 149–152, 216–217 (*see also* colonialism: in New Zealand); in Nicaragua, 64, 155, 157, 159, 162, 166–167,
181–182, 184–186, 203, 217 (*see also* colonialism: in Nicaragua); statues and, 89, 228n5
Commander in Chief (TV show), 37, 42–50, 57
commodification, 37, 89, 134, 195, 231n5
Computer Weekly, 210
CONADETI (National Commission for Demarcation and Titling), 165
confiscation line, 126, 128, 139
conjuncture, 5, 29, 108, 135–136, 152, 165–166; conjunctural analysis, 8, 129, 131, 144, 147–150, 161, 200, 211, 215; conjunctural crisis, 64, 100, 167–168, 232n3; conjunctural shift, 188; conjunctural struggle, 217–218
conquest (of America), 69, 166, 223
conquista. *See* conquest (of America)
Conrado, Alvaro, 203
Conservative government (U.K.), 209, 213
conspiracy theories, 13, 28, 30, 219, 225n10
Contras (Nicaragua), 163, 172, 201, 231n10
Cooper, Anderson, 73
Corona, 4
Coronation Street (TV show), 49
Costa Rica, 161–162, 166, 222n7, 230n2; calypso and, 179, 190–196, 212, 231n4; history of, 157, 159; media and, 8, 156, 170, 173–175, 188–189; Nicaraguan refugees in, 172, 204, 206
Costeños, 70–72, 82, 156, 159, 161–164, 167, 178, 187–188
counterintelligence, 25
counterknowledges, 24–25, 27, 30–31, 66, 184
countersurveillance, 25–26, 28, 66, 107, 187, 219
counterterrorism, 14, 50, 52, 54, 57
country music, 162
COVID-19, 62, 100–102, 213, 219, 228n7, 232n2
Creole (language), 156, 159–160, 166–167, 172, 189, 196, 231
Creole (people), 156–157, 160–162, 164, 166; autonomy and, 158; as concept, 226, 230n2; development and, 165; identity, 167, 182; media and, 155, 171–173, 177, 179, 183; spirituality and, 158; working in Miskito Keys, 78, 227n9
Crimea, 218
criminality, 109, 112–123, 161

criminalization: as authoritarian strategy, 165, 168, 200, 204; of Indigenous people, 7, 112–114, 123–125, 133, 135, 220
criminal justice system, 29, 112–116, 119–123, 141, 211
Crown, British, 108, 126, 128–129, 137–140, 150, 230n5 (chap. 6)
CSI (TV show), 74
Cuba, 136, 160, 222n7, 224n8, 229n12
cultural citizenship, 2, 5, 9, 37, 43, 57; coloniality and, 111; construction of, 35, 67, 168; practices of, 107, 179, 219; struggles for, 133, 137
cultural studies, 3, 49, 57, 68, 131, 144, 168, 211, 221n4, 224n1
Curtis, Cliff, 142

Daily Show, The (TV show), 29, 222n5
Dancing with the Stars (TV show), 148
da Silva, Lula, 218
Davey, Ed, 211
Dávila, Tamara, 207, 231n13
Day That Changed My Life, The (film), 88
debt crisis, 165, 223n10
decoloniality, 2, 4, 104, 152, 155, 219–220; decolonial ethos, 117, 119; decolonial forces, 136; decolonial politics, 156, 179; decolonial struggles, 7–9, 115, 137, 155, 187; disaster and, 76–77, 89, 101–102; theories of, 68–69, 103
Demarcation Now (radio program), 176
democratization, 1, 155, 199; authoritarianism vs., 165–166, 197, 208, 221n1; media events and, 15; neoliberalism vs., 98–100; participatory media and, 9, 63–65, 104, 107, 169, 219
dependency theory, 68, 169
D'Escoto, Miguel, 207
development: capitalism and, 113, 133; cultural, 9, 160; economic, 160, 173, 189, 219; interoceanic canal and, 165, 184–185; as practice, 31, 133, 157, 168–170, 174, 186; theories of, 169
digitalization, 111, 199–200
digitization, 7
Di Gud Frenz, 193–195
Dirty War, 169
disarticulation. *See* articulation/disarticulation/rearticulation
disaster capitalism, 83–84, 97–98, 228n1

disasters, 3, 5–6, 155–156, 218–220, 227n5; calypso and, 193; cinema and, 18–19; coloniality and/as, 94, 183, 216, 223n11; media and, 61–69, 72–92, 99–102, 104, 107, 170; 9/11 as, 38; TV and, 42, 95. *See also* coloniality; earthquakes; hurricanes; 9/11
displacement (after disaster), 18, 79, 82, 87, 93–96, 100, 165, 193
Divergentes, 206, 231n11
drones, 50–51, 53–57, 219
drugs: drug addiction, 71, 174, 188; drug dealing, 44, 71, 170–171; drug taking, 38, 78; drug trafficking, 44, 171; U.S. war on drugs, 42, 44, 49

Earthquake Commission (EQC), 83, 91–92, 94–100
earthquakes, 61, 72, 80, 169, 194. *See also* Christchurch earthquakes; disasters
Eating Media Lunch (TV show), 131
elections, 167; electoral fraud, 175, 218; in Nicaragua, 165, 175, 178, 203, 204; in United Kingdom, 213; in United States, 2–3, 23, 25, 218, 221n3, 225–226n17
El País, 205
El Salvador, 166, 222n7
Eminem, 29, 225n10
Enlightenment, 30, 69
ER (TV show), 38
Escape from New York (film), 18
estrangement, 149
Eurocentrism, 64–65, 69, 102, 107, 109, 113, 160, 163, 169, 212, 216; assimilation and, 156; control and, 125; discourses of, 120; incarceration and, 122; media and, 109, 111, 114, 120; *mestizaje* and, 161
extractivism, 64, 70, 158, 167–169
Extreme Makeover (TV show), 74

Facebook, 3, 6, 170, 207, 225n14; Afro-Costa Ricans and, 189, 194, 212; cinema and, 147; Costeños and, 133, 172, 174, 179, 182, 187; disaster and, 67, 88, 99, 101; TV and, 34, 97, 110, 122–123, 145–146; 2018 Nicaraguan uprisings and, 197–199, 204
Fahey, Morgan, 85
fandom, 35–36, 52, 138
femininity, 51

feminism, 36, 46, 47–48, 51, 53, 57, 176, 196, 200
Ferguson, Missouri, 65, 226n1
Ferguson, Walter, 191–194
Fiji, 137
Financial Times, 210
Finlayson, Chris, 150
First Time in Prison (TV show), 116
fiscal envelope, 138
Five Days in the Red Zone (film), 88
Flavell, Te Ururoa, 229n9
Flint, Michigan, 94
Floyd, George, 7, 107
Forbes, Mihingarangi, 230n7
fourth world, 1, 8, 100, 218, 220, 221n1
Fox (TV channel), 13–14, 225n15
Fox News, 27, 31–32, 217, 218, 224n6, 225n14
Friday Night Lights (TV show), 39–40
FSLN. *See* Sandinistas
Full Frontal with Samantha Bee (TV show), 222n5
Fujitsu, 209–211, 232n1

Gahona, Ángel, 177, 198
Gap Filler, 86, 101, 104
Garífuna, 71, 159, 166
Garvey, Marcus, 188–190
Gaza, 6, 65
gender, 3, 36, 66, 78, 155, 226n1; gender-based violence, 214; incarceration and, 118; struggles over, 168; TV drama and, 37–39, 42–43, 46–49, 51, 53, 57
geopolitics, 37, 43, 53, 57, 62; "development" and, 169; feminist geopolitics, 57; Indigeneity and, 127, 130; popular geopolitics, 5, 10, 15, 33–34, 47, 49, 51–52, 170, 211; post-9/11 and, 4–5, 14, 19, 25, 32, 36, 40, 51, 167
Geraldo at Large (TV show), 31, 214
Ghana, 192
Gillies, Amanda 128
Glinton, Herbert "Lenky," 193
Godley, John Robert, 89
Goodman, John, 75, 79–80, 101
Goulbourne, Alfonso, 193
Gramsci, Antonio, 3, 66, 131, 169, 211, 221n4
Grant, Ulysses, 193, 231n5
Greening the Rubble, 86, 104
Grenfell, 213
Guardian, 205

Guatemala, 132, 166, 222n7
Güegüense, 202–203
Gurdián, Pinita, 207

Haiti, 29, 68, 70, 75, 160, 222n7
haka, 141
Hamas, 6, 223n13
hapu, 121, 145
hashtags, 3, 67, 88, 197–198, 203
HBO (TV channel), 28, 31, 75, 102
Heavenly Creatures (film), 85
hip-hop, 29, 189, 194, 225n10
Holland, Semiramis, 128
Hollinrake, Kevin, 210
Hollywood, 2, 15, 19, 22, 142, 147, 208, 212, 216
Homai Te Pakipaki (TV show), 118
Homeland (TV show), 37, 42, 50–57, 214, 219
homelessness, 42
Honduras, 159, 163, 166, 172, 187, 222n7
Hope and Wire (TV show), 88, 220
Horizon (software), 209–211, 232n1
Horomia, Parekura, 127, 131
hospitality, 121–122, 143, 145
House (TV show), 74
human rights, 42; abuses of, 99, 183, 188, 198, 202; Inter-American Commission of, 180, 185; Inter-American Court of, 198; in Nicaragua, 180, 204, 207, 208; organizations of, 179, 180, 182, 198; struggles for, 200
Hurricane Felix, 9, 64, 73, 75–78, 81–82, 100–101, 155–156, 227n9
Hurricane Katrina, 5, 64, 73–78, 94, 100–101, 219, 227n6, 227n8; disaster capitalism and, 83–84; race and, 62, 73–74, 81, 94, 212; YouTube and, 66, 73, 75, 82
Hurricane Maria, 94
hurricanes, 61, 63, 72, 194. *See also* Hurricane Felix; Hurricane Katrina; Hurricane Maria
hypermediation, 4, 135

If God Is Willing and Da Creek Don't Rise (film), 74, 80–81
Immortal Technique, 27, 29, 225n10
imprisonment. *See* incarceration; political prisoners; prison

incarceration, 7, 42; African Americans and, 113, 229n6; Eurocentrism and, 122; of Indigenous peoples, 112, 133; of Māori, 42, 112–113, 116, 119–121, 140, 148; media and, 118, 122; in Nicaragua, 204, 208. *See also* political prisoners; prison
Independence Day (film), 18
Independent Police Conduct Authority (IPCA) (New Zealand), 149
India, 67
Indio Maíz, 164, 197, 214
infected blood scandal, 213
Infosys, 211
Inside Death Row (TV show), 118
Instituto de Investigaciones y Gestión Social (INGES), 205
insurance, 67–68, 83, 91, 94, 96, 98, 228n1
Interamerican Commission of Human Rights, 180, 185
Interamerican Court of Human Rights, 164, 198
interculturality, 71, 155–156, 170, 173, 175, 182
intermediality, 8
International Labour Organization Convention, 169, 108, 165
interoceanic canal (Nicaragua), 165, 175, 177, 179, 181, 184–186, 196
Iran, 41, 50
Iraq, 38–41, 48, 124
Iraq War, 5, 33, 38–41
Islam, 20, 22, 28, 50
Islamabad, 52, 54
Islamophobia, 51
Israel-Palestine conflict, 6, 42, 53, 223n13
Iti, Tame, 8, 126–132, 135–152, 215, 229n2
iwi, 85, 118, 121, 130, 136, 140, 145, 150, 229n7

Jackson, Hardy, 74, 77–78, 81–82, 101
Jackson, Moana, 113–114, 117, 124
Jackson, Peter, 85
jail. *See* prison
jailing. *See* incarceration
Jamaica, 29, 157, 159, 162, 188, 191, 222n7
January 6, 2021, insurrection, 217
Jones, Alex, 219
Joseph, Mike, 194–196
Just Speak, 114, 117

Kabu Yula (radio station), 171
Kahi, Tearepa, 116, 141–142

Kaitiaki o te Maungarongo (TV show), 116
kaupapa Māori, 119–120
Kayapo, 132, 134
Kenana, Rua, 110, 126–127
Keskidee Aroha (film), 150
Key, John, 97, 150, 228n4
King, Mike, 148
King, Rodney, 107
King Pulanka festival, 72, 104
Kruger, Tamati, 129, 149
Kurdish separatist movement, 42
K-Ville (TV show), 74

La comunidad en su casa (TV show), 173, 214
La Prensa, 206, 231n11
laughter, 128, 131, 142
La Vida Después del Viento (TV show), 75, 77, 81
Law and Order: Special Victims Unit (TV show), 74
Law 28 (Nicaragua), 164
Law 445 (Nicaragua), 164–165, 178, 180, 185
Law 840 (Nicaragua), 184–185
Leche de Coco, 193–194
Lee, Spike, 74–76
Le Monde, 205
levees, 73–75, 80–81, 219
levees.org, 75, 101
LGBTQ+ movements, 198, 201, 214
Life in Vacant Spaces, 86
Limón, 156, 162, 166, 170, 175, 188, 190–191, 193–194, 196
LimónTV (TV channel), 175, 189–190, 231n1
liquefaction, 84, 86, 92, 99
Lockup (TV show), 118
Lone Gunmen, The (TV show), 13
Loose Change (film), 5, 27–28, 225n11
Lord Cobra, 192
Los Angeles, 13, 38
Lost (TV show), 36

mainstream media, 3, 7, 35, 65–66, 81, 102, 107, 152, 168, 212, 220; appropriation of, 169–170; Bilwi and, 71; celebritization and, 132, 134; in Central America, 216; in Costa Rica, 189, 195; disaster and, 28, 62, 77, 134; Indigenous media vs., 110, 128–129, 144–147, 150–151; New Orleans and, 71; in New Zealand, 8, 92, 109, 114,

119, 125, 128–131, 137–144, 148–149, 152; in Nicaragua, 183, 204, 207; 9/11 and, 28, 30, 140
Mais ne nous délivrez pas du mal (film), 85
mana, 119, 122–123, 130, 229n10, 230n5 (chap. 6)
Managua, 87, 158–159, 176, 179–180, 185, 197–198, 205
Māori (people and culture): criminalization of, 112–124, 229n6, 229n12 (*see also* 2007 terror raids); Māori activism, 8, 90, 108, 110, 113, 126–127, 130–131, 135–137, 140, 145, 151, 217, 220 (*see also* Iti, Tame); Māori history, 84–85, 90, 108–110; Māori knowledges, 101–102, 111, 118, 126, 151–152, 228n2; Māori language (see *te reo* Māori); Māori media, 8, 114–119, 143–144, 146, 148, 155, 212, 215 (*see also* Whakaata Māori); Māori Party, 229n9; Māori sovereignty, 123–124, 136, 217; Māori Television (*see* Whakaata Māori)
marae, 215
Marae (TV show), 103, 143
Marae DIY (TV show), 118
Marae Kai Masters (TV show), 118
Margarula, Yvonne, 132
Mardi Gras, 79–81, 219
Mardi Gras Indians, 72, 104
Marley, Bob, 191
Marshall, Peter, 149
Martí, José, 160
masculinity, 43, 46, 48, 53, 228n1
mash-ups, 6, 88–89
Mayangna (people), 157, 164, 166, 179, 183
Mayerle, Jennifer, 78, 81
McDonald, Trevor, 118
McLean, Mere, 129
media convergence, 7–8, 15–16, 22, 34–36, 56–57, 65, 99, 111–112; activism and, 135, 197; postdisaster waiting and, 92; TV textuality and, 52, 77
media events, 1, 23–26, 31, 61, 66, 68, 85, 209. *See also* transmedia events
media spectacle, 32, 211; disaster event and, 26, 77; elections and, 23, 32, 225; terrorism and, 25; tourism and, 174; war and, 33, 38
mediation, 24–25, 31, 56, 155, 188, 191, 199, 205–206, 213–214, 218; disaster and, 5–6, 15, 61–63, 81, 88–89, 98–101, 216;

Indigeneity and, 8, 114, 135–136, 174, 179; remediation and, 66, 73, 87
mediatization, 25, 65, 75, 213–214
Meet the Prick (film), 139
memes, 67, 187, 197
Menchú, Rigoberta, 132
mestizaje, 159–161, 165, 182, 193, 196, 216, 230n3
mestizos, 156, 169, 216, 229n6, 231n4; in Costa Rica, 159, 161, 179, 193; nation-building and, 160, 193; in Nicaragua, 71, 159–161, 163–164, 173, 179, 182, 185. See also *mestizaje*
Metuktire, Raoni, 132, 134
Mexico, 4, 63, 132, 159, 170, 174, 175, 222n7, 226–227n4; border with United States, 126, 221n5; Mexico City, 169, 229n1. *See also* Zapatistas
Middle East, 23, 39, 44
Misión Bosawás, 179
Miskito (people), 164, 166–167, 187; history of, 157–158, 162–164; Hurricane Felix and, 78, 155, 227n9; identity, 167; land rights and, 179–183; media, 170–172, 177, 179, 187; working in Miskito Keys, 78, 227n9
Miskito Keys, 78, 227n9
Miskitu (language), 166–167, 171–172
Miss Universe, 205–206
Mita, Merata, 137
modernity, 69, 156, 213, 217–219, 223n12, 226n2; Global South and, 8–9, 68–69, 160, 167; Indigenous people and, 151, 185; visuality and, 15–16, 22; waiting and, 93
modernity/coloniality/decoloniality (MCD) research program, 68–69. *See also* coloniality; decoloniality
modernization, 8, 167, 169, 217
moko, 126, 136, 143
Monestel, Manuel, 193–194
Monkey Point, 184
Morales, Evo, 69
Morales-Garro, Ramón, 190, 193
Moravian Church, 157–158, 166
Morrah, Michael, 143–144
Morris, Ashley, 79–80, 101, 227n12
Mos Def, 27, 29–30, 225n10
Mosquitia, 157–158
Mosquito Reserve, 158
motherhood, 46, 49–51, 53, 169, 198, 201–202

Mould, Francesca, 127, 130
Mr Bates vs the Post Office (TV show), 209–214
Murillo, Rosario, 198, 200, 214–215, 218; authoritarianism and, 175, 177, 197, 206, 218; interoceanic canal and, 175–177, 185; media and, 176, 197, 203, 205, 212, 231n12; repression and, 175–177, 183, 198, 200, 205, 212
Muru (film), 141–142
music, 134, 162, 167, 179, 189–196, 199, 225n12, 227n11; disasters and, 67, 77–79, 81–82, 86; enslaved people and, 9; prisoners and, 117, 119, 122

narcocorridos, 174
National Party (New Zealand), 138–139
Native Affairs (TV show), 128, 144, 230n7
Navidad Roja (Red Christmas), 163
neoliberalism, 62–65, 80, 84, 91–92, 113–115, 120, 152, 223n10, 224n14; authoritarianism and, 218; disaster and, 6, 62, 72, 76, 83, 96–101, 228n1; globalization and, 1, 5, 217; Indigenous people and, 125, 133–136, 186; Latin America and, 9, 155, 167–168, 214, 216; New Zealand and, 84, 91–92, 96–100, 108, 114–115, 120, 227n1
neoliberal multiculturalism, 58
Nepal, 137
Netflix, 118, 207, 216
New Orleans, 5, 70–72, 162, 226–227n4; bloggers, 73, 75, 76, 79–80, 227n12; George W. Bush and, 73–74, 78, 227n6; Hurricane Katrina and, 5, 64, 73–81, 83, 94, 100, 219; Mardi Gras, 72, 79–81, 104
news and current affairs, 6, 65–67, 187, 207, 210–212, 214, 217–218, 224n6; calypso as, 193, 195; disasters and, 67, 74, 88, 102; geopolitics and, 33–34, 37–38; Indigenous people and, 110, 127–128, 130–131, 142–143, 146, 148, 175, 229n9, 230n7; internet and, 3–4, 9, 20, 23, 27, 31–32, 182
New York, 4, 14, 28–29, 80, 162
New Yorker, The, 222n5
New York Post, 52
New York Times, 3, 205, 223n13
New Zealand, 1, 3, 82, 132, 136–137, 140, 215, 220, 221n2, 228n3, 229n7, 230n5; coloniality and/in, 6–7, 100, 109, 113, 115, 120, 128, 138–142, 144, 147, 149–152, 216–217; colonization of, 145; criminal justice system in, 112–116, 119–123, 141, 211; flag of, 127, 138–140, 142–146; government of, 83–86, 91–92, 99, 108, 114, 124, 138, 149, 215, 227–228n1; history of, 84–85, 90, 108, 124, 149–150, 152, 227–228n1, 228n4; mainstream media in, 91, 109–112, 114–115, 119, 121, 125, 127–128, 130, 140, 143, 145–146, 148, 152, 155, 215; neoliberalism in, 1, 84, 91–92, 99, 100, 108, 223n10, 227–228n1; police of, 126, 131, 151. See also Māori media; Treaty of Waitangi; 2007 terror raids; Whakaata Māori
New Zealand Corrections Department, 120–123
New Zealand Herald, 98
Ngāi Tahu, 85
Ngā Pirihimana Hou (TV show), 116
Ngā Tamatoa, 110, 137
Ngā Tamatoa: Forty Years On (film), 144
Nicaragua, 6, 8–9, 73, 87, 155, 159–168, 188, 191, 205, 214, 216–218; authoritarianism in, 175–176, 179, 196, 205–208; Caribbean Coast of, 155–167, 170, 178–188, 226n3, 230n4; flag of, 158, 203, 205; government of, 168, 175–176, 180, 184; history of, 70–71, 157–165; media in, 170, 175–176, 179–182, 185, 199, 204, 208, 231n11; 2018 Nicaraguan uprisings, 9, 196–208, 214. See also Hurricane Felix; Nicaraguan Revolution
Nicaraguan Revolution, 155, 162–164, 182, 197–202, 204, 206, 231n10
Nigeria, 47
9/11, 4–6, 13–57, 225n10; coloniality and, 8, 112, 124, 140–142, 220; Hurricane Katrina and, 62; Latin America and, 9, 216; memorialization and, 67
9/11 Truth movement, 16, 26–32, 212, 219, 225n9, 233n13
nongovernmental organizations (NGOs), 165, 169, 176, 196, 204, 214
No Reservations (TV show), 80
North Korea, 41–42, 44–45, 48–49
nuclear weapons, 44

Obama, Barack, 27, 29, 32, 52–54, 225n17
October 15: After the Raids (film), 126, 130, 144

Office, The (TV show), 222n5
official knowledges, 26, 28, 30, 62–63, 65, 187; expert knowledges, 26, 57, 76, 81, 97, 101–102, 169, 212
Onion, The, 222n5
Operation 8, 126, 149–150
Operation 8 (film), 130, 144
Operation Northwoods, 26, 224–225n8
Orange Is the New Black (TV show), 118, 119
Organization of American States, 198, 207
Orientalism, 20, 25, 32, 45, 54
Ortega, Daniel, 73, 183, 198–199, 200–201, 204–208, 214–215; authoritarianism and, 175–176, 184, 197, 206, 218; interoceanic canal and, 175–177, 184–185; media and, 175–177, 182, 185, 200, 203, 205–206, 212; repression and, 175–177, 183, 198, 200, 205, 212
Palacios, Sheynnis, 205–206, 231nn11–12
Palin, Sarah, 43
Pākehā (people or culture), 108–110, 113–114, 116, 121, 126, 136–141, 144–145; audiences, 110, 118–119, 123, 147; colonialism and, 228n4; media, 109; ways of knowing, 152
Pakistan, 51, 53–56
Palestine, 53, 124. *See also* Gaza; Israel-Palestine conflict
Panama, 159, 162, 166, 187, 191–193, 207, 222n7
Panama Canal, 159, 162
pandemic. *See* COVID-19
Panorama (TV show), 210
Paraguay, 185, 222n7
Parihaka, 110
participatory media, 1, 4, 6, 9, 111, 169, 186, 216; calypso and, 191, 196; convergence and, 22, 168; disaster and, 90, 92; in New Zealand, 90, 92; in Nicaragua, 72, 75, 156, 168–171, 173; reception practices and, 56; Whakaata Māori and, 110
Partido Revolucionario Institucional (PRI), 63
Partygate (TV show), 232n2
Patene, Rawiri, 144
Patu (film), 137
Pearl Lagoon, 156
Pentagon, 4, 28
Peru, 68, 222n7
pink tide, 9, 167, 168
podcasts, 31, 34, 65

Poke, The, 224n5
police, 107, 113, 142; New Zealand Police, 110, 116, 121, 126–127, 129–131, 140, 142, 144, 147, 149–152; New Zealand police commissioner, 126, 131, 149–150, 230n7; Nicaraguan police, 165, 171, 179, 197–199, 203–204; police brutality, 7, 29, 107, 113, 140, 142, 165, 179, 197–199, 203, 226n1; U.S. police, 23, 29, 50, 62, 226n1
political prisoners, 197–199, 204–208
popular culture, 71, 103–104, 212; cultural citizenship and, 37, 57; in Latin America, 162, 168–170, 173, 179, 203–204
popular knowledges, 81, 102, 187, 212
postcolonialism, 68, 89, 108, 134, 151–152, 157, 212; postcolonial nation-states, 7, 82, 108–109, 112, 129–130; postcolonial present, 94, 212
postmodernity, 15, 18, 68
Post Office scandal (U.K.), 209–214, 232n1
Pouwhare, Robert, 139
power blocs, 26, 90, 113, 187, 214, 221n4
premediation, 14, 66
Price of Peace, The (film), 147
prison, 28, 29, 47, 112–113, 118, 229n6; British postmasters and, 209; Māori population in, 112, 116–117, 119–121, 123, 127, 149, 229n6; in Nicaragua, 165, 171, 197–199, 204–208, 216, 231. *See also* incarceration; political prisoners
Private Eye, 210
privatization, 63, 76, 84, 94, 98, 113, 223n10, 227n1
public sphere, 2, 25, 30, 35, 37, 98
Puerto Cabezas. *See* Bilwi
Puerto Rico, 94
Puerto Viejo, 156, 166, 189–190, 193
Puntos de Encuentro, 205
Putin, Vladimir, 4, 197, 218

QAnon, 31, 219
Quake City, 102
quake refugees, 95–97
quakes. *See* earthquakes
queering, 43, 47–49

RACCN. *See* Autonomous Region of the North Caribbean Coast
RACCS. *See* Autonomous Region of the South Caribbean Coast

racialization, 1, 124–125, 212, 216–217, 220; coloniality and, 70, 130; *Commander in Chief* and, 46–47; of criminality, 7, 127–128; of disasters, 62, 68, 73, 76, 78, 86, 94, 100, 104; Latin American, 159, 161, 165, 168, 170, 200, 216; 9/11 and, 20; of policing and incarceration, 107, 113, 226n1 (chap. 3); 2000 presidential election and, 23

racism, 125, 160–161, 163, 166, 189, 196, 216; activism and, 149; coloniality and, 70, 108–110, 114, 137, 140–141, 157, 219; in *Commander in Chief*, 47; conjunctural analysis and, 131; criminalization and, 112–113; disasters and, 68, 73, 101, 156; foreign policy and, 48; in *Homeland*, 51–53; neoliberalism and, 6, 3, 133; participatory media and, 76, 145; recoded, 124; Whakaata Māori and, 118, 122

radio, 65, 67, 87, 132, 193, 211, 217; Bribri radio, 173–174; in Costa Rica, 9, 156, 166, 170, 173–174, 188–189, 193; Kabu Yula, 171; in New Zealand, 99, 136, 139, 147–148; in Nicaragua, 9, 75, 156, 166, 170–172, 176–177; pirate radio, 228n1; Radio 4 (U.K.), 210; Salem talk radio, 217; Sandinista radio, 176

Radio 4 (U.K.), 210
Radio Pacific, 139
Rama (language), 166, 184
Rama (people). *See* Rama-Kriol
Rama-Kriol (people), 163, 166, 179, 184–186
Ramírez, Sergio, 160, 205
"Rapist in Your Path, A," 214
Rastafarianism, 191
Reagan, Ronald, 2 162, 227n1
reality television, 2, 7, 49, 116, 118, 148
rearticulation. *See* articulation/disarticulation/rearticulation
refugees, 52, 172. *See also* quake refugees
reggae, 189, 191, 194
reggaeton, 194, 212
remediation, 66, 73, 76, 77, 82, 87
resilience, 62, 72, 92, 98, 112, 121, 149, 215
restorative justice, 121, 123, 142
Riverdale (TV show), 207–208, 214, 231n14
Roderick, Maramena, 117
Rolleston, William, 89
Rūaumoko, 101–104
Ruatoki, 126–127, 129–131, 136, 139, 143, 149, 151

Rugama, Leonel, 201
Rumsfeld, Donald, 131
Russia, 218

Salem Radio, 217
Sandinistas, 163, 165, 177, 181, 186, 197, 200–201, 204, 207; guerrilla fighters, 204, 208; Sandinista army, 163, 172; Sandinista Front for National Liberation (FSLN), 163, 165, 172, 196–197, 200, 203; Sandinista government, 164–165, 168, 175–177, 179–180, 183–184, 197–198, 231n10; Sandinista media, 176, 185–187, 197, 205; Sandinista Revolution (*see* Nicaraguan Revolution); Sandinista-YATAMA alliance, 178
saneamiento, 178, 180, 184
San Francisco, 19, 80
San José, 193
Santí, Marlon, 132
"Satan in the smoke," 20–21, 224n5
Saturday Night Live (TV show), 222n5
Scott, Robert Falcon, 89
securitization, 5–6, 41, 51, 53, 57, 113, 124, 152, 176
security, 17, 42, 69, 165; on Caribbean Coast of Nicaragua, 179, 182; geopolitics and, 5, 42–43, 46, 48, 51–53; Indigenous people and, 124, 129, 179, 182
Se Humano, 206
seismic activity. *See* earthquakes
Sesame Street (TV show), 23
Shanty y su Calypso, 193
Shearer, Harry, 74–75
Shocking Reminder, A (film), 88
sitcoms, 49, 66
Six Feet Under (TV show), 38–39
slavery, 70, 125, 169, 219; calypso and, 212; in Central America, 9, 70, 159, 161, 167, 188, 212; in United States, 70, 75
smartphones, 15, 34, 170, 187. *See also* cellphones
soap operas, 37, 49
solidarity, 9, 63, 65, 81, 128, 132–133, 148, 186, 200, 203
Somoza dictatorship (Nicaragua), 63, 162, 175, 201, 204, 207–208
Songs from the Inside (TV show), 7, 116–123, 214
South Africa, 112–113, 136–137

sovereignty, 47–48, 149; Nicaragua and, 159, 207; struggle for Māori sovereignty, 123, 129–130, 136, 145, 149–150, 217; third space of, 151
spectacularization, 5, 15, 18, 24, 32, 38, 75, 114, 120, 142
Springboks, 137
Steens, Maria, 130, 143, 229n9
Stewart, Jon, 224n6
stigmatization, 112, 125, 149, 152, 170, 174, 188, 196, 213
Sting, 134
St. Vincent, 159, 222n7
Subcomandante Marcos, 132, 134, 229n1
Sudan, 40–41
Sunak, Rishi, 210–211
Sunday (film), 88, 228n4
Suppression of Rebellion Act, 124
surveillance, 1, 5, 14, 17, 23–24, 65, 113, 124–125, 216; drones and, 53–56; Indigenous peoples and, 7–8, 121, 124, 126, 141–142; in New Zealand, 90, 121, 126, 141–142; in Nicaragua, 176, 197, 216, 218; reality television and, 223–224n14; system of, 125, 176, 197, 218
Sykes, Annette, 124
Sylvan, Cyril, 193
Syria, 218

tablets, 15, 34, 187
Tahiti, 137
Tame Iti: The Man behind the Moko (film), 143
Tāneatua, 137, 147
Tasba Pri, 163
Tawan Inangka (TV show), 177
Tearepa, Kahi, 116, 141–142
Te Kāea (TV show), 144
Te Karere (TV show), 110, 143
telenovelas, 216
television drama, 6, 35, 37, 66, 118, 214; British, 209–214, 232n2; disaster and, 65, 73–77, 79, 101–102; geopolitical, 33–56, 211; New Zealand, 88; prison, 118; teen, 9, 207, 212
Television New Zealand (TVNZ), 110, 147
te reo Māori (Māori language), 3, 108, 110–111, 119, 129–130, 136–137, 141–143, 148, 150

terrorism, 29, 35, 42, 57, 220; Indigenous people and, 6, 8, 112, 124, 127–131, 140–142, 144–145, 148–149, 229n8, 229n12; in United States, 14, 19, 28–29, 40, 43, 45, 48, 50–54, 224n8; use by Rosario Murillo, 205, 231n12
Terrorism Suppression Act (TSA), 124
terror raids (New Zealand). *See* 2007 terror raids
Te Whiti, 110
Thatcher, Margaret, 84, 227
theatricality, 136–139, 144, 202–203
3rd Degree (TV show), 143–146, 214
third world, 1, 22, 27, 45, 100, 169, 218
TikTok, 189
Times-Picayune (New Orleans), 76
Torres, Hugo, 204
torture, 28, 35, 45, 199, 207, 221n5
tourism, 79, 173–174, 189, 190–191
Townbook Limón, 188–189, 231n1
transmedia events, 4, 15, 32, 66, 76, 211. *See also* media events
transmediality, 7–9, 66, 220
transmediation, 2, 6–7, 22, 79, 100, 115, 182, 205–206, 212–213, 218–220, 221n5
transmodernity, 69
Treaty of Managua, 158
Treaty of Waitangi, 108–110, 113, 126, 138, 150, 229n7
Treme (TV show), 74–80, 101, 214, 220, 227n11
tricksterism, 137–138, 192, 202–203
Trinidad, 9, 159, 191, 212, 222n7
trolls, 197
Trump, Donald, 2–4, 32, 63, 221n3, 221–222n5
Tūhoe, 116, 136–139, 145, 148, 215–216, 229n7; Crown apology to, 150; fiscal envelope and, 138; history of, 126–128, 140–141, 143–144; struggle for sovereignty, 129–130, 136, 150; Te Urewera and, 145, 150, 230n5; terror raids and, 126, 129–131, 140, 144, 147, 149–150; Treaty of Waitangi and, 113, 138, 146, 149. *See also* Iti, Tame; 2007 terror raids
Tumblr, 34
Tún, Papa, 193
Tupac Amaru rebellion, 68
Turia, Tariana, 131, 229n12
TVNZ (New Zealand), 110, 147

TV1 (New Zealand), 127, 130, 143
TV3 (New Zealand), 116, 127–128, 130, 143, 145, 147
TV7 (Nicaragua), 75, 77, 175, 177, 182
24 (TV show), 35
Twitter, 34, 65, 207; Black Twitter, 192; disaster and, 67, 88, 97, 101; Indigenous people and, 110, 132–133; Nicaraguan uprisings and, 197, 199, 203–204
2007 terror raids (New Zealand), 126–131, 140–152, 215

Ukraine, 198, 218
United Airlines, 15
United Fruit Company (UFCO), 159
United Kingdom, 62–63, 84, 113, 135, 210, 213, 223n10
United Nations Decade for People of African Descent, 173, 189
United Nations Declaration on the Rights of Indigenous Peoples, 109, 165, 228n3
United Nations Permanent Forum on Indigenous Issues, 108–109
United Negro Improvement Association (UNIA), 188
United States, 1, 14, 23–24, 26–32, 71, 217–218, 223n10; coloniality and, 69–70, 137, 151, 216–217, 228n3; Costa Rica and, 188–189; Cuba and, 224n8; disasters and, 6, 62–64, 70, 73, 75, 82, 94, 100; Donald Trump and, 3–4, 221n5; George W. Bush and, 27, 33, 38; global financial crisis and, 227n1; incarceration in, 113; Latin America and, 4, 71, 157–160, 162–163, 165–167, 222nn6–7; media spectacle and, 225–226n17; media studies and, 8, 66; Mexico and, 4, 126; Nicaragua and, 73, 198, 200–201, 205, 207, 231n10; 9/11 and, 16, 18, 28–32, 223n13, 224n7, 225n10; race and, 81, 107, 112, 226n4, 228n1; surveillance, securitization and, 17, 124, 229n8; television in, 9, 38, 40–57, 221n3
university, 26, 67, 83–84, 161, 166, 169–170, 197–198
Unmanned aerial vehicles (UAVs). *See* drones
Urewera, Te, 126, 128–130, 136, 140, 143, 145, 150, 229n7, 230n5 (chap. 6)
U.S.-Mexico border, 126, 221n5

Venezuela, 167–168, 175, 203, 222n7
Vennells, Paula, 210
vidding, 29, 225n12
Vietnam, 41
Vijil, Ana Margarita, 207
visuality, 15–18, 22–23, 25
Volunteered Geographic Information (VGI), 67
vulgarity, 139–140
vulnerability, 32, 53, 62–63, 72, 96, 98, 227n5

Wairarapa Times-Age, 147
Waitangi Day, 110, 137, 229n3
Waitangi Tribunal, 108, 127, 138–140, 143
waiting, 80, 92–96, 98–100
Waka Huia (TV show), 143
war on terror, 38–42, 51–56, 58, 65, 67, 124, 127, 130, 140
Washington, D.C., 4, 46–48, 54
Washington, George, 29
Washington Consensus, 167, 223n10
Washington Post, 51
Webby, Kim, 147
Wellington, 3, 114, 117, 137, 148
West, Kanye, 73–74
West Bank, 6
West Wing, The (TV show), 43
Whakaata Māori, 7, 101–102, 108, 110–111, 118, 129, 139, 145, 147, 155, 220; audiences of, 110–111, 119, 145, 215, 228n5; crime and, 112, 114, 116–117; disaster and, 101–102, 228n7; impact on mainstream media, 112, 143–147, 151–152; racism and, 118, 122; terror raids and, 127–131, 140, 142, 144, 230n7. *See also* Māori; Māori media
whakapohane, 139
Whakatane River, 137
When a City Falls (film), 88
When the Levees Broke (film), 74, 80
White House, 3, 23, 42, 44, 46, 48–49
whiteness, 69, 124–125, 225n13
Wikipedia, 4, 223n9
Windrush scandal, 213
WKRG, 81
Women behind Bars (TV show), 118
World Trade Center: 9/11 attacks, 4, 14–15, 20–22, 25, 27–32, 38, 48, 223n13, 224n5, 224n7

X. *See* Twitter
X-Files, The (TV show), 13

YATAMA, 163–165, 178, 187
YouTube, 5–6, 27, 29, 39, 54, 56, 102, 110, 133, 186–188, 204, 207; Afro–Costa Ricans and, 189; calypso and, 212; Costeños and, 78, 170, 180–182, 184–187; disaster and, 64, 66–67, 75, 77–78, 82, 87–88, 101–102 (*see also* Hurricane Katrina); Nicaraguan uprisings and, 188, 199, 204

Zapata, Rafael, 193
Zapatistas, 68, 132, 134, 136, 169, 175, 229n1
Zondag met Lubach, 222n5

About the Authors

KEVIN GLYNN is an associate professor at Northumbria University in the United Kingdom. He is the author of *Tabloid Culture: Trash Taste, Popular Power, and the Transformation of American Television* and coauthor of *Shifting Nicaraguan Mediascapes: Authoritarianism and the Struggle for Social Justice* and *Communications/Media/Geographies*. He has published widely in anthologies and international journals in media and cultural studies, as well as critical/cultural geographies. He has taught in departments of media, communication and cultural studies, American studies, and geography at universities in the United States, Aotearoa New Zealand, and the United Kingdom.

JULIE CUPPLES is a professor of human geography and cultural studies at the University of Edinburgh. She is the sole or joint author or editor of eight books, including *Development and Decolonization in Latin America*, *Shifting Nicaraguan Mediascapes*, *Communications/Media/Geographies*, *Unsettling Eurocentrism in the Westernized University*, and *The Routledge Handbook of Latin American Development*. She works at the intersection of human geography, media and cultural studies, and Latin American studies, and does most of her research in Central America.